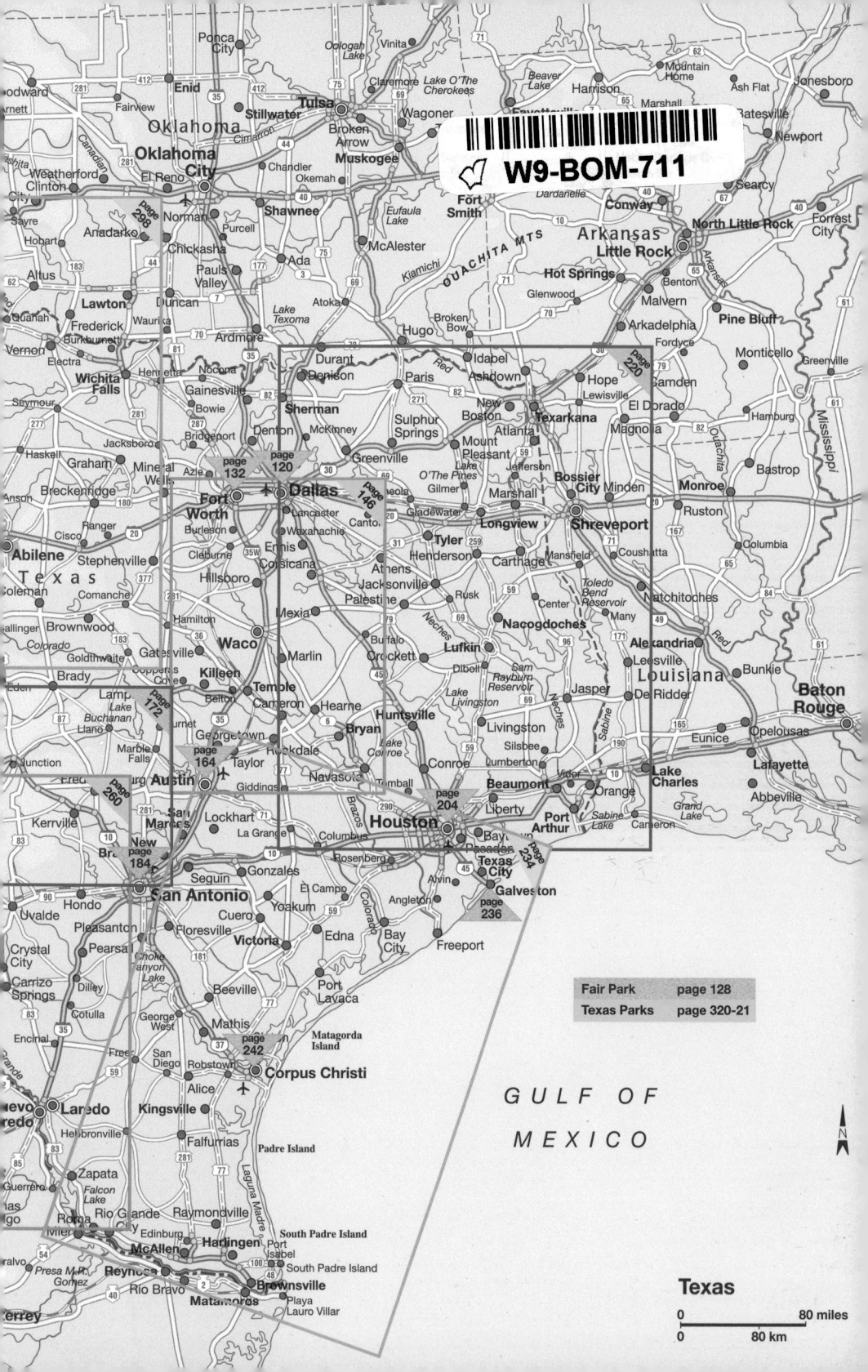
W9-BOM-711
Fair Park page 128
Texas Parks page 320-21
GULF OF MEXICO
Texas
0 80 miles
0 80 km
Oklahoma
Oklahoma City
Tulsa
Arkansas
Little Rock
North Little Rock
Louisiana
Texas
Dallas
Fort Worth
Houston
San Antonio
Austin
Corpus Christi
Laredo
Waco
Abilene
Lubbock
Amarillo
Shreveport
Baton Rouge
Lake Charles
Beaumont
Galveston
Texas City
Port Arthur
Brownsville
McAllen
Harlingen
Matamoros
Reynosa
Enid
Stillwater
Muskogee
Norman
Shawnee
Lawton
Wichita Falls
Denton
Sherman
Tyler
Longview
Bossier City
Monroe
Alexandria
Lafayette
Victoria
Kingsville
Alice
Laredo
Padre Island
South Padre Island
Matagorda Island
Texarkana
Hot Springs
Fort Smith
Pine Bluff
Jonesboro
Newport
Searcy
Conway
Forrest City
Greenville
Monticello
Hamburg
Bastrop
Ruston
Columbia
Natchitoches
Bunkie
Opelousas
Eunice
Abbeville
Lake Charles
Orange
Port Arthur
Cameron
Jasper
Nacogdoches
Lufkin
Huntsville
Bryan
College Station
Conroe
Galveston
Texas City
Freeport
Port Lavaca
Victoria
Corpus Christi
Kingsville
Harlingen
McAllen
Brownsville
Matamoros
Reynosa
Rio Bravo
Playa Lauro Villar
Port Isabel
South Padre Island
Raymondville
Falfurrias
Beeville
Kerrville
Fredericksburg
Marble Falls
Llano
Brady
Coleman
Abilene
Stephenville
Cisco
Ranger
Breckenridge
Graham
Haskell
Jacksboro
Bridgeport
Decatur
Gainesville
Denison
Durant
Paris
Idabel
Ashdown
Texarkana
Hope
Lewisville
El Dorado
Magnolia
Camden
Malvern
Arkadelphia
Hot Springs
Benton
Little Rock
Conway
Searcy
Jonesboro
Mountain Home
Harrison
Ash Flat
Batesville
Fordyce
Greenville
Monticello
Hamburg
Bastrop
Ruston
Columbia
Natchitoches
Bunkie
Opelousas
Eunice
Abbeville
Lafayette

INSIGHT GUIDES

TEXAS

APA PUBLICATIONS

Part of the Langenscheidt Publishing Group

INSIGHT GUIDE
TEXAS

About This Book

Editorial
Project Editor
Alyse Dar
Editorial Director
Brian Bell

Distribution
North America
Langenscheidt Publishers, Inc.
36–36 33rd Street, 4th Floor
Long Island City, New York 11106
orders@langenscheidt.com

UK & Ireland
GeoCenter International Ltd
Meridian House, Churchill Way West
Basingstoke, Hampshire RG21 6YR
sales@geocenter.co.uk

Australia
Universal Publishers
1 Waterloo Road
Macquarie Park, NSW 2113
sales@universalpublishers.com.au

New Zealand
Hema Maps New Zealand Ltd (HNZ)
Unit 2, 10 Cryers Road
East Tamaki, Auckland 2013
sales.hema@clear.net.nz

Worldwide
Apa Publications GmbH & Co.
Verlag KG (Singapore branch)
7030 Ang Mo Kio Avenue 5
08-65 Northstar @ AMK
Singapore 569880
apasin@singnet.com.sg

Printing
CTPS - China

©2008 Apa Publications GmbH & Co.
Verlag KG (Singapore branch)
All Rights Reserved
First Edition 1986
Fourth Edition (updated) 2008
Reprinted 2010

CONTACTING THE EDITORS

We would appreciate it if readers would alert us to errors or outdated information by writing to:
Insight Guides, P.O. Box 7910, London SE1 1WE, England.
insight@apaguide.co.uk

NO part of this book may be reproduced, stored in a retrieval system or transmitted in any form or means electronic, mechanical, photocopying, recording or otherwise, without prior written permission of *Apa Publications*. Brief text quotations with use of photographs are exempted for book review purposes only. Information has been obtained from sources believed to be reliable, but its accuracy and completeness, and the opinions based thereon, are not guaranteed.

www.insightguides.com

The first Insight Guide pioneered the use of creative full-color photography in travel guides in 1970. Since then, we have expanded our range to cater for our readers' need not only for reliable information about their chosen destination but also for a real understanding of the culture and workings of that destination. Now, when the internet can supply inexhaustible (but not always reliable) facts, our books marry text and pictures to provide those much more elusive qualities: knowledge and discernment. To achieve this, they rely heavily on the authority of locally based writers and photographers.

Texas lends itself especially well to Insight Guides' approach. As the writer John Steinbeck, in his book *Travels With Charley,* observed: "Texas is a state of mind, Texas is an obsession."

How to use this book

The book is carefully structured both to convey an understanding of the state and its culture, and to guide readers through its sights and activities:

- To understand Texas today, you need to know something of its past. The first section covers the state's past and culture in

lively, authoritative essays written by specialists. This section includes essays on the state's **History** and **Features** on its culture today.

◆ The main **Places** section gives a full run-down of all the attractions worth seeing, divided by geographic areas. The principal places of interest are coordinated by number with full-color maps.

◆ The **Travel Tips** listings section provides comprehensive information on travel, hotels, restaurants, sports and festivals. Facts may be located quickly by using the index printed on the back cover flap.

◆ The photographs are chosen not only to illustrate geography and attractions but also to convey the many moods of Texas and its people.

The contributors

The original edition of *Insight Guide: Texas* was edited by **Diana Ackland** and **Janie Freeburg**. They assembled a team of fine Texas writing talent, including **John Smith**, **Paul Powell**, **Mel McCombie**, **A.C. Greene**, **Lisa Jones**, **Sue Winton Moss**, **Winston Derdon**, **John Minton**, **Gary Taylor**, **Michael Murphy**, **Pamela Jantzen**, **Fernando de Luna**, **Lisa Germany** and **Louis Dubose**.

That edition was taken over by Insight's editor-in-chief of North American titles, **Martha Ellen Zenfell**. This thoroughly revised and reorganized edition was edited by **Jeff Evans**, a freelance journalist specializing in guidebooks and leisure-activity writing. **John Wilcock** provided new essays and was assisted by two Texas-based writers, **Ann Mills** and **Christopher Walters**.

But a guidebook is only as good as its most recent incarnation, and a team of Texas-based writers fully updated this current version. **Helen Bryant**, **John Davis**, **Eileen Mattei**, and **Ed Proctor** contributed to the Features and Places sections. **Teresa Gubbins** covered the Travel Tips. It was edited by **Alyse Dar**, a native Texan now working as an editor for Insight Guides. Text was copy edited by **Paula Soper** and proofread by **Susan Howarth**. The picture researcher was **Tom Smyth**.

Map Legend

- International Boundary
- State Boundary
- Border Crossing
- National Park/Reserve
- Airport: International/Regional
- Bus Station
- Parking
- Tourist Information
- Post Office
- Church/Ruins
- Monastery
- Mosque
- Synagogue
- Castle/Ruins
- Archeological Site
- Cave
- Statue/Monument
- Place of Interest

The main places of interest in the Places section are coordinated by number with a full-color map (e.g. ❶), and a symbol at the top of every right-hand page tells you where to find the map.

INSIGHT GUIDE
Texas

CONTENTS

Maps

Texas **114**

Downtown Dallas **120**

Fair Park **128**

Fort Worth **132**

Central Texas **146**

Austin **164**

Hill Country **172**

San Antonio **184**

Houston **204**

East Texas **220**

Gulf Coast and Rio Grande Valley **234**

Galveston **236**

Corpus Christi **242**

Del Rio to Laredo **260**

El Paso **270**

The Trans-Pecos **278**

Big Bend National Park **290**

West Texas and the Panhandle **298**

Texas Parks **320**

Introduction

Best of Texas **6**

Where Big is Beautiful **15**

The Lone Star State **19**

History

Decisive Dates **26**

Six Flags Over Texas **29**

The Tale of the Longhorn **39**

Modern Times **49**

Features

Texans **59**

The Texas Rangers **71**

Don't Fence Me In **79**

Musical Traditions **91**

Texan Architecture **99**

El Capitan Peak, Guadalupe Mountains National Park

Information panels

Samuel Maverick **42**
Movies in Texas **52**
Black Cowboys **84**
Neiman Marcus **126**
Texas Wines **177**
The Chisholm Trail **194**
Tex-Mex Food **265**
Desert Plantlife **282**
The Marfa Lights..... **287**
Buddy Holly **312**

Insight on ...

Texas Customs and Festivals **178**
Spanish Missions **198**
Houston: Space Capital **214**
Wildlife **294**

Travel Tips

Transportation **340**
Accommodations **343**
Eating Out **355**
Activities **364**
A–Z **370**
Further Reading **376**

◆ **Full Travel Tips index is on page 339**

Places

Introduction **113**
Dallas **119**
Fort Worth **131**
Waxahachie to Waco **145**
Waco to Austin **155**
Hill Country **171**
San Antonio **183**
Houston..... **203**
East Texas **219**
The Gulf Coast **233**
Rio Grande Valley **249**
Del Rio to Laredo **259**
El Paso **269**
The Trans-Pecos **277**
Big Bend National Park **289**
The West **297**
Amarillo to Lubbock **309**
Texas Parks **319**

THE BEST OF TEXAS

From unique attractions, top beaches, best Western wear... here, at a glance,are our recommendations, plus some tips and tricks even the locals won't always know

BEST MUSEUMS AND GALLERIES

- **Kimbell Art Museum** (Fort Worth) is human-sized with a wide collection that is constantly being expanded. *See pages 135–6.*

- **Amon Carter Museum** (Fort Worth) has collections of works by Frederic Remington and Charles M. Russell, who specialized in depicting life on the range and along the cattle trails. *See page 136.*
- **Panhandle-Plains Historical Museum** (Canyon) contains an art collection, geological exhibits and a reconstructed pioneer town of a century ago. *See page 309–10.*
- **Nasher Sculpture Garden** (Dallas) is the outdoor setting and perfect backdrop for more than 300 modern works. *See page 123.*
- **The Menil Collection & the Rothko Chapel** (Houston) have collections ranging from medieval and Byzantine art to contemporary works. *See page 206.*

ONLY IN TEXAS

- **Cadillac Ranch** Tongue-in-cheek sculpture of buried Cadillacs on the prairie. *See page 310.*
- **Luckenbach** Celebrated in song by Waylon Jennings and Willie Nelson, the bite-sized Hill Country town where "everybody's somebody." *See pages 174–5.*
- **The Orange Show** Folk art at its zenith in suburban Houston. *See page 208.*
- **Galveston, Mustang, Padre Islands** Three of Texas' 350 miles of barrier islands offer history, world-class birdwatching, beachcombing and camping. *See page 328.*
- **The Alamo** Shrine of Texas liberty, site of one of history's most famous battles. *See page 184–5.*
- **The Austin Bats** Ann Richards Congress Avenue bridge in the Texas capital is home to a huge colony of Mexican freetail bats, which swirls forth at dusk in a crowd-pleasing spectacle. *See page 164.*

ABOVE: nose-down in the Panhandle plains – the sculpture known as Cadillac Ranch.
RIGHT: summer evening flight of the bridge-dwelling Austin bats.

BEST FESTIVALS AND EVENTS

- **Austin City Limits Music Festival** 150-odd bands perform each September for three days on the shores of Town Lake in downtown Austin, the self-proclaimed "Live Music Capital of the World." *See page162.*
- **Luling Watermelon Thump** One of the best of the small-town festivals, this one celebrates the humble watermelon. *See page 178.*
- **Kerrville Folk Festival** Springtime homage to folk and acoustic music, in the heart of Texas Hill Country. *See page 171–2.*
- **State Fair of Texas** Home of Big Tex, the corny dog and the Cotton Bowl Texas vs O.U. football shoot-out held each October in Dallas. *See page 128.*
- **Cinco de Mayo and Diez y Seis**. *Tejanos* (Hispanic Texans) celebrate these Mexican independence holidays on May 5 and September 16.
- **Texas vs Oklahoma University or Texas vs Texas A&M** These two college football classics pit the University of Texas against their arch foes in a pair of near century-old rivalries.
- **Spring Wildflowers** Wildflowers are one of the glories of spring in Texas and driving in the Hill Country to see bluebonnets and other Texas flora is a time-honored Lone Star tradition.
- **Juneteenth**. Commemorates June 19, 1865, when Texas slaves learned they were free. *See page 178*
- **Willie Nelson's Fourth of July Picnic**. Fireworks, hot sun, cold beer, hours of music and Willie Nelson make for an only-in-Texas blowout.

BEST TASTES OF TEXAS

Here is but a small selection of the many restaurants serving the best of Texas cooking around the state.

- **Barbecue** The Salt Lick (Austin). *See page 355.*
- **Chicken-Fried Steak** Massey's (Fort Worth). *See page 357.*
- **Tex-Mex** Mi Tierra (San Antonio). *See page 359.*
- **Gulf Coast Seafood** Gaido's Seafood Restaurant (Galveston). *See page 361.*
- **Southern "Comfort" Food and Soul Food** Threadgills's (Austin). *See page 358.*
- **High End Texas/Southwestern** Reata (Alpine and Fort Worth). *See page 357–62.*

TOP RIGHT: the James Smooth "Steppers" march in the Juneteenth Parade, Austin. **ABOVE:** fresh corn tortillas are a staple ingredient of Tex-Mex cooking.

Best State and National Parks

- **Big Bend National Park** Showcases mountains, canyons, rivers, deserts and more. *See page 289.*
- **Lost Maples State Natural Area** A Hill Country treasure whose rare outcroppings of Bigtooth Maples and Texas Madrones provide the state's most beautiful autumn color. *See pages 176 and 330.*
- **Padre Island National Seashore** Mile after mile of unspoiled, undeveloped uninhabited beach and dune lets you indulge your inner Robinson Crusoe. *See page 328.*
- **Palo Duro Canyon State Park** Texas' Grand Canyon, a dramatic slash in the Panhandle replete with history and natural beauty. *See page 329.*
- **Franklin Mountains State Park** Skyline drives reveal dramatic views of El Paso and its sister city of Juárez, across the Rio Grande in Mexico. *See page 271.*
- **Aransas National Wildlife Refuge** A birdwatchers' paradise along the middle of the Texas Coast, and home to the largest migrating colony of endangered whooping cranes. *See pages 245 and 330.*
- **San Antonio Missions National Historical Park** Spain's and Mexico's ongoing legacy in Texas had its origins in this ruggedly beautiful chain of churches (of which the Alamo is but one) in the San Antonio metropolitan area. *See pages 196 and 333.*
- **Caddo Lake State Park** Texas' only natural lake (the others are man-made reservoirs) is a watery wilderness of cypress-shadowed sloughs and channels for canoers, kayakers and fishermen to explore to their hearts' content. *See page 323.*

Above Right: a natural wonder of the Franklin Mountains State Park – the giant Southwest barrel cactus. **Below:** sweeping views from a lookout point on a Chisos Basin hiking trail, Big Bend National Park.

Great Books to Read

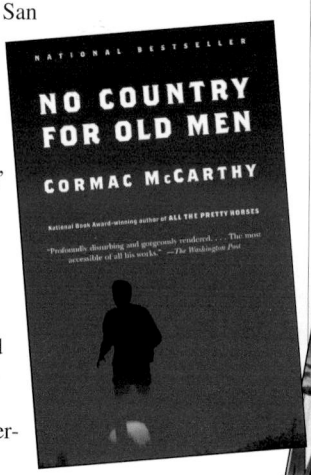

- **La Relación** by Alvar Nuñez Cabeza de Vaca. Historic account of Texas' first "tourist," shipwrecked at Galveston in 1528.
- **The Gay Place** by Billy Lee Brammer. Indelible portrait of freewheeling politicos in Austin in the 1950s.
- **Lonesome Dove** by Larry McMurtry. The definitive Western novel, based loosely on larger-than-life people and events.
- **I Say for Me a Parable** by Glen Alyn. Oral history of East Texas' black community.

- **Caramelo** by Sandra Cisneros. Multigenerational saga that follows a family from Mexico to Chicago to San Antonio.
- **No Country for Old Men** by Cormac McCarthy. Bloody doings in the desolate brush country along the Texas/Mexico border.

BEST WESTERN WEAR

See pages 368–9.

- **M.L. Leddy's** This family-run operation in Fort Worth has specialized in fine handcrafted boots and saddles since 1922.
- **Cavender's** A Texas-based chain stocking enough boots, jeans and hats to outfit a King's Ranch-worth of cowboys.
- **Rocketbusters** (El Paso) Custom bootmakers to the stars.
- **Texas Hatters** Custom hats from derbys to ten-gallon Tom Mix specials. The "High Roller" and "Half Breed" original styles are their signature *chapeaux*.

FAMOUS TEXANS

- **Willie Nelson** (b. Abbott). Ageless country music icon with a unique style of performing. *See page 92.*
- **Dixie Chicks** (members raised in Dallas, Lubbock). Chart-topping, politically controversial country trio. *See page 91.*
- **Larry McMurtry** (b. Archer City). Celebrated Pulitzer Prize-winning author of *The Last Picture Show* and *Lonesome Dove*. *See page 52.*
- **Lance Armstrong** (b. Plano). Seven-time Tour de France winner and cancer treatment advocate.
- **Ornette Coleman** (b. Fort Worth). Pulitzer Prize-winning jazz trailblazer. One of the innovators of the free jazz movement. *See page 94.*
- **Flaco Jimenez** (b. San Antonio). Pioneer of conjunto music and an accordion maestro legend. *See page 95.*

ABOVE RIGHT: a clutch of Grammys for the Dixie Chicks. **LEFT:** "Big Tex," the waving, talking four-story-tall icon of the State Fair of Texas, models the latest line in western wear.

TOP TIPS

Rent A Car Public transportation and taxis are rare even in the big cities. A car is a must, especially considering the vast distances between some Texas destinations. Avoid renting from an airport counter if possible as fees and taxes are steep.

Texas State Parks Pass An annual pass conveys free admission to the holder and a guest in all state parks and historic sites. To purchase, call 512-389-8900 or log onto www.tpwd.state.tx.us

Ask A Stranger The origin of the name Texas is "Tejas," a Caddo Indian word meaning "friendship." Most Texans are happy to assist visitors by pointing out directions and local highlights.

Pack Everything Texas has several countries worth of climates within its borders. A blue norther can freeze the Panhandle while vacationers are sunbathing on Padre Island, all on the same day. From tropical Houston to arid Amarillo, Texas offers a full menu of weather conditions.

Think Local From Blue Bell ice cream to Shiner Bock beer to Rio Grande Valley grapefruit to Stubb's barbecue sauce to Texas 1015 onions to Elgin hot Sausage, Texas is replete with native foods and beverages and condiments.

Eat Cheap Texas food is delicious and diverse and is best savored in casual venues such as barbeque shacks, hamburger joints, taco stands, seafood markets and small-town cafes. There is no end of eating opportunities.

WHERE BIG IS BEAUTIFUL

The myths are magnificent but so is the reality. What appeals most about Texas – and Texans – is the huge diversity

There's one word people use more than any other to describe Texas: "big." Big ranches, big cities, big money, big sky, big smiles, big mountains, big fun and, above all, big hearts. Plain and simple – Texas is a big place, and its image in the American mind has always been larger than life. It's been said that the US is a frontier nation and that distinctly American notions like "rugged individualism" were shaped by the vast wilderness that beckoned at the country's western border. Possibly more than any other state, Texas epitomizes this frontier ethic. And, as some people see it, the American spirit has blossomed here more fully than anywhere else.

For many people, Texas *is* America – the one place where the American dream is still alive, where the values and traditions that helped build the nation are still a viable part of the culture. Think, for example, of all the American icons that come from Texas: the cowboy, the sheriff, the six-shooter, the 10-gallon hat, the maverick, the oil baron, the longhorn and the open range, just to name a few. And how many times have you seen the big-hearted, drawling Texan used to represent Americans as a whole, slapping the world on the back and inviting it in for a barbecue? Distortions they may be, but they evoke an image of an America recognized around the world.

Getting to know a place that is as broadly mythologized can be difficult because often we mistake myth for reality, settling for stereotypes or caricatures. So it's important for travelers to strip away their preconceptions and try to pry the real Texas away from its image. Sometimes they are the same thing, but usually not.

The best way to approach the state is to forget about "Big Texas" and concentrate on something smaller. Texas isn't a single place, after all, and Texans aren't a single people. There is as much diversity here as there is anywhere else in the country and when you begin to focus on specific people, towns or places, the stereotypes will quickly fall away. Yes, there are cowboys and wealthy oilmen. Also ranchers, Native Americans, Latinos and plenty of horse traders. But there are also things that you never expected: a Vietnamese fishing community along the Gulf Coast, a Czech farming town out on the plains, or a community of artists in a dusty border town.

"Texans want to believe they're different, a reverberating quality that other places don't have," said the late author James Michener, who made the state the subject (and the title) of his 32nd novel and then came to live here. "Texas has a rather logical pull on the imagination of the creative artist. I have great respect for the Texas legend. How you specify that it is a legend and how it became a legend and so on is a tough artistic problem. But I have great respect for it." ❑

PRECEDING PAGES: "Big Tex" at the State of Fair in Dallas; Houston skyline Tranquility Park.
LEFT: cowboy in contemplation.

THE LONE STAR STATE

Cultural traditions, economic realities and the sheer distances involved mean that Texas could actually be five different states under its Lone Star

Texas is a world in itself. To understand this, one starts with size. With 267,000 sq. miles (692,000 sq. km) in land area, Texas is larger than many nations of the world, including every country in Europe. Size creates space, space makes for distance, and distance creates differences. These are the basic ingredients that have helped make Texas and Texans outstanding in the eyes of the world. Although sometimes treated as a kind of international joke, the truth is that Texas is enormous and its inhabitants inordinately proud of it.

These facts go to explain not only the wide geographic choices for the visitor but how diversified are its peoples and their cultures: there is no such thing as "a Texas" or "a Texan." These are collective names.

Distance and difference

Because of its size, traveling the entire state takes a good deal of time. It is not the kind of place that can be covered in a day or two. There are 940 highway miles (1,500 km), for example, between Texline on the northern border of the Texas Panhandle, and Brownsville at the mouth of the Rio Grande across from Mexico. From Texarkana in the northeast corner, beside the Arkansas border, to El Paso at the state's extreme western tip is 810 miles (1,300 km).

As one crosses this vast surface, everything changes: the configuration of the earth, the economy, time zones, and even the seasons. It is feasible to be snowbound in Amarillo one day and the next day to be sunbathing on the beaches of South Padre Island. Out west, in the mountain areas of the Big Bend and around Fort Davis, the torrid summer endured in most of the state is pleasantly tempered by altitude. It takes only a little traveling around to understand why Texans never think of their province as one place, one thing or one society.

PRECEDING PAGES: "nodding donkey" painted pump jacks at Post.

LEFT: Hispanic Texan all dressed up in San Antonio.

RIGHT: a big welcome to big Texas.

Cattle and oil

It was cattle and then oil that originally fueled the state's economy and made it what it is, and both can be found, or have thrived, in almost every part of the state. In the early days, land and cattle were pretty much the only assets of the fledgling republic, which wasted no time

in converting them into money, selling land to the Federal government and longhorn steers by the millions to buyers in the north and west.

Oil and gas, of course, are almost everywhere in the state with only 34 of Texas' 254 counties not having found oil or natural gas within their boundaries. Texas is the largest petroleum-producing state in the US, and it has been estimated by economists that, if Texas were an independent nation, it would rank as the world's fifth-largest petroleum-producing country. The diminishing oil, however, is getting more and more expensive to pump out of the ground and no major new wells have been discovered for half a century or more.

Though one's sense of the past comes from human works – the buildings, roads and other monuments resulting from centuries of creative efforts – what is under the land has often been more important in Texas than what is on top. Faults, folds, intrusions and other geological movements, beginning 250 million years ago, formed the hidden reservoirs and basins that contain the great supplies of petroleum, natural gas, coal, salt, sulfur and other minerals.

Not only has Texas increased in wealth and importance because of its subsurface minerals, but, in its most important agricultural region, the High Plains, water pumped to the surface from underground aquifers has transformed a "desert" into one of the world's great cotton- and food-producing areas.

Five states

When the old Republic of Texas joined the United States a century and a half ago, it retained the right to divide itself into as many as five states, should it so decide. And, although this option has so far been eschewed, it still lurks at the back of some minds. Certainly it would make this huge behemoth more manageable. The so-called "Five States of Texas" are recognizable by the manner in which the inhabitants earn their living, the crops they farm, and their attitude toward their own and other people's customs, religions and traditions.

Boundaries

The exact boundaries of North, South, West, East and Central Texas may vary, but the inhabitants of each seem to accept the fairly general definitions. For example, when a Texan mentions "West Texas," it is not just the geographical portion of the state that is being described: it is also a collection of traditions associated with that part of Texas and attached to its residents. And each major region contains its subregions, which are also recognizable to most Texans, such as the Gulf Coast, the Rio Grande Valley, the Panhandle and the High Plains, although these subregions have not acquired their own unique cultural patterns in the way the larger "states" have.

Plenty of time

West Texans are considered highly individualistic, quick to react but free with their purse and time. In West Texas one is seldom told, "I don't have time to see you now." Because so many of the region's leaders have associated themselves with ranching and the oil business, West Texans are seen as people willing to gamble – forced to gamble by the nature of their enterprises.

Ranching, whether cattle or sheep and goats, is a very cyclical undertaking, dependent on the fluctuations of both the weather and the market.

Oil is famous for not always being where the prospector drills, but it can also reward its finder, and the landowner, with instant wealth. Most West Texas ranches today depend on oil and gas from their vast acres for economic survival. But all over Texas, the sight of the "horsehead" pump is common, some towering as high as a three-story building, pulling oil from those ancient reefs and seabeds many meters below the surface. One is bound to see more pump jacks than cowboys even in West Texas, which was once informally known as "Big Ranch Country." The stark flatness of the area, the open spaces that seem to go on forever, and the huge sky are often startling to newcomers, who will immediately understand the meaning of the term "high lonesome." Natives insist on the distinction between West Texas, which stretches from the western edge of Hill Country to El Paso, and the northwestern Panhandle, which includes the cities of Lubbock and Amarillo.

LEFT: Work Project Administration mural, Fort Worth.
ABOVE: the 1841 cabin of John Neely, the founder of Dallas.

"Coonier" folk

East Texas natives, especially old timers, are held by the rest of Texas to be shrewder, more Southern-rural, often gifted with a special kind of earthy humor and wisdom. Or, as one may still hear in certain parts of East Texas, they're "coonier," a tribute to the clever tactics of the raccoon, an animal quite prevalent in the region. This was the part of Texas most like the Old South, with cotton plantations and slow, unhurried ways back in the time of its agricultural dominance. Here one finds dense forests, humid swamps and wide, slow-moving rivers, while, at its western edges, some 500 miles (800 km) away, there are arid deserts, barren mountains and streams that, although furious when full, are often dry.

Even today, East Texas is a region of mostly smaller towns and many rural communities of the crossroads variety, consisting of a general store, a service station, a couple of churches (usually Protestant) and maybe a schoolhouse, left empty when the country schools were consolidated years ago. East Texas, incidentally, has produced some of Texas' better-known writers and other artists, many of them working from the strong sense of tradition that seems to come with the land. The late William Goyen's writings were filled with East Texas imagery.

Alvin Ailey, the renowned choreographer, was born in East Texas. And sculptor James Surls is based in East Texas and uses woods found in the area as his main medium.

Down to the border

South Texas starts (in the Texas mind) at San Antonio and continues southward to the Rio Grande. Along its edges it supports two separate cultures: the long, well-populated curve of the Gulf Coast and that other world of mostly Hispanic Texans along the river border with Mexico. South Texas was the birthplace of the Texas cowboy, who began as a Mexican

vaquero (origin of the Western term "buckaroo"), and of the 19th-century trail drives made famous in story, film and song. It remains a spread out, sparse land containing several of the state's major ranches, including the famous 825,000-acre (334,000-hectare) King Ranch.

Owing to the centuries-old Hispanic influence (some land deeds in South Texas go back to the Spanish kings), South Texans have the reputation of being easy-going, and are passionate and fiercely loyal to their families and political leaders. The lower Rio Grande Valley, called simply "The Valley" by Texans, furnishes a significant percentage of the citrus fruit and vegetables for sale in the US.

Selling the goods

North Texans share fewer traditional traits, probably because of the region's long-time role as merchant to all the rest of Texas and the Southwest. Storekeepers have always had to learn to be all things to all customers, and North Texas has found customers all over the world for everything from clothing to electronics. Because Dallas and Fort Worth are its key metropolises – their combined areas go by the name "The Metroplex" – North Texas assumes more sophistication than other parts of Texas, although the statement meets fierce and determined resentment if repeated too often. Citizens of Austin and Houston are not known for their high opinion of Dallas, though almost everyone praises Fort Worth for its old-fashioned charm.

An atmosphere of promotion and display has influenced an unusual number of film and theatrical figures to come out of North Texas, including two Dallas playwrights: the late Preston Jones, with his *Texas Trilogy*, and Don Coburn, whose *Gin Game* won a Pulitzer Prize in 1978. Larry L. King's musical *Best Little Whorehouse in Texas* was one of the most durable theatrical productions of the 1970s and 1980s. Not to be overlooked are the screenwriter Robert Benton from Waxahachie, and the Oscar-winning film actress Sissy Spacek from Quitman.

In the middle

Central Texas is not as well-defined geographically as the other sections, often overlapping them. But the folklore of its people is strong. Perhaps from the fact that it contains Austin, the state capital and hotbed of liberalism, or because it has had to learn political compromise with its bordering regions, Central Texas has contributed a large proportion of political figures to the lore of the Lone Star State.

The foremost example, of course, is Lyndon Johnson, US president from 1963 to 1969. He was born in the Hill Country, to the north and west of the capital, yet he never attempted to pull up those roots during his rumbustious journey to the White House.

Central Texas is also home to large German and Czech populations, which moved into the state during the 19th century. ❑

LEFT: Cowboy of the West.
RIGHT: Texas' highest point, Guadalupe Peak.

W
E
S

Decisive Dates

1519 Spain lays claim to the region comprising the present state of Texas.
1685 La Salle lands in Matagorda Bay and sets up a short-lived French colony.
1718 The *presidio* (president) San Antonio de Bexar and the mission San Antonio de Valero (the Alamo) are established on the San Antonio River.
1754 Construction begins on the present Alamo chapel.
1793 San Antonio de Valero mission is closed and its lands are divided up among Indian families.
1801 A Spanish cavalry unit from San Carlos del Alamo de Parras occupies the mission as a garrison.

GEN. ANTONIO LOPEZ DE SANTA ANNA.

1823 Stephen F. Austin brings the first 300 families to help Mexico settle Texas.
1824 Mexican constitution promises Texas statehood.
1830 Law of April 6 toughens restrictions on immigration from the US into Texas, heightening tensions between Anglo settlers and Mexico.
1834 Santa Anna is elected president and starts to centralize the Mexican government.

Revolution

1835 Texas revolt begins; San Antonio is occupied. The Texas Rangers are officially instituted.
1836 Santa Anna invades. Texas declares independence. Siege and battle of the Alamo. All defenders of the mission are killed. Santa Anna is later defeated at San Jacinto. Texas becomes an independent republic.
1839 Austin, formerly the village of Waterloo, is established as the new nation's capital.
1841 Republic of Texas' President Mirabeau Lamar sends a small armed force to New Mexico in a vain attempt to seize territory from Mexico.
1842 Santa Anna retaliates by twice seizing San Antonio, leading to an expedition by mutinous Texas volunteers which ends in disaster at Mier.
1844 US Senate rejects annexation treaty with the Republic of Texas, dashing hopes until the election of US President James K. Polk, who revives the annexation effort; it passes the following year.
1846 Ending almost a decade of independence, Texas joins the US. War breaks out between Mexico and the US.
1848 War ends. The Rio Grande becomes a permanent international boundary in the Treaty of Guadalupe Hidalgo.
1850 US Army repairs the Alamo.
1853 The Buffalo Bayou Brazos and Colorado – the first railway chartered by Texas – begins operating.
1854 The state establishes two Indian reservations.
1858 The army imports camels for use in the arid western part of the state.
1861 Texas secedes from the Union in favor of the Confederacy. The Alamo is used by the Confederate Army during the war between the states.
1865 Final battle of the Civil War fought near Brownsville, Texas, after the war's official end. Announcement at Galveston that slavery has been abolished.
1866 Large-scale cattle drives to the north begin.
1870 Texas is readmitted to the Union.
1873 Record annual rainfall (109 inches/279 cm) at Clarksville.
1875 Comanche Chief Quanah Parker loses his last fight and is forced onto a reservation, effectively ending Indian wars in Texas.
1876 Charles Goodnight founds the J.A. Ranch at Palo Duro Canyon, the first cattle ranch in northwest Texas.
1884 Fence cutting wars; new laws ban the practice.
1888 The Alamo chapel, having been used as a warehouse, is sold by the Catholic church to the state.
1894 Oil is discovered at Corsicana.

Early 20th Century

1900 Hurricane destroys half of Galveston and kills 6,000 people.
1901 Mining engineer Captain A.F. Lucas discovers the Spindletop gusher near Beaumont.
1905 State of Texas grants custodianship of the Alamo to the Daughters of the Republic of Texas.

1907 Neiman Marcus department store opens in downtown Dallas.
1910 First military airflight in a Wright Brothers plane at Fort Sam Houston.
1916 Pancho Villa and his men cross the border to raid Texas communities.
1917 Race riots occur in Houston. Texas legislature votes to impeach Governor Jim Ferguson for mismanagement of state funds.
1920 Texas-Mexico border skirmishes come to an end.
1925 Miriam "Ma" Ferguson, wife of impeached Governor Jim Ferguson, becomes the first female Governor of Texas. She is re-elected for a second term in 1933.
1930 Oil strike by C.M. "Dad" Joiner 100 miles (160 km) east of Dallas becomes the East Texas Oil Field, the largest petroleum deposit on earth at that time.
1932 Texas Babe Didrikson Zaharias wins three Olympic gold medals.
1933 Texan Wiley Post makes first solo flight around the world.
1934 Career of Depression-era bank robbers Bonnie Parker and Clyde Barrow ends in a hail of bullets, after a 102-day manhunt led by Texas Ranger Frank Hamer.

POST-DEPRESSION TEXAS

1947 Fiery chain explosions demolish much of the coastal refinery town of Texas City, killing almost 600 and injuring almost 4,000.
1953 Dwight D. Eisenhower becomes the first Texas-born President of the US.
1956 George Stevens' movie of Edna Ferber's novel *Giant* is released to wide popularity, forever fixing the myth of tough Texas oilmen in American folklore.
1958 Texas Instruments' Jack Kilby ushers in the electronics age with his revolutionary development of the silicon chip.
1959 Lubbock-born rock 'n' roll singer Buddy Holly dies in an airplane crash.
1962 NASA opens Manned Spacecraft Center at Houston.
1963 President John F. Kennedy is assassinated while touring Dallas in a motorcade with Texas Governor John Connally. Kennedy's Texan-born Vice-President, Lyndon B. Johnson, is elevated to presidency.
1964 Lyndon B. Johnson wins election for the presidency in the largest landslide in US history.
1969 Apollo 11 commander Neil Armstrong calls Houston from the moon.
1976 Houston Democrat Barbara Jordan becomes the first African-American woman to deliver a keynote address at a party conference.
1978 *Dallas* TV drama series begins and is soon screened all over the world.
1985 Larry McMurtry's novel *Lonesome Dove*, about a Texas cattle drive, is published to immense popular and critical acclaim; TV adaptation follows.
1988 Sometime Houstonian George H.W. Bush is elected US President.
1993 Federal agents storm the compound of the Branch Davidians near Waco, resulting in more than 80 deaths. El Paso author Cormac McCarthy wins the National Book Award for *All the Pretty Horses*.
1998 Murderess Karla Faye Tucker, becomes the first woman to be executed in Texas since 1863.

2001 Texas Governor George W. Bush, Jr, son of George H.W. Bush, is sworn in as the 43rd President of the US. Tropical Storm Allison claims 23 lives. Thousands lose their jobs as Houston-based energy company, Enron, collapses.
2005 When Hurricane Katrina devastates the city of New Orleans in neighboring state Louisiana, Texas takes more than 100,000 refugees. Years later, many still live in the state.
2006 The Dallas Cowboys start construction on a new stadium, moving the team from the suburb of Irving to the suburb of Arlington.
2007 Former First Lady and conservationist, Lady Bird Johnson, dies at age 94. ❑

PRECEDING PAGES: the storming of the Alamo.
LEFT: Antonio Lopez De Santa Anna.
RIGHT: Republican Governor of Texas, George W. Bush, Jr is elected President of the US.

SIX FLAGS OVER TEXAS

Control of Texas has been handed from one external power to another, but independence and self-determination remain the watchwords of its people

A Texan's love of, and zeal for, Texas is stronger and more important than any regional affiliation. And the thing that binds Texans tightest is history.

Pass through a few Texas towns large enough to have an independent school system, and the names on the schools will begin to take on a familiar sound: Austin, Crockett, Fannin, Bonham, Lamar, Travis, Houston. Every town will have buildings or streets carrying one or more of those names, too.

Schoolchildren, taught Texas history by legislative decree, grow up on stories about its legendary heroes. Today, with thousands of Hispanic and black students, schools are beginning to be called by the names of ethnic heroes such as Benito Juárez, Emiliano Zapáta or Martin Luther King. Historical mythology is strong in all ethnic groups.

Unlike New England or the Atlantic seaboard states, Texas had no single source of settlement. White men came quite early to some parts of the state and arrived 350 years later to the others. The famous "Six Flags Over Texas" theme is rooted in historical fact. Each flag – those of Spain, Mexico, France, the Republic of Texas, the Confederacy, and the United States – represented a separate, if brief, period of the state's history.

The Texan coast may have been sighted by Amerigo Vespucci as early as 1497, but there is evidence of much earlier inhabitants – some possibly as far back as 37,000 years. Archeological studies have revealed no grand past civilizations in Texas such as were found in Mexico and Central and South America, but there were interesting cliff dwellers in the Texas Panhandle, and cave dwellers left traces of their fascinating paintings for us to ponder throughout western Texas. The Caddo confederations encountered in eastern Texas by the first Europeans were an agricultural people.

LEFT: three of the flags to have flown over Texas – the Mexican, the French and the Spanish.
RIGHT: trading with the natives.

The natives

Along the Gulf Coast, from Galveston Bay southwestward to Corpus Christi Bay, lived the nomadic Karankawas. Practitioners of ceremonial cannibalism, and always incredibly fierce, they had been wiped out by the white man's diseases and bullets by the 1850s. The Native

Americans that the Texas settlers battled against were Plains tribes who rode in from the north on horses descended from those brought to the New World by early Spanish explorers.

One of these, Alvar Núñez Cabeza de Vaca, was cast ashore on what is believed to have been Galveston Island, working his way across Texas for eight years before finally reaching Spanish Mexico in 1536.

He and three other shipwrecked survivors of the Narvaez expedition were enslaved by the Karankawas, but, after escaping, gained such reputations as medicine men that, when they approached a strange tribe, everyone turned out to welcome them.

When Cabeza de Vaca returned to civilization with tales of cities of gold and pearl "to the north," the myth of the Seven Cities of Cibola became the motive for several Spanish expeditions to Arizona, New Mexico and Texas. These golden cities and the equally mythical Gran Quivira were never found, of course, but the search for them led to Spanish colonization of the Southwest.

It was France laying claim to the area around Matagorda Bay that caused the Spanish to begin settling Texas. In 1685, French explorer René Robert Cavelier, Sieur de La Salle, had landed on the Texas coast and built a fort. By the time Spanish authorities in Mexico heard of the French intrusion, La Salle had been killed by his own men and the colony wiped out by Native Americans. Nevertheless, the nervous Spanish began to build missions on the border between French Louisiana and Spanish Texas.

In East Texas, they met Native Americans who greeted them with the cry "Tejas!." Thinking this was the name of a large tribe, the Spanish explorers called the area Tejas, or Texas. Later, settlers realized the word was a widely used greeting meaning "friend."

FRIENDS

The Native American cry "*tejas*" ("friend"), from which the state derived its name, has been translated over the years into the Texas state motto: "friendship."

Spanish heritage

Despite owning Texas for nearly three centuries, the Spanish settled it only for protection, in narrow strips along the coast and the rivers. Even San Antonio, the major Spanish settlement, was more important militarily and as a mission than as a commercial center.

Spain's mark, however, is still strong in Texas, with many of the outstanding geographical features and major rivers bearing Spanish names. Numerous Spanish missions still stand, at least partly restored, and various Spanish legal terms and property laws survive as Texas statutes.

Perhaps the most important Spanish inheritance was passed to cattle ranching. Almost every practice and piece of equipment used by ranchers has a Spanish name and origin. These range from *chicote*, a rawhide whip, to *tumbador*, someone who throws calves ready for branding.

The older regions of greatest Spanish colonization, from San Antonio and Laredo south, especially those along the Rio Grande river, still show evidence of this influence in their architecture, language, religion and everyday customs.

SAM HOUSTON

DAVID CROCKETT.

Between 1811 and 1821, Spain found itself continually putting down rebellions in Texas. In 1811, the young Santa Anna, later to be the scourge of the Alamo but then still a junior officer, was in one of these disciplinary forces. At the same time, the Spanish authorities recognized that the sparsely occupied parts of Texas were always under threat unless developed, so they encouraged immigration. Moses Austin was among the men who applied for an *empresario* grant but, when he died just after receiving it, his son, Stephen Fuller Austin (today known as the "Father of Texas"), renegotiated it in his own name and brought in 300 settlers.

The Texas nation

"Texians" (as they were then called) never learned to get along well with the Latin laws, religion and political practices of Mexico. Aggravated by the unpopular Law of April 6 1830, which aimed to restrict Anglo immigration, the inevitable break came in 1835 when the Anglo-American majority in Texas led a rebellion against what were considered despotic governmental practices. In reality, the despotism was mainly created by Mexican dictator Santa Anna.

The Texas Revolution lasted only eight months, but it gave Texas the myth and image which Texans are exhorted to live up to. It was this short but successful period of rebellion that created the Texas Valhalla, with such heroes as Ben Milam, James Fannin, Jim Bowie, William B. Travis, James Bonham, Davy Crockett with his fellow Tennesseeans, and General Sam Houston.

Those first colonists are to Anglo-Texas what the passengers of the *Mayflower* are to Massachusetts: the proudest blood lines go back to "The Old 300." In 1821, Mexico gained its independence from Spain and, within the next decade, 41 *empresario* contracts were signed, permitting the arrival of nearly 14,000 Anglo-Americans to supplement the original Spanish population. Eventually hundreds more settlers joined the Austin colonists.

FAR LEFT: Sam Houston, Governor and Senator of Tennessee, involved in the Texas Revolution.
LEFT: Congressman Davy Crockett.
ABOVE: Texas battle flag in Austin's State Capitol.

From the Texas Revolution came the stories of the Alamo, those 13 fateful days in 1836 when 189 patriots held out against the fierce onslaught of 4,000 Mexicans, who eventually overran the fort, killing all its defenders, save a few women, children and slaves.

Minimizing his losses, Santa Anna said: "It was but a small affair," and ordered the bodies

of the heroes to be burned. His aide, noting that he took many casualties, losing many of his best men, muttered: "Another such victory and we are ruined."

Forty-six days later, the Texans got their revenge. Along with a group of American volunteers, and led by General Sam Houston, they gained vengeance at San Jacinto.

Taking Santa Anna and his 1,500 men by surprise, Houston's force, though greatly outnumbered, routed the Mexicans within minutes. "Remember the Alamo," they shouted to each other as they charged, and it has never been forgotten. Santa Anna was captured, 600 of his

troops were killed, and Texas was free. A new republic was born.

The period that followed was the seedbed for the feelings of loyalty for which Texans are so famous. And no matter how diverse their lives, or how far from Texas they may wander, all Texans hold the Alamo in common ownership.

From 1836 to 1845, the Republic of Texas was an independent nation with its own flag, its own ambassadors, its own President and Congress, and, after some moving around, its own specifically designed national capital at Austin. It is true that millions of Texans today may recall the Republic only occasionally, but they have never entirely forgotten it.

Their self-reliance and fierce loyalty (which has not always endeared Texans to their fellow American citizens) come from that decade of independence. The state seal and the Lone Star flag, which is still displayed as frequently as the national banner, remain from that independent government.

First president

Commander of the army Sam Houston was elected as first President of the new Republic of Texas, his 5,119 votes far outnumbering the total votes of his rivals (Henry Smith, 743; Stephen F. Austin, 587).

The Mexicans were still to cause major trouble in the next decade, when, in 1842, they invaded Texas and briefly captured San Antonio before withdrawing. And there was also the Indian problem.

Houston had lived among the Cherokees, and understood the Indian mentality more than most. He wanted to stabilize the situation, and proposed a guarantee of Indian rights through legal title to Indian lands. But he found that he was unable to keep the promises he made to the Cherokees. When Houston's term expired, the new president, Mirabeau Lamar, proposed that all Indians be expelled from Eastern Texas: "Nothing short of this will bring us peace and safety," Lamar thundered, "the white man and the red man cannot live in harmony together... Nature forbids it..."

The republic expanded rapidly, tripling its population, but the influx of slaves – brought by southerners settling on the Gulf Coast to develop the cotton crop – was to prove disputacious when Texans voted to join the Union in 1845.

As part of the annexation arrangement, the Federal Congress assumed the Texas Republic's $5 million in debts and allowed Texas to retain possession of all undistributed land (although, in the 1840s and 1850s, much of it was still in the possession of the Comanches). There were no federal taxes in effect but Texas had no wealth, only land. It sold to the US its rights to New Mexico and Colorado, and Sam Houston and other conservatives supported the Boundary Act on the grounds that the state had more desert land than it could use.

Pressing for funds for frontier defense, Texas persuaded Congress to give it an extra $7.75 million in 1855. With the money, the state

launched a major building program of state structures, courthouses, schools, transportation systems – all of which was achieved without imposing taxes. This then conditioned Texas to look for sources other than taxes to finance its activities.

By 1860, when Sam Houston was elected Governor for a second term, Texas was again in debt. The following year, when the Civil War broke out, Houston was forced to resign after he refused to swear allegiance to the Confederacy.

THE LAND IS OURS

Unusually, Texas still owns all its public lands. If the Federal government wishes to create a park, or cut a stand of timber, it has to ask the state's permission.

so little ideology other than a profound belief in the American nation and its destiny..."

Three months after Houston's burial, in 1863, the Confederate legislature of Texas passed a resolution: "His public services through a long and eventful life, his unblemished patriotism, his great private and moral worth, and his untiring, devoted and zealous regard for the interests of the state of Texas command our highest admiration, and should be held in perpetual remembrance by the people of this state."

American giant

"In retirement and isolation at Huntsville, Houston was a tragic figure. He did not live out the war," wrote historian T.R. Fehrenbach. "He was a giant of the American 19th century who had outlived his time and the full understanding of his countrymen. Houston confused men; he had the politician's knack of listening attentively to everything brought before him, saying little and always giving the impression he might go along with every argument. He had

LEFT: the capital of Texas in Austin.

ABOVE: a cowboy at an annual western festival at Fort Worth Stockyards.

Newcomers

During the period of revolution, resettlement and republic, thousands of people came to Texas to get away from whatever their life had been "back home." They weren't always fleeing from the law. More often, the new Texans came west to escape failure or some sort of unhappiness that could be left behind. This is very much a continuing tradition as, even today, Texas becomes home for thousands who leave other parts of the nation every month to seek new opportunities in the Lone Star State. When one recalls that a high percentage of the dead at the Alamo, and a majority of the unfortunates who were slaughtered earlier at Goliad, were

recent arrivals in Texas, and that even Davy Crockett, the superhero of the Alamo, had only been in Texas for a few weeks, the tradition of the newcomer hero becomes understandable.

At the time of the Civil War, most Texas settlers were from the agricultural South. A plantation economy, with its accompanying slavery, controlled East Texas and the Coastal Plains, where cotton was a profitable crop. Thus, Texas was overwhelmingly drawn into the Civil War on the side of the Confederacy. It was never torn by any major battles, and, after the war, sectional wounds healed quicker in Texas than in any other southern state. Within a decade,

newcomers from northern states were not only arriving in great numbers but were assuming positions of business and economic leadership.

Opportunity frontier

When the Union blockaded the Gulf Coast during the Civil War, Texas managed to smuggle some cotton across the Rio Grande for shipment to world markets, but the blockade was serving another purpose, then unknown. Unable to export its cattle even to the Confederate Army, Texas' herds built up during the Civil War to more than 3 million. Once the war was over, there was tremendous demand for this beef in northern and western states.

Texas went through relatively little of the sorrow and desperation of the Reconstruction period. And because it was the only ex-Confederate state that offered its southern sister states hope of a new beginning, southerners flocked there. The 15 years that followed Appomattox saw Texas emerge as the opportunity frontier of the whole nation, north and south alike. It has retained that position, and has continued to uphold that reputation.

Families from every social level picked up and moved to Texas, bursting the old frontier boundaries until, like a flooding river, they swept out onto the prairies and battled with Native Americans for the wealth of grass and soil which was once thought to be the "Great American Desert." This movement to the frontier created two new Texas myths: one was the frontiersman and his sturdy pioneer wife, and the other was the cowboy.

Texas was readmitted to the Union in 1870 and, with the 1875 surrender of Comanche Chief Quanah Parker at Fort Sill, Oklahoma, the far western portion of the state was finally ready for ranching on a large scale. Barely a decade later, though, the wide open spaces were being fenced and confined as settlers and sheep farmers fought to contain the open range.

Oil was discovered at Corsicana in 1894 by workers drilling for water. With the discovery of the major gusher at Spindletop in 1901, Texas entered the new century with an economic boom.

The Texas style

The state's tradition of independence has had a direct influence on both the business climate and the political philosophy of modern Texas, creating a sense of self-sufficiency which, critics say, amounts at times to the conviction of Divine Destiny in the minds of some residents.

Whether embodied in the bygone wildcatter oilmen or contemporary computer magnates who amass fortunes at breakneck speed, the old ethos of resourcefulness and individual initiative still holds sway in Texas. Everyday life is infused with a dramatic tension between the legacy of the frontier past and the imperatives of the urban present. ❑

LEFT: Houston's Ship Canal, vital access to the sea.
RIGHT: the historic Strand district, Galveston, survivor of the mighty 1900 hurricane.

ELISSA
STOP

Coca-Cola
WESTERN
HATTERS
COKERS
HATS

GHT
HOTEL
FORT WORTH STOCK YARDS

Jared L. Brush.
Charles Lux.
R. G. Head.
John H. Iliff.
Thos. H. Lawrence.
John W. Snyder.
John T. Lytle.

THE TALE OF THE LONGHORN

With hardy livestock and even hardier cowboys, life on the great cattle trails was no picnic

The first cattle known to have entered Texas were 500 cows brought in by Coronado in 1541. Subsequent explorers also brought cattle, which gradually wandered into the wilderness. By 1757, Reynosa (pop. 269) had 18,000 head of cattle.

A fat cow was worth four pesos in 1779, with hides and tallow more valuable than beef. Mission Espiritu Santo, on the banks of the winding Guadalupe river, between present-day Victoria and Mission Valley, was the first great cattle ranch in Texas. Around 1770, it claimed 40,000 head of cattle.

Ideal trail cattle

The definitive Texas cow was the longhorn – a hybrid breed from Spanish *retinto* (criollo) stock and English Hereford and Bakewell cattle that were brought in from Ohio, Kentucky and other southern and midwestern states in the 1820s and '30s. These longhorns had a spread of 5 or 6 ft (1.5 or 2 meters), with some spanning a full 8 ft (2.5 meters) from tip to tip. They were apparently "tough to eat and tougher to handle" but, with their long legs and hard hooves, were ideal trail cattle which gained weight even on the way to market.

"No animal of the cow kind will shift and take care of itself under all conditions as will the longhorns," declared a veteran rancher, Charles Goodnight. "As trail cattle, their equal has never been known. They can go further without water and endure more suffering than others."

By the mid-19th century, great hordes of Texas longhorns that had been roaming freely, and shaped by nature and environmental conditions, were being gathered into herds for the trail drive north. "No other industry in the Southwest had such an economic significance or such picturesque aspects. The driving of herds caused towns, customs and a distinctive type of people to grow up beside the trails," was the assessment of a 1930s writer for the *WPA Guide.*

Cattleman Edward Piper made what may have been the first northern drive in 1846, moving a herd from Texas to Ohio. He was followed almost immediately by many other contractors, especially after the end of the Civil War. Eight to 20 hands were needed to trail a herd of 2,000–3,000 cattle, about one man per 250–350 animals, with crews including a trail boss and cook plus a horse wrangler (usually a young boy), to handle the six or eight mounts needed for each man.

The boss

The all-important trail boss had "as many duties as the captain of a steamboat." He arose early to wake and assign the men, ensured there were always enough provisions, settled all disputes, kept counting the cattle to see none had been

PRECEDING PAGES: cattle and cowboy nostalgia for Fort Worth's Stock Yards.

LEFT: a gallery of Texas cattlemen.

RIGHT: Chisholm Trail round-up, Fort Worth.

lost and rode ahead to check on water supplies. "A boss," explained one, "rides about three or four times as far as the herd goes." Exploring ahead, the boss would ride part way back and, from some hilltop, wave his hat to indicate which direction the herd should take.

Points and drags

The herd itself was usually a mix of beeves – mature steers – and cows (who walked with a less steady stride). It had a head (point) and feet (drag), with swing men watching the "shoulders" and flank men watching the "hips." Riders bringing up the drag, sometimes physically pushing the laggards ahead, were enveloped in dust, especially on the alkali flats, and kept a "wipe" across their faces. The best place to learn cuss words, recalled one veteran, was always on the drag. "There is a Homeric quality about the cowboys' profanity and vulgarity that pleases rather than repulses," concluded John A. Lomax, the music historian: "He spoke out plainly the impulses of his heart."

It was crucial to keep the herd moving, although the trick to successful trail herding was to keep the cattle from knowing they were under restraint. One drawback to mixed herds was the almost daily arrival of new calves, which usually had to be shot or abandoned, as they could rarely keep up with the demanding pace of their elders.

NEVER CROSS A COOK

After the trail boss, the cook held the most authority and, for obvious reasons, it paid to stay on his good side. In addition to driving the chuck wagon, serving up grub and acting as doctor to both men and animals, a cook might also serve as a custodian for personal belongings, a stakeholder for bets and even be ready to pull a tooth. As for what he cooked, the mainstays were fluffy sourdough biscuits, accompanying pork and beans or the inevitable steak, with occasionally son-of-a-gun stew, which appeared to contain everything except horns, hide and hooves. Accompanying this came six-shooter coffee, strong enough to float a pistol.

Branding

Cattle drives began in early spring when new grass was emerging but before the rivers were swollen with heavy run-offs. In the north, drives had to be completed before the autumn snowfalls.

As the hundreds of cattle bore the brands of many different owners, they would be fed through a chute where each beast would be lightly slashed with a road brand, on the left side behind the shoulder. The owner's brand

would have been applied by the *marcador* when, as a calf, it was flanked, mugged or bulldogged, each of which methods "throws" the animal on its right side, leaving its left side upwards for branding. Branding required skill and experience because, if the irons were pressed too hard, the mark would go too deep and leave sores. There were other preliminaries too: the male calves had to be castrated (the roasted testicles were a much-prized snack), and horns had to be trimmed to prevent the animals injuring each other.

Brands were not widely used by Spanish and Mexican ranchers because their *ranchos* operated on the *patrón* system. The *patrón*, in the manner of a feudal lord, owned all the cattle and land within the "fiefdom" of his *rancho*, so there was very little need to establish his ownership by branding. If the cattle were on his land, they were his.

Each Texas ranch had its own distinctive brand, which was registered with the Cattleman's Association, and established brands were recognized by their distinctive pattern everywhere on the range. Before the Civil War, it was not uncommon for a South Texas rancher to start a herd by rounding up unbranded cattle and giving them his brand. "Mavericks," or unbranded cattle, are said to have gotten their name from Samuel Maverick, the Matagorda County entrepreneur of the 1840s.

On the move

Once under way, the trail drive would cover up to 16 miles (26 km) per day, although a herd making only 10 or 12 miles (16 or 19 km) could take a leisurely lunch by grazing and thus put on some weight en route. The easiest part of each day was the afternoon, when the thirsty cattle were eager to reach water – the basic secret of successful trailing being the grazing and watering: well-fed cattle were less likely to stampede.

At night, the foreman would bed down the animals in some cool, dry spot well away from woodland (that might hide Indians) or ravines (into which they might stampede) and the two men on watch would ride slowly around the herd, usually humming or crooning softly, which the cattle appeared to find soothing.

The watchmen, judging time by the stars, changed every two hours – a pot of coffee was kept hot on the coals all night – and the guard waking his successor always made sure

LEFT: branding a cow.

ABOVE: contemporary engraving of a longhorn cattle drive to Abilene, Kansas, in the 1870s.

Samuel Maverick

Samuel Maverick, born in South Carolina in 1803 to a prosperous family, arrived in South Texas at Matagorda Bay in 1835. He had been a lawyer back home and planned to start a new career as a land speculator in this promising new territory, but almost immediately he found himself caught up in frontier politics and the Mexican War. At one point he was almost executed by the Mexicans as a spy, but, after an appeal by the wife of a fellow prisoner, all were reprieved.

Before long, Maverick was busy selling his properties back East and buying land at 15¢ per acre. By 1842, he was said to have become the biggest landholder in the state and his stated ambition was to travel on his own land all the 600 miles (960 km) from San Antonio to El Paso. Later that year, Maverick was caught during the invasion of San Antonio and imprisoned in Mexico for seven months. On his return, he reluctantly accepted 400 cattle from a neighbor in lieu of a debt, thus becoming a rancher.

His spread was amidst the tall grass and wild clover of the Matagorda Peninsula, a 70-mile (112-km) long sandbar off the Gulf Coast as much as 5 miles (8 km) wide, with an irregular grass-covered prairie running down the center. Without much interest, he placed the cattle under the indifferent care of his black slaves, who are said to have reported that their boss was not enthusiastic about applying a burning iron to flesh. The slaves branded about one-third of the growing herd, many of which eventually strayed to the mainland.

Charlie Siringo, who in 1885 published the first cowboy biography, referred to Maverick as "being a chickenhearted old rooster," who "wouldn't brand or earmark any of his cattle." Another story, however, says that he had just too many cattle to brand. There did exist an "MK" brand but it was never extensively used.

At one meeting of neighboring cattlemen, Maverick supposedly told them that if they all made sure their own cattle were branded then the ones left over would clearly be his, a naive attitude one might think, except that naive might not be the precise word to describe the largest landowner in the entire state.

Stray cattle were hardly a rarity but, in those parts, when cowmen came across unbranded ones, it was usually assumed they were Samuel Maverick's. Naturally, many of Maverick's unmarked herd were seized by other, less scrupulous ranchers, who stamped them with their own brand. It being the custom of the times, nobody regarded it as stealing: if cattle were unbranded or the brand was unregistered, there was simply no recourse in law, although it was widely accepted that suckling cows belonged to their mothers and shared the same brand. Some heartless but enterprising "maverickers" were not averse to slitting a calf's tongue so that it could not suckle nor cry for its mother. According to an old saying all it took to make a cowman was "a rope, nerve to use it and a branding iron."

Some ranchers hired "maverickers" to brand as many as 18 "mavericks" per day, at 50 cents to a dollar apiece. Eventually, in 1854, Samuel Maverick sent a party of *vaqueros* to round up his herd, which numbered several hundred, and move it to Rancho Conquista, a spread he'd acquired on the San Antonio river, 50 miles (80 km) from the city.

More than ever disenchanted with the cattle business, Maverick later sold his herd, but the use of his name to describe stray cattle spread beyond the state of Texas and lives on today to signify people who make their own way in life, independent of the crowd. ❑

LEFT: Samuel Maverick, the unconventional rancher and one-time biggest landowner in Texas.

to call him by his name. "No one liked to touch a sleeping man," wrote historian Wayne Gard, "lest he become so startled that involuntarily he would reach for his six-shooter."

The drive cost the herd's owner about $500 per month, worked out on the basis of about 75¢ per head of cattle for three months.

MAKING BIG MONEY

In 1884, the cattle-driving Pryor brothers were contracted to deliver 45,000 head in 15 separate lots, earning themselves a handy net profit of around $20,000.

Breaking the ban

When shipping began to California and New Orleans (after the cattle had been driven to the nearest railheads in Kansas and Missouri – some 1,000 miles/1,600 km away), cows were fetching only three or four dollars a head in Texas, while they were worth upward of $30 apiece in the North. In 1867, defying a ban by several neighboring states (imposed because local ranchers feared the spread of the deadly Texas tick fever), Illinois cattle dealer Joseph G. McCoy managed to persuade Kansas Pacific officials to lay a siding to Abilene in Kansas, at the edge of the quarantine area. From there, he began shipping cattle to the Union Stockyards in Chicago. He sent 35,000 head the first year and kept doubling the figure until 1871, in which year cowboys pushed about 600,000 animals north from Texas. Over the next 20 years contractors drove 5–10 million cattle out of Texas, becoming the state's first big income producer. Longhorns with their stamina and endurance became a symbol of the state.

After the slaughter of the buffalo herds, and after the Indians (who, anyway, usually preferred to eat buffalo rather than beef) had been confined, the ranches spread north onto the Great Plains, where windmills and wells solved the problem of water supplies.

Ranchers claimed as much land as they needed and enforced their "property rights" with six-shooters.

ABOVE: re-creating a trail ride at Gainesville, near the Texas-Oklahoma border.

Barbed reply

By the 1880s, with the state trying unsuccessfully to ban foreign ownership, would-be ranchers from all over the world were flocking to Texas, but overstocking, followed by a severe drought, led to the inevitable bust.

New procedures were desperately needed; people believed that stock had to be both con-

served and contained. Such fencing as there had been in the past in Texas had been constructed primarily from the osage tree, but this changed in 1874, when an Illinois man, Joseph F. Glidden, was granted a patent for new fencing material which consisted of barbs wrapped around a single strand of wire. There were hundreds of competing designs but Joseph Glidden's was the one which eventually predominated. It was praised as being "light as air, stronger than whisky and cheap as dirt."

ART ON THE TRAIL

Charles M. Russell was the major painter of the longhorn's "fire, muscle and movement," while Frederic Remington specialized in depicting trails and stampedes.

Fence cutting

Battles between cattlemen and the "nesters" (small farmers, sheep ranchers, etc.) broke out, with thousands of incidents of wire cutting – a Fence Cutting War that soon embroiled the Texas Rangers. Nevertheless, sheep ranching persevered and, by early in the 20th century, Texas had become the major state for wool production, a $23 million crop from several million sheep.

When fencing began there were other problems. For instance, those with legal title to land were prone to fencing it off and thus barring others' cattle from grass and water. Compromises eventually had to be made, such as openings for public roads every 3 miles (5 km) and amending English common law to recognize that, in arid country, all people living in a watershed had rights to flowing water. Similarly, individual preferences had to be taken into account in a state so large, where different counties held different views of segregation, alcohol and carrying arms. "It was firmly established in the Texan mind that men make laws to their need and satisfaction and for no other reason," wrote the historian T.R. Fehrenbach, explaining that trying to impress a Texan with a notion of a higher law was like impressing a Comanche with the wisdom of the Great White Father in Washington.

Last of the longhorns

With the end of unlimited free range grass, it became more economical to raise cattle that developed faster than longhorns, which, by the 1920s, had been almost bred out of existence. Shorthorns and Herefords predominated.

Longhorns were saved from probable extinction by Will C. Barnes and other Forest Service men, who collected a small herd of breeding stock for Oklahoma's Wichita Mountains Wildlife Refuge. A few years later, oilman Sid W. Richardson financed the acquisition of small herds for Texas state parks. Eventually, cattlemen rediscovered the longhorn's longevity, its resistance to disease, fertility, ease of calving, ability to thrive on marginal pastures, and also the fact that its leaner beef was in tune with the times.

One result of the cattle drives was that ranches were established not only in the uninhabited parts of Texas but also on the hitherto remote plains of the Middle West and in the Indian Territory that is now the state of Oklahoma. As the Indians were pushed further and further back, even the mountains and desert plains in the far-Western parts of the state, beyond the Pecos river, became valuable property. Indeed, these are the major cowman's strongholds today, and they contain some of the largest ranches in the state. ❑

LEFT: pioneering rancher Charles Goodnight.
RIGHT: longhorn at the enormous King Ranch in southern Texas.

SHRIMP
FLOUN
12
CHICKEN NECKS
LIVE SHRIM
FREE PARKIN
FOR SALE
MORE
(409) 68

HEADQUA
CHIPS
NORTH JETTY
BAIT SHOP
NORTH JETTY
OPEN
AND THE
FISHING IS GREAT!
LIVE BAIT
OD AND REEL
WATER
SIT A SPELL !!
25
HEAD

MODERN TIMES

After the legacy of the longhorn came the bounty of black gold, and with it an increasingly urban sophistication for the rural state of Texas

Although at least a dozen western states contributed to the cowboy legend, Texas has done more than its share to make the cowboy an American icon. Several thousand cowboys can still be found doing all the traditional cowboy chores, except fighting Native Americans – which was never a cowboy chore in the first place. The traditional garb of the cowboy is also seen today in hundreds of Texas cities, towns and villages, although not every pretender wearing high-heeled boots and a cowboy hat will be a cowboy.

"The first sign that someone is becoming a real Texan," said the author James Michener, appears to be "that first big purchase of cowboy hat and boots... then you're on your way." Boots, oversized buckle belts, denims and rodeo shirts are everyday wear for millions of Texans – not a costume – and a visitor who wishes to dress in the same manner should feel perfectly free to do so, though you're likely to look out of place in such garb in most of the Dallas, Houston and Austin areas: Texans not only accept but encourage visitors to wear traditional clothes.

Frontier heritage

In a sense, the frontiersman and his mate survive, although the conditions and the times that made them have long since passed. It is the frontier that still provides so much of the motivation for today's Texas: self-sufficiency, a sense of obligation to one's fellow citizen, openness, mutual trust and a sense of sharing by people living under the same pressures. A lot of Texas business, including big business deals, is conducted on the basis of a handshake or a telephone conversation; sadly, it is rapidly becoming rarer in Texas.

The frontier was a mutually dependent society: if someone was lazy, weak or careless, everyone might be hurt and thus all were expected to shoulder their share of community work and duty. Hard work and shrewdness were valued over the creative arts and purely intellectual pursuits. Today, most Texans are still deeply influenced by these values, although by now they are far more receptive to intellectual and artistic accomplishment.

The great oil rush

The greatest change in the way Texas lived and viewed itself began in 1901, when the Spindletop oil field near Beaumont, in the southeastern corner of the state, blew in with billions of barrels of oil each year. Spindletop was where the world's modern petroleum industry was born. No field like it had been dreamed of before and, with the later development of the East Texas oilfield in Rusk County, it ensured that Texas, and the world, would never be the same again.

With the Spindletop discovery, the state had jumped from an agricultural economy to a financial-industrial economy. At first, Texans were slow to recognize change and many still

PRECEDING PAGES: bait shop on the Bolivar peninsula.
LEFT: cowboy boots come in all guises in Texas.
RIGHT: not-so-lonesome cowboy.

haven't fully accepted it. To this day, the struggle between rural and urban values continues to divide the state. In the 1960s, the trend toward suburbanization increased, as more and more farmers preferred to live in town and visit their fields by car. Indeed, most Texans now live in urban areas, a fact not always apparent from the many movies and novels about the state that turn on the romance of the past.

Since Spindletop, Texas has rarely failed to lead the US in petroleum production. In the early days, it led the world. This added to the state's tendency to measure itself not against sister states but against the world.

Recent decades

The 1960s produced a series of events bigger even than the state itself. The traumatic assassination of President John F. Kennedy in Dallas in 1963 was followed by the succession of the vice president, Lyndon B. Johnson – a Texan – as the 36th US President. The year before had seen the opening of NASA's Manned Spacecraft Center at Houston, and, before the decade was over, Apollo 11 astronaut Neil Armstrong was transmitting the first words from the surface of the moon: "Houston, Tranquility Base here. The Eagle has landed." Somehow, it seemed appropriately Texan in style.

A TEXAS PRESIDENT

Lyndon Baines Johnson (1908–73) was born into a Texas Hill Country farming family. Ruthlessly ambitious, he became a senator in 1948 and John F. Kennedy's Vice-President in 1960. Three years later, aboard Air Force One, he was sworn in as US President, just 99 minutes after Kennedy's assassination in Dallas.

In the 1964 election, Johnson had a landslide victory but his years at the White House, dedicated to creating "the Great Society," were darkened by the shadow of the Vietnam War. Vociferous domestic opposition to the conflict persuaded "LBJ" to step down in 1968 and he retired, with his wife, Lady Bird, to their Texas ranch.

In the 1970s, while price freezes, gas shortages and minority rights became as familiar concepts to Texans as to the rest of the country, the state continued to grow. In 1973, it became the fourth most populous state in the Union.

The Arab oil embargo increased domestic production in Texas oilfields. Towns such as Lubbock, Abilene and Odessa doubled in size. But no big new fields have been discovered for 50 years now and, with the cost of bringing up existing supplies double what it was in the 1970s, the state has increasingly found itself supplying oil equipment to other producers, such as Mexico. Texas crews now operate offshore oil rigs all over the world.

In the 1990s, Texas replaced Democratic Governor Ann Richards (1991–94) with the future US President, the Republican George W. Bush. However, through Mrs Richards, women had finally cracked the political glass ceiling, and, in 1993, Texas elected its first woman senator, Kay Bailey Hutchison.

Superlative Texas

Texas facts and figures are seldom expressed in other than superlative terms: *The* biggest; *The* best. And Texas planners tend to think along the same lines. That's one of the reasons why such a high percentage of recent US building and real estate development has taken place in cities such as Dallas, Houston and Austin. Some Texas cities have experienced the disadvantages of uncontrolled growth. But this fact has not discouraged Texas developers.

Today, in the wake of the Iraq War and the soaring price of oil, the commodity itself is of critical importance. Aside from that, though, oil is an element of Texas' identity. Even in the 34 non-producing counties, oil plays a vital part in local business. Dallas is a perfect example: it is a city legendary the world over for its involvement in the oil business, but it is located in a section of Texas that has never produced any.

However, Texas' rich oil resources are a double-edged sword. On the one hand, oil has brought immeasurable wealth to the state, especially now that domestic sources of energy are so highly valued. But Texans' reliance on oil has also made the state vulnerable. The crash in world oil prices caused a great deal of hardship in Texas in the early 1980s and was followed by the shock of the Savings and Loan crisis of the late 1980s, when over a million Texans lost their homes. Now, state leaders recognize the importance of economic diversification and go out of their way to attract high-tech firms. Computer chip fabrication and software development have found a receptive home in Austin.

FAR LEFT: John F. Kennedy, assassinated in Dallas.
LEFT: Ann Richards, Governor in the 1990s.
ABOVE: President George W. Bush speaks in the Rio Grande Valley about immigration policy.

The new economy

Everything – from the fashion industry to movie and television production – is currently taking root in Texas, and all of these new players are challenging the oil industry's long tenure at the head of the state's economic pyramid. The new economy is based on a more general and sounder combination of technology, manufacturing and finance.

Movies in Texas

For a long time after William Wellman cast the big sky near San Antonio as a featured lead in his seminal airplane drama *Wings* (1927), major movie production in Texas was a rare event. Notable movies made in Texas were virtually unheard of during the glory days of the Hollywood studio era, when even Howard Hawks' *Red River* (1948), the saga of a Texas cattle drive, employed Arizona locations. The lonely house on the West Texas plain in George Stevens' *Giant* (1956), filmed near Marfa, echoed that movie's solitary eminence among film stories about Texas that were actually shot in the state.

A case can be made for Texas novelist Larry McMurtry as author of the soaring popularity Texas now enjoys as a film location. The adaptation of a McMurtry novel, *Hud* (1963), was the first major hit movie shot in Texas since *Giant*, and was followed by Warren Beatty's *Bonnie and Clyde* (1967), shot near Dallas. Peter Bogdanovich's film of another McMurtry novel, *The Last Picture Show* (1971), shot in and around McMurtry's hometown of Archer City in West Texas, created an even bigger stir.

Despite accelerating activity throughout the 1960s, 1970s and 1980s, the dream of a film industry to match Texas' increasing opinion of its importance was still a chimera, when another Larry McMurtry yarn rode to the rescue. His big mid-career best-seller, *Lonesome Dove*, an elegiac epic about a cattle drive, became an enormously popular TV mini-series in 1989.

The timing was probably coincidental and its significance more symbolic than real, but after *Dove* came the deluge: Oliver Stone's *JFK* (1991), Clint Eastwood's *A Perfect World* (1993), *What's Eating Gilbert Grape* (1993), *Dazed and Confused* (1993), *The Underneath* (1995), *Lone Star* (1996), *The Whole Wide World* (1996), *Michael* (1996), *Suburbia* (1997), *The Newton Boys* (1998) and *Hope Floats* (1998) – all but the Stone picture shot in or near Austin. Notable television movies include *The Good Old Boys* and a sequel to *Lonesome Dove*, *Streets of Laredo* (both 1995).

Lonesome Dove was adapted by Austin screenwriter William Wittliff, and most of it was shot near the capital city. It was Austin's charms that finally attracted enough stars for a permanent movie colony in Texas. Houston and Dallas could match Austin's non-union labor costs and exceed its technical facilities, but they could not compete with its easygoing hedonism and plentiful live music – both appealing to movie folk – nor the diversity of nearby locations.

Pine forests, scrubby hills, vast prairies, small town squares, and, during the odd rainy year, lush pastures and sparkling creeks can all be found within striking distance of the capital city. And a typical winter in Austin is sunny and agreeable.

A base of competent film crew personnel developed in Austin, many of whom cut their teeth on independent features such as Richard Linklater's *Slacker* (1990), made for milk money and entirely devoted to a ramble through everyday Austin bohemia. Linklater's decision to remain in Austin while he pursued his career gave heart and employment to other young filmmakers, and, within a few years, Hollywood producer Lynda Obst chose the area for a second home.

By the turn of the millennium, Dallas was generating the greatest sums of money as the base for two popular TV series, *Walker Texas Ranger* and *Barney*, while feature filmmakers virtually tripped over each other in Austin, where Hollywood features were regularly in progress.

Dallas money versus Austin cachet: a vintage Texas state of affairs that is likely to endure. ❑

LEFT: James Dean and Elizabeth Taylor on the set of *Giant*, filmed at Marfa.

Texas has taken over national leadership in many phases of the chemical industry (not just petrochemicals). It has remained an important aerospace center, and is attracting more and more technological manufacturing firms. Still a major farm and ranch center, it contains the most farmland of any American state and ranks third among the states in total agricultural income. It is first in the production of cotton, cattle, sheep, goats and, in most years, rice.

Its location in the US "sunbelt" is also enticing. All kinds of corporations are shifting their headquarters to the Lone Star State, not just for its more favorable climate but also for its access to world markets, its central location and its eagerness to acquire fiscal and industrial families. Major international corporations, too, have opened branches in Dallas and Houston.

Tradition and pragmatism

Despite their strong sense of history, Texans have always been receptive to new ideas, never holding on to some outdated asset for sentimental or historical reasons. Although they quite clearly appreciate tradition, they are also a pragmatic people, and they are willing to make changes in the name of progress. Even the Alamo, the sacred shrine of Texas liberty, had to be rescued from commercial development in 1905. In most cases, historical and sentimental concerns take a back seat when they involve anything less than the biggest and the best. This attitude might strike some observers as rather hard-hearted, but Texans are so frank that most people find it endearing.

Friendliness and hospitality

Friendliness and hospitality are Texan traditions that are quickly adopted by new residents. Visitors will find Texans, in general, helpful and gracious. They are never too busy to answer questions, give directions or help out people in need. The smaller the town, the more likely you are to receive this personal attention, but even the big cities of Texas have more public heart than most other big cities.

Most Texans show a great deal of public respect for the elderly and for women. Even street urchins use such terms as "ma'am" and "sir" to adults. Many Texans see themselves as the highest expression of the American character. To them, Texas epitomizes the American dream, and is valid in every way. They believe in Texas in a way more often found in older,

ABOVE: a group of Hurricane Katrina refugees reunite in Fort Worth. They were among the 100,000 who fled to Texas in September 2005.

more chauvinistic cultures. But Texas is also maturing, taking on an international viewpoint as more and more of its young people travel outside its borders.

Sporting artists

Texas is growing swiftly and coming of age, socially and artistically, with a speed to match its technology. Although in some parts of the state artists are often not given the respect and support they receive in other societies, Texas is beginning to accept more responsibility for supporting the arts in their varied forms. And there are few visitors who will not find some expression of their native or national tradition honored in one of the Texas museums, galleries or parks.

Texas also plays a lot and is dedicated to sports, particularly baseball and American football, although soccer has become popular with younger Texans, more and more of whom are playing the game. Texas athletes of both sexes have established themselves as stars and record-holders in track and field, swimming, gymnastics, golf, baseball, basketball, tennis, motor and horse racing, sailing and polo. There is scarcely a Texas town that cannot volunteer the name of some native son or daughter who has gone on to receive national or international sporting acclaim. And visitors who participate in such activities as golf or tennis will find doors opened to them.

ALL EYES ON DALLAS

The TV series *Dallas* first aired in the US in April 1978 and ran until May 1991. The drama topped ratings charts all over the world.

Increasingly urban

Although in the eyes of the United States, as well as the rest of the world, the prevailing image of Texas remains rural, it is solidly urbanized by a ratio of 10 to one. Life today in the larger Texas cities has scant connection with the Texas of history and romance. Nevertheless, these metropolitan people were fascinated, along with everybody else, by the TV drama series *Dallas,* which – despite the cast working in high-rise offices – pictured the ranch as the center of Texas family life, even if the Ewings were not exactly an average family.

The depiction of smart, sophisticated shopping centers and cosmopolitan boutiques as typical of Texas, as in some recent films and television dramas, violates some of the world's most precious preconceptions (or misconceptions). Yet the urbanity is all true, and in the major cities one can find virtually every famous retail name and designer label offered in the capitals of Europe and Asia, or in New York or Los Angeles.

As a matter of fact, many Europeans and glamorous figures from the rest of the US come to Texas to shop in such exclusive stores as the world-renowned Neiman Marcus. Few people realize that Dallas ranks as the second- or third-largest fashion marketing center in the country. But, of course, as Texas has grown, it has acquired the vices and problems it long scorned as "big city" or "foreign." It houses three of the largest US cities, so slums, pollution and traffic are a part of the urban scene.

A mini-US

Texas is said to be modern America in microcosm, bowing to changes while proclaiming a rugged individualism.

Perhaps this is the best way for personal independence in the US to survive – honoring traditions while, at the same time, regarding them with a flexible state of mind. ❑

LEFT: Cheerleading for the NFL Houston Texans.
RIGHT: the mustang sculptures of Las Colinas, Irving, near Dallas.

FORT WORTH
CHANGE
Dash For The Timbers
By Frederic Remington

TEXANS

Peoples from all over the world have made Texas – the land of opportunity – their home, bringing with them their own individual cultures and traditions

One of the saddest sights in New Orleans or Galveston is the daily arrival of hundreds of refugees from the older Southern states, seeking homes on the Texan prairies. The flood of emigration from South Carolina, Alabama and Georgia is formidable... Old men and little children, youths and maidens clad in homespun, crowd the railway cars, looking forward eagerly to the land of promise...The ignorance of these people with regard to the geography of the country in general, is dense. "I never travelled so much befo'," is a common phrase; "is Texas a mighty long ways off yet?"

— Edward King, 1874

Anglo immigrants established the overall trends of the state's cultural development, when they wrested the area from Mexico in the 19th century. But there have been other cultural influences: Texas is crosshatched with a complicated pattern of regional and ethnic divisions. According to the latest edition of the *Texas Almanac*, Texas ranks fourth in rates of foreign immigration, as of 2002.

"Anglos" – American citizens – who settled in Texas before annexation, were mainly from the South, although, even within this group, there were major cultural differences. Immigrants from the Deep South, where slavery was deeply rooted, tended to settle east of San Antonio, in the wetter agrarian sections of the state. Those from the mid-Atlantic states, where slavery was less pervasive, tended to settle to the north and west of the Colorado River.

Like Southerners today, these settlers held a wide range of political, religious and moral views, some of them in direct opposition to each other, and to those of foreign "Anglo" emigrants from the British Isles and central and eastern Europe.

PRECEDING PAGES: cowboy culture past and present, Fort Worth.

LEFT: Mexican-American, Rio Grande City.

RIGHT: Tyler Rose Festival Queen, East Texas.

The cowboy image

For a long time, the homesteading, agrarian Anglos east of San Antonio set the tone for the whole state. East Texas was not just Southern – it was an extension of the Deep South. In the early 20th century, thanks to the ubiquitous presence of the cowboy in the

societal media of the day, their influence in the popular imagination waned, while the West, with its powerful icons, became more influential. Denim overalls and cotton growing gave way to cowboy boots and cattle raising as essential elements in the international image of Texas – at least until the wildcatter and the oil baron joined the cowboy in the Lone Star pantheon. Non-Southern dishes like chicken-fried steak, tortillas and chili con carne have by and large replaced the traditional offerings of grits, greens and cornbread on the Anglo table.

Today, Texas is identified much more readily with the American West than with the South,

and recent immigrants seem to prefer the state's "cowboy image" to its connection with the Confederacy. Although for the most part cowboys are a thing of the past, the cowboy image seems more in keeping with the state's vitality than the cultivation of Southern memories. And, because being a cowboy was never an exclusively Anglo experience, it tends to run right across Texas' many ethnic boundaries.

Anglo-Southerners are not just being Westernized, they are disappearing. Whites of Old Southern descent make up less than half the population, especially after heavy immigration from California, the Midwest and the Northeast during the mid-1990s boom years. And, due to the large number of Mexican-Americans in Texas, white non-Hispanics form a smaller percentage of the population here than in the country as a whole.

The composition usually called "Anglo" is likely to consist of several European and possibly some non-European elements. Texas was the location of the earliest Polish community in the United States and some of the first Irish ones. The largest group of immigrants to come directly from Europe was German.

HUGO THE RED

Even though Hugo O'Conór was a Spanish governor, it was clear he was not of Hispanic origin – he was called the "Red Captain" for the distinctive color of his hair.

Intermarriage between American Anglo-Southerners and recently arrived continental colonists, and later between this mixed group and Hispanics, occurred as soon as they began to live within sight of each other. The taboo against Anglo African-American marriages – though fading – is still rarely broken, however, if the great-great-grandparents of typical Texas blacks could be assembled, some of them would be black, but a number would, in fact, be white.

Irish or Spanish

The Irish were among the first Europeans in Texas. In fact, Hugo O'Conór was a Spanish governor of Texas in the late 18th century. Where O'Conór came from and how he ended up in the employ of the Spanish are questions to which the answers are lost. More Irish arrived in Texas in the 1820s and 1830s, when the Spaniards granted what are now the counties of Refugio and San Patricio (St Patrick) to Irish settlers. The Mexican government evidently wanted an Irish Catholic buffer between the areas of Protestant-born Anglo settlements and the Spanish-speaking Catholics.

After the Republic of Texas was declared in

1836, the Europeans viewed the area as more stable politically than when it was part of Mexico. Leaders of the Republic encouraged immigration more actively than had the Mexican government. Whether Texas would be annexed by the United States was then unknown, but these factors combined to open Texas up to a flood of Europeans whose imagination had been captured by the Texas Revolution.

From the beginning, the Texas government saw to it that new settlers received land, and immigrant aid groups, like the Adelsverein, who settled New Braunfels and Fredericksburg, organized migration to Texas. However, the group was not well-administered and ran short of badly needed relief funds.

The Germans

The largest European ethnic group in Texas, the Germans' first permanent settlement was Industry, in Austin County, west of Houston, so-called for its cigar factory. Many Germans settled in the port cities of Galveston and Indianola. Typically, they wrote home an "America letter" that described – often with exaggerated, if not downright false, hopefulness – the human happiness, fertility and wonderful climate of Texas. Their letters were shared among a village or other group of acquaintances from which more brave Germans, despite the danger, would set out. German immigrants tried to bring along an entire support group, motivated in varying degrees by wanderlust, political idealism and the desire for social and economic improvement. Some stayed in the relatively urban ports, while others settled for a while in the interior where there were friends and relatives. After they had found their bearings, they proceeded to establish daughter communities. Constrained by the settlement patterns of previous groups and the threat of Comanche raids farther west, most Germans made their homes in a 10-county strip north of San Antonio, designated as the "German Belt," which became the center of German influence in the state.

LEFT: two Pleasanton cowgirls.
ABOVE: German Texans in Fredericksburg.

The German immigrants came from all walks of life. Some were peasant farmers, while others were well-educated. Some brought with them libraries that were extensive for the time and place, and they belonged to learned organizations such as the Goethe Society. Some formed orderly farming communities, while others organized into utopian-style communes, such as Bettina and Tusculum.

In *Journey Through Texas,* Frederick Law

Olmsted, who traveled throughout the South from 1856–7, wrote with surprise and admiration about the intellectual attainments of the German colonists in Texas. He described their primitive but neat log cabins, plastered and stuccoed, and their books, musical instruments and paintings. Olmsted hoped their liberal influence would move Texas out of the Old Southern sisterhood of slave states.

Olmsted recorded: "One of the party said to me: 'I think if one or two of the German tyrants I could mention could look in upon us now, they would display some chagrin at our enjoyment,...I have been assured, I doubt not, with sincerity, by several of them, that never in Europe had they had so much satisfaction – so much intellectual enjoyment of life, as here."

Most of the Germans disliked slavery. In fact, at least 19 German-born Union sympathizers were killed by Confederate troops near the town of Comfort in 1862. Nor did they wish to annihilate the Native American, who considered Germans a distinct tribe, superior to the loathsome Spaniards, Mexicans and Anglo-Americans. German influence can still be felt today in the music (polkas and conjuntos), the bock and lager-style native-Texas beers and the architecture (the churches, courthouses and "Sunday Houses") of Central Texas and the Hill Country.

BARBECUES AND SCHNITZELS

German settlers often gathered on market days and holidays to sell their produce or celebrate. On these occasions, whether revisiting a large market city such as San Antonio or just celebrating at one of their villages, they roasted a calf, sheep or goat. Their mastery of sausage-making and of the slow smoking of meats made an essential contribution to the art of that typically Texan food, barbecue. Some people also believe another unique Texas preparation, chicken-fried steak, is of German derivation. They point to its obvious similarities with the German schnitzels, which are also breaded and pan-fried cuts of meat.

Latin colonies

In the German agricultural villages of Sisterdale, Bettina and Comfort, Latin was spoken in everyday life; the communities are remembered as "Latin colonies," and, understandably, they mystified their Anglo neighbors at the time. It is just as well that the neighbors understood little of what the Germans had to say, for their beliefs were on the whole very different from those of the Anglo-Southerners. Not only were many of them opposed to slavery, as Olmsted noted, but several communities – Sisterdale and its daugh-

ter village of Comfort, in particular – were the centers of free thought and agnosticism. Many of the German settlers were Lutheran, and a few Catholic, but their free-thinking may have been unique on the frontier.

Broad German influence continues to this day in certain parts of Texas. Until the 1950s, the Tex-Deutsch dialect, an amalgam of English and German, was spoken in many settlements of San Antonio, such as the King William District. Today it has almost disappeared, and the Germans of the Texas Hill Country are becoming more like the Anglo majority and less like a true minority group.

Deliberate attempts to preserve German festivals have resulted in the regular celebration of the Fredericksburg Easter Fires and the *Wurstfest* in New Braunfels. The Easter Fires are lighted on the hills surrounding Fredericksburg on the Saturday before Easter. While local legend holds these fires were originally set by Comanche Indians, scholars have demonstrated that they were probably a custom brought from southern Germany which can be traced to pagan roots. The *Wurstfest* in New Braunfels usually comes in fall, at more or less the same time as the German *Oktoberfest*. Sausage and beer consumption, and a *gemütlich* sociability, link this New World celebration to the boisterous beer halls and *kellers* of Munich.

The Slavs

The Texas State Historical Marker at Serbin, Texas, makes interesting reading: "Trilingual (Wendish-German-English) community founded in 1854 by 588 Wends under the leadership of the Rev. John Kilian. The Rev. Kilian (Evangelical Lutheran) named the place Serbin because the Wends were descendants of Lusatian Serbs (or "Sorbs"). A thriving town 1865–1890; had grocery, dry goods, jewelry, drug and music stores, shops of wagon maker, blacksmith, saddler, post office, three doctors, two dentists. On Smithville-Houston Oxcart Road – sending out cotton, other produce, and hauling in staples. Decline began about 1890 as railroads bypassed settlement by several miles."

Just as German communities have adapted more and more to the dominant Anglo culture, other small groups, have been similarly absorbed. A group of Polish Catholics followed their priest southeast of San Antonio in 1854 to set up the first Polish colony in the US, Panna Maria. Later, several more Polish towns were established in Texas.

Two other major Slavic groups in the state are the Czechs (more of a cultural designation now, since Czechoslovakia was dissolved in 1993) and the Wends. Together, several central and eastern counties still have the largest rural populations of Czechs in the US. Czech settlements are generally agricultural, and most Texas Czechs have made their names and fortunes as farmers. Not as numerous as the Germans, the Czechs have nevertheless preserved many of their culinary traditions.

Several Czech communities hold celebrations to honor their heritage. Annual festivals in West, Taylor and Ennis draw city-dwellers to eat sausage and sauerkraut and dance the polka.

Wends are a German-speaking group who left their homes in Prussia in the 1840s. Those in Texas settled in two counties east of Austin, Lee and Fayette. The church and farm were the centers of Wendish life. Today most Wends have left the smaller towns for the city, but their colony in Texas was the only such community located in North America.

The Cajuns

French colonization of Texas was sporadic. While La Salle and other French explorers were among the early visitors to Texas, and Jean Lafitte and his pirate band established an early enclave in Galveston, the French influence seen today has mainly come from a group of French-

ADDITIONAL ANGLOS

Other smaller groups have blended into the Anglo culture. A substantial Scandinavian population immigrated to Texas; Greeks settled along the coast, particularly around Galveston; and a small Italian contingent lived in the larger cities but also had agricultural settlements in the Brazos Valley. The Jews' principal migration took place in the 19th century, when German and eastern European Jews came to Texas. Today, Jews are an urban group in the state, but synagogues in small towns like Brenham and Corsicana are reminders that they have been in Texas as long as many other European settlers. Jewish merchants founded several thriving Texas mercantile chains.

LEFT: hot competition at the World's Championship Bar-B-Que Contest held annually at the Houston Livestock Show.

American settlers who traveled to Texas from Louisiana. The Cajuns are descendants of the Acadians, who were removed from their Canadian homeland in the 1760s to 1780s. After resettling in French-owned Louisiana, they developed their own culture, combining French, Spanish, Indian and Creole elements.

At the turn of the 20th century, the discovery of oil in East Texas lured Cajuns to the area. The Texas Cajuns retained – (and still retain) – their regional French patois, their string-band music and bayou-bred culinary traditions, and a certain *laissez les bon temp roulez* outlook towards life. They lend a distinctive flavor to the East Texas and Gulf Coast areas where they have settled. Jambalaya, gumbo, and crawfish étouffée are eaten throughout the bayou country of East Texas. Cajun music is also enjoying renewed popularity. Usually played on accordions and guitars, and sung in the Cajun French patois, this music enlivens many East Texas dancehalls.

Hispanics

In his book of essays, *In a Narrow Grave*, Larry McMurtry put forward the view that Texas cities are always improved when the Hispanic culture influences the Anglo. If this is true, Texas cities must be improving: their Hispanic populations are increasing steadily. San Antonio, Houston and El Paso are among the top US metropolitan areas in total Hispanic population, and Texas follows only California in the number of Hispanics: people with Spanish surnames make up more than a quarter of its population. In big cities like Dallas and Houston, where blacks used to be the largest minority, Hispanics are gaining on, or surpassing, them. In the state as a whole, Hispanics overtook blacks as the dominant minority group in the late 1940s.

Spanish-speaking peoples are gradually re-Hispanicizing the state, following much the same immigration patterns as Anglos. Hispanics are no longer confined behind the imaginary boundary that once kept them west and south of the San Antonio river. Today there are *barrios* in Dallas and Fort Worth, Corpus Christi, El Paso and even in the Texas Panhandle, bringing Mexican and Central and South American customs, traditions and color the length and breadth of the state. Hispanics are integrated into every element of public and private life in the state. Cinco de Mayo and Diez y Seis, two holidays celebrating Mexican independence, are widely celebrated outside of Hispanic communities as well.

The Spanish-ruled Mexicans were the first non-Native American Texans, or *Tejanos*, and

descendants of these original settlers form a small, stable and often wealthy core of the Spanish-speaking population of Texas. Sometimes intermarrying with wealthy Anglos, these *Tejanos* have succeeded in preserving a culture distinct even from the rest of the Spanish-speakers.

Hispanic influence is strongly felt at the dinner tables and snack bars of Texas. More than any other minority group, Spanish-speaking Texans have made their cuisine part of the mainstream of Texas life and, increasingly, that of the rest of the nation. Tacos, enchiladas, fajitas and all the rest of the Tex-Mex menu (a culinary style derived from the cross-cultural influences of the border regions of both countries) are found as often on the Texas table as chuck roast and iced tea.

It was remarked upon, though not with surprise, when, a few years ago, salsa eclipsed ketchup as the leading condiment in the US.

The African-Americans

The state's other major minority group, African-Americans, have not been absorbed by the Anglo culture as the Germans and Czechs have, but they have lived in Texas as long as the Spaniards. When Cabeza de Vaca was shipwrecked on the Gulf Coast in 1528, an African slave named Estebanico was with him. Blacks, enslaved or free, were found in subsequent Spanish settlements, and intermarriage resulted in a significant *mulatto* population in Spanish Texas. The first large infusion of blacks came after the Republic of Texas was established. The Mexican stand against slavery had made owners reluctant to import their human chattels, and the absence of slavery had created a haven for free blacks. But, after independence, slavery became legal, and former Deep Southerners began to bring in slaves. Slavery tended to be concentrated east of the Texarkana-San Antonio line, where the Anglo masters were settled, and where the agrarian economy was more conducive to farms and plantations. Following Emancipation (which Texas slaves learned about on June 19, 1865 – two and a half years after its issue, giving rise to the state holiday of Juneteenth), and into the 20th century, blacks often lived a rural life on scattered farms or in small black "freedman" communities. Today, as they move to cities within Texas and elsewhere, the rural communities

LEFT: recent arrivals at the Annunciation House migrants' shelter, El Paso.

ABOVE: Hispanic restaurant owner in Dallas.

that preserved black culture are dying out or, as in the case of Austin's historic Clarksville neighborhood, becoming gentrified by an influx of affluent white homeowners.

Black migration to cities outside the state is partially responsible for the decline in the share of the general population that is African-American. Geographer Terry Jordan believes that Texas' transition from a Southern to a Western self-image is linked to this shift in the most visible minority. Blacks are part of the Southern tradition, while Hispanics seem to belong to later 19th-century frontier history.

The popularly accepted idea that blacks were not an important part of western frontier life ignores some significant black history. Many runaway slaves and free blacks joined the Native Americans and lived with them, not just on the frontier but beyond it.

The black soldiers of the ninth and 10th Cavalry and the 24th and 25th Infantries who fought the Native Americans were called "buffalo soldiers" by the tribes (owing to the coarse, kinky quality of the troopers' hair). After they mustered out of the service, many of these soldiers stayed out West to ranch, raise crops on dryland farms or work as cowboys. Despite this role played by black soldiers in the Indian wars and the settling of West Texas, most Texans continue to associate blacks only with the Southern strands of Texas' history.

Blacks are more often urban now, so that their political and cultural influence is most strongly felt in the cities. Texas' most famous African-American politician, the late US Senator Barbara Jordan, came from the heart of Houston's inner city black wards.

Throughout their history in the state, African-Americans have enjoyed the benefits and suffered the inequities of the best and the worst Texas has to offer. As *The Handbook of Texas* puts it: "On the one hand, blacks have worked with others to build the state's unique cultural heritage. But on the other hand, African Americans have been subjected to slavery, racial prejudice, and exclusion from the mainstream of state institutions. Their contributions to the state's development and growth in spite of these obstacles have been truly remarkable."

The Native Americans

Texans tend to think their Native American population was simply dispersed to other states. In fact, many Texas tribes were totally destroyed, including the Hasinai and other East Texas tribes who gave the state its name (*tejas* meaning "friendship"). For many years, it was com-

monly believed that the only unassimilated Native Americans in the state were the Alabama and Coushatta, two Southern tribes who migrated to East Texas where they lived on one of the state's three reservations.

Other important groups include the Tigua, who preserved their culture almost in secret in the *barrio indio* of El Paso, and the Kickapoo, who migrate annually from Mexico across the Rio Grande to Eagle Pass in South Texas.

KICKAPOOS CROSSING

Kickapoo Indians enjoy special dispensation from both US and Mexican governments, allowing them to roam freely across the border between the two countries.

Recently, Native Americans have been staging a comeback in Texas. Oklahoman and New Mexican Indians, especially Cherokee and Navajo, have moved to the larger cities. In Dallas and Houston, which have the largest Native American populations, they live in distinct communities, but not along tribal lines.

The Asians

Asians were the last group to be added to the Texas mix. They first came to the state on their eastward trek after the California gold rush. Chinese laborers worked on the railroad, but were abandoned by the rail companies when the tracks were finished. Isolated in a strange world, the Chinese were then usually hired as cheap labor to undercut emancipated blacks.

The first wave of Chinese immigrants did not have much lasting impact on Texas, since US immigration laws banned most Chinese women from the country. Some agricultural laborers in Robertson County intermarried with local women, producing the "Black Chinese" of Calvert. More or less permanent Chinatowns were formed in El Paso, and later in San Antonio, but restrictive immigration policies kept the Asian population to a low level in Texas until fairly recent times.

In the early 20th century, Japanese settlers started experimental rice-farming communities along the coast, while Chinese and Japanese merchants set up small businesses in San Antonio and other cities. Until recently, Asian-run groceries served the black community, but a new influx of Southeast Asians has made Asian products more profitable.

The latest Asian migration, the result of the Vietnam War, has included Vietnamese, Cambodians and others. Many have settled on the Texas Gulf Coast where they fish in areas traditionally harvested by other groups, particularly Anglos.

Misunderstandings and prejudice at first resulted in several killings and other ugly incidents that involved the influence of the Ku Klux Klan. However, the coast is now fairly calm, and Texas seems ready to add another piece to its mosaic of cultures. The most famous assimilation story may be that of Dat Nguyen, the son of Vietnamese "boat people" who grew up to be a star defensive player on "America's Team," the Dallas Cowboys.

While a distinctive Vietnamese culture might seem most likely to thrive in fishing settlements along the coast, not all Vietnamese live in these areas, nor do they all earn a living by fishing. Many of the latest immigrants are technicians and other highly trained people who have settled in Texas' urban areas (the Asian populations of Austin and Houston more than doubled in the 1980s and '90s). Others are found in rural communities as professional workers, farmers and ranchers. ❑

LEFT: urban Texas park rangers.

RIGHT: young Asian Texan at an assembly plant in the Panhandle city of Amarillo.

THE TEXAS RANGERS

Efficient, tough and uncompromising: the Texas Rangers are a remarkable band of law enforcers, a legion of heroes with a reputation second to none

For most of the first century of Texas history, the Texas Rangers were almost synonymous with that history. No police force in the country had the prestige of the Rangers. The *WPA Guide* noted in 1940: "The man in the tan trousers and shirt, wide-brimmed Western hat, black tie, leather holster and sidearms not only commands respect but admiration."

Today, the Rangers badge, traditionally carved from 1940s-era silver Mexican five-peso coins, is one of the most famous law enforcement emblems in the world. Texas Rangers were "one of the most colorful, efficient and deadly bands of irregular partisans on the side of law and order the world has ever seen," one historian noted... "called into being by a society that could not afford a regular army." Many of these adventurers were famous before reaching their thirties, men who showed "an utter absence of fear," superb psychologists at understanding not only the enemy but also the men around them.

There is an apocryphal story still told of a 1930s oilfield boom town in east Texas caught up in the grip of a riot. Frantic with fear, the local sheriff wired the governor in Austin for help in the form of the Texas Rangers. A day later, the train pulled into the boom town station, from which alighted a single Ranger. "They only sent one?" asked the incredulous sheriff. The Ranger did not bat an eye. "You've only got one riot, don't you?" he replied.

In the 1880s, Texas Ranger Captain Bill McDonald, who was known for his readiness "to charge hell with a bucket of water," confronted three gunmen who had tried to ambush him. He dropped one, and, after taking bullets through his left side and right wrist, was busy cocking his pistol with his teeth when the other two outlaws fled. "No man in the wrong can stand up against a man in the right who keeps on a-coming," was the romantic assessment of this episode by a fellow Texas Ranger.

PRECEDING PAGES: custom-made saddles at Capitol Saddlery in Austin.

LEFT: Texas Rangers, *circa* 1900–1905, pose with one of their wives who is carrying a Colt revolver.

RIGHT: star of the Texas Rangers.

Origins of the force

"In 1823," wrote journalist Pamela Colloff in the April 2007 issue of *Texas Monthly* magazine, "Stephen F. Austin hired ten men 'to act as rangers for the common defense.' Nearly two centuries later that group – known as the Texas Rangers – is alive and well, having adapted from being frontier lawmen to an elite investigative force, trading their horses and bedrolls for cellphones and laptops." In 1835, the Texas legislature instituted the Texas Rangers as an official body: 56 men in three companies, each with a captain and two lieutenants.

The Head Ranger, a major, was subject to the army's commander-in-chief. Earning the same pay as the army ($1.25 a day), Rangers supplied their own mounts and rations and had to be equipped with "a good horse (and) one hundred

rounds of powder and ball" at their own expense. They protected the frontier against raiding Mexicans, and fought against outlaws and Indians.

Rangers in the Republic

Throughout the years of the Republic of Texas (1836–45), the Rangers worked as scouts and couriers during the first presidency of Sam Houston, who fostered friendship with the Indians. But, from December 1838, under the presidency of Mirabeau B. Lamar, 13 new Ranger companies were commissioned, which "over the next three years...waged all-out war against the Indians," according to *The Handbook of Texas*.

The army and the Rangers were often at odds, due to conflicting sets of rules and orders; the former sought to police the frontier and keep peace, while the Rangers rode to push back and punish the Indians.

When Sam Houston was re-elected in 1841, he realised that the Rangers were the most effective and economical way of protecting the frontier, when Captain John Coffee "Jack" Hayes and 150 Rangers helped repel an 1842 invasion from Mexico.

A few years later, the Mexican War of 1846 brought the Rangers worldwide fame. "Armed to the teeth," they successfully guided the US Army to Monterrey and were at home in the remote deserts of northeastern Mexico, where, battling guerrillas, they earned a fearsome reputation as *los diablos Tejanos* (Texan devils). Between 1845 and 1875, Rangers fought in the big and little wars against Indians and Mexicans, as well as tracking down robbers and horse thieves.

Revolver revolution

In 1851, when 21-year-old former sailor Samuel Colt began manufacturing the first .34-caliber six-shooter weapon, nobody seemed particularly interested. Then one of the revolvers found its way into the hands of a veteran Ranger, Captain Samuel Walker, who saw its potential for a man fighting on horseback. At his suggestion, Colt designed a heavier .44-caliber gun (later .47), which became the standard weapon for US cavalrymen.

The first to use Colt's new six-shooter on the Plains Indians was the aforementioned Captain Jack Hayes, a 23-year-old former Tennesseean who had arrived in Texas as a surveyor, before he was appointed by President Lamar to be Chief of Rangers at San Antonio. All the ideal requirements for a Texas Ranger seemed to come together in this handsome, quiet "gentleman of purest character," and, when he ended his service, at 34, he was the model to which all

Rangers aspired. One Comanche war chief swore never to confront Hayes, "who has a shot for every finger on his hand." Largely thanks to Hayes and his men, the Rangers learned to embrace the most advanced technology of each era, which has enabled them to stay relevant to their times.

PISTOL PACKING

The Department of Public Safety issues each Ranger a SIG Sauer P226 pistol, but many prefer the 1911 Army Colt .45 automatic.

Taking out bad men

After the end of the Mexican War (February 2 1848), the Rangers went into a decline and were little used. One Ranger captain, arriving to help a community fight off the Indians, said that all he was doing afterwards was hearing complaints from farmers about Rangers killing their hogs. At the onset of the Civil War (1861), many joined the Confederate forces.

State Democrats, back in power in 1874, declared Texas was "overrun with bad men," and, to counter these, plus Indian attacks on the western frontier and border raids by Mexicans, the Rangers were regenerated. Their Special Force unit gained a fearsome reputation, on one occasion stacking a dozen dead rustlers "like cordwood" in a Brownsville square "as a lethal response to the death of one Ranger." Among the 3,000 desperadoes they "thinned out" was the multiple killer John Wesley Hardin.

The Rangers endured another lean period at the beginning of the 20th century, when the force was trimmed down to just four 20-man companies.

But the 1910 revolution against Mexico's president Porfirio Diaz created unrest at the border. Then the onset of World War I, with its need to counter German intrigues and protect internal Texas security, was followed by Pancho Villa's raid on Columbus, New Mexico, in 1916, which fueled antagonisms between the two nations.

LEFT: inside the Texas Rangers Hall of Fame, Waco.
ABOVE: Samuel Colt, gun-manufacturer.
RIGHT: John Wesley Hardin, one of the outlaws gunned down by Rangers.

Executed without trial

In responding to these challenges, sometimes, critics charged, the Texas Rangers' actions were high-handed and they were not being held accountable. If an ethnic Mexican, be he a Tejano US citizen or Mexican national, was found armed, he was often accused of banditry and killed outright. In 1915, a group of Rangers, having captured a carload of Mexi-

cans suspected of robbing a train near Brownsville, took them into the bushes and shot them. The indiscriminate killing of approximately 5,000 Hispanics between 1914 and 1919 (according to *The Handbook of Texas*) became a source of "scandal and embarassment" and, in 1919, prompted a legislative investigation which discredited Ranger tactics. The force was overhauled by recruiting "men of high moral character." Higher salaries – as well as more restraints – were introduced.

RANGERS' REPUTATION

One early writer once said of the Texas Rangers that they "could ride like Mexicans, shoot like Tennesseeans and fight like the very devil."

The Prohibition years

Prohibition found Rangers patrolling the border against tequila smugglers, protecting Federal tick inspectors, monitoring labor and Ku Klux Klan demonstrations, and taming the lawless oil boom towns. The Rangers were often at odds with local lawmen, who preferred to leave gambling casinos and illegal drinking joints alone.

In 1932, the Rangers ill-advisedly backed Governor Ross Sterling in the Democrat primary, and, when his opponent, Miriam "Ma" Ferguson, took office, all 44 Rangers were fired or resigned in protest. Ferguson politicized the force, handing out Ranger badges as political favors to contributors and cronies. Salaries were slashed and Texas became a haven for the likes of George "Machine Gun" Kelly and Bonnie (Parker) and Clyde (Barrow). Parker and Barrow were eventually hunted down by renowned Ranger Frank Hamer.

New qualifications

In 1935, under Governor James Allred, the Rangers became part of the Texas Department of Public Safety, which included the Texas Highway Patrol. New qualifications were laid down for Rangers, who had to be between 30 and 45 years of age (later extended to 50), 5 ft 8 inches (1.74 meters) tall and "perfectly sound" in mind and body. Each Ranger was required to be "a crack shot" and underwent extensive training in ballistics and investigation techniques.

Rangers were spread throughout the state, becoming plain-clothes officers and sometimes a sort of rural constabulary. When World War II arrived, they were kept busy rounding up enemy aliens and helping protect vulnerable sites. Their attitude toward America's Mexican neighbors changed as a modern era between the two countries began.

The job of the Rangers widened enormously in the 1960s, when the 8,000 cases they had been dealing with annually almost doubled, due to increasing urbanization. Rangers became involved on both sides of labor and civil rights issues. Rangers sometimes acted as strikebreakers against farmworkers in south Texas, even while they helped guarantee voting rights and civil rights in other areas. Some of the old complaints began to resurface, as the Rangers again began to hear accusations about their attitude toward brown-skinned citizens. Today, however, around a quarter of the Ranger force is of Hispanic heritage. "We are attached at the hip to Mexico," says one Ranger.

Today's Rangers, 117 men and one woman as of Spring 2007, are supplied with powerful cars and sophisticated weapons, and forensic and communications equipment. "Our job is assisting local law enforcement agencies that don't have a lot of resources," says one. Noted *Texas Monthly*: "a typical day (for the Rangers) looks more like CSI than *The Lone Ranger*." ❑

LEFT: Lieutenant Clete Buckaloo, Texas Ranger, Waco.
RIGHT: the Texas Rangers Hall of Fame in Waco.

NAT
COWGIR
A
HALL

L
SEUM
AME

DON'T FENCE ME IN

A real Texas cowboy bore little resemblance to the Indian-fighting, songs-around-the-campfire hero created by Hollywood

To much of the world, the cowboy is the embodiment of the American character; stoic, self-reliant, loyal, taciturn, hardy and – sometimes – reckless or violent. His iconic status has outlasted two World Wars, the Space Age, rock 'n' roll, the onset of the Internet and the whole of the 20th century. And, nearly a decade into the new millennium, his heroic aura remains undiminished, nearly 150 years after his brief heyday.

He has been celebrated in books such as Owen Wister's *The Virginian*, Teddy Blue Abbott's *We Pointed Them North*, and Larry McMurtry's *Lonesome Dove*; in the paintings and sculptures of Charles Russell and Frederic Remington; in the photographs of Erwin E. Smith and Richard Avedon; in song, from cowboy ballads collected by Texas folklorist John Lomax to the chart-topping hits of Waylon Jennings and George Strait; and on film in John Ford's *The Searchers*, Howard Hawks' *Red River* – both starring John Wayne – and Fred Zinnemann's *High Noon*.

The zenith of the American cowboy was brief, roughly the last 25 years of the 19th century. And, contrary to the tall-in-the-saddle imagery perpetuated by the movies and television, the typical cowboy was a wiry man – be he Anglo, African-American or Hispanic – of slight stature whose six-shooter was most typically drawn to defend against a rattlesnake or coyote, not a bandit or Indian.

He was a blue-collar workingman, a laborer who toiled for seldom more than a dollar a day. But what set him apart from the rest of mankind, in his eyes, was that he was first and foremost a horseman, heir to a centuries-old tradition.

"The cowboy's contempt of the farmer was not unmixed with pity," wrote Larry McMurtry, "Cowboys could perform terrible labors and endure bone-grinding hardships and yet consider themselves the chosen of the earth; and the grace that redeemed it all in their own estimation was the fact that they had gone a-horseback."

Though his lineage belongs to history, he has an enduring hold on our imagination, and his descendants still practice his craft today.

The working cowboy

Underneath the storybook and movie glitter, there was always a real working cowboy, and there still is today. Not until the Comanche and Kiowa were largely "subdued" in the mid-1870s by the army and the Texas Rangers could much of the vast Texas prairie be safely opened to rancher, and so the working cowboy did not fight nearly as many Indians as we see him fighting in the movies.

When he was on the trail, the cowboy lived out under the stars and he had a closeness to nature. He supplied his own strong code of frontier ethics in a land with no established law, and he enforced it with a gun – though the gun-

PRECEDING PAGES: National Cowgirl Museum facade, Fort Worth, depicting women of the American West.
LEFT: modern-day cowboy enjoys a gallop.
RIGHT: saddle and rifle, timeless cowboy icons.

fighter was a rare and endangered species in the West, compared to the ubiquitous cowboy.

The history of the working cowboy begins with the introduction of cattle into the New World by Spanish explorers as early as the 16th century. Most of the details of cattle ranching had been worked out by the Spaniards in northern Mexico and southern Texas by the time the first Anglos came into the area in the 1820s.

The Spanish cattle-ranching vocabulary was assimilated by the early Texas cattlemen, along with the rest of Spanish/Mexican cattle culture. Words like *lariat* (rope), *remuda* (string of riding horses), *corral* (holding pen for cattle) and *dally* (from "dar la vuelta," or "take a turn") are still in use today. Words for land forms, such as *mesa* (high plateau) and *arroyo* (dry wash), were also adopted.

No Fancy Boots

The boot was one of the cowboy's tools: he had no need of the exotic leathers and elaborately stitched tops seen on today's fashionably macho and expensive footwear.

Cowboy costume

Much of the Texas cowboy's costume came from the *vaquero*, as the Mexican cowboy was called. The angled high-heeled boots helped to keep a cowboy's feet in the stirrups when he was riding his horse. The narrow toes of the boots and the slick, treadless leather sole were designed to slide easily into the stirrup, while the boot tops were 12–16 inches (30–40 cm) high and perfectly plain in design. The leather was good quality and durable.

Being generally concerned with the well-being of his animals, the Texan cowboy replaced the sharp, revolving roweled spurs favored by the *vaquero* with larger, blunt wheels, in order to protect his horse's flanks. The jingle of spurs was "saddle music" to the cowboy. While the *vaquero* usually wore spurs only for work, many a Texas cowboy felt naked without them, and only removed them upon entering his house.

For a long time, cowboys wore a very characteristic pair of striped breeches. These gave way in the 1870s to the blue denims manufactured by the Levi-Strauss Company of San Francisco. A cowboy covered his breeches with heavy leather leggings, called chaps, when he rode through brushy country. "Chaps" is a corruption of the Spanish word *chapparal*, meaning heavy brush.

The bandana, an oversized neckerchief, was the Swiss army knife of the West. It was invaluable to cowboy and *vaquero* alike: it kept the sun off the back of his neck and mopped the

sweat from his face; it could be a sling for a broken arm or a mask to filter the acrid dust; wrapped around a couple of biscuits, a bandana could serve as a lunchpail.

The tall-crowned, wide-brimmed *sombrero* worn by the *vaquero* was never favored by the Texas cowboy; nor was the fabled ten-gallon hat ever worn by anyone but movie cowboys. There was a wide variety of headwear among real cowboys, from the cavalry-style fedora to the shapeless farmboy's hat, but, by the 1870s, the hats made by John B. Stetson of Philadelphia had become standard western wear.

Cowboys who worked for a dollar a day would pay $10 to $20 for a good hat and $20 to $30 for a good pair of boots.

Shirts were widely varied, some no more than homemade flour-sack affairs. As likely as not, they were covered with a vest. The sleeveless vest gave warmth and protection, but did not bind the cowboy's arms while he worked. For cold weather, a cowboy wore a blue denim jacket or a fleece-lined leather shortcoat. An oilcloth slicker kept off the rain. A cowboy rarely carried more than one change of clothes, which he packed into a bedroll.

LEFT: Texas cowboys in traditional costume, *circa* 1890.
ABOVE: a cowboy works long hours!

Trail driving days

The cowboy's life was a hard one. As many a "greenhorn" quickly learned, a cowboy had to have common sense and a head for survival. The heyday of Texas cowboying was the trail-drive years from the mid-1860s through the 1880s. Prior to this time, the cattle business in Texas was rather low-key. It centered on Spanish-style ranches that were loosely run and generally unfenced – prime conditions for creating "mavericks" in the rich South Texas grasslands where the hardy longhorn cattle could easily survive on their own.

After the Civil War, a flood of immigrants from the South entered Texas, many of them young single men looking for a new life. They found it as cowboys.

The price of cattle in the industrial cities of the north was as much as $40 a head, whereas, in south Texas, longhorns could be bought for $4 apiece. Thus, there was plenty of work for cowboys, driving cattle from Texas to the railheads in Kansas, from where beef was shipped to city markets. The great cattle trails of the era – the Chisholm Trail, the Goodnight-Loving Trail, the Western Trail and others – came into being to transport cattle across the unfenced plains to railheads or army posts in New Mexico, Kansas, Missouri or even Wyoming or Montana.

A cowboy's work began in spring with the cattle roundups or "cow hunts." Nursing calves followed their mothers as the cattle were herded into holding pens. There the animals were separated by their brands and claimed by their owners. Young calves were marked with the same brand as their mothers. They came to be known on the trail as "dogies," from the short rope that tethered the new-born calf to its mother. As herds became larger and cattle thieves began to alter brands, some ranchers took to cutting notches in the ears of their cattle as a secondary form of identification.

Trail ballads

After all the rounding up and branding, the trail drive began. Many a cowboy ballad was composed on the open trail, as the cowboys sang to comfort their cattle and keep them from stampeding. Cowboy ballads were usually laments about loneliness, lost love, and the hard life on the trail. Many, such as *Streets of Laredo*, derived from English or Celtic ballads. "The chief contribution made by white men of America to the folksongs of the world," observed Texas folklorist J. Frank Dobie, are "the cowboy songs of Texas and the West… rhymed to the walk, the trot and the gallop of horses."

Hollywood Western stars like the late Gene Autry and Roy Rogers capitalized on this aspect of cattle trail life, making their careers as "singing cowboys." But historians point out that a hard day's drive more usually ended with conversation around the fire, or perhaps a game of poker. Few cowboys would have had room in their saddlebags for musical instruments any larger than a harmonica or a concertina.

Beginning the drive

To start a drive, small herds of cattle, rounded up in south Texas by four or five cowboys, would be driven toward a pre-arranged point where a trail herd was formed. The trail drives then followed well-known routes that were determined by designated passes or river fords. Small operators with only 10 or 12 cowboys went up the same trails used by big outfits with 50 or more cowhands. The biggest drive recorded, in 1869, set out from Texas with 15,000 head of stock. Between 1865 and the mid 1880s, some 10 million animals went up the trails, the largest artificial migrations in history.

With the sale of the cattle in Abilene, Kansas (or Dodge City, Denver, Cheyenne or Kansas City), the cowboys were paid for the first time on their long ride from Texas. For many of them, all the nights of sleeping on the ground and days of herding cattle over the open plains were erased in wild drinking and carousing in brothels. When the last dust of the trail drive had been washed away, the cowboys mounted up for the long ride home.

Not all cowboys wasted their money in the saloon and the bordello for, as often as not, the wages of the trail drive were used to buy cattle back in south Texas or in Mexico. A cowboy might also take his pay in cattle when he returned home, driving them north as part of a larger herd the following summer. In this way some working cowboys, such as the legendary Charles Goodnight, became great ranchers. They invested their profits in land and cattle, building up small spreads of their own.

The fenced range

When J.F. Glidden was issued the first patent for barbed wire in 1874, it portended the end of the open range and the great cattle drives. At the same time, the railroad was expanding. In Texas, Fort Worth became the major railhead. Slaughterhouses and packing companies were built in Fort Worth and San Antonio, making it unnec-

essary to drive cattle to Kansas. Additionally, the introduction of refrigerated boxcars meant beef could be shipped longer distances. Amarillo and Abilene became active markets in Northwest Texas.

It was not uncommon for a rancher to marry a woman much younger than himself, his own younger years being given to building up a ranch that would support a family. Charles Goodnight, at age 91, married a woman 65 years his junior. This practice left many women widowed and in charge of ranches. Some women took an active part in the management of Texas ranches and still do so today.

Hard work was and is still a major part of life for the ranch cowboy. In addition to the spring round-up and branding, the ranch cowboy had to look after his cattle year-round. Cowboys still practice their riding and roping, but now they work in the corral or inside the fences of the ranch, rather than on the open range. In the fall and winter, cowboys ride the fencelines in order to mend them. Winter is also a time for repairing saddles, bridles and other pieces of important ranch equipment.

KING OF RANCHES

The enormous King Ranch in southern Texas was modeled so closely on the Spanish *rancho* that *patrón* King even led an entire village out of Mexico to work on it.

Gigantic spreads

It was in the era of the open range that the great ranches of Texas began to form. The King Ranch in south Texas is the largest in the state. Texans measure the ranch's current size as 1.23 RIs (Rhode Islands), or 823,000 acres (333,000 hectares). It was founded in 1853 by a former Rio Grande steamboat captain, Richard King. Even though the original boundaries of the ranch are no longer the same, the King Ranch is substantially intact and still family owned. There are organized tours, and any highway that goes to Kingsville will cut through some part of it.

The celebrated XIT Ranch in the Texas Panhandle was started by Midwestern and British land and cattle syndicates and was the largest range in the world under fence. In the 1870s and 1880s, the state sold the land to the syndicates to finance the present State Capitol in Austin. Originally a monstrous 4.54 RIs (more than 3 million acres or 1.25 million hectares), the XIT was split up in later years as the out-of-state investors went their separate ways. At its

LEFT: strong coffee fortified cowboys on the long trail rides.
ABOVE: faces of the west.

Black Cowboys

Although it is a lesser-known fact, some of the best cowboys to come into Texas were black Americans leaving the war-ravaged states of the South. African-Americans in the West often met the same prejudice they faced elsewhere. Few acquired property or social distinction. But, to a range boss, character and willingness to work trumped skin color. It was estimated that about one-quarter of the cowboys on the northbound traildrives between 1866 and 1895 were black.

Many of the early black cowboys had been born as slaves or sons of slaves and eventually found more freedom on the open ranges than in urban areas. Others were army veterans from the corps of black cavalrymen called "Buffalo Soldiers". After the Civil War, some 5 million head of loose stock roamed the Texas plains and cowboys of all color were in high demand. Some ranches east of the Trinity river had all-black crews, and many became horsebreakers, but very few achieved the elevated status of foremen or managers. A handful became Federal peace officers or took up careers as rodeo performers. One Texas-born African-American cowboy, Bill Pickett, achieved enormous fame by inventing the rodeo sport of bulldogging (or steer wrestling). A life-size bronze statue of Pickett subduing a steer stands today in the historic Stockyards District in Fort Worth.

Bose Ikard, a slave born in Mississippi in 1843, was brought to Texas by his master in 1852 and learned the cowboy trade on a ranch near Weatherford. Freed as a result of the Civil War, he went to work for the famed Western rancher Charles Goodnight, eventually becoming the cattle baron's right-hand man. Goodnight said he trusted Ikard "farther than any living man." Ikard's story was among those told in fictional fashion in the novel and TV mini-series *Lonesome Dove*.

Another former slave, Isom Dart – who was born Ned Huddleston in Arkansas in 1849 – had an early career stealing horses in Mexico and swimming them across the Rio Grande to sell in Texas. Later his gambling and fighting in Northwest Colorado entangled him with the law. After that, he changed his name to Isom Dart, bought a ranch and tried to go straight but was tracked down and killed, at the age of 51, by bounty hunter Tom Horn.

The 1993 made-for-television movie *Return to Lonesome Dove* featured a fictional character named Isom Pickett, who was a composite of the real life Dart and Bill Pickett.

A cowboy and broncbuster named Nat (or Nate) Love was one of many who claimed to have been the original model for Deadwood Dick, saying he had acquired the nickname by winning a roping contest in Deadwood, Arizona in 1876.

Today's black cowboys can showcase their skills through a series of African-American rodeos, sponsored by the Cowboys of Color, the Bill Pickett Invitational Rodeo and other organizations.

In recent years, blacks have begun to assume their rightful roles in the cinematic history of the West via such actors as Woody Strode *(Sergeant Rutledge, The Man Who Shot Liberty Valance)*, Morgan Freeman *(Unforgiven)*, Danny Glover *(Lonesome Dove, Silverado, Buffalo Soldiers)* and Louis Gossett, Jr. *(Return To Lonesome Dove)*. Mel Brooks used his 1974 parody Western, *Blazing Saddles*, to send up modern racial attitudes.

Charles Goodnight composed this epitaph for his friend in 1929: "Bose Ikard served with me for four years on the Goodnight-Loving Trail, never shirked a duty or disobeyed an order, rode with me in many stampedes, participated in three engagements with the Comanches, splendid behaviour." ❑

LEFT: the Black Cowboy was much respected by his Anglo peers.

peak, the ranch was bounded by more than 1,500 miles (2,413 km) of fencing.

Texas ranches have become more mechanized and modernized. The only contemporary ranch of any size doing business in the 19th-century way is the Kokernot 06, between Fort Davis and Balmorhea in Davis County.

However, large modern-day Texas ranches such as the Green, the Matador, the 6666, the Waggoner, the Y.O, and, of course, the mighty King Ranch still endure and thrive, though some have had to incorporate oil exploration and tourism into their traditional livestock vocations.

Cowboy spectaculars

Rodeo is the sport of cowboys, developing naturally out of their skills and tasks as they worked with livestock. Early rodeos were just informal gatherings of locals who all pitched in to provide the livestock, riders and entertainment. Pecos, in far west Texas, claims to have held the first rodeo in 1883. Rodeo is now controlled by the Professional Rodeo Cowboys Association (PRCA), which sanctions more than 650 rodeos each year all over the United States – even in places such as New York City. There are National Finals held annually in mid-December in Las Vegas, Nevada, and the top rodeo cowboys make six-digit salaries competing in as many as 125 competitions a year.

The traditional rodeo events are bull riding, bareback bronc riding, calf roping, steer wrestling, saddle bronc riding and, for women, barrel racing. In the 1930s and 40s, there was an extensive women's rodeo circuit. Women competed in the same events as men and added gymnastic trick riding, too. However, during World War II, women's rodeo was discontinued and never regained popularity. There is still today a thriving circuit of African-American rodeos officiated by several organizations.

Rodeo contests can be held indoors or out, but the basic requirement is a large, dirt-floored corral or arena, with chutes along one side and escape gates for the livestock opposite them. The arena is surrounded by stands, and behind the stands are barns and holding pens. Bull and bronc riders mount up in small pens that open directly into the arena.

When the gate swings open, a rider tries to stay on the animal for eight seconds. Half of the points scored in a ride come from the total time the rider stays mounted; the other half are awarded for the competitor's style and daring.

Rodeo can be dangerous: the animals are wild, and often try to trample or gore dismounted rid-

ABOVE: over the fence at a Texas rodeo.

ers. The rodeo cowboy's best friend is the clown, who runs into the arena to distract the mount while the rider is on the ground. Elaborately inscribed belt buckles, displaying the cowboy's name and the event, are presented as trophies.

Cowboy heritage

The world of the cowboy and the Wild West has been preserved in several modern museums dedicated to its memory. One of the finest collections can be found in the Panhandle-Plains Museum in Canyon, Texas. The T-Anchor Ranch Headquarters, built in 1877, is on the museum grounds. Another fine collection is in the Longhorn Museum in Pleasanton, which claims to be "the birthplace of the American cowboy." Exhibits in this museum document the cowboy and his Indian and Hispanic antecedents. San Antonio has The Trail Drivers Association and the Institute of Texan Cultures, both displaying collections of cowboy – and cowgirl – memorabilia. Austin's Bob Bullock Texas State History Museum details the Lone Star State's frontier past. The XIT Museum in Dalhart chronicles the history of that famous old ranch, while the National Cowgirl Museum and Hall of Fame in Fort Worth has a collection celebrating women in the West. Also in Fort Worth, the Amon Carter Museum (in that city's Cultural District) and the smaller downtown Sid Richardson Collection feature large quantities of Western art and photographs, including masterpieces by Charles Russell and Frederic Remington.

The National Ranching Heritage Center on the campus of Texas Tech University in Lubbock is the home of 20 buildings representing ranch housing from the Spanish days to the large family ranch houses of 1890s cattle barons. Almost any county historical museum in any town in cattle country preserves some artifacts from the trail driving and cowboy era.

Lost skills

The visitor looking for working cowboys today is at something of a loss. Modern equipment has made many of the cowboy's traditional jobs obsolete. Consequently, contemporary cowboys and ranchers have learned to combine traditional roping and riding skills with modern tools, from DNA breeding research to computers and "green" technology. A modern cowboy might ride the range on an all-terrain vehicle, with a cellphone in the pocket of his Levis. The best ranch to visit is the Y.O. Ranch near Kerrville. The King Ranch offers tours, as do some of the surviving West Texas spreads. Dude ranches in the Bandera area also offer a taste of ranch life. But, a rodeo is the most accessible form of cowboy life available today.

Beware of imposters

Not all the folks you see strolling around in boots and jeans are cowboys. People who look like cowboys may never have been astride a horse. Cowboy hats, Western-cut shirts with pearl snaps, big buckles on tooled leather belts and leather boots are standard fashion for many modern Texans. By contrast, some of today's younger working cowboys wear "gimme" caps and T-shirts emblazoned with the names of rock 'n' roll bands. Find a fellow who takes things too far by adding a swagger and some big talk to this costume and you have what's popularly referred to as a "drugstore cowboy." He's the cowboy who spends more time at the drugstore lunch counter than he ever does astride a horse. A real cowboy is apt to say of such a fellow, "He's all hat and no cattle." ❑

LEFT: a face of the West at Fort Worth Stockyards.
RIGHT: fancy cowboy boots – as *not* worn by the trail riders, who preferred plainer, more functional styles.

EXIT

MUSICAL TRADITIONS

From country, blues and folk to conjunto, Western Swing and good ol' rock 'n' roll – musically, Texas has it all

The enduring glory of the music from the Lone Star State is rooted in its free-form eclecticism, its gumbo of cultural influences and a cheerful disregard for the artificial boundaries erected between musical genres in other parts of the country. Texas has always been a crossroads, and over the past 300 years Texas music has been informed and enriched by Anglo-Celtic ballads, Mexican norteño, Appalachian mountain folksongs, African/Caribbean blues, Cajun and zydeco music from the wilds of Louisiana, Bohemian oompah polka bands and British invasion pop, not to mention the various practitioners of punk, rap, reggae, jazz, techno, funk and rock who have managed to find a home within the joyfully elastic boundaries of the state's musical community. The constant cross-fertilization of distinct ethnic sources accounts for both the diversity and the similarity of traditional Texas music.

Home of country

The tendency to think of Texas as the home of country and western and cowboy music is understandable (no matter what those folks in Nashville say). Texans have made some of the most important contributions to the development of country music. Texan Vernon Dalhart's 1924 recording of "The Wreck of the Old 97" was the first million-selling country album; Bob Wills and his Texas Playboys took Western swing to the world; Ray Price and Ernest Tubb formulated the hard-edged honky-tonk sound which dominated country music in the post-war era; the Dixie Chicks, from Dallas, became the best-selling female group of all time.

When they came to the South, the early Anglo-Irish settlers brought with them a vigorous heritage of folk songs, ballads and fiddle music. In Texas and the surrounding region, unique Southwestern forms soon developed, like the cowboy songs that were documented extensively in the early 20th century by the Texan John A. Lomax, one of America's earliest and most prodigious folk-song collectors.

Texans also developed distinctive instrumental styles, like the swinging, fluid Texas fiddle style that can be heard at the many annual fiddle and bluegrass contests across the nation. One of the Texas fiddle style's earliest practitioners, the legendary A.C. Eck Robertson, was also one of, if not *the* first country musicians to record commercially. In the early 1920s, he waxed such classics as "Sally Gooden" and "Brilliancy".

The continued vitality of country music in Texas is seen in the ongoing popularity of small dancehalls that are dotted throughout the state (such as Austin's Broken Spoke and Gruene Hall in the Hill Country near New Braunfels) and, of course, in the revolving cast of larger nightclubs in the major cities (Billy Bob's Texas, in Fort Worth, bills itself as the "world's largest honky-tonk.") The 1970s saw the emer-

PRECEDING PAGES: musical parade in Fort Worth.
LEFT: Buddy Holly Center, Lubbock.
RIGHT: the late bluesman Clarence Gatemouth Brown, who was born in Louisiana and raised in Texas.

gence of the "Outlaws" led by native Texans Willie Nelson and Waylon Jennings, who spearheaded a movement out of Austin that flew in the face of Nashville conformity by blending rock, country and blues, and appealing to younger rock audiences. Today, a new "Texas Music" country-rock movement mixes regional pride with a high-octane rock urgency. Younger performers such as Pat Green, Cory Morrow and Cross Canadian Ragweed are appealing to the children of the Waylon 'n' Willie audience.

FIFTY YEARS OF SWING

Pioneer of Western swing, Bob Wills was one of Texas' most durable musicians. His career stretched from the 1920s all the way into the 1970s.

Unconventional

While Texas continually generates conventional country stars who succeed in logging big chart hits – including George Jones, Ernest Tubb and Ray Price over three decades ago, and more recently George Strait and the Dixie Chicks – it is the iconoclasts who make the most compelling music. Grandfathered by the tion of storytelling Texas singer-songwriters, including Billy Joe Shaver, Rodney Crowell, Steve Earle, Lyle Lovett and Robert Earl Keen.

Austin City Limits

The capital of Texas continues to supplement Nashville as the country music capital of the United States. There is a wide audience for the television series *Austin City Limits*; the widely popular show has featured more than 800 musicians and bands. In recent years it has reached out to embrace alternative rock, rhythm and blues and singer-songwriters.

Willie Nelson likewise achieved the status of American institution many years ago, his weathered visage a national icon, his laconic vocal style and fluid guitar playing still refreshing and instantly recognizable.

He also has become godfather to a generation of storytelling Texas singer-songwriters, including Billy Joe Shaver, Rodney Crowell, Steve Earle, Lyle Lovett and Robert Earl Keen.

Western swing

Perhaps Texas' most original contribution to country music is the musical style known as *sui generis* rock 'n' roll ancestor Buddy Holly of Lubbock, they make a kind of Texas music that belongs to no one genre. Joe Ely, Jimmie Dale Gilmore and Butch Hancock, all from Lubbock, seamlessly mix folk, country and rock in their own performances or collectively as The Flatlanders. They and other west Texas musicians such as Waylon Jennings and Roy Orbison (and, before them, Bob Wills), took a perverse pride in bending musical rules and leaping over stylistic boundaries.

Western swing. It was developed by two Fort Worth bands, Milton Brown and his Musical Brownies, and the Light Crust Doughboys in the early 1930s. However, most people agree that the genre was perfected by Bob Wills and his Texas Playboys. Wills turned traditional string-band dance music on its head by introducing elements of hot jazz, blues, pop and even Tex-Mex ranchera strains. Soloing and improvisation were encouraged, and Wills' twin-fiddle attack, augmented by a keening steel guitar and the soulful vocals of Tommy Duncan made for one of the swingingest sounds in any genre. Wills sometimes even included brass in his line-up. The Western-swing torch is still carried today by performers such as George Strait and Asleep At the Wheel.

The blues, R & B and hip-hop

"Blues came to Texas, lopin' like a mule," sang the famous Texas bluesman Blind Lemon Jefferson. Texans were certainly indispensable to the style's development. After the Civil War, freed slaves and free migrant black people followed the harvests and worked in the sugar plantations and lumber camps of east Texas. Their field hollers and acoustic "country blues" informed the music of Texas bluesmen like Mance Lipscomb, Huddie "Leadbelly" Ledbetter and Sam "Lightnin'" Hopkins.

In the 1930s, Dallas' Aaron "T-Bone" Walker was one of the first electric blues guitarists to coin an original style: the single-string solo. A master showman (he did splits while playing the guitar behind his head), Walker was a pivotal influence on B.B. King, Eric Clapton and others. Walker's contemporary, the late Clarence "Gatemouth" Brown bristled at being called "just" a bluesman, when he played country, jazz and Cajun music as the spirit moved him.

After World War II, Houston and Dallas/Fort Worth became the state's hotbeds of electric, urban blues and rhythm and blues. The Duke and Peacock record labels in Houston waxed hits by Bobby "Blue" Bland, Junior Parker and "Big Mama" Thornton, while the "Texas Tenors" – a group of hard-charging saxophonists led by King Curtis, Illinois Jacquet and David "Fathead" Newman – set the standard for sax players in R & B, soul and jazz bands. Other great jazzmen who hail from Texas include the avant-garde master

LEFT: The Flatlanders – Joe Ely, Jimmie Dale Gilmore, and Butch Hancock.

ABOVE: the late King of Western Swing, Bob Wills.

RIGHT: R & B singer, Beyoncé Knowles.

Ornette Coleman, ragtime king Scott Joplin and keyboardist Teddy Wilson). Today, Houston's R & B heritage is carried on by Destiny's Child and its breakout superstar frontwoman, Beyoncé Knowles.

Additionally, Houston, along with New Orleans and Atlanta, has become the headquarters for rap and hip-hop in the South. After the success of the Geto Boys in the 1990s, Houston hip-hop (characterized by its slowed-down, hypnotic "screwed" grooves) is dominated by the influence of the late D.J. Screw, and current performers Mike Jones, Slim Thug and Bun B.

ZZ Top, from Houston, also emerged from the blues-rock scene of the 1970s and notched huge hits by combining John Lee Hooker-style boogie with over-the-top Texas braggadocio. Texas rock is a wellspring of raucous, often bizarre music, stretching from the 1960s-era psychedelic anthems of the 13th Floor Elevators to the avant-punk noise of the Butthole Surfers in the 1980s and 1990s, and today's 20-member rock choir, Polyphonic Spree.

Conjunto and Tejano

Like their Anglo-American counterparts, Mexican immigrants and Tejanos (Texans of Hispanic heritage) brought a vast store of folk songs and ballads, many in the styles of norteño, mariachi or corridos. Tejanos were innovators and helped develop a distinctive Tex-Mex dance music called conjunto. While the distinguishing instrument of conjunto, the accordion, was introduced to Mexicans by the Germans in the 1840s, by the late 19th century they had developed their own accordion style, while retaining the polka and waltz melodies of their European antecedents. Conjunto was not insulated from other ethnic traditions. The early performer Narcisco Martinez, who is sometimes called "the Father of Conjunto Music," even recorded a version of the Bob Wills standard "San Antonio

From blues to rock

Texas has also been home to younger white artists who draw their inspiration from the blues, a trend which stretches from Janis Joplin – who was part of Austin's folk revival scene in the 1960s before moving on to California, where her rapid rise to stardom ended in a tragic death – right through vocalists such as Fort Worth's Delbert McClinton and the late guitarist Stevie Ray Vaughan. The Vaughan brothers, Jimmie and Stevie Ray, amassed an international reputation as electric blues guitarists of the first order, Jimmie with the Fabulous Thunderbirds and Stevie Ray with his band Double Trouble.

Rose." Corridos, the storytelling songs of the border country, have kept pace; recently a new strain has arisen, the *narcocorrido*, chronicling the exploits of drug smugglers and outlaws. Conjunto has had an interesting influence on Texas rock 'n' roll, which could be heard in the early 1960s in the Tex-Mex rock 'n' roll hits ("She's About a Mover", "Mendocino") of the Sir Douglas Quintet. Doug Sahm and Augie Meyers, two of the SDQ founders, went on to form another Tex-Mex group in the 1990s, the Texas Tornados, which featured conjunto master accordionist Flaco Jimenez and vocalist Freddie Fender.

Tejano, an amped-up, electrified rock 'n' roll cousin of conjunto, received national attention when its brightest young star, Selena Quintanilla Perez, was killed by an employee in 1996. While a clear successor to Selena has yet to emerge, tejano's popularity has continued to simmer in the dancehalls and music festivals of the Rio Grande Valley, Corpus Christi and south Texas.

Cajun and zydeco

Before and after World War II, immigrants from Louisiana flowed west in search of work in the oil refineries of Houston and the cities of Beaumont, Orange and Port Arthur. The two musical forms they brought with them, Cajun and zydeco, are roughly analogous to country music and the blues. White Cajun musicians tended to adhere to the traditional sounds of the button accordion, the triangle, the fiddle and guitar. The peppery, volatile dance music called *zydeco* is powered by the keyboard accordion and a heavy rhythm section. It was introduced to Texas by black Creoles from the Lafayette, Louisiana area (principally Clifton Chenier, the late "King of Zydeco").

Clubs and festivals

The club scene is capricious, with venues opening and closing, or changing ownership or location, continuously. One Austin club, Antone's, is a good example. In 1997, it opened in its fourth location in 30 years. Most of the larger cities have free "alternative" weekly newspapers, such as the *Austin Chronicle* and the *Dallas Observer*, which are good sources for club and concert listings. Texas' annual music festivals are usually well-advertised. The Texas Folklife Festival every June offers a fairly comprehensive sampling of authentic traditional Texas music, as well as revival forms. For folk-music fans, the Kerrville Folk Festival in May is mandatory, and every kind of global and regional pop music can be found at Austin's gigantic South By Southwest festival, which overwhelms the capital city every March. Over the past five years, the three-day Austin City Limits Music Festival, in the heart of the city, has earned a permanent spot on the music fan's calendar every September. And Willie Nelson's Fourth of July Picnic is a holiday event as revered as parades and fireworks. ❑

LEFT: attending a class at the Tejano Conjunto Music Festival in San Antonio.

RIGHT: in the clubs and on the streets, Austin nurtures its live music scene.

TEXAS ON DISC

In an era of iTunes, Amazon, satellite radio and other ubiquitous music resources, Texas music is more accessible than ever. The music magazine *No Depression* is an excellent source for information on Texas and Americana artists, as is the website www.lonestarmusic.com, and the various alternative weeklies cited above. One of the best independent record stores in the country, with an exhaustive selection of Texas music, is Waterloo Records in Austin. The Arhoolie record label is particularly rich in archival recordings of old-time Cajun, folk, blues, country, zydeco and conjunto artists.

IMAGINE PEACE

TEXAN ARCHITECTURE

From adobe huts and primitive log cabins to glistening glass towers, the state's architecture is a fascinating mix of the functional and the inspired

In Texas today, the words "Remember the Alamo" also have a special relevance to Texas architecture. For most of the 20th century, and especially in recent years, a battle has been waged between people who want new Texas architecture to reflect native values and styles and those who want to move beyond regionalism to the very cutting edge of international design.

It's an issue that is not likely to be resolved soon, because, at a deeper level, it is a struggle over the image of Texas itself. The conflict between regional design and international design isn't just about architecture. It's part of an ongoing struggle between rural and urban Texas, between native architects and outsiders, and between the mythical Lone Star State and the real, contradictory, contemporary Texas.

Beginning with adobe

To remember the Alamo in San Antonio is, of course, to remember the Spaniards – Texas' first European settlers. The Spaniards gave architectural life to the creamy white limestone of Central Texas, and introduced skill and efficiency to the simple adobe technique of the Native Americans. Although the late 19th-century Spanish architect, Antonio Gaudí, would have approved of the tribes' method of globbing one handful of mud on top of another to make a wall, the 18th-century Spanish friars taught them to mold heavy, regular adobe bricks in wooden frames.

Adobe, together with wood and stone, was used by the Native Americans, and later the Spaniards, all along the lower Rio Grande river. It was easier to make adobe bricks than to quarry stone, and an adobe wall protected the interior of a house or church from the heat just as well as stone. Not only is adobe sturdy and well-suited to the hot, dry Southwestern climate, it is a sensuous material that affords all sorts of stylistic features. For instance, because the walls are so thick, all windows have window seats; and because steps and oven hoods are also made of adobe and plastered over, in the same manner as the walls, the interiors have a sculpted all-of-a-piece quality.

The Missions

The Spanish missionaries in Texas, used to the Renaissance churches of their homeland, took pains to create an architecture that went beyond function. They wanted their buildings to express beauty in the wilderness. The Alamo is remembered as the bloody place where early Texans sacrificed their lives for freedom, but the building itself, in the heart of downtown San Antonio, is the image of quiet repose. The stone arches and carved niches suggest that the Alamo deserved a different kind of fame. The bell tower and "rose window" of San Antonio's San José Mission are proof that the Spaniards intended not just to survive, but to glorify, too.

PRECEDING PAGES: reaching for the sky in Houston.
LEFT: Dallas Hyatt Regency, adjoining the geodesic dome-topped Reunion Tower.
RIGHT: Mission Concepción, San Antonio.

Farmhouse style

Such a claim can hardly be made for the early Anglo-American settlers of the 1820s and 1830s. When farmers from Tennessee, Kentucky, Mississippi and Alabama rolled into Texas, they brought with them the only architecture they knew – the plain log house and its cousin, the functional frame house of roughly hewn boards. There was nothing extra in these houses, nothing to make life on the Texas frontier a little sweeter or softer.

And yet, as is often the case with architecture, function led people to design structures that were, if not beautiful, still comfortable in the landscape. The deep porch offered protection against the sun, the dog or possum "trot" (an open breezeway between two essential rooms or cabins) was used for such things as curing meat and for sleeping outdoors, and the steeply pitched gable roof protected the house from the pounding rain. These features not only eased the hardships of frontier life, they created a simple, graceful, appealing style.

Even the Germans who emigrated to Texas from the 1840s onwards modified their age-old method of building stone and timber *(Fachwerk)* houses in order to incorporate elements of the Anglo farmhouse. Their hewn frameworks were joined with mortise and tenon joints, secured by wooden pegs. In the 1850s, Frederick Law Olmsted, traveling to San Antonio, slept in New Braunfels in a "small cottage of a single story, having the roof extended so as to form a verandah, with a sign hanging before it, *Guadalupe Hotel, J. Schmitz.*"

Formality and grace

Before the Civil War, most people in Texas did not live in houses as snug and pleasant as those of the Germans in Central Texas. They were only too glad to leave behind their relatively crude houses when life grew easier, and when the classic Greek Revival and later Victorian styles were brought into the eastern, central and southern parts of the state.

The Greek Revival put classical columns on the porches of even the simplest log houses, and gave a touch of Southern formality and grace to larger buildings. Greek Revival is found in Austin (for instance, in the Governor's Mansion), but it flowered in East Texas. Crockett, Jefferson, Marshall, Tyler and Houston all have charming and varied examples of the Greek Revival, which remained popular into the 1870s when Victoriana became all the rage. The Victorian buildings of Nicholas Clayton of Galveston, and the Richardson-Romanesque courthouses of James Riley Gordon in many of

the county seats (look for his buildings in such places as San Antonio, Waxahachie, La Grange, Stephenville, Sulphur Springs, Giddings and New Braunfels) are evidence of the growing influence of gentility. When Texans began to concern themselves with porticoes and turrets, high culture had clearly arrived.

VICTORIAN GENTILITY

One of the most elegant Victorian buildings in Texas, Austin's Driskill Hotel, designed by Frederick E. Ruffini, is still open for business.

Modern Texas

Beaux-arts eclecticism held sway in Texas briefly, just long enough to influence some public and university buildings. The trickle-down popularity of the Arts and Crafts Movement in Britain found expression in thousands of Texas bungalows.

During the Great Depression, courthouses and other public buildings were built by government labor. Their blocky, repetitive shapes and flat reliefs in the Art Moderne style make it easy to date such monumental buildings as the Fort Worth City Hall and the distinctive courthouses of Travis, Brazoria and Eastland Counties to this period.

FAR LEFT: German-style architecture, Fredericksburg.
LEFT: ornate column at Rice University, Houston.
RIGHT: Bishop's Palace, Galveston.

Not many skyscrapers were built in Texas in the 1920s and 1930s. The few that did go up, like Houston's Esperson Building, were in the then-popular eclectic style.

Within a period of about 50 years, roughly between 1870 and 1920, domestic architecture in the state was seen to mature. Indeed, wealthy Texans systematically demonstrated that what was fashionable in Paris or London was fashionable in Houston, or even on the ranch. The set for the 1956 film *Giant* (about a Texas rancher and oilman) captured this spirit of brashness, while the movie's Second Empire mansion, silhouetted against endless West Texas ranchland, carried it to absurd limits.

Self-conscious insecurity

Some of the houses in Houston's River Oaks section are only a little less self-conscious. Even when the stylistic adaptations are imaginatively and tastefully handled, and local stone, such as pink granite, has been used, there is often a feeling of insecurity about the homes of newly rich Texans. Sometimes those who made it felt the need to rise above their architectural roots – sullied as they were by poverty, struggle and, not infrequently, illiteracy.

Exterior influences

In the 1920s and 1930s, small groups of architects abroad – in California, New York and Spring Green, Wisconsin (at Frank Lloyd Wright's Taliesin compound) – formulated new ideas about Modern architecture that would eventually make it acceptable for Texans to look upon their architectural heritage without shame. Their new ideas ranged from the "organic naturalism" of Wright's "Prairie Style" to the "machines for living" of the Frenchman Le Corbusier, but all of them respected what was functional in architecture – and opposed what was merely applied and decorative. In this light, the functional and formal aspects of missions and ranch houses were re-evaluated. If early Texans had allowed form to "follow" function out of necessity, a later generation of Texans made a conscious choice to do so. The result was the flowering of Texas architecture in the mid-20th century.

It was at this time that Texas buildings began to show not contempt, but deference to their older neighbors. San Antonio architect O'Neil Ford, who, along with others, became interested in the accurate restoration of Spanish colonial architecture, taught Texans to respect the scale and character of indigenous buildings, and to appreciate the native materials used in them. Ford's own Trinity University campus in San Antonio (begun in 1949), a group of brick buildings that beg comparison with Italian hillside villages, is faithful to the nature of the hilly Texas landscape. His Johnson City Post Office (1970) is a modified ranch house of limestone blocks with a wide front porch and a sloping roof. His Cowboy Artists of America Museum in Kerrville (1983) is both a fortress built of creamy limestone and a gallery of near-forgotten building techniques. Throughout his life (he died in 1982), Ford had great influence on Texas architects. His teachings still form the basis of the regionalist school of thought.

DON'T FORGET THE KIMBELL

Fort Worth's much-admired Kimbell Museum, opened in 1972, draws from the past in subtle ways. Its barrel vaults, which allow light to stream down along interior walls, may recall the silos that architect Louis Kahn admired in the Texas landscape, but this is, at best, conjecture. What makes the Kimbell appropriate to Texas is its strength, tranquility and aura of permanence. It looks back to the years before Texas dressed its buildings up in the styles of the East, beyond the Victorian and Greek Revival periods to the simple, functional early Texas buildings. It is regional in the finest sense of the word. Remember the Alamo, but don't forget the Kimbell.

Boxy towers

Ironically, the Modern emphasis on function, which prepared the way for a new appreciation of Texas' early buildings, was also responsible for giving birth to the attitude that the architecture of the past did not stack up well against the box. When the German Bauhaus architects sold Americans on their philosophy in the 1940s, cities like New York and San Francisco began to build boxy skyscrapers.

Texas cities were still young at that time, and possessed a few fine old buildings and almost no tradition of urban architecture. Thus, when cities like Houston and Dallas began to expand, much of their growth took the logical form of the Modern glass box. Their new urban buildings delivered a message as honest as that conveyed by the early settlers' houses: unadorned simplicity was still at home in Texas. Later, the boxes were criticised for their brutality.

Early Texas structures were admired for their utility and for their rural beauty, but they certainly didn't influence high-rise architecture in the heyday of the box. A golden sunset reflected by the limestone facades of Central Texas could evoke the memory of Coronado and his search for the Seven Golden Cities; or a lonely wind whistling through a broken windmill near an isolated ranch house could conjure up romantic images of the hard frontier life. But what, after all, did rough-cut limestone blocks or pitched roofs have to do with multi-story, steel-framed buildings?

In the years when the glass box dominated, Houston architecture came into its own. The Tenneco skyscraper (1963), with its exposed steel frame, and One Shell Plaza (1965), with its clean white facades, were as sophisticated and current as any new buildings, anywhere.

Philip Johnson set the stage for his Houston breakthroughs with his Amon Carter Museum in Fort Worth (1960), which has the stately order of a Greek temple. Later, by breaking up the rigidity of the Bauhaus box with the trapezoidal towers of his Pennzoil Place and his round-cornered Post Oak Central buildings (both 1976), Johnson drew international eyes to Texas architecture. The state that was famous for its rugged individualism at last had a Mod-

PEI IN THE SKY

Chinese-born architect I(eoh) M(ing) Pei, responsible for some of the most distinctive modern buildings in Texas, is also famous for the Louvre's glass pyramid in Paris.

LEFT: the Kimbell Art Museum, Fort Worth.
ABOVE: Hill Country general store built in the 19th century of native limestone blocks.

ern architecture that expressed it. Even the more conservative Dallas received oddly shaped, shimmering, reflective glass buildings and a City Hall (dedicated 1978) which broke out of the box completely. I.M. Pei's design, which took the form of an immense triangle balancing on one edge, sent cantilevered floors of offices precariously (it seemed) out over a plaza. O'Neil Ford was outspokenly annoyed by the City Hall, believing its effectiveness depended on playing tricks with the viewer's expectations. It was intentionally unnerving. Ford and his opinions are relevant to the shift in taste in skyscraper design in the early 1980s.

Once again, with his Houston skyscrapers, Philip Johnson led the way for developer Gerald Hines, but this time he did more than break out of the box. His designs now referred openly to the architectural styles of the past. His lighthouse-like Williams Tower, with Art Deco setbacks, and his Gothic Republic Bank tower were the world's first postmodern skyscrapers.

And that wasn't all. By sheathing Republic Bank in red granite, Johnson made an oblique reference to Texas' many granite public buildings. His 1983 Crescent complex in Dallas (offices, hotel and shopping court) was said to draw inspiration from early Texas architecture. Suddenly, the regional architecture that pragmatists like O'Neil Ford had championed became popular with postmodern architects, interested in its romantic connotations.

Muddying the waters

A thin sheath of limestone or granite on a steel-framed skyscraper does not, however, make a regionalist building. If anything, it only serves to muddy the water between the opposing regional and international camps. For the most part, regionalist architecture is still practiced by Texas architects on a small scale in rural areas. Many large urban commissions still go to outsiders. In recent years, for instance, the green glass Wells Fargo Bank Plaza, by Skidmore, Owings and Merrill; the steel and glass Four Leaf Towers, by Cesar Pelli; and the silvery granite needle of I.M. Pei's JPMorgan Chase Tower were added to Houston's skyline.

Dallas, meanwhile, is becoming somewhat more daring. The designs for new office towers have not been innovative – most go no farther than the now-clichéd sawtooth edge – but things are changing. I.M. Pei has designed two 60-story rockets of glass docked in a water garden downtown, and Philip Johnson plans a postmodern building whose arches allude to the work of the Italian architect Palladio.

The challenge

As Texas grows, its architecture continues to change. Houston has attracted attention as a center of new architecture by the country's best-known architects. But, in days ahead, the cities to watch may be San Antonio – the controversial library is particularly noticeable – and Austin, where local architects are at last being given important commissions. Already in Austin – a town rich in Victorian structures – one of the new office buildings on Congress Avenue, which leads to the pink Capitol, is made of granite from the same quarry and has a gable roof. Over the past few years, Austin buildings have increasingly reached for the sky, as the city strives to create a dense urban core.

The challenge for architects is to keep buildings honest and original – learning from Texas' past, but anticipating a new Texas. ❑

LEFT: I.M. Pei's JPMorgan Chase Tower, Houston.
RIGHT: Wise County Courthouse, Decatur, built by James Riley Gordon from pink granite in 1895.

PLACES

A detailed guide to the entire state, with principal sites clearly cross-referenced by number to the maps

Texas has it all: sophisticated cities, beautiful beaches, colorful deserts, sleepy border towns, wide open plains and dramatic mountains. In both geography and culture, it is a microcosm of the entire country. Texas contains as much diversity and internal contradictions as any other part of the United States. You'll find wild rodeos and honky-tonks, but also fine museums and elegant restaurants; towering glass skyscrapers and bustling sidewalks, but also quaint Victorian homes and old-time country fairs.

Texas is a place where all sorts of social, economic and geographic boundaries intersect, and each part of the state has a distinct character. You'll notice the influence of the Old South in East Texas, and the vital mix of Mexican and American cultures along the Rio Grande. You'll find that Texans are still struggling with the conflict between rural and urban values, and that there are more "cowboys" walking the streets of Houston or Dallas than there are on the range.

Tours of Texas generally start in the Dallas-Fort Worth Metroplex, two cities that have grown into a single bustling metropolitan area. The Metroplex has been a major business center for years, but recently the cities have made strides in the cultural arena as well. Fort Worth's museum district houses some of the finest collections in the state and the new Dallas Arts District is quickly becoming a hub of culture and entertainment.

To the east, Houston is Texas' largest city, and with its rich ethnic mix, great wealth, exciting architecture and thriving arts community, it is also one of the liveliest. People don't often think of Texas as a coastal state, but Texans have been enjoying the warm breezes, glorious sunshine and brilliant blue waters of the Gulf of Mexico since the early 1900s. America's "Third Coast" has over 300 miles (500 km) of white, powdery beaches, quaint Victorian villages, modern resorts, bustling fishing towns and major ports.

As you travel south, toward the Rio Grande, Texas' Hispanic roots become apparent. San Antonio is the urban capital of Hispanic politics and culture in Texas – as well as the home of the Alamo – but it is in the small towns along the Rio Grande that the Tex-Mex blend of *la frontera* is most distinct.

The scene changes dramatically as you travel west. In Central Texas, the land begins to open up and the towns grow farther apart. In the state's westernmost corner, the plains give way to desert. El Paso, this region's largest city, has more in common with its New Mexican neighbors than it does with its sister cities to the east. ❑

PRECEDING PAGES: Lajitas in the Trans-Pecos region; "El Capitán," Guadalupe Mountains National Park; East Texas lakes. **LEFT:** Thanksgiving Square, Dallas.

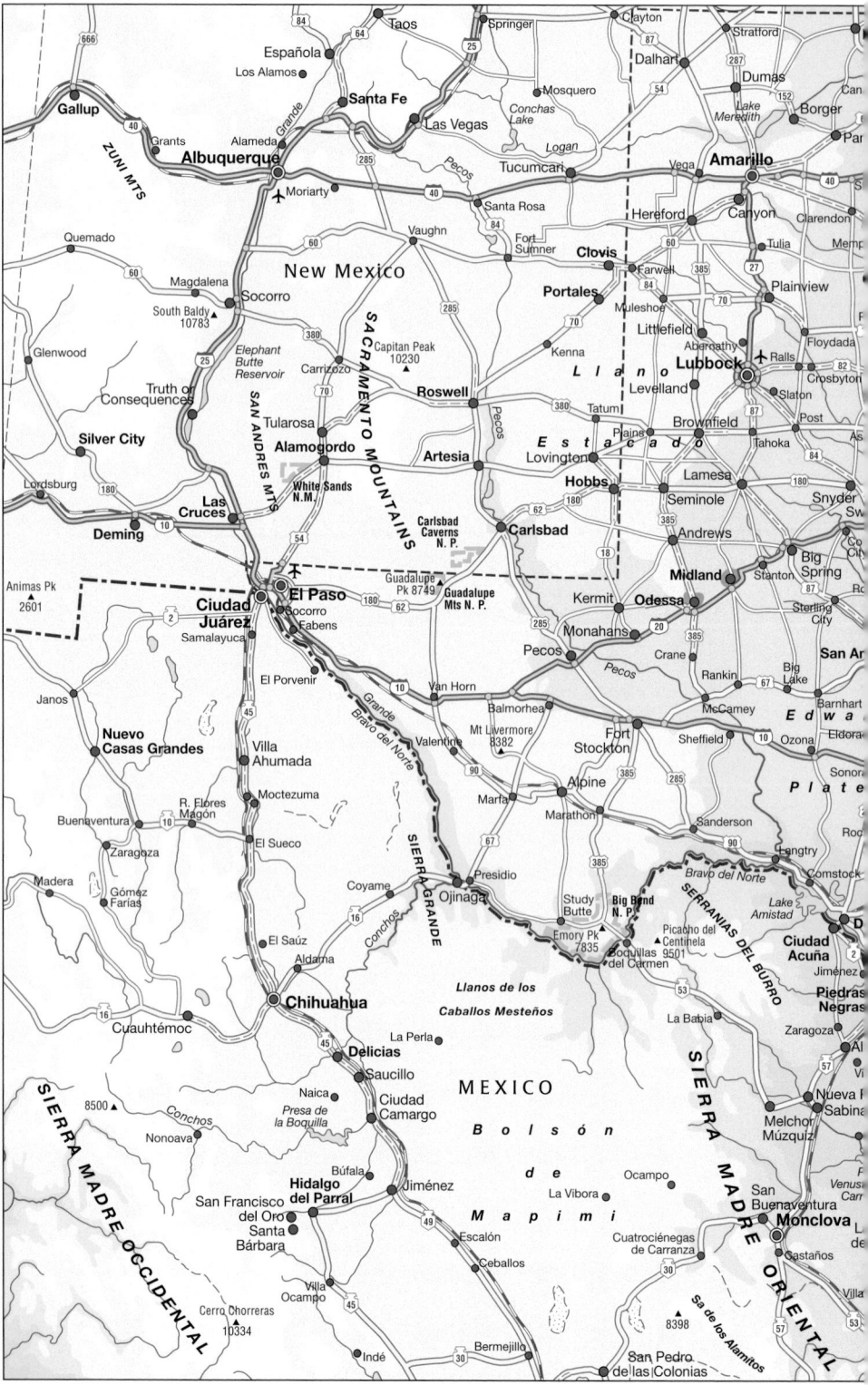
Taos
Springer
Clayton
Stratford
Dalhart
Dumas
Española
Los Alamos
Mosquero
Conchas Lake
Lake Meredith
Borger
Gallup
Santa Fe
Las Vegas
Grants
Alameda
Albuquerque
ZUNI MTS
Grande
Logan
Tucumcari
Pecos
Amarillo
Vega
Moriarty
Santa Rosa
Hereford
Canyon
Clarendon
Quemado
Vaughn
Fort Sumner
Clovis
Tulia
New Mexico
Farwell
Portales
Plainview
Magdalena
Socorro
South Baldy 10783
Muleshoe
Littlefield
Floydada
Glenwood
Elephant Butte Reservoir
Capitan Peak 10230
Kenna
Abernathy
Ralls
Lubbock
Llano Estacado
Truth or Consequences
Carrizozo
Roswell
Levelland
Crosbyton
Slaton
Tatum
Brownfield
Post
Silver City
Tularosa
Alamogordo
Artesia
Plains
Tahoka
Lovington
Lamesa
Lordsburg
White Sands N.M.
Hobbs
Seminole
Snyder
Las Cruces
Deming
Carlsbad Caverns N. P.
Carlsbad
Andrews
Big Spring
Animas Pk 2601
Guadalupe Pk 8749
Guadalupe Mts N. P.
Midland
Stanton
Ciudad Juárez
El Paso
Socorro
Fabens
Kermit
Odessa
Sterling City
Samalayuca
Monahans
Pecos
Crane
San Ar
El Porvenir
Van Horn
Rankin
Big Lake
Janos
Balmorhea
McCamey
Barnhart
Edwa
Nuevo Casas Grandes
Mt Livermore 8382
Fort Stockton
Sheffield
Ozona
Eldora
Villa Ahumada
Valentine
Sonora
Plate
Moctezuma
Alpine
R. Flores Magón
Marfa
Buenaventura
Marathon
Sanderson
Zaragoza
El Sueco
Langtry
Madera
Presidio
Comstock
Gómez Farías
Coyame
Ojinaga
Study Butte
Big Bend N. P.
Bravo del Norte
Lake Amistad
Ciudad Acuña
El Saúz
Emory Pk 7835
Picacho del Centinela 9501
Boquillas del Carmen
Jiménez
Aldama
Chihuahua
Llanos de los Caballos Mesteños
Piedras Negras
Cuauhtémoc
La Babia
Zaragoza
La Perla
Delicias
Saucillo
MEXICO
Naica
Ciudad Camargo
Presa de la Boquilla
Nueva I
Sabina
8500
Nonoava
Melchor Múzquiz
Bolsón de Mapimí
Búfala
Jiménez
Ocampo
Hidalgo del Parral
San Francisco del Oro
La Víbora
San Buenaventura
Monclova
Santa Bárbara
Escalón
Cuatrociénegas de Carranza
Ceballos
Gastaños
Villa Ocampo
Cerro Chorreras 10334
8398
Sa de los Alamitos
Indé
Bermejillo
San Pedro de las Colonias
SIERRA MADRE OCCIDENTAL
SIERRA MADRE ORIENTAL
SIERRA GRANDE
SERRANIAS DEL BURRO
SACRAMENTO MOUNTAINS
SAN ANDRES MTS

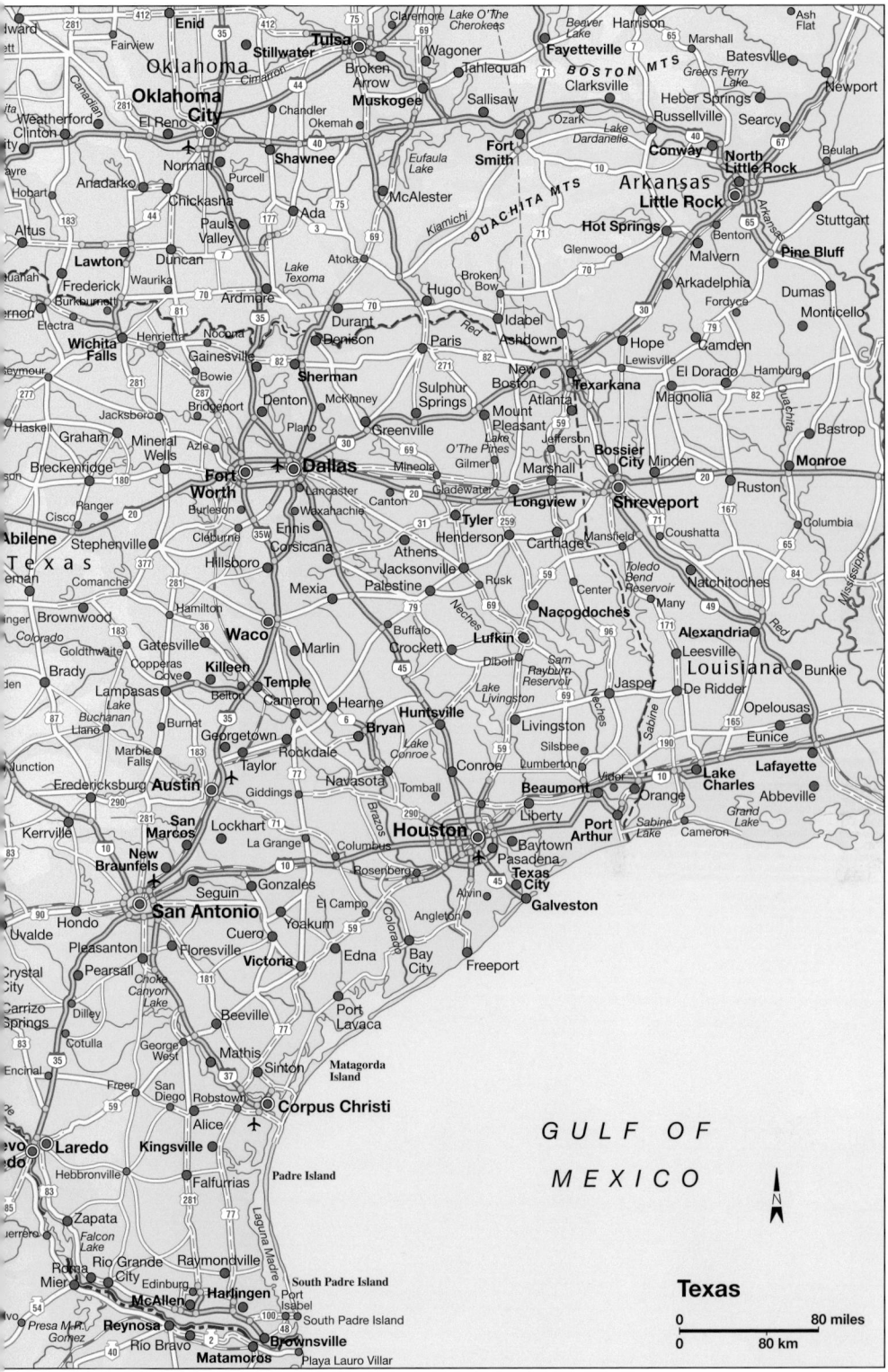
Oklahoma
Oklahoma City
Tulsa
Enid
Stillwater
Fairview
El Reno
Weatherford
Clinton
Norman
Shawnee
Purcell
Anadarko
Hobart
Chickasha
Ada
Pauls Valley
Altus
Lawton
Duncan
Frederick
Waurika
Ardmore
Lake Texoma
Atoka
Durant
Denison
Hugo
Broken Bow
Idabel
Ashdown
Paris
Red
Kiamichi
Wichita Falls
Henrietta
Nocona
Gainesville
Bowie
Sherman
Denton
McKinney
Bridgeport
Jacksboro
Haskell
Graham
Mineral Wells
Azle
Breckenridge
Fort Worth
Dallas
Plano
Greenville
Sulphur Springs
Mineola
Lancaster
Waxahachie
Canton
Burleson
Ranger
Cisco
Cleburne
Ennis
Corsicaria
Abilene
Stephenville
Texas
Hillsboro
Comanche
Mexia
Hamilton
Brownwood
Colorado
Waco
Marlin
Gatesville
Goldthwaite
Copperas Cove
Killeen
Brady
Lampasas
Belton
Temple
Cameron
Hearne
Lake Buchanan
Burnet
Llano
Georgetown
Marble Falls
Taylor
Rockdale
Fredericksburg
Austin
Giddings
Navasota
Tomball
Huntsville
Bryan
Lake Conroe
Conroe
Lumberton
Kerrville
San Marcos
Lockhart
La Grange
Columbus
Houston
Baytown
Pasadena
Rosenberg
New Braunfels
Seguin
Gonzales
San Antonio
El Campo
Hondo
Uvalde
Yoakum
Cuero
Angleton
Alvin
Texas City
Galveston
Pleasanton
Floresville
Victoria
Edna
Bay City
Freeport
Pearsall
Choke Canyon Lake
Dilley
Beeville
Port Lavaca
Cotulla
George West
Mathis
Sinton
Matagorda Island
Encinal
Freer
San Diego
Robstown
Corpus Christi
Alice
Laredo
Kingsville
Hebbronville
Falfurrias
Padre Island
Zapata
Falcon Lake
Laguna Madre
Rio Grande City
Raymondville
Roma
Mier
Edinburg
Harlingen
South Padre Island
McAllen
Port Isabel
Reynosa
Presa M.R. Gomez
Rio Bravo
Brownsville
Matamoros
Playa Lauro Villar
Claremore
Lake O'The Cherokees
Wagoner
Tahlequah
Muskogee
Sallisaw
Fort Smith
Eufaula Lake
McAlester
Beaver Lake
Fayetteville
Harrison
Marshall
Batesville
Greers Ferry Lake
Newport
Clarksville
BOSTON MTS
Heber Springs
Russellville
Searcy
Ozark
Lake Dardanelle
Conway
North Little Rock
Beulah
Arkansas
Little Rock
Stuttgart
OUACHITA MTS
Hot Springs
Benton
Malvern
Pine Bluff
Glenwood
Arkadelphia
Dumas
Fordyce
Monticello
Hope
Camden
Lewisville
El Dorado
Hamburg
Texarkana
Magnolia
Atlanta
Mount Pleasant
Lake O'The Pines
Jefferson
Bossier City
Minden
Monroe
Marshall
Gilmer
Longview
Shreveport
Ruston
Bastrop
Tyler
Henderson
Carthage
Mansfield
Coushatta
Columbia
Athens
Jacksonville
Palestine
Rusk
Toledo Bend Reservoir
Center
Many
Natchitoches
Nacogdoches
Neches
Buffalo
Crockett
Lufkin
Diboll
Sam Rayburn Reservoir
Lake Livingston
Jasper
Alexandria
Leesville
Louisiana
Bunkie
De Ridder
Opelousas
Eunice
Livingston
Silsbee
Sabine
Vidor
Beaumont
Orange
Lake Charles
Lafayette
Abbeville
Liberty
Port Arthur
Sabine Lake
Grand Lake
Cameron
Brazos
Colorado
Mississippi
GULF OF MEXICO
N
Texas
0
80 miles
0
80 km

DALLAS

Map on page 120

The city is a good-living, skyscraper settlement with a penchant for the arts and some of the best shopping in the land, though it is still best-known for the tragic events of November 22 1963

It's no accident that the famous television series was called *Dallas* and not, say, *Houston*. Echoing the inter-city rivalry of other places, sophisticated Dallasites are confident about proclaiming their superiority. "Houston? Why would anyone want to go there?" asks a Dallas tourist official with puzzled disdain, an attitude bolstered by her home town's world-class architecture, esteemed art collections and glittering shopping malls that lure big spenders from around the world.

Downtown

The easiest way to explore downtown Dallas is via the expanding light rail system which runs predominantly on the west side of town. This rail system (DART) shares Union Station with Amtrak and here, beside the Stemmons Freeway (I-35) in the southwest corner of town, is a good place to begin.

Four stepped, perpendicular glass boxes house the **Hyatt Regency Hotel**, connected to which is the 560-ft (172-meter) **Reunion Tower** ❶ (open daily; entrance fee; tel: 214-712-7146). Topped by a geodesic dome with 260 lights, the tower adds a dramatic night-time star to the city's skyline. An observation deck, revolving restaurant and lounge are accessible via fast elevators and the views, understandably, are the best in Dallas. **Reunion Arena**, just to the south, was the home of the Dallas Mavericks basketball team and the Dallas Stars hockey team until they moved to the American Airlines Center in 2001. Reunion Arena is now mostly used for rock concerts.

The city began in this area, in the **Cabin of John Neely Bryan** ❷ beside the nearby Trinity river, which Bryan mistakenly believed to be navigable for trade all the way to the Gulf of Mexico. An earlier colony, La Réunion, founded by French settlers, had failed, largely because the colonists had been artisans in Europe, not farmers. Bryan, however, survived and lived long enough to welcome, in 1872, the first passengers arriving on the Houston and Texas Central Railroad. This was the beginning of the city's major expansion. Between 1880 and 1890 Dallas' population tripled to 38,000, the mule cars that transported passengers around town were replaced by electric trams, *The Dallas Morning News* began publication, and the forerunner of the annual State Fair of Texas began. Bryan's reconstructed cabin now sits on a grassy sward across from the Old Red Courthouse on Houston Street.

Just east of the Reunion Tower is the city's huge **Convention Center** ❸, flanking a grassy hillside which is home to a herd of longhorns. This exhibit, which shares **Pioneer Plaza** ❹ with an ancient ceme-

PRECEDING PAGES: Dallas skyline.
LEFT: the landmark revolving Pegasus.
BELOW: ready to march in the State Fair of Texas parade.

The Pioneer Plaza exhibit covers over 4 acres (1.6 hectares) and pays tribute to the Texas trail-driving days. It was unveiled in 1994.

tery, is collectively the world's biggest bronze monument. Dozens of longhorns and three cowboys by Texan sculptor Robert Summers sprawl down a realistic cattle trail in a setting enhanced by native plants and a stream that cascades over a miniature limestone cliff. Beyond the Plaza, facing the public library, the futuristically stepped-back **City Hall** ❺ is the work of Sino-American architect I.M. Pei.

From the Reunion Tower's observation deck, it is easy to be impressed by Dallas' architecture. This tangible display of big-money investment began way back in 1908, when Texas law demanded that every insurance company doing business in the state should keep a substantial part of its assets in Texas. Insurance remains essential to the city's economy, along with banking, merchandising, and, most recently, high technology. For many years Dallas was the world's largest inland cotton market, and all the farmers of North Texas did their banking here. But it was after World War II that the city began its most accelerated growth. Two large aircraft factories were built in the suburbs, and, for a time in

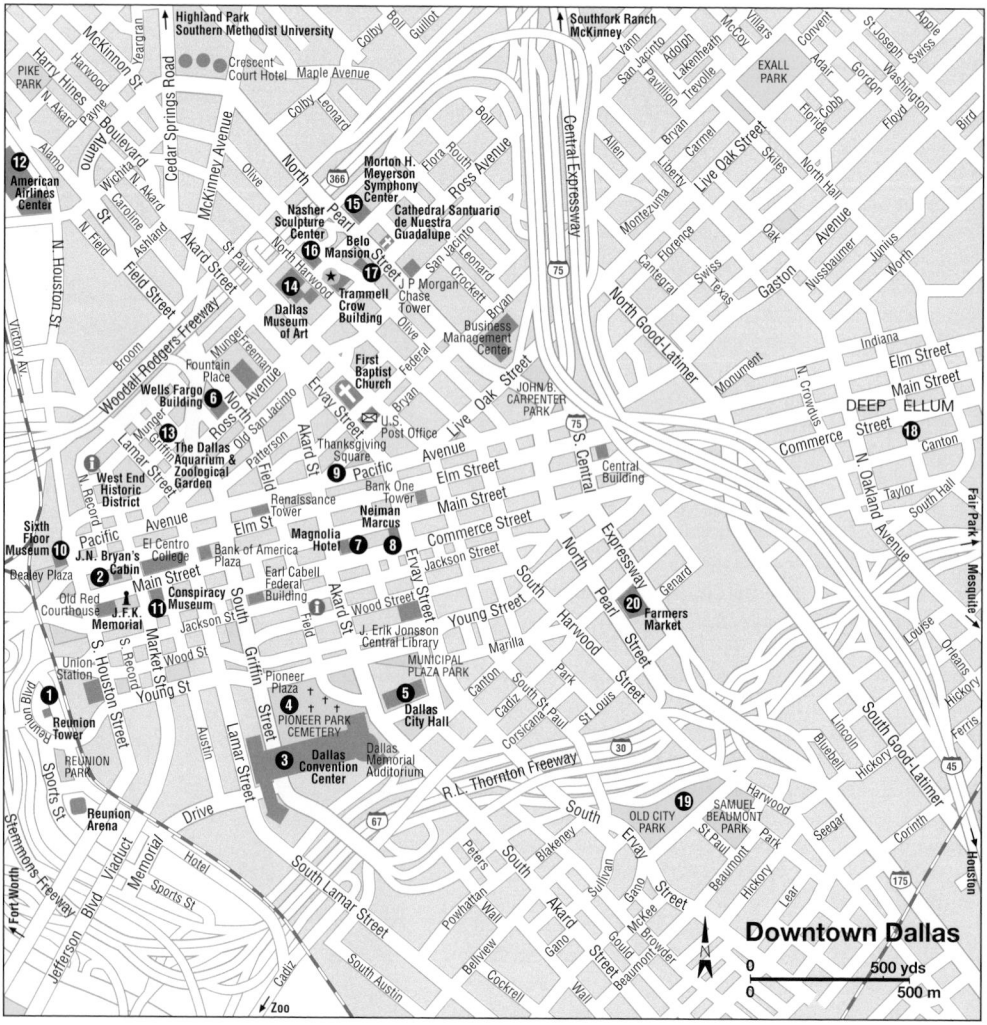

the 1950s, oil companies swarmed to Dallas, where banks were eager to finance them. At least 17 Fortune 500 companies, including Exxon, J.C. Penney, and Kimberly-Clark, currently have their headquarters in the Dallas area.

Map on page 120

Northeast, on Main Street, is the **Bank of America Plaza**, a 72-story giant outlined with 2 miles (3 km) of green neon; while the sharp angles of I.M. Pei's 60-story **Wells Fargo Building** ❻ (Field Street and Ross Avenue) near Fountain Place, catch one's eye from everywhere in the city. Also distinctive are the octagonal Thanksgiving Tower (Elm and Ervay) and the J.P. Morgan Chase Tower (Pearl and San Jacinto), whose slit tower had to be modified to cut down its wind tunnel effect. Almost hidden by the huge behemoths surrounding it is Pegasus, the flying red horse trademark (reconstructed in 1999) atop the **Magnolia Hotel** ❼ (formerly Magnolia Petroleum) at Main and Akard streets. This was the tallest building in the South when it went up in 1922. Behind it, at Main and Ervay, is the **Neiman Marcus** ❽ department store and, two blocks north, close to the light-rail line, is **Thanksgiving Square** ❾. This tranquil oasis, by architects Philip Johnson and John Burgee, incorporates a spiral-shaped chapel with stained-glass ceiling, a reflecting pool, waterfalls, a copse of sweet gum trees and a tower with bells.

The minimalist John F. Kennedy Memorial.

JFK Memorial

Just north of the Reunion Tower is the **West End**. With many of the city's oldest buildings restored as shops and cafés, the area is filled with arts and crafts, pushcart traders, clubs and boutiques. If walking is too much trouble, visitors can take horse-drawn carriage rides around the area.

Head up Houston Street, past the unmistakable Old Red Courthouse (behind which, at Main and Market, is the simple **John F. Kennedy Memorial**, designed by Philip Johnson), and ahead on the left is the most-visited site in Dallas: the former Texas School Book Depository building, from which Lee Harvey Oswald shot President Kennedy. Here, the **Sixth Floor Museum** ❿ (open daily; entrance fee; tel: 214-747-6660; www.jfk.org) overlooks Dealey Plaza, through which the President was riding in a motorcade on November 22 1963 when he was assassinated. Oswald – later arrested and murdered on live television while in police custody – fired the fatal shots from a corner window on the building's sixth floor, a site roped off in the museum.

BELOW: the building from which JFK was assassinated.

Don't underestimate the time needed to see the museum: it is immensely interesting (and moving), and, to the uninitiated, serves as a quick course about a significant era in US history. Among the messages in the visitors' book is one from a child who observed it was the first time he had seen his father cry. The museum, which gets an average of 1,000 visitors each day, houses exhibits about JFK's campaign; his social and economic programs; the space race; and the "Red Threat". Reproductions of newspaper stories from around the world are on show, including the full-page advert in *The Dallas Morning News* on the day of his visit to the city, in which his right-wing enemies accused him of communist sympathies. Cameras used by spectators watching the motorcade can be seen, as

can the famous Zapruder camera and some of the footage it recorded of the assassination. A videotape of the dramatic events of that day includes a tearful Walter Cronkite announcing the President's death.

President John F. Kennedy was on his way to make a speech at the Dallas World Trade Center when he was assassinated. The shots rang out at 12.30pm; the President was pronounced dead in hospital at 1pm.

Conspiracy theories

Kennedy's assassination understandably spawned endless speculation about who was to blame, with the skeptics ranging from those who felt that Oswald had been a patsy for the Cubans, or the Mafia, to dyed-in-the-wool conspiracy theorists who believed it to be the latest chapter in a chain of events masterminded by unspecified secret forces. Despite the conclusions of four major investigations into the crime, almost four out of five Americans believe that the killing was the result of a conspiracy.

Opposite the Kennedy Memorial, at 110 Market Street, **The Conspiracy Museum** ⓫ (open daily; entrance fee; tel: 214-741-3040) serves as a focus for all who reject the findings of the Warren Commission, which named Oswald as the sole assassin. "We just want people to think", says museum director Tom Bowden. "Maybe that way we can correct the textbooks so that they contain information about the larger conspiracy."

The West End continues north of the DART rail line, whose station at Pacific and Lamar (shared with a bus transfer station) is almost surrounded by parking lots, which accommodate visitors to the neighboring streets. Here bars, saloons, restaurants and cafés keep pedestrian traffic on the move.

Bringing new business to the West End is the striking **American Airlines Center** ⓬ (2500 Victory; tel: 214-222-3687), a state-of-the-art sports stadium that has superseded the Reunion Arena as the home of the major sports fran-

BELOW: carriage for hire in the West End Historic District.

chises and is surrounded by hip restaurants, shops and hotels, including the gleaming 33-story W Hotel. Designed by architect David Schwarz in retro style, with Art Deco touches, it was built at a cost of $420 million on an old railway yard and opened, with a concert by the Eagles, in July 2001. New transport links all around have revitalised the area.

Map on page 120

Another recent development in the area is the **Dallas World Aquarium & Zoological Garden** ⓭ (1801 N. Griffin; open daily; entrance fee; tel: 214-720-1801; www.dwazoo.com). Two once-derelict warehouses now house this extremely popular attraction, which opened in 1992 and was expanded in 1996. It is home to the world's largest freshwater aquarium, containing manatees, turtles, giant catfish and more, plus a saltwater aquarium with rays and sea turtles among its inmates. The other major draw here is a South American rainforest, featuring exotic plants and wildlife, from toucans and sloths to monkeys and crocodiles, along its jungle walkway.

Note that it is not the custom to hail taxis in Dallas. Cabs should be requested by telephone.

Culture District and Uptown

One block northeast of the distinctively shaped Fountain Place (Wells Fargo Building) is the **Dallas Museum of Art** ⓮ (DMA), designed by Edward Larrabee Barnes (1717 N. Harwood; closed Mon; entrance fee; tel: 214-954-0234; www.dma-art.org). Its collection is impressive: there are American artifacts dating from the pre-Columbian and Spanish eras; Greek and Roman antiquities; a model of a boat from the Egyptian Middle Kingdom, *circa* 2000 BC; a magnificent Hindu shrine of silver and wood; plus 18th-century Gilbert Stuart and Copley portraits, 19th-century landscapes, and works by Toulouse-Lautrec, Léger, Picasso, Mary Cassatt, Georgia O'Keefe, Giacometti, Edward Hopper, Andrew Wyeth and the Modernists. One room alone includes millions of dollars' worth of art by Courbet, Boudin, Pissarro, Degas, Cézanne, Monet, Rodin, Van Gogh and Vuillard. Contemporary artists represented include Pollock, Rothko, Stella and Warhol.

BELOW: museum browsing in the Culture District.

Between the DMA and the **Morton H. Meyerson Symphony Center** ⓯ (financed by Meyerson's friend Ross Perot, the billionaire founder of Electronic Data Systems who garnered 19 percent of the vote when running for president in 1992) is the **Nasher Sculpture Center** ⓰ (opening hours, entrance fee; tel: 214-242-5100; www.nashersculpturecenter.org). The $50-million building and outdoor sculpture garden designed by Renzo Piano will house more than 300 modern works. Adjacent stands the **Trammell Crow Building** surrounded by a score of valuable sculptures, including Rodin bronzes, and displaying a collection of Asian art. Note the enormous Ellsworth Kelly painting in the building's east lobby and the 68-ton (62-metric ton) steel sculpture by Eduardo Chillada, which was requested by the building's architect, I.M. Pei. In front of the building, and flanked by the 1898 Cathedral Santuario de Nuestra Guadalupe, is **Artists' Square**, a venue for craft shows, with a stage for concerts and cultural events.

Uptown begins on the other side of the freeway. At Olive and Ross, **Belo Mansion** ⓱, a building now housing the Dallas Bar Association, was, in 1932, the funeral home where the body of Clyde Barrow once

lay. The 25-year-old bank robber and his companion, 23-year-old Dallas-born Bonnie Parker, were both shot dead driving down a Louisiana country road. Their four-year crime spree had earned them headlines throughout the country. The gas station at 1620 Eagle Ford Road, built by Clyde's father, has been replaced with a new structure, but the Barrow house behind it still stands.

To head into northern Dallas, take one of the venerable 90-year-old streetcars (with velvet seats and stained-glass windows) that start from outside the DMA and run along bustling, brick-tiled **McKinney Avenue**, which is lined with restaurants, boutiques and galleries.

The multi-million dollar Morton H. Meyerson Symphony Center is home to the Dallas Symphony Orchestra, rated one of the finest orchestras in the US.

Northern Dallas

Visitors come from all over the US to shop in Dallas and, of course, thousands of locals spend countless hours in the malls that continue to spring up, largely in the northern part of the city. The very first was **Highland Park Village**, a pseudo-Colonial complex with outdoor cafés, posh stores such as Hermes, and an old theater now converted into a cinema. It was designed by William David Cook, who also designed Beverly Hills, and it is America's second-oldest shopping center. It is located on Mockingbird Lane near the Dallas north Tollway. A couple of miles north, on Northwest Highway abutting US 75, is North Park Center, filled with such prestigious stores as Neiman Marcus, Nordstrom and Barney's New York.

Nearby, on the other side of US 75, is the new shopping area known as **Mockingbird Station**, home to some local craft shops, boutiques and restaurants, as well as an **Angelika** cinema which shows many art films that aren't on general distribution. DART trains can take you to this area from downtown.

BELOW: the DART light rail system links many downtown points of interest.

One of only three theaters built to a design by Frank Lloyd Wright, Dallas Theater Center's **Kalita Humphreys Theater** is on Turtle Creek Boulevard. Not far away is one of the most expensive institutions of higher learning in Texas, **Southern Methodist University** (SMU). One of its benefactors was the late Algur H. Meadows, an oil magnate who in middle age began using his large fortune to build up a private art collection. He was aggrieved to discover that he was the owner of a number of Spanish School paintings wrongly attributed to masters, and that many of his supposed Braques, Picassos and Modiglianis were in fact counterfeits by the Hungarian master forger Elmyr de Hory. Meadows righted his collection with the help of an art historian and kindly donated it to the university. The hundred or so Spanish paintings now displayed at SMU's **Meadows Museum** (5900 Bishop Boulevard; closed Wed; Sun pm only; entrance fee; tel: 214-768-2516), by such masters as Murillo, Velázquez, Goya and Miró, are all of unquestioned authenticity.

A popular attraction in suburban Las Colinas is the spectacular Flower Clock, at the junction of State Route 114 and O'Connor Road. The beds are refreshed no less than eight times a year.

Opulent hotels and homes

Dallas has some world-famous hotels, among which are the **Mansion on Turtle Creek** and the **Crescent Court** nearby. The latter, which is more "public", is so opulent that even the house cats live in their own designer "mini hotel" in the grounds. The surrounding Turtle Creek area has some of the classiest homes in the city, as does Mockingbird Lane, which heads west from Highland Park to Love Field airport. Further north is the upscale **Galleria** (LBJ Freeway and Dallas Parkway; tel: 972-702-7100; www.dallasgalleria.com), modeled after a prototype in Milan and housing a Westin hotel, dozens of restaurants, hundreds of shops and an ice rink.

BELOW LEFT: Thanksgiving Square chapel.
BELOW RIGHT: Fountain Place skyscraper.

Neiman Marcus

The Dallas-based Neiman Marcus department store, world-renowned for its Christmas Book offering such "His and Her" gift suggestions as $1,600 mummy cases or pairs of matched camels ($16,000), prides itself on unstinting service. At the request of one customer, for example, the store discreetly investigated Queen Elizabeth's stocking size so that she could be sent a pair of nylons.

Customers were made and kept, Stanley Marcus once explained, "by (the) ability to remember small details, such as anniversary dates... a promise to get a certain evening bag for a specific social occasion... a promise that the dress bought for a girlfriend would be billed to the Mr and not the Mrs account." This was not trivia: "... it's what specialty store retailing is all about."

Stanley, one of the sons of co-founder Carrie Marcus, has been probably the most responsible for the developing the store's modern image, but Neiman Marcus – now a chain with outlets in 38 US locations – was a success from the its start in 1907. Soon after that, Nebraska-born Al Neiman teamed up with (and married) Kentucky-born Carrie Marcus who, aged 21, had already proved herself to be the most successful saleswoman at the Dallas department store A. Harris & Co.

Together with Carrie's brother, Herbert, the trio set up a sales promotion business in Atlanta which was so successful that they sold the company from the Missouri franchise for a new bottled drink, Coca-Cola. It became a family joke down through the years that Neiman Marcus was founded on a bad business judgment.

They soon set up their Neiman Marcus store in central Dallas. Neiman, the flamboyant and egotistical buyer, traveled regularly between Dallas and New York City, acquiring clothes and constantly clashing with his partners over style and design. In the 1920s, Herbert bought him out for $250,000 and the Neiman marriage broke up at the same time.

At first, the store's wealthier clientele was, to a large extent, the state's cotton aristocracy but, just after the Great Depression began (as the store was completing a major expansion), oil was discovered in East Texas. This produced a new group of millionaires who soon became Neiman Marcus customers.

In a history of American department stores, published in 1979, author Robert Hendrickson wrote that Neiman Marcus operated on the premise that "if we can please the 5 percent of our customers who are the most discriminating we will never have any difficulty in satisfying the other 95 percent who are less critical."

Certainly millions of recipients of the store's Christmas Book seem satisfied. Eight customers, for example, splashed out on the $11,200 Chinese junks offered one year. One page of the catalog is devoted to "How to Spend a Million Dollars at Neiman-Marcus," although other pages offer gifts for $25 and under. ❑

LEFT: the world-famous Neiman Marcus department store.

Between the small Love Field airport and Dallas/Fort Worth International Airport is the fast-growing area of **Las Colinas**. Here, gleaming corporate headquarters are surrounded by acres of wide-open spaces and some upscale housing, set beside a winding, artifical lake called the Mandalay Canal. Part of the canal is lined wih a tree-dotted walkway of restaurants and boutiques. In Williams Square, on O'Connor Road, a group of nine oversized bronze mustangs, sculpted by Robert Glen, gallop across a stream. A short film about the work of Nairobi-born Glen is shown in the adjoining **Mustang Sculpture Exhibit** (Tue–Sat; free; tel: 972-869-9047; www.mustangsoflascolinas.com).

Another Las Colinas attraction is the **Dallas Communications Complex** (6301 N. O'Connor Road), which, as well as a communications museum, houses a highly active movie studio where such films as *Silkwood*, *RoboCop* and *JFK* were filmed. Visitors taking a tour here (closed Sun; entrance fee; tel: 972-869-0700) can inspect movie sets and props, watch a show explaining special effects and visit a museum that includes such artifacts as a Superman suit, Judy Garland's dress from the *The Wizard of Oz* and the costumes worn in *The Sound of Music*.

"Big Tex" – mascot of the Texas State Fair – personified.

Las Colinas is but one section of the thriving town of **Irving** (pop. 191,000), irrevocably associated with the Dallas Cowboys football team, who play in the Texas Stadium (2401 E. Airport Freeway, just east of the University of Dallas). In 2009, the team will move to a new stadium in nearby Arlington. Irving Arts Center (3333 N. MacArthur Boulevard; tel: 972-252-7558) is an active cultural focus and draws visitors for its symphony concerts, dance performances, puppet theater, plays and gospel events. Its sculpture garden features the work of Texan artists. Irving's downtown **Main Street**, lined with quaint shops and a drugstore complete with old-fashioned soda fountain, has been revitalized. In addition, its 1920s railroad station in **Heritage Park** has been restored, along with its primitive teletype machine.

Midway between the two major cities, the Dallas/Forth Worth International Airport has been growing at a phenomenal rate. Covering 30 sq. miles (78 sq. km) – larger than Manhattan Island – with seven runways, it could contain the main airports of New York, Los Angeles and Chicago combined. American Airlines maintains its headquarters in Dallas and runs its own museum, named after its founder, **C.R. Smith** (near the airport at 4601 Highway 360; closed Mon; Sun pm only; free; tel: 817-967-1560; www.crsmithmuseum.com).

BELOW: the Mustangs of Las Colinas.

Deep Ellum

East of US 75 and running roughly parallel to it is Greenville Avenue, whose lower end is jammed with hip bars, dance clubs and pool halls. It's the area to find ethnic restaurants of all kinds, although **Deep Ellum** ⓲, further to the south, offers a more concentrated experience (drive or take a taxi down Elm Street from midtown). Deep Ellum, which comes alive late at night, has been renowned for its blues and jazz clubs since the 1920s. It was here that famous Texan bluesmen like Blind Lemon Jefferson and Huddie "Leadbelly" Leadbetter began their careers, and today it is also the home of artists, unusual shops and some of the city's best restaurants. The 12-block area, which

housed a community of freed slaves after the Civil War, has always attracted the avant garde and owes its current revival to the "outlaw parties" in renovated warehouses that a group of musicians organized in the 1980s. Clubs began to open up, followed by art galleries, funky shops and eating spots.

The big Ferris wheel at Dallas' Fair Park.

Across I-30 from Deep Ellum is **Fair Park**, site of the 1936 Texas Centennial Exposition, which celebrated the battle at which Texans won their independence from Mexico. Every autumn here, the largest talking dummy in existence, Big Tex, greets visitors to the State Fair of Texas.

The park is also home to the largest collection of Art Deco buildings in the country. Included among the attractions are the **Texas Hall of State** Ⓐ (open daily; only Sun pm; free; tel: 214-421-4500; www.hallofstate.com), complete with mammoth murals and statues of heroes; the 68,000-seat **Cotton Bowl Stadium** Ⓑ; the **Dallas Aquarium** Ⓒ (open daily; entrance fee; tel: 214-670-8443), with sharks, piranhas and 5,000 other water-loving creatures; an amusement park dominated by what is probably the country's biggest Ferris wheel, and several theaters. Next to the park's band shell, pleasant gardens and a conservatory make up the **Texas Discovery Gardens** Ⓓ (closed Mon; Sun pm only; entrance fee; tel: 214-428-7476; www.texasdiscoverygardens.com), which include a collection of plants indigenous to Texas.

Fair Park also has seven museums. **The Science Place** Ⓔ (open daily; entrance fee; tel: 214-428-5555; www.natureandscience.org) features an IMAX Theater and has hands-on exhibits for the whole family, including an active cutaway beehive and a car that gets progressively drunker to demonstrate the dangers of drink driving. Also worth visiting are the **Dallas Museum of Natural History** Ⓕ (open daily; entrance fee; tel: 214-421-3466), the **African-American Museum**

BELOW: West End Cattle Drive.

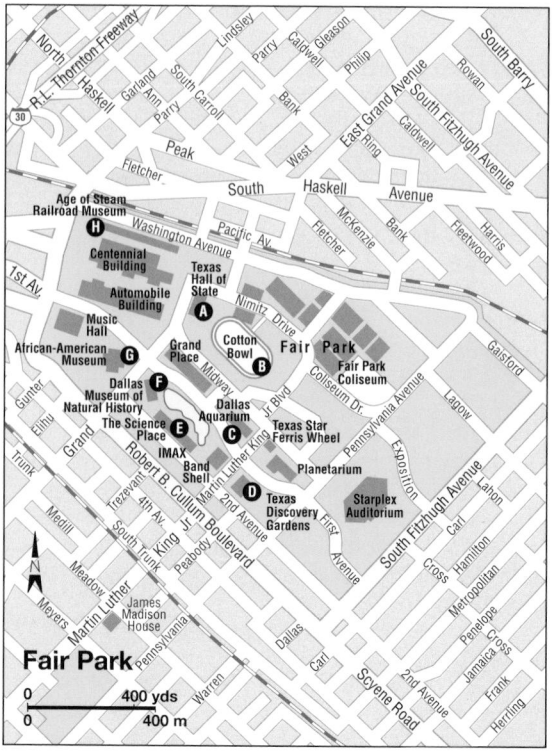

Maps: City 120 Park 128

Ⓖ (closed Mon; Tue–Fri and Sun pm only; free; tel: 214-565-9026; www.aamdallas.org), and the **Age of Steam Railroad Museum** Ⓗ (open Wed–Sun; entrance fee; tel: 214-428-0101; www.dallasrailwaymuseum.com).

East of Fair Park is the little community of **Mesquite**, which stages a rodeo every Friday and Saturday evening between April and September. Here, you can eat Texas barbecue and watch champion cowboys compete at roping, steer wrestling and bareback riding (for information tel: 972-285-8777).

Heading south

Interesting sites in the southern part of town include the **Dallas Zoo** (650 S.R.L. Thornton Freeway; open daily; entrance fee; tel: 214-670-5656; www.dallaszoo.org), which offers a 20-minute narrated monorail safari through half a dozen African habitats. Not far away is **Old City Park** ⑲ (1717 Gano Street; closed Mon; only Sun pm; entrance fee; tel: 214-421-5141; www.oldcitypark.org), which has a collection of century-old buildings and a Victorian bandstand on its village green. Nearby is the enormous **Farmers' Market** ⑳ (1010 S. Pearl Street; open daily), one of the largest surviving fresh produce markets in the US.

Larry Hagman as sleazy oil executive J.R. Ewing in the TV series Dallas, *set at Southfork Ranch just north of the city.*

Out of town

The television series *Dallas*, which ran from 1978 to 1991, probably did more to spread the city's fame than anything else, even if the image of greedy oilmen and dysfunctional families was not what the city fathers might have chosen. It made the **Southfork Ranch** (open daily; entrance fee; tel: 972-442-7800; www.southfork.com), half an hour's drive north of downtown via US-75 (take the Parker Road exit), where the Ewing clan supposedly lived, familiar to viewers in around 100 countries. Today, more than a decade after the series ended, Southfork remains the area's major tourist attraction. The family who lived there was forced to move out by the hordes of tourists, and the ranch has now become a popular location for events such as weddings and private rodeos. Tours start from J.R.'s Den.

McKinney, a historic county seat 20 miles (32 km) northeast of Dallas, is a fine example of a small town (pop. 54,000), with numerous Victorian houses, that has worked hard at retaining its old-time flavor. Victorian and Greek Revival houses around Chestnut Square, dating back to 1853, are furnished in period style and can be toured (Tue, Thur and Sat 11am; no tours August; entrance fee; tel: 972-562-8790; www.chestnutsquare.org). In the sleepy center of town, many old buildings – with their tin ceilings preserved – have been refurbished as shops selling arts and crafts. On Kentucky Street, the Collin County Jail (1880), popular with moviemakers, once housed Frank James of the infamous James gang.

The **Heard Natural Science Museum** (open daily; only Sun pm; tel: 972-562-5566; www.heardmuseum.org) pays tribute to its founder, Bessie Heard (1884–1988), scion of a venerable local family, meticulously documenting her life. The museum sits in a 287-acre (116-hectare) wildlife sanctuary with trails, a garden and a picnic area. ❑

BELOW: Dallas Farmers Market.

FORT WORTH

Map on page 132

From cowtown to cultural and commercial center: Fort Worth has become a modern, sophisticated city but has never forgotten its dusty, cattle-trading roots

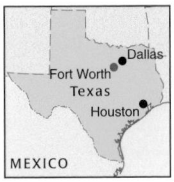

Fort Worth, which began life as a bastion against rampaging Comanche Indians, spent its first half century as a rough and tumble frontier town, dusty and lawless. The bad guys were quick to take advantage of the situation, and the area became a haven for bandits, outlaws and military deserters. One neighborhood famous for its notorious residents – including bank robbers Butch Cassidy (George Parker) and the Sundance Kid (Harry Longabaugh) – was known as Hell's Half Acre until its destruction in the early 1900s.

What brought international fame and fortune to what had been just another dusty Western backwater, however, was the longhorn steer. By 1870, large numbers of cowboys had begun to take their rest and pleasure in Fort Worth as they drove great herds of longhorns along the Chisholm Trail from the South Texas ranches to railheads in Kansas. In Fort Worth, the trail's last major stop, they bathed, drank, gambled and whored to forget their arduous, lonely and monotonous trail-driving. After resting and having provisioned themselves, the cowboys went on their way with thousands of cattle, through dust or mud.

With the arrival of the Texas and Pacific Railroad in 1876, hundreds of miles were cut off the cattle drives, and eight lines eventually connected Fort Worth with northern markets. The cattle were, of course, the worse for wear – and thinner – for every mile they traveled, thus cattle freighted from Fort Worth were in much better condition than they would have been had they struggled all the way to Kansas. Acres of pens were built to receive the herds, which were fattened up before transportation.

LEFT: western festival, Fort Worth Stockyards.
BELOW: the Live Stock Exchange.

Attendant industries such as meat-packing – the Armour and Swift companies became major players – developed here and remained Fort Worth's most important source of income through the 1920s. However, just as improvements in transportation had brought the cattle business to Fort Worth, further improvements took part of it away. Larger trucks and better highways made centralized marketing and fattening of cattle unnecessary. Cattlemen could fatten and auction herds locally, for truck delivery.

The Stockyards

Today, Fort Worth's **Stockyards National Historical District** Ⓐ, its streets cobbled and gaslit, looks much as it did a century ago. The cattle pens have been restored and Exchange Street is lined with the shops of artisans hand-crafting saddles, chaps and boots. Even today, in this sleek, modern city, one might still see a Stetson-wearing businessman, or a lawman on horseback.

At the famous **White Elephant Saloon** (tel: 817-624-8273), noted for its bullet-splintered floorboards,

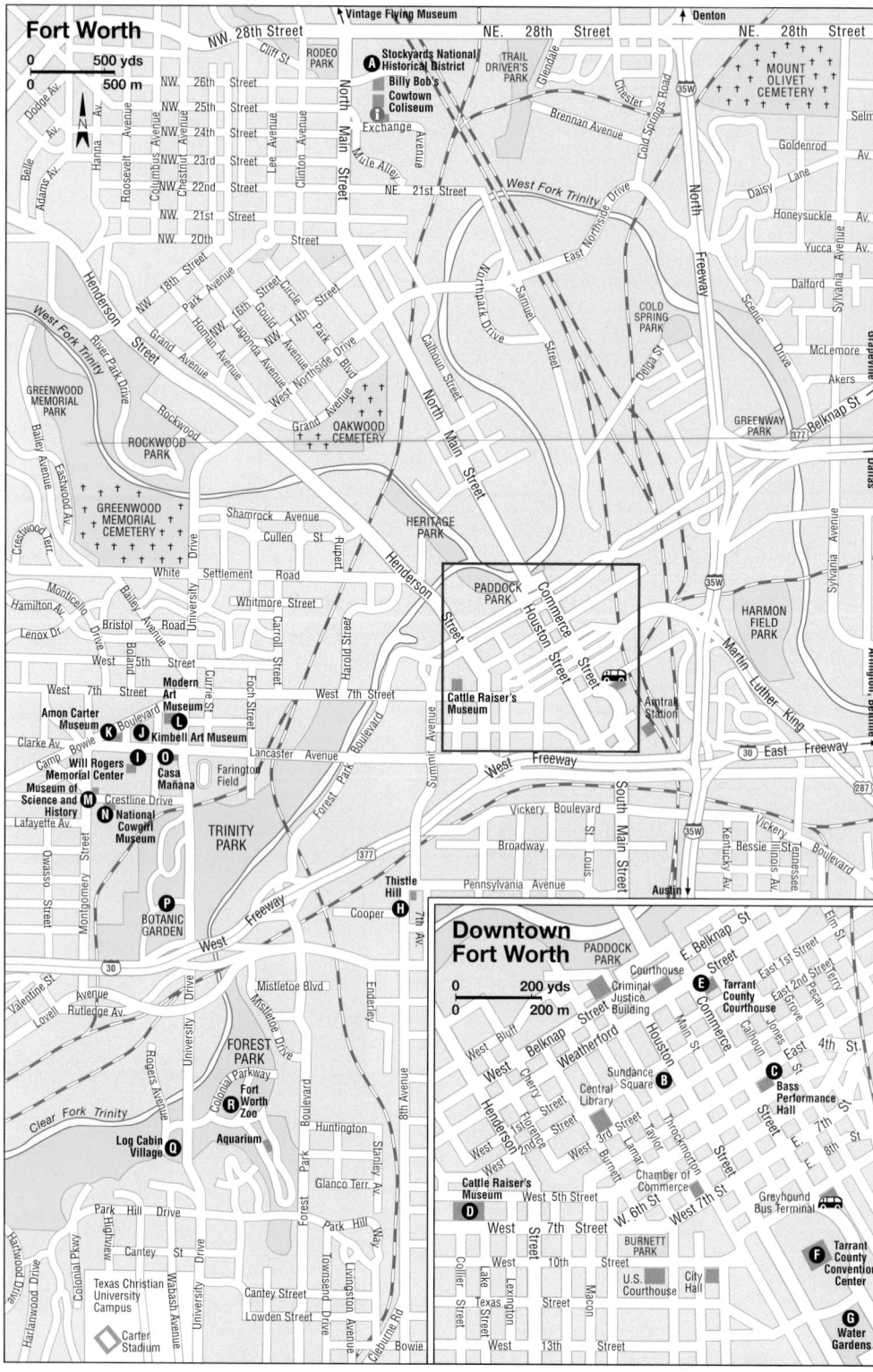
Fort Worth
0 500 yds
0 500 m
N
Vintage Flying Museum
Denton
NW. 28th Street
NE. 28th Street
Cliff St
RODEO PARK
A Stockyards National Historical District
Billy Bob's Cowtown Coliseum
Exchange
TRAIL DRIVER'S PARK
Glendale
Chester
Cold Springs Road
MOUNT OLIVET CEMETERY
Brennan Avenue
Selma
Goldenrod
Av.
Dodge Av.
Av.
Belle
Adams Av.
Hanna
Roosevelt Avenue
Columbus Avenue
NW. 26th Street
NW. 25th Street
NW. 24th Street
NW. 23rd Street
NW. 22nd Street
NW. 21st Street
NW. 20th Street
Lee Avenue
Clinton Avenue
North Main Street
Mule Alley
Avenue
NE. 21st Street
West Fork Trinity Drive
Daisy Lane
Honeysuckle Av.
Yucca Av.
Dalford
Sylvania Avenue
Scenic Drive
East Northside Drive
North Freeway
Henderson Street
NW. 18th Street
Park Avenue
Circle Street
NW. 16th Street
Gould Avenue
NW. 14th Street
Park Avenue
Lagonda Avenue
West Northside Drive
Grand Avenue
Horton Avenue
River Park Drive
West Fork Trinity
Northpark Drive
Samuel Street
Calhoun Street
COLD SPRING PARK
Delga St
McLemore
Akers
Grapevine
GREENWOOD MEMORIAL PARK
Rockwood
ROCKWOOD PARK
OAKWOOD CEMETERY
GREENWAY PARK
377
Belknap St
Dallas
Bailey Avenue
Eastwood Av.
GREENWOOD MEMORIAL CEMETERY
Shamrock Avenue
Cullen St
Rupert
HERITAGE PARK
Sylvania Avenue
Creekwood Tarr.
White Settlement Road
Drive
Monticello
Hamilton Av.
Bailey Avenue
University
Whitmore Street
Lenox Dr.
Bristol Road
Carroll Street
Harold Street
PADDOCK PARK
Commerce Street
Houston Street
35W
HARMON FIELD PARK
Martin Luther King
Arlington, Bethlehem
West 5th Street
Boland
West 7th Street
Curie St
Foch Street
West 7th Street
Modern Art Museum
Amon Carter Museum
K
J
Kimbell Art Museum
L
Cattle Raiser's Museum
Amtrak Station
Clarke Av.
Bowie
Camp
I
Will Rogers Memorial Center
O
Casa Mañana
Lancaster Avenue
Farrington Field
Forest Park Boulevard
Summit Avenue
West Freeway
30
East Freeway
287
Museum of Science and History
M
Crestline Drive
N
National Cowgirl Museum
Lafayette Av.
TRINITY PARK
Vickery Boulevard
South Main Street
Broadway
Louis St
Kentucky Av.
Illinois Av.
Bessie St
Tennessee
Vickery Boulevard
Owasso Street
Montgomery Street
377
Thistle Hill
H
Pennsylvania Avenue
Austin
P
BOTANIC GARDEN
Cooper
7th Av.
West Freeway
30
Valentine St
Avenue
Lovell
Rutledge Av.
Drive
Mistletoe Blvd
Mistletoe Drive
Enderley
FOREST PARK
Colonial Parkway
Rogers Avenue
University
R
Fort Worth Zoo
Clear Fork Trinity
Log Cabin Village
Q
Aquarium
Huntington
Boulevard
Forest Park
Stanley Av.
8th Avenue
Glanco Terr. Av.
Park Hill Drive
Park Hill Way
Highview
Cantey St
Drive
Colonial Pkwy
Hartwood Drive
Hartwood Blue
Texas Christian University Campus
Wabash Avenue
University
Cantey Street
Lowden Street
Townsend Drive
Livingston Avenue
Clebourne Rd
Bowie
Carter Stadium
Downtown Fort Worth
0 200 yds
0 200 m
PADDOCK PARK
E. Belknap St
Courthouse
Criminal Justice Building
E
Tarrant County Courthouse
East 1st Street
East 2nd Street
Elm St
Terry
Eastgrove
Pecan
Commerce Street
Houston
Main St
Calhoun
Jones St
East 4th St.
West Bluff
Belknap Street
Weatherford
West Cherry Street
Sundance Square
B
Central Library
C
Bass Performance Hall
Henderson Street
1st
Florence
2nd
Street
West 3rd Street
Lamar
Taylor
Throckmorton
Burnett
Street
7th St
8th St
Cattle Raiser's Museum
D
West 5th Street
Chamber of Commerce
W. 6th St.
West 7th St
Greyhound Bus Terminal
West 7th Street
BURNETT PARK
F
Tarrant County Convention Center
West 10th Street
Collier Street
Lake Street
Texas Street
Lexington Street
U.S. Courthouse
City Hall
Macon
G
Water Gardens
West 13th Street

there's nightly country and western music, and the notorious 1887 gunfight between owner Luke Short and former marshall Jim Courtright is re-enacted on February 8 each year. The **Stockyards Hotel** (where Bonnie and Clyde once stayed) has been decorated in "cattle baron baroque," its saloon bar stools sporting saddles, while the mission-style **Cowtown Coliseum** (121 E. Exchange, tel: 817-625-1025), which since 1908 has featured performers as varied as Enrico Caruso and Elvis Presley, offers weekly rodeos. The world's first indoor rodeo was held here in 1918. Even the 6,000-capacity **Billy Bob's Texas** (tel: 817-624-7117), which describes itself as "the world's largest honky-tonk," has live bulls posturing in its indoor ring, inviting visitors to see how long they can stay aboard the pesky critters.

Map on page 132

This way for bronco bustin'!

Next to the old hog and sheep pens (now housing art galleries, shops and eateries), the **Grapevine Vintage Railroad** operates steam-train trips (tel: 817-625-RAIL), pulled by its 1896 engine (Fri–Sun; diesel replacement Wed and Thur) to the little town of Grapevine *(see page 139)*, 21 miles (34 km) northeast. Up on the hill, the old Swift meat-packing plant is decorated with early 20th-century antiques, and houses an Italian restaurant.

Livestock auctions are still held weekly in Fort Worth and, in keeping with modern technology, entire herds of cattle are bought and sold via satellite communications. The city has also profited from the West Texas oil boom and serves as a base for many oil companies.

Although the size of sprawling Fort Worth (pop. 624,000) makes it a bit of a problem to negotiate without a car, it has only two other major areas that draw most visitors – the historic downtown area, 2 miles (3 km) to the southeast of the Stockyards, and the Cultural District, a mile or two west of that. The three areas make up what is termed a "Western Triangle" and, sensibly, the city runs a shuttle between them.

BELOW: the Grapevine Vintage Railroad steam train at Stockyards Station.

Downtown

At the heart of downtown, **Sundance Square** Ⓑ, between 2nd and 5th streets at Throckmorton, is especially lively at night, with crowded bars and clubs, and musicians entertaining the patrons of packed sidewalk cafés. In the old days, when rowdy cattlemen came here to celebrate, they were sometimes amused by a tightrope walker negotiating the wire between the Plaza Hotel and the Adelphi Theater across the street. Close by the original 1908 hotel, long ago converted into offices, is the **Sid Richardson Collection of Western Art** at 201 Main Street (closed Mon; Sun pm only; free; tel: 817-332-6554), a permanent collection acquired by the late oilman. At one time, Richardson, who died in 1959 aged 67, owned 125 producing oil wells. His nephew, Perry Bass, and his sons acquired 38 square blocks of downtown after inheriting the Richardson fortune, and the Bass family – unsurprisingly among the nation's wealthiest individuals – have been major local philanthropists.

Surrounded by the collection's 56 paintings, primarily by Frederic Remington and Charles M. Russell, is a magnificent, silver-studded saddle by Ed Bohlin, given to Richardson by his close friend and

Cowboy's lariat.

fellow oilman Amon Carter. Almost everybody who's watched a Western movie has seen some of the art of Ed Bohlin, the Swedish-born farmer who migrated to the US with the dream of becoming a cowboy. He was commissioned by Buffalo Bill Cody to repair leather harnesses used in his traveling show, and then moved to Hollywood to create saddles, holsters and other leather tack for the studios. Among his customers were Roy Rogers, Tex Ritter, Gary Cooper, the Cisco Kid (Duncan Renaldo) and John Wayne, who habitually donned a Bohlin-made gunbelt and silver hatband.

The **Bass Performance Hall** Ⓒ (4th and Calhoun streets; tel: 817-212-4280), home of the city's symphony orchestra, ballet and opera companies, is an awesome masterpiece designed by the Washington architect David M. Schwarz and completed in 1998. It is hoped that the 2,000-seat hall will last 300 years – as long as some of its European counterparts: "Great concert halls," Schwarz muses, "are symbols of an age. If they're done well they reflect a great moment in history." Surmounted by Hungarian sculptor Márton Váró's gigantic granite angels, blowing 6-ft (2-meter) trumpets, this hall is also noted for such extravagant decorative features as the cloud-filled, 80-ft (25-meter) wide Great Dome, which soars high above the auditorium. This, and the hall's other artwork, was the creation of Scott and Stuart Gentling.

Sundance Square is backdropped by the block-long (and very luxurious) Worthington Hotel, which is convenient to everything downtown, including Outlet Square, a vast indoor mall to which it is connected by a mezzanine passageway. This enables guests to bypass the scorching streets. A huge mural flanks the parking lot on 3rd Street: a three-story *trompe l'oeil* by Richard Haas of cowboys and longhorns on the Chisholm Trail.

BELOW: the covered sidewalks of Fort Worth, Exchange Street.

Raising cattle and falling water

Map on page 132

Famous branding irons and "a talking longhorn" can be inspected in the **Cattle Raiser's Museum** **D** (1301 W. 7th Street; open daily; entrance fee; tel: 817-332-8551). One exhibit here explains the importance of the brand inspector in the never-ending fight against rustlers.

At one end of what was once Hell's Half Acre, not far from the history exhibits in the newly refurbished Fire Station No. 1 (2nd and Commerce streets; open daily; free), is the **Tarrant County Courthouse** **E** (100 E. Weatherford), dating from the late 1900s. At the other end is the **Fort Worth/Tarrant County Convention Center** **F**, between Houston and Commerce. Opposite are the delightful **Water Gardens** **G** at Commerce and 15th streets, created by architect Philip Johnson and his associate, John Burgee, and imitated all over the country. Slabs are tipped at delicate angles to carry, direct, or stop water that is swirling, falling, sprinkling, or lying still. Closed in 2004 after a tragic drowning incident, the gardens recently re-opened with new safety features and a plaque commemorating the victims. The effects of the pouring, pounding water are not intended to rival nature – rather, they bring to mind leaking dams or streams of industrial coolant in flow to prevent meltdown.

One of the most remarkable features of the Kimbell Art Museum is the clever use of natural light, which allows exhibits to be seen to their best advantage.

Cultural District

The third region of the city's Western Triangle, the Cultural District, is 1½ miles (2 km) west of downtown. Roughly halfway between the two areas can be found **Thistle Hill** **H** (tours Mon–Fri and Sun pm; entrance fee; tel: 817-336-1212), an imposing example of a cattle baron's mansion dating from the turn of the 20th century. Cattleman W.T. Waggoner began building the house at 1509 Pennsylvania Avenue for his daughter in 1903, and another cattleman, Winfield Scott (one-time owner of the Plaza Hotel), completed it in 1910. The landscaped grounds are as interesting as the house restoration, which contains period furnishings and original pieces.

Dominant in the Cultural District is the **Will Rogers Memorial Center** **I** (3401 W. Lancaster Avenue, tel: 817-392-7469), but, apart from the staging of specific events (such as the annual Southwestern Exposition and Livestock Show in January), it requires less attention than other major museums here.

One of these, the **Kimbell Art Museum** **J** (3333 Camp Bowie Boulevard; closed Mon; Fri and Sun pm only; free; tel: 817-332-8451), designed by the late Louis Kahn, has long been regarded as one of the top two or three museums in America. Kahn, revered by many of his fellow architects, also designed La Jolla's Salk Institute, and his work, according to *Contemporary Architects* "had an absolutely monumental impact on the development and redirectioning of progressive design."

Combining concrete, marble, glass and vegetation with subtle modulations of natural light in a simple, exquisitely detailed whole, the Kimbell is human-sized with a wide collection that is constantly being expanded. There are objects which would, on their own, justify a visit: a Duccio, a Giovanni Bellini, Vuillards, a Cézanne, a Rubens, a Rembrandt and a

BELOW: red brick Main Street leading to the Tarrant County Courthouse.

The National Cowgirl Museum is devoted not just to women who have worked the ranches. Entertainers like Dale Evans and Patsy Cline are also members of the Hall of Fame.

spectacular Oriental collection. The museum, founded with the art collection of oil tycoon Kay Kimbell on his death in 1964, explains its rationale: "that the individual work of outstanding merit and importance is more effective as an educational tool than a large number of representative examples."

Situated near the is the **Amon Carter Museum** Ⓚ (closed Mon; Sun pm only; free; tel: 817-738-1933), the work of Philip Johnson, one of the many American architects who were influenced by the work of Louis Kahn. Founded by the Fort Worth publisher whose name it bears, the museum has just been given a $39 million extension (again by Philip Johnson) – the new building opened in October 2001. The museum is best known for collections of works by Frederic Remington and Charles M. Russell, who specialized in depicting life on the range and along the cattle trails.

In addition to the museum's collection of significant paintings by such revered American artists as Thomas Eakins and Winslow Homer, there are numerous intriguing paintings by anonymous 19th-century artists and some wonderful sepia prints. These feature gold mining scenes and were taken in an era when advances in photography had reduced the time needed for exposures to a mere 30 seconds. The pioneering "animal movement" photographer Eadweard Muybridge is also represented with an 1887 shot of a horse that shows all four of its feet off the ground.

The permanent collection of the **Modern Art Museum** Ⓛ (3200 Darnell Street; closed Mon; free; tel: 817-738-9215) – ironically the city's oldest – includes works by such 20th-century favorites as Frank Stella, Mark Rothko, Clyfford Still, Morris Louis, Joseph Cornell and even Pablo Picasso, with contemporary sculpture dotting the adjoining garden.

BELOW: inside one of the five pavilions comprising the Modern Art Museum designed by Japanese architect, Tadao Ando.

Map on page 132

The Fort Worth Museum of Science and History Ⓜ (1501 Montgomery Street; open daily; Sun pm only; entrance fee; tel: 817-255-9300) employs every inch of space to entertain and educate its visitors, with even its restroom walls adorned with charts explaining aspects of the human body. Notes by the fountains reveal that water covers three-quarters of the earth's surface, with only 3 percent of it fresh. The museum is exceptionally friendly to kids who can sit in a helicopter or dig for dinosaur bones. Additional attractions are an Omnimax theater, astronomy programs and daily shows at the Noble Planetarium.

For information about the women who worked the ranches on horseback, there's the **National Cowgirl Museum & Hall of Fame** Ⓝ (1720 Gendy Street; open daily; Sun pm only; free; tel: 817-336-4475), whose 153 inductees include Henrietta Chamberlain King, co-founder of the enormous King Ranch; sharpshooter Annie Oakley; world champion bull rider Lynn Jonckowski; and trick rider and calf roper Dixie Reger Moseley.

Casa Mañana Ⓞ (West Lancaster at University Drive; tel: 817-332-9319) is a venue for Broadway-style musicals whose roof is an early example of the geodesic dome invented by R. Buckminster Fuller. It was one of the city's tributes to the 1936 Texas Centennial Celebration. Based on the triangle, and requiring no internal support, the geodesic dome grows stronger as it grows larger, can withstand hurricanes and, unlike domes in general, has good acoustics. A later example forms the top of the Reunion Tower in Dallas.

One plot at Fort Worth's Botanic Garden has been planted particularly for the strength and variety of its scent, in anticipation of blind visitors.

Walks on the wild side

Several blocks to the south, near the intersection of I-30 and South University Drive, is the **Botanic Garden** Ⓟ (open daily; free; tel: 817-871-7686), a 114-acre (46-hectare) park watered by natural springs and containing more than 50 species of tree, all sorts of roses, and a Japanese Garden.

Further south still on Colonial Parkway, west of University Drive, is **Log Cabin Village** Ⓠ (closed Mon; Sun pm only; entrance fee; tel: 817-926-5881), featuring seven homes from the 1850s, with costumed pioneers, a grist mill and spinning wheels.

A short distance away is the **Fort Worth Zoo** Ⓡ (1989 Colonial Parkway; open daily; entrance fee; tel: 817-759-7555) in Forest Park. Set among natural habitats along winding paths are 5,000 animals, birds and reptiles. The zoo's art gallery contains 28 enormous paintings by the German artist Wilhelm Kuhnert, who went to the East African bush for inspiration. Several American buffalo live here on a 3,400-acre (1,375-hectare) range of their own. There is a prairie dog "town," where small burrowing owls may be seen creeping in and out of abandoned prairie dog holes. Trails of many descriptions divide the refuge.

Aviation buffs will enjoy the **Vintage Flying Museum** at Meacham Airport (505 NW 38th Street; open weekends, weekdays by appointment; entrance fee; tel: 817-624-1935). Some planes in this collection of historic aircraft and WWII memorabilia still fly, and each October the museum hosts a fly-in of rare and vintage aircraft.

BELOW: Cowtown Coliseum, with *The First Bulldogger* out front.

Arlington

Though a separate town, **Arlington** (pop. 375,000) has become something of an eastern adjunct to Fort Worth. Its many residents are fans of the Texas Rangers and thus flock to the magnificent **Rangers Ballpark**, which costs as much as a Las Vegas hotel and offers almost as many attractions. The complex was designed by Washington architect David M. Schwarz, the man who designed the Bass Performance Hall and the new American Airlines Center in Dallas. An entire entertainment complex is rising around it, but already thousands come to enjoy the walking trails, admire the 19-ft (6-meter) architectural friezes depicting scenes from Texas history, see the huge murals of famous baseball heroes, visit the baseball museum, and view construction of the new Dallas Cowboys football stadium.

The Six Flags Over Texas amusement park specializes in white-knuckle rides, but there is plenty to entertain all ages, including mock shoot-outs, ice shows and appearances by popular "Looney Tunes" characters.

During games, no fan is ever further than about 75 ft (23 meters) from a bright television monitor – there are 2,000 in the park. In the basement, enormous tanks pump soda to dozens of concession stands.

Visitors who take the 50-minute Ballpark tours (daily, game days am only; Sun pm only; entrance fee; tel: 817-273-5098) view the vast, open-air arena with its 49,000 seats, the dugouts, the luxurious player lounge displaying posters of every baseball movie, and the huge press balcony. Then many tourists spend hours in the **Legends of the Game Museum**, where all the heroes – Ty Cobb, Hank Aaron, Lou Gehrig and Babe Ruth among them – are represented through videos, trophies, jerseys and other memorabilia. One section is devoted to the little-known women's leagues. Upstairs in the Learning Center, baseball history is taught through interactive video quizzes, and there are various exhibits showing how bats and balls are made.

BELOW: riding the mechanical bull, Fort Worth Stockyards.

Fun and games

Heading away from the Ballpark, past Arlington's Convention Center, you reach **Six Flags Over Texas** (open daily; weekends only spring and fall; often closed winter; entrance fee; tel: 817-640-8900), at the junction of I-30 and Highway 360. This is the state's biggest tourist attraction and the original base of what is now a nationwide chain.

The theme park devotes an area to each of the nations whose flag has flown over Texas – Spain, Mexico, France, Texas, the Confederacy and the US, and there are other attractions, too.

Next door, **Six Flags Hurricane Harbor** is the largest water park in the US, and offers a cool respite from the searingly hot temperatures that summer visitors to Texas can always expect (1800 E. Lamar Boulevard; open daily; limited opening spring and fall; closed winter; entrance fee; tel: 817-265-3356). Nearby, the **Air Combat School** (921 Six Flags Drive; open daily; entrance fee; tel: 817-640-1886) offers a chance to make a simulated jet fighter flight while strapped into an actual cockpit.

Louis Tussaud's Palace of Wax & Ripley's Believe It or Not! (open daily; entrance fee; tel: 972-263-2391) is to the east, along I-30 at Beltline, and there are attractions further afield: the **Johnson Plantation Cemetery** (open by appointment; entrance fee;

tel: 817-460-4001), featuring an historic log cabin, lies at Center and Arkansas Lane, and, at the entrance to the River Legacy Parks near the lake at the west side of town is the **Living Science Center** (703 NW Green Oaks Boulevard; closed Mon; Sun pm only; closed Sun Nov–Mar; entrance fee; tel: 817-860-6752), housing environmental exhibits for all ages.

On the far side of Highway 360, which runs north to south on the eastern edge of Arlington, are shopping opportunities at Six Flags Mall (2911 E. Division), and the enormous Traders Village Flea Market (2602 Mayfield Road), which displays the wares of 1,600 dealers at weekends. The return trip west to Fort Worth on I-20 passes the gargantuan Parks Mall (Cooper at I-20).

Arlington's downtown attractions are clustered within walking distance of each other around Main Street. These include the perennial Johnny High's Country Music Revue at the **Arlington Music Hall** (224 N. Center; entrance fee; tel: 817-226-4400) and the 200-seat Theatre Arlington (305 W. Main Street; tel: 817-275-7661). The **Arlington Historical Society Museum** (1616 W. Abram; closed Mon and Tue; Sat and Sun pm only; donations accepted; tel: 817-460-4001) includes a veteran barber shop and general store. The **Arlington Museum of Art** (201 W. Main Street; open Wed–Sat; free; tel: 817-275-4600) concentrates on Texan artists.

Consider Arlington as a base for a visit to Dallas or Fort Worth. Not only is it halfway between the two centers, but it also has numerous attractions of its own, as well as plenty of restaurants and hotel rooms.

Grapevine

More than 30 19th-century buildings have been preserved and restored in the little town of **Grapevine**, which sits at the other end of the Tarantula railroad line which begins at the Fort Worth Stockyards. Named for the wild mustang grapes prevalent in the area, the town dates back to 1843 when General Sam Houston

BELOW: dressed up for a Fort Worth art festival.

camped nearby before signing a peace treaty with Indian tribal leaders. There are numerous wineries in the area, the nearest being the château-style **Delaney Vineyards** (2000 Champagne Boulevard; tours Sat pm and weekdays by appointment; free; tel: 817-481-5668).

In celebration of the local wine industry, Grapevine stages an annual "Grapefest" every September.

Grapevine is dotted with historical markers, and much of its Main Street is listed in the *National Register of Historical Places*. The tourist office (tel: 800-457-6338) is situated in the artfully reconstructed Wallis Hotel building, once filled with turn-of-the-20th-century traveling salesmen. *The Sidewalk Judge,* a lifelike sculpture by J. Seward Johnson, sitting on a bench outside, is an irresistible photo opportunity.

Across Main Street, at No. 300, the old **Palace Theater** (tel: 817-410-3100) has been restored as a home for the Grapevine Opry, and in the next block is the former **Grapevine Home Bank**, which was robbed by some of the Bonnie and Clyde gang back in 1932. Many of the buildings on Main Street now sell predominantly tacky souvenirs, but some display genuine arts and crafts. These include the Pueblo Connection (a range of Native American items), Beaux Arts Galleries and Off the Vine – a shop selling wine-related art such as hand-blown goblets.

What's known as the **Torian Log Cabin**, built in 1845, inhabited until the 1940s and still primitively furnished, sits near the gazebo in Liberty Park at the northern end of the street. The more interesting old homes are behind Main Street at the other end: a group of Victorian houses on College Street. One block west back on Main Street are the Heritage Center and the **Grapevine Depot**, the latter serving as the town's railroad station before being converted into an historical museum.

BELOW: Cowtown camaraderie.

The St Louis and Southwestern (Cotton Belt) Railroad depot once stood here and today, near the classic 1933 **Aeromotor Windmill**, which at one time pumped water for a nearby farm, is the terminal for the Tarantula steam train, plying daily between here and Fort Worth. At the blacksmith's shop, with its wild mustang grapevine, genial Jim White demonstrates forging brands while posing happily for visitors, and his neighbor, saddlemaker Aubrey Mauldin, presides over a leather shop filled with custom-made boots.

Map on page 132

The cowboy boot is something special and the state produces more of them than any other place in the world. There were 600 Texas bootmakers at one time. Now only about one-tenth of that number still painstakingly cut and stitch every inch by hand, from pointed toe (to slip easily into the stirrup) to elevated arch and heel (to hold the foot firmly in place).

A cowboy's best friend.

At the far end of the depot is **Grapevine Heritage Garden**, featuring such specimens as the swamp rose, the pink-flowered bouncing bet (once used as a soap substitute) and the crinum lily, all attracting butterflies and hummingbirds, and making the garden a visitors' delight.

North of town, 19-mile (30-km) long **Grapevine Lake** is a cool recreational oasis offering boating, swimming, fishing and all kinds of water activities. Beyond the lake, off Highway 26 at 3000 Grapevine Mills Parkway, near the airport, is the huge, brightly lit Grapevine Mills shopping mall, which is not a bad place to pass away a couple of hours between flights. A convenient shuttle bus runs to and from the airport.

Denton

Thirty-five miles (56 km) northeast of Fort Worth, on US-35, is **Denton**. Its century-old limestone and granite courthouse dominates a square lined with renovated old buildings that now house restaurants and antiques and specialty stores. The **Courthouse-on-the-Square Museum** in the courthouse focuses on the history of the region (closed Sun; free; tel: 940-349 2850); bizarrely, the town's pioneer founder, Captain John B. Denton, is buried beneath the lawn.

BELOW: Denton County Courthouse.

Numerous movies (including the 1998 film, *Armageddon*) have been shot in Denton, especially among the old homes of the Oak-Hickory Historic District and at the Evers Hardware Store (109 W. Hickory; closed Sun), which has remained family owned ever since its founding in 1885.

To the south of town, the **Texas Motor Speedway** (I-35 and Highway 114) will be of interest to auto-racing enthusiasts, while the **Hangar 10 Airplane Museum** (open Mon–Sat; tel: 940-565-1945) at Denton Municipal Airport has vintage aircraft on display and will appeal to flying buffs.

Also in this area is the Texas Women's University (TWU), the largest of its kind in the nation, containing the **Daughters of the American Revolution Museum** (open by appointment; tel: 940-898-2000), which displays gowns worn by the First Ladies of Texas. In the vicinity is the **University of North Texas** (tel: 940-565-2000), which has a fashion collection of its own, as well as a famous library. ❑

PAT NEFF HALL
OF HISTORY

WAXAHACHIE TO WACO

Map on page 146

It's easy to zoom by this stretch of Central Texas, but a detour from the Interstate is rewarded with a string of quirky towns, fine man-made lakes, distinctive architecture and absorbing museums

Central Texas is the backyard of Texas – not such a bad thing to be in a state with so many glamorous frontyards. Too often travelers, unless headed for the lakes or elderly relatives, race from Dallas to Austin without ever exiting the Interstate. Really to understand Texas, leave the causeway between Waxahachie and Waco and "come on around to the backyard."

Waxahachie

Waxahachie ❶ (pop. 22,000), located 35 miles (56 km) south of Dallas, is one of the latter's bedroom communities. Take the exit from I-35 East, the Dallas arm of the Fort Worth-Dallas "Y." The town's name derives from a Native American expression for buffalo creek; white settlers arrived here in the 1840s.

Much of the honey in Texas supermarkets comes from Waxahachie, a town that has become increasingly industrialized. Nevertheless, it still proudly preserves hundreds of Victorian and early 20th-century houses, many of which can be toured along a "Gingerbread Trail" marked on a free map. This is available from the city's Visitors' Bureau (102 YMCA Drive; tel: 972-937-2390).

Photographs and pioneer artifacts in the **Ellis County Museum** (closed Mon; Sun pm only; free; tel: 972-937-0681), a former Masonic meeting-house on the **Courthouse Square**, are devoted to the history of Waxahachie. The red sandstone and granite 1895 Ellis County Courthouse (open Mon–Fri; free), a product of Texas courthouse architect James Reily Gordon, is one of the most-photographed buildings in the state. It cost $150,000 to construct – a substantial sum in the 1890s. According to legend, an Italian stonecutter who was working on the building is thought to have fallen in love with a Waxahachie telegraph operator, Mabel Frame, whose carved face is a recurring exterior motif.

The museum owns the red-brick Greek Revival **Jenkins Home** (604 W. Main; open during the Gingerbread Trail Days festival in early June; entrance fee; tel: 972-937-0681), packed with antique fans, furniture and Bohemian glass. It was built in 1904 at the height of Waxahachie's prosperity (based on cattle, grain and cotton), along with the **Chautauqua Auditorium**, still in use in Getzendaner Park. From the same era is the ornate Roman Revival **Nicholas P. Sims Library** (515 W. Main), with a richly decorated Carrara marble and gold interior.

Waxahachie, close to Dallas' already established film industry, and with its abundant period architecture, has become popular as a movie location. The 1985 *Peyton Place* remake was filmed here, as, more recently, were the movies *Tender Mercies* and *Places in the Heart*.

PRECEDING PAGES: the spring-fed Blue Hole, near Austin. **LEFT:** Baylor University, Waco. **BELOW:** Ellis County Museum/Old Masonic Lodge, Waxahachie.

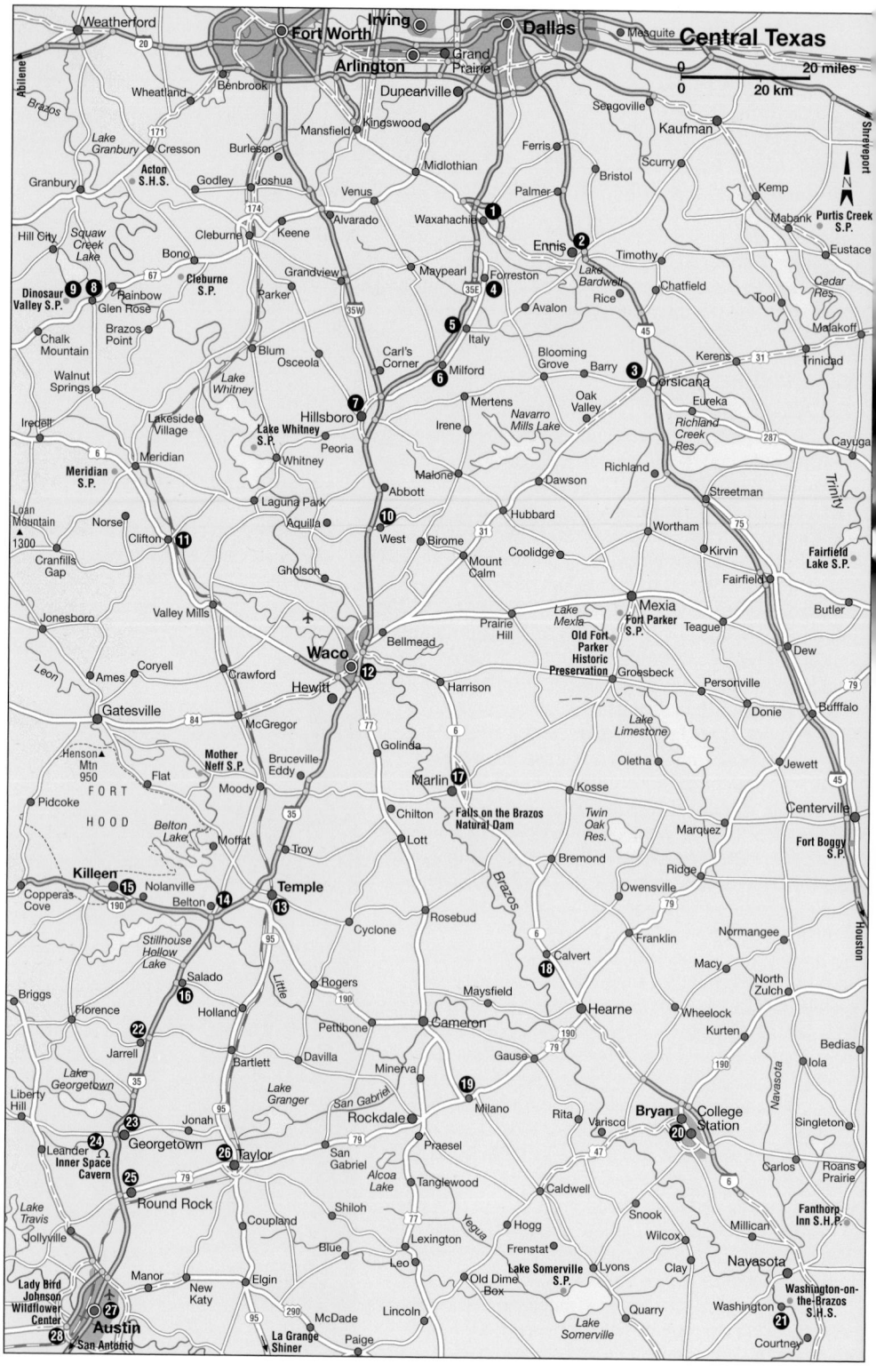
Central Texas
0 20 miles
0 20 km
N
Weatherford
Fort Worth
Irving
Dallas
Mesquite
Arlington
Grand Prairie
Duncanville
Benbrook
Wheatland
Abilene
Brazos
Lake Granbury
Cresson
Burleson
Mansfield
Kingswood
Midlothian
Ferris
Seagoville
Kaufman
Scurry
Bristol
Palmer
Kemp
Shreveport
Acton S.H.S.
Granbury
Godley
Joshua
Venus
Alvarado
Waxahachie
Ennis
Mabank
Purtis Creek S.P.
Eustace
Timothy
Hill City
Squaw Creek Lake
Cleburne
Keene
Bono
Cleburne S.P.
Grandview
Maypearl
Forreston
Lake Bardwell
Chatfield
Cedar Res.
Tool
Dinosaur Valley S.P.
Rainbow
Glen Rose
Parker
Avalon
Rice
Malakoff
Brazos Point
Italy
Chalk Mountain
Blum
Osceola
Carl's Corner
Blooming Grove
Barry
Corsicana
Kerens
Trinidad
Walnut Springs
Lake Whitney
Milford
Mertens
Oak Valley
Eureka
Iredell
Lakeside Village
Hillsboro
Lake Whitney S.P.
Peoria
Irene
Navarro Mills Lake
Richland Creek Res.
Cayuga
Meridian
Meridian S.P.
Whitney
Malone
Richland
Dawson
Streetman
Trinity
Loan Mountain 1300
Norse
Laguna Park
Abbott
Aquilla
Hubbard
Wortham
Clifton
West
Birome
Coolidge
Kirvin
Fairfield Lake S.P.
Cranfills Gap
Gholson
Mount Calm
Fairfield
Jonesboro
Valley Mills
Prairie Hill
Lake Mexia
Mexia
Fort Parker S.P.
Teague
Butler
Bellmead
Waco
Old Fort Parker Historic Preservation
Dew
Leon
Ames
Coryell
Crawford
Hewitt
Harrison
Groesbeck
Personville
Gatesville
McGregor
Lake Limestone
Donie
Bufffalo
Henson Mtn 950
Mother Neff S.P.
Bruceville-Eddy
Golinda
Oletha
Jewett
Flat
Moody
Marlin
Kosse
FORT HOOD
Pidcoke
Chilton
Falls on the Brazos Natural Dam
Twin Oak Res.
Centerville
Belton Lake
Moffat
Lott
Marquez
Fort Boggy S.P.
Troy
Bremond
Killeen
Nolanville
Temple
Ridge
Copperas Cove
Belton
Brazos
Owensville
Rosebud
Cyclone
Stillhouse Hollow Lake
Franklin
Normangee
Calvert
Macy
Salado
Little
Rogers
North Zulch
Briggs
Florence
Holland
Mayfield
Hearne
Wheelock
Pettibone
Cameron
Kurten
Jarrell
Bartlett
Davilla
Gause
Bedias
Iola
Lake Georgetown
Minerva
Liberty Hill
Lake Granger
San Gabriel
Milano
Rita
Bryan
College Station
Navasota
Singleton
Jonah
Rockdale
Varisco
Leander
Georgetown
Inner Space Cavern
Taylor
San Gabriel
Praesel
Carlos
Roans Prairie
Alcoa Lake
Tanglewood
Caldwell
Round Rock
Lake Travis
Shiloh
Coupland
Snook
Fanthorp Inn S.H.P.
Jollyville
Vegua
Hogg
Millican
Lexington
Wilcox
Blue
Frenstat
Leo
Lake Somerville S.P.
Lyons
Clay
Navasota
Manor
Elgin
Old Dime Box
Lady Bird Johnson Wildflower Center
New Katy
Washington-on-the-Brazos S.H.S.
Austin
McDade
Lincoln
Quarry
Washington
San Antonio
La Grange
Shiner
Paige
Lake Somerville
Courtney

Polka Festival

Map on page 146

Many of the state's Czech immigrants settled in this fertile, Central Texas cotton-growing belt, and almost all of them did well as cotton farmers here. Their descendants make up approximately half the population of **Ennis** ❷, on I-45 between Dallas and Houston. Since 1966, Ennis has sponsored the **National Polka Festival** in May, attracting crowds of 30,000. A parade of polka bands rolls down the main street, which may be the widest in Texas – divided into East and West Main by railroad tracks, it is 340 ft (104 meters) across. The town also has a **Railroad and Cultural Heritage Museum** (105 NE. Main Street; open daily; Sun pm only; entrance fee; tel: 972-875-1901), which showcases the Czech influence as well as railroad history.

Faces carved into the columns of Ellis County Courthouse, Waxahachie.

On the water

Since 1900, more than 200 lakes have been created in Texas. **Lake Bardwell**, or the Bardwell Reservoir, on Waxahachie Creek, 4 miles (7 km) outside Ennis, was built by the US Corps of Engineers in the early 1960s. Like the other new lakes near Navarro Mills and Mexia, it is a popular recreation area, with pretty lakeside parks and camping. It also acts as the water supply for Ennis, Waxahachie and Corsicana. Visitors from out of state – especially New Englanders, whose reservoirs are fenced and carefully patrolled – are often surprised to find Texans fishing, water-skiing and sailing on theirs.

Corsicana ❸, the Navarro county seat, is 19 miles (30 km) south of Ennis on I-45. It is named for Corsica, home of the parents of the Texas hero José Antonio Navarro of San Antonio, who signed the Texas Declaration of Independence and helped write the first constitution. The first Texas gusher was not drilled at Corsicana as is commonly believed. However, a 12-year oil boom began in 1894 when the city dug an artesian well and struck oil instead of water. The strike made Corsicana the first oil boomtown in Texas. A current attraction, **Pioneer Village** (912 W. Park Avenue; open daily; Sun pm only; entrance fee; tel: 903-654-4846) is made up of reconstructed 19th-century log buildings, including an Indian trading post and slave quarters.

Corsicana has achieved a minor sort of fame from a special local delicacy, the "Deluxe" fruit cake made by the **Collin Street Bakery** (401 W. 7th Avenue; open daily; tel: 800-292-7400; www.collinsstreet.com), which has been exported all over the world – 1.6 million fruitcakes per year, to be exact. An essential ingredient is the inimitable Texas pecan, more than a million pounds (just under half a million kg) of which are used by the bakery annually.

BELOW: dolls in Czech national costume at Ennis Railroad Museum.

Nameless place

Forreston ❹, 10 miles (16 km) south of Waxahachie on the Interstate, is the oldest town in the area. Another 5 miles (8 km) south, near **Italy** ❺, the Confederates operated a hat factory.

Italy was originally called "Houston Creek," because Sam Houston was reported to have camped nearby. Reputedly the post office would not issue a postmark unless the name of the town was changed

and, after six different names had been rejected, settlers wrote back: "Let the post office be nameless, and be damned." The community was Nameless, Texas, from 1880 to 1890, and there is still a Nameless Schoolhouse and Nameless Road. Houston Creek eventually became Italy – a tribute, it is said, to the sunny Central Texas climate. The population of Italy has never exceeded 1,300, but it did receive the first fully endowed public library in Texas – the **Dunlap Library** – from businessman S.M. Dunlap.

Texas-born Audie Murphy (1924–71) was able to build on his honorable service record by becoming an actor, starring in a series of war and western films, most notably the Civil War movie The Red Badge of Courage *(1951).*

Historical towns

Back on I-35 or via State Route 22 from Corsicana, you arrive at **Milford** ❻, a town settled in the 1850s that once adopted the good-humored city motto: "The home of 700 friendly people and three or four old grouches." It is nothing more than human nature to leave the freeway in the hope of catching a glimpse of one of the grouches. The town of **Hillsboro** ❼, just below the point where I-35 West joins I-35 East from Dallas, has been a crossroads since the 1850s, when there was a dirt-floor, elm-pole courthouse here. Today's limestone Hill County Courthouse was built in 1890, burned down in 1993 and was restored in 1999, with the help of a fund-raiser headlined by Willie Nelson, who grew up in nearby Abbott. At Hill Junior College, the **Harold B. Simpson History Complex** (open Mon–Fri; entrance fee; tel: 254-582-2555, ext. 256) displays paintings, photographs and documents from the Civil War, around 200 guns and other weaponry from the Civil War to the present, and the uniform worn by Audie L. Murphy, the most decorated American soldier of World War II.

Northwest of Hillsboro on State Road 144 is **Glen Rose** ❽, where it is rumored John Wilkes Booth once lived – under the name John St Helen – after

LEFT: Ellis County Courthouse depicted on the backdrop of the Chautauqua Auditorium. **RIGHT:** the real thing.

he assassinated President Lincoln. Glen Rose is sometimes known as the "Petrified City," because petrified wood is a popular building material here. Local history is explained in the **Somervell County Museum** (Mon–Fri; Sun pm only; weekends only in winter; free; tel: 254-898-0640) at Vernon and Elm streets.

Jurassic Park

Numerous dinosaur tracks can be found in Glen Rose and in the 1,270-acre (514-hectare) **Dinosaur Valley State Park** ❾ (open daily; entrance fee; tel: 254-897-4588), 4 miles (6 km) west of the town. The tracks are easy to spot, but there is a steep trail to the river. The Bosque River Valley was once coastal swampland and dinosaurs left their tracks – some of the best-preserved examples in the world – in the limestone river bed here. There are no "taildrag marks" in the dinosaurs trackway – the water here was deep enough for the dinosaurs' tails to float – but you can see where the mud oozed up between their toes. The park has facilities for camping, picnicking, hiking, biking and horse riding, and is one of the state parks in which part of the official State Longhorn Herd is kept.

Acrocanthosaurus footprint in Dinosaur Valley State Park.

West, Texas

The small town of **West** ❿, halfway between Hillsboro and Waco, is sometimes confused with the region "West Texas," so it is called "West, Comma, Texas." Forty thousand people came here on September 15 1896 to view the ridiculous, staged spectacular of two locomotives of the Missouri, Kansas and Texas Railroad crash into each other. Their throttles tied back to 50 mph (80 kmph), the trains exploded on impact, killing two spectators. The agent who dreamed up this reckless stunt was merely fired – and promptly rehired the next day.

BELOW: house on Waxahachie's Gingerbread Trail.

The Bosque

The town of Waco was founded, and initially thrived, on the profits of five "C"s: cattle, cotton, corn, culture and collegians.

Twenty miles (32 km) west of Hillsboro, across the Brazos River, is the region known as **Bosque County** (Spanish for "woods" and pronounced "boskay"). A number of Norwegians settled here as farmers between 1850 and 1875. They fiercely defended their log houses from attacks by the Kiowa and Comanche Indians and many relics and household items used by these early Scandinavian settlers have been collected for display in the **Bosque Memorial Museum** (open Tue–Sat; entrance fee; tel: 254-675-3845; www.bosquemuseum.org) on Avenue Q in **Clifton** ⓫ (pop. 3,200). Clifton's Nordic heritage is also celebrated with a smorgasbord each November at **Norse**, near Clifton.

Waco

Until they were driven out, the Waco were a Wichita tribe occupying a site by the 840-mile (1,344-km) long Brazos River in Central Texas. When the whites first settled the area 160 years ago, they took **Waco** ⓬ as the name for their town. First came Fort Fisher, then and now a Texas Ranger outpost, but what really brought attention to the town was the construction, in 1870, of a massive suspension bridge across the river.

"That bridge was very important," explains local historian Roger Conger. "The Brazos was a veritable iron curtain across the center of Texas. After the Civil War many Southerners were going west. They had to come to Waco to cross the river."

Six bridges span the river within the city today but the antique suspension bridge (now pedestrian-only) is still the most significant. When the 475-ft (145-meter) bridge supplanted the ferry, it was the longest single-span suspension

BELOW: Dr Pepper Museum, Waco.

bridge west of the Mississippi River, and the second longest in the world. Supported by wire cables and 2,700,000 Waco bricks, it was built by New York engineer Thomas Griffith from the plans of New York's Thomas Roebling, designer of the Brooklyn Bridge. Longhorns and wagon trains bound for the Chisholm Trail traversed it in its earliest days and, until 1889, a toll was charged: "five cents for each loose animal of the cattle kind."

Map on page 146

Earliest site

Some of the settlers who followed the Texas Rangers to this beautiful valley on the Brazos in the 1840s lived in log cabins on the site of what is now Cameron Park on Rotan Drive. Here are woods, hiking trails, the natural habitat **Cameron Park Zoo** (open daily; Sun pm only; entrance fee; tel: 254-750-8400; www.cameronparkzoo.com) and Miss Nellie's Pretty Place, a wildflower preserve donated to the city by a former congressman's mother.

What the earliest settlement probably looked like can be seen adjoining the riverside Fort Fisher Campground, at **The Governor Bill and Vara Daniel Historic Village** (closed Sun; entrance fee; tel: 254-710-1160), on the campus of Baylor University. The largest Baptist university in the world, Baylor also houses the **Strecker Museum** (closed Sun; free; tel: 254-710-1110), devoted to natural history, and the fascinating marble-columned **Armstrong Browning Library** (closed Sun; Sat am only; free; tel: 254-710-3566) with portraits of, and 4,000 letters written by or to, the Victorian poets Robert and Elizabeth Barrett Browning. The library's collection – assembled by Baylor's late Professor A.J. Armstrong – is supplemented by 50 lovely stained-glass windows depicting verses by the poetic pair.

Dr Pepper has a taste all of its own.

BELOW: the Texas Ranger Museum, Waco.

MAKE MINE A DR PEPPER

Probably the most unconventional cultural center in Waco is the Dr Pepper Museum, based at 300 S. 5th Street (open daily; Sun pm only; entrance fee; tel: 254-757-1025).

Dr Pepper was invented in 1885 in Waco's Old Corner Drug Store by pharmacist Charles Alderton. His boss, Dr Morrison named it Dr Pepper but why remains unclear. The museum, housed in a bottling plant opened in 1906, covers the history of Dr Pepper and the entire soft drink industry: "We're proud of our display on Waco's other soft drink, Big Red, invented about half a block from here," declares director Joe Cavanaugh. The site is now featured on the National Register of Historic Places but Dr Pepper has not been produced here since the 1920s.

If you want to visit the oldest working Dr Pepper plant (since 1891), make a trip to Dublin, 94 miles (150 km) west of Waco. Here you can sample Dr Pepper made to the original recipe, incorporating cane sugar rather than other sweeteners. Tours of the factory are offered and visitors on Tuesdays can see the bottling taking place.

The Waco site also includes an early soda fountain where you can sample traditional sodas and sundaes. There is no entrance fee if you just go in for a drink.

Map on page 146

Between the Baylor campus and US-81 is the Tourist Information Center (tel: 800-321-9226), adjoining the **First Street Cemetery**, which houses Confederate graves. Other attractions are the **Texas Sports Hall of Fame** (1108 University Parks Drive; open daily; Sun pm only; entrance fee; tel: 254-756-1633), where kids can try on helmets of the Houston Oilers or Dallas Cowboys, and the **Texas Ranger Hall of Fame & Museum** (open daily; entrance fee; tel: 254-750-8631). Jim Bowie's knife and the rifle he carried at the Alamo are here, as well as a jewel-studded saddle (which cost $5,800 in 1903), novelist James Michener's typewriter, the pistol Pat Garrett used to kill Billy the Kid and enough of the early Rangers' Colt revolvers to equip an army.

Six-shooter junction

In its prime, Waco was a rough cowtown. "Next stop, Waco," the train conductors would yell as the train approached, "Get out your six-shooters." The last legal hanging in Texas occurred here in 1923, witnessed by over 4,000 people, and, in 1955, a Waco television station was the first in the world to broadcast a murder trial. A more genteel era is reflected by the city's group of 19th-century homes, operated from the gingerbread-style Hoffmann House by the Historic Waco Foundation (810 S. 4th Street; tel: 254-753-5166; www.historicwaco.org). The Foundation also hosts the annual Brazos River Festival in April.

Two of these Victorian homes lie between I-35 and Waco Drive and can be toured on Saturday and Sunday afternoons (except December). They are the Greek Revival **Earle-Napier-Kinnard House** (814 S. 4th Street), completed in 1869, and **Fort House** (503 S. 4th Street), in which Alabama planter William Aldridge Fort lived with dozens of relatives and slaves in the 1870s.

BELOW: McLennan County Courthouse, Waco.
RIGHT: the famous bridge over Waco's Brazos River.

Across the river, at 100 Mill Street, is the Italianate **East Terrace**, shielded by large elm and pecan trees, with walks down to the river. Home of industrialist John Wesley Mann, *circa* 1872, it contains original furniture.

Confederate support

At 1901 N. Fifth Street, the **Earle-Harrison House** (tel: 254-753-2032), sitting in 5-acre (2-hectare) gardens, is gloriously furnished. Portraits of General Robert E. Lee abound in some of these old homes, a reminder that Waco's men marched off to support Confederate armies in the Civil War.

A total of six Confederate generals hailed from Waco, which has also been home to former Texas Governor Ann Richards and Madison Alexander Cooper Jr, whose 840,000-word novel, *Sironia, Texas* – on view in the public library – is said to be the longest ever written.

Another among Waco's dozen or more museums is the **Helen Marie Taylor Museum of Waco History** (open Tue–Sat; entrance fee; tel: 254-752-4774), whose location at 701 Jefferson sits on the site of one of the Waco Indian tribe's main villages.

In 2001 a downtown park was opened in front of City Hall (3rd and Austin). The walkways and fountains of **Heritage Square** were constructed on the site of an area devastated by a tornado in 1953. ❑

WACO TO AUSTIN

Map on page 146

Austin – college town, state capital and home of live music – dominates this part of Central Texas, but the many small towns around the city are worth a visit, too

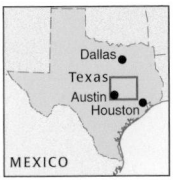

The impression is unavoidable: the young of Central Texas migrate to larger cities like Austin and Dallas as soon as possible. A disproportionately large percentage of the population remaining in rural areas appears to be old or very young. Past Waco, the pull of Austin, which is filled with students and ex-students, is unmistakable. Cars speed up, responding to the attraction of Texas' magnetic capital. Temple – with its fenced stretch of Interstate that does not look as if it is supposed to be exciting – Belton, Killeen and Salado (it rhymes with Laredo) zip by most I-35 drivers unnoticed, unless they are searching out the Dairy Queen. But this series of former railroad stops is more interesting than it looks, and repays a visit if examined with the eye of the novelist or sociologist.

Like most towns south of Waco, **Temple** ⓭ and **Belton** ⓮ were originally built around loading pens and general stores about a century ago. Today, the area is known primarily for the commanding presence of **Fort Hood**, the largest military base in the US, which is set on no fewer than 217,000 acres (87,800 hectares), near Lake Benton. The base is one of the primary training grounds for US soldiers dispatched to Iraq and other global assignments. The main drag of nearby Harker Heights is lined with car dealerships, eating places and fairly rowdy nightclubs.

LEFT: the Governor's Mansion, Austin. **BELOW:** hay bale Jack-o'-Lantern in Central Texas.

Two historic army divisions maintain museums at Fort Hood: the **1st Cavalry Museum** on Headquarters Avenue and the **2nd Armored Division Museum** on Battalion Avenue (both open daily; Sat and Sun pm only; free). These and the many reconstructed frontier forts in Texas, along with gun museums and collections of artifacts, they feed the imagination.

Life and death

There are a number of eateries in the Temple-Killeen area, and, in addition to plenty of hearty Texan specialties, they offer a good opportunity to observe small-town life. In fact, Texan-watching is at its best while sawing a batter-fried "corny dog" or a chicken-fried steak, a cheap cut of hammered beef breaded like fried chicken and served with potatoes and gravy.

The point of bars, clubs, honky-tonks, ice-houses and beer-joints in Texas is friendliness, not fighting. But making some new friends by fighting, particularly in hole-in-the-wall joints and motel rooms, is an ongoing frontier tradition. Invitations to do so should be firmly refused. Pistol-packing is not entirely unheard of, but is thankfully rare.

In towns like Temple, Belton and **Killeen** ⓯, there is still much pleasure to be taken in day-to-day proceedings. There are as many original characters, language tricks and private jokes as anywhere else,

Restaurants, hotels, museums, wildlife refuges and zoos are likely to change their names and hours, if not just disappear completely, in booming Texas. Where distances are great, telephone ahead or inquire at a Chamber of Commerce or other tourist agency.

possibly more, since the storytelling tradition remains strong in both rural and urban Texas. In this region, times are changing: Temple-Killeen's Standard Metropolitan Statistical Area is one of the 10 fastest-growing in the US.

Local history

I-35 follows the railroad – beside the Chisholm Trail, along which cattle were driven to rail-heads farther north – so busy Temple is a logical place to find the **Railroad and Pioneer Museum** (315 W. Avenue B; Tue–Sat 10am–4pm, Sun 12–4pm; entrance fee; 254-298-5172) in the 1910 Santa Fe depot at 31st Street and Avenue H. It houses a steam engine and railroad equipment.

The **Czech Heritage Museum** (515 N. Main Street; closed Sat and Sun; free; tel: 254-899-2935) exhibits an unusual collection related to Czech immigration at the Slovanska Podporujici Jednota Statu Texas (SPJST; Benevolent Order of the State of Texas) Insurance Building. Preserved artifacts include a bible dated 1530. There are SPJST halls in many Central Texas towns.

The **Bell County Museum** in Belton (201 N. Main Street; open Tue–Sat pm only; free; tel: 254-933-5243), is a local history museum occupying a 1905 Carnegie Library building.

Farms and plantations

The pretty little town of **Salado** ⑯, once a stage halt on Salado Creek, a few miles south of Killeen, is best known for its popular and picturesque Stagecoach Inn (1 Main Street), a restaurant with mid-19th century antecedents and modern motel additions. Across the street is the Central Texas Area Museum, where Sam Houston delivered an anti-secession speech from the balcony.

BELOW: Heep Ranch in Buda, near Austin.

Texas' first chapter of the Grange, an important organization of anti-corporate American farmers that flourished during the Progressive era, was founded at Salado in 1873. The related Farmers' Alliance, which had several million members throughout the country in its most successful days, originated at Lampasas, about 50 miles (80 km) west of Fort Hood, in 1875. Together they helped elect the famous Populist James Stephen Hogg, who was Governor of Texas 1891–95.

Near the I-35 access road at Salado, the antebellum **Robertson Plantation House** is unusually complete, with outbuildings, slave quarters and a family cemetery. It was built in 1856 by E.S.C. Robertson, son of Sterling Clack Robertson, who settled 600 families in the Brazos River Basin, northwest of Stephen F. Austin's colony.

The name "Salado" means "salty" in Spanish.

The steady character, intelligence and diligence with which Austin won the respect of his fellow "Texans" were also displayed by Robertson. One of the directors of his "Nashville Company" was Sam Houston, who had already been the Governor of Tennessee and later became both President and Governor of the state of Texas.

The complex, ultimately unsuccessful attempt to turn the early settlers into Mexican citizens makes a long and stirring story. The patriarch Moses Austin, father of Stephen, who did not live to see the Anglo-Southerners enter the Promised Land, had wished to give his name to a great port, Austina, which would rival New Orleans. Instead, a new capital in the wilderness was named for the Father and Grandfather of Texas. The now-abandoned town of **Nashville**, one of the principal settlements of Robertson's colony, was also considered for the capital. If Nashville had been made capital of Texas instead of Austin, Robertson would be better-known today.

BELOW: Hamilton Pool, a popular swimming place, west of Austin.

Once Bucksnort

There are a number of interesting cities to the east of I-35, where Central and East Texas merge. **Marlin** ⓱, 25 miles (40 km) east of Eddy, between Waco and Temple on State Route 7, was settled by Alabama and Tennessee farmers brought to Texas by Sterling Robertson. It was originally "Bucksnort." The Marlin for whom it is named was the first farmer to return after the "Runaway Scrape," when almost the whole population of the rebellious Republic fled before the invading Mexican army and the Indians from which their own army could not protect them. Local artifacts in the **Falls County Historical Museum** (145 Heritage Row; open Mon–Fri pm only; free; tel: 254-883-9101), include the gallows from the county jail.

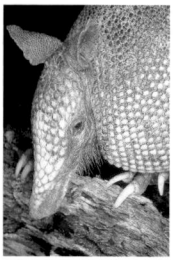

The armadillo, the "State Mammal," is commonly found in rural Central Texas.

As the style of some of its architecture may suggest, Marlin has been one of the Central Texas spas since 1891, when hot water – not oil, as is often the case elsewhere – was struck in drilling an artesian well. The grand, château-like **Highlands Mansion** (1413 McClanahan Road; tel: 254-803-2813), built in 1900 and now a bed and breakfast inn, is a reminder of the prosperous times that arrived a considerable while after the Revolution. Between Marlin and Lott, the land office for Robertson's colony of Sarahville de Viesca was located at Falls on the Brazos Natural Dam. Fort Milam, a Texas Ranger outpost, was founded nearby.

Reconstruction

Below: water skier on a central Texas lake.

Calvert ⓲, 41 miles (66 km) southeast of Marlin on State Route 6, is named for Robert Calvert, a descendant of Lord Baltimore and owner of one of the large cotton plantations in the area. The fields here were worked by slaves and, after the Civil War, by black convicts and Chinese and Italian immigrants. The theory was that Northern Europeans were incapable of laboring long in such a climate.

At Calvert, the reconstruction period was punitive and violent, in a manner reminiscent of the deep South. A cage for unreconstructed Confederate sympathizers, called a "sky parlor," was placed in a tree or atop a wooden pole where **Virginia Field Park** is now. But the cotton continued to grow: in the early 1870s, Calvert believed it possessed the world's largest cotton gin.

It is said that **Milano** ⓳, 15 miles (24 km) southwest of Hearne on State Route 79, owes its name to a post office blunder. At the time it applied for a postmark, it was called Milam, in honor of the Texas Revolutionary hero Ben Milam. Apparently there was some confusion in Washington, and authorization was ultimately given to use the misspelling.

A number of Italian immigrants, especially Sicilians, settled close by, in the flood-prone Brazos bottomland between Hearne and Bryan, and many Italian surnames are still found on country mailboxes.

College Town

Although Austin, home of the University of Texas (UT), is possibly the state's best-known college town, the huge campus of Texas A&M University at

Bryan/College Station ⑳, 18 miles (29 km) southeast of Hearne, is nearly as large. There are over 46,000 students studying here (UT has 50,000). A great rivalry exists between A&M and UT, if only because, whereas A&M receives a third of the oil revenue from public lands (endowed before the hidden oil was discovered on them), UT receives the remainder.

Map on page 146

Many Texans have warm feelings for Aggies – trusting, stalwart and stupid, as portrayed in the innumerable Aggie jokes. In the budget wars between the Austin campus and the state government, politicians, including several colorful governors, have depicted UT to rural and poor voters as an arrogant, wasteful, rich man's school. Part of this has to do with the liberal politics of Austin, in contrast to the state's general conservatism.

The settlement of Bryan/College Station is actually two towns, not one. Bryan, founded in 1859, was joined, in 1877, by College Station, developed as a railroad stop and new site for A&M University.

Tours of the A&M campus, including the **Sanders-Metzger Gun Collection** (free), displaying famous Colt pistols, can be arranged at the Information Center in the Rudder Tower. Also in College Station is the **George Bush Presidential Library and Museum** (1000 George Bush Drive West; open daily; Sun pm only; entrance fee; tel: 979-691-4000). Bush senior was an A&M student, and the museum houses a record of, and papers from, his presidency.

Independence site

Continuing its journey down to the Gulf of Mexico, the Brazos river reflects significant dates in Texas history at many points along its route. Eighty miles (128 km) southeast of Waco, at **Washington-on-the-Brazos** ㉑ in 1836, Texas declared its independence from Mexico. Then the river was the lifeblood of the fledgling republic, as can be seen in the **Star of the Republic Museum** (open daily; entrance fee; tel: 936-878-2461; www.starmuseum.org).

BELOW: country mailboxes in central Texas.

Expanding suburbs

At Temple, you may choose to proceed down I-35 to Austin through **Jarrell** ㉒, an old Czech community which was a stage-coach stop, or head south on State Route 95, a picturesque alternative with interesting small towns. This highway by-passes Austin so keep an eye out for west-bound US-79 or US-290, to reach the city. Austin's rapid growth brought rediscovery and development in communities like **Georgetown** ㉓ in Williamson County. They are enjoying a rebuilding period after many years of declining population, and, in uncovering their Victorian facades, they develop, just like Congress Avenue or 6th Street in downtown Austin, a solid sense of their history. The north and south forks of the San Gabriel river flow together at Georgetown. **San Gabriel Park**, on the river east of the Interstate, and 1,200-acre (486-hectare) **Lake Georgetown** are splendid places to have a picnic. There are good-looking late 19th-century buildings in the **Courthouse Square**, a National Historic District.

Lake Georgetown is a popular angling center, attracting fishermen with its stocks of smallmouth bass, channel cat and walleye.

Williamson County was originally to be called San Gabriel, but its state senator, "Three-Legged Willie" Williamson, is said to have protested that there were enough saints in Texas already. The upshot of his display of anti-Mexican sentiment was that the county was named for him.

East-west divide

Inner Space Cavern ㉔ (open daily; entrance fee; tel: 512-931-2283; www.innerspace.com), on I-35 between Round Rock and Georgetown, is one of Texas' most accessible caves. Its large rooms are unusual in this part of the state, and the tour takes visitors into the most beautiful of them.

Such caves, the springs that one finds here, and the change in topography

BELOW: two of a kind in Georgetown.
RIGHT: central Texas caves.

which at times is very noticeable, especially between Austin and San Antonio, are due to the activity of the **Balcones Fault Zone** that runs alongside I-35 from Mexico up to Oklahoma. To the west, the ground rose up producing what the Spanish called *Los Balcones* (balconies). The springs, around which early settlements grew, gush up through fissures in the rock. This important geological formation divides eastern and western Texas.

Map on page 146

Stalactites and stalagmites in one of Texas' many natural caves.

Round Rock

In **Round Rock** ㉕, 10 miles (16 km) south of Georgetown on Brushy Creek, they celebrate the founding of the county with an Old Settlers Week. The eroded round rock, for which the city was named, was used to gauge the depth of the water of Bushy Creek, which was crossed by the old Chisholm Trail. Some of the buildings here alongside the stage route were built as early as the 1850s.

Sam Bass, the legendary train and stage-coach robber, who claimed never to have killed a man, was ambushed by Texas Rangers in the 100 block of East Main on July 19 1878. Businesses and condominium blocks are named after the outlaw, who became more famous after he was killed than he had ever been when alive. His grave is in the northwest corner of **Old Round Rock Cemetery** on Sam Bass Road, west of the intersection with Old Chisholm Trail. Covered with wildflowers in spring, the cemetery is easy to find and has an Anglo section, with crooked and cracked Victorian monuments, and a more colorful, smaller Mexican section, with paper and plastic flowers on the graves.

The **Palm House Museum** (212 E. Main; open Mon–Fri; free; tel: 512-255-5805) doubles as the Round Rock Chamber of Commerce office and adjoins a pharmacy that still has the pressed-tin ceiling once common in small-town

BELOW: slave cemetery at Round Rock.

stores. Another famous Round Rock son was Vander Clyde, a renowned aerialist, who had great success in Paris in the 1920s. Clyde made his entrance in an evening dress, completely convincing as a woman, and performed to the music of Wagner and Rimsky-Korsakov.

Notorious bandit Sam Bass was high on the Texas Rangers' wanted list. They finally got their man in 1878, after a tip-off about a planned bank raid in Round Rock. They set an ambush, and Bass was badly injured in the gunfight. He died two days later.

Snake sacking

US-79 East is the road to **Taylor** ㉖, famous for its barbecue and annual snake sacking contest. Snake sacking is highly controversial. Have the rattlesnakes been stunned or their mouths sewn up with monofilament? Animal lovers demonstrate outside, while the snake handlers, usually covered with bites, say all that preparation would be too much trouble.

State capital

Austin ㉗ (pop. 656,000) is the capital of Texas but is better known in many circles for its boast of being "the live music capital of the world." This reputation has been bolstered for decades by a popular, much-syndicated musical performance show, *Austin City Limits,* which features many local and national artists from the various roots music genres, especially country and folk. The show has given birth to an annual Austin City Music Festival in Zilker Park. The festival is as popular with fans as the longer-running, more industry-geared South By Southwest (SXSW) which draws acts from all over the world. As the home of the University of Texas, the city melds an air of youthful exuberance with legislative seriousness, but it is primarily a college town with all that that implies. Only a few blocks from the Capitol complex – the heart of state government – renowned 6th Street reverberates with rock, jazz, blues, country and reggae until the early hours.

BELOW: Sixth Street, the heart of Austin's live music scene, during the South By Southwest festival.

A growing city

Austin has, for years, been growing, partly because there was room for it to grow, though this period of over-development is coming to an end. Whole series of hilltops on which there were only trees and scrub a few years back were turned almost overnight into neighborhoods of slab-on-grade ranch houses, insensitive to the environment both esthetically and structurally. Compared with those elsewhere, costs and profits for developers here are good: Austin land prices are high, although not compared with the prices in bigger cities, while the cost of housing has recently caught up with the major metropolises. But nobody likes traffic, air, water or noise pollution, so city council members often run as development or environmentalist (or "neighborhood") candidates. Running against the developers is a good way to get elected.

Between the mid-1970s and mid-1980s, the strong anti-growth movement hoped to discourage development by refusing to provide roads and other utilities. But Austin has continued to grow anyway, fueled by a high-tech boom and faster than other "Sunbelt" cities.

Maps: Area 146 City 164

The SXSW music convention also includes a film festival – a sensible move in as much as the city of Austin is also a focal point for movie fanatics – along with an online interactive festival.

Walking downtown

Despite the city's sprawl, the downtown area is relatively easy to get around. It is dominated by government buildings, notably the pink granite **State Capitol Building** Ⓐ (12th Street and Congress Avenue; free guided tours; tel: 512-463-0063), which, in typically Texas style, is just a few feet higher than its model in Washington, DC.

Construction began in 1882, but the building was not completed until 1888. A thorough renovation was completed in 1997 and includes an underground

BELOW: inside the State Capitol, Austin.

The Texas State Capitol Building is the largest of all the state capitols in the United States and, on completion, was thought to have been the seventh biggest building in the world.

extension, its roof landscaped to fit in with the historic wooded grounds. The State Capitol's tourist information office is in the Old Land Office building (11th and San Jacinto streets; tel: 512-305-8400). Informative 2-hour walking tours down historic Congress Avenue and along 6th Street leave the Capitol steps at 9am on Thursday, Friday and Saturday; also Sunday at 2pm (contact the Austin Visitor's Center, 209 E. 6th Street; tel: 800-926-2282). Across from the Capitol is the Greek Revival **Governor's Mansion** Ⓑ (1010 Colorado Street; free tours Mon–Thur; tel: 512-463-5516), built in 1856 by Abner Cook.

Bat Heaven

Surely one of the most unusual tourist attractions must be the colony of more than a million Mexican free-tailed bats which congregate under **Congress Avenue Bridge** Ⓒ over Town Lake. At dusk, they set off in search of food. Between spring and fall, crowds gather every evening for a spectacle that can be thrilling.

The Austin-San Antonio area was called "bat heaven" by Dr Merlin Tuttle, the founder and president of Bat Conservation International. Most of the bats in this part of the country are Brazilian or Mexican free-tails. The largest known bat colony in the world is found in the "nursery cave," Bracken Cave near San Antonio, where experts say there are an estimated 200 baby bats per square foot.

Beside Town Lake (actually the Lower Colorado river), on the south side of the bridge, is Zilker Park, home of **Barton Springs Pool** (open daily; entrance fee; tel: 512-476-9044), generally regarded as the city's crown jewel. Thirty-two million gallons (121 million liters) of water a day flow from Barton Springs into

BELOW: leader in the fight for Texas independence, Stephen Austin.

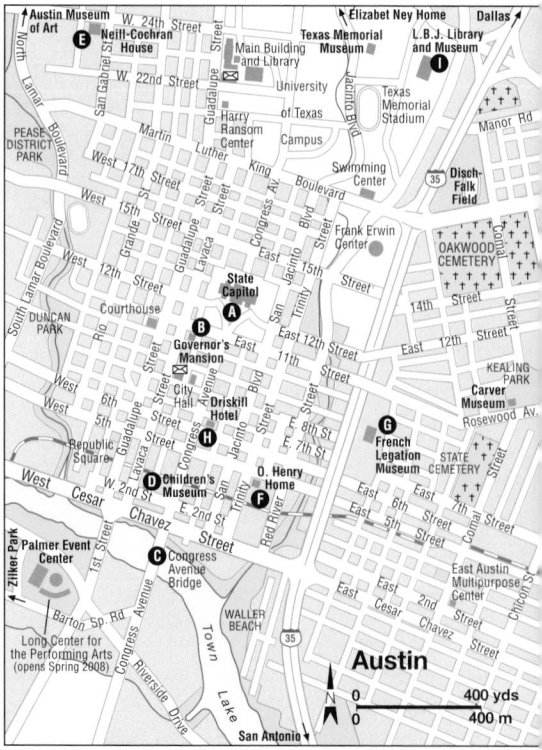

this idyllic swimming hole, which was reinforced as a pool almost as long as a football field in 1930. The water temperature supposedly hovers around 68°F (20°C), but it feels much colder at first splash.

Bats also figure in the **Austin Children's Museum** Ⓓ (201 Colorado Street; closed Mon; Sun pm only; entrance fee; tel: 512-472-2499), a fun, hands-on, educational facility that opened in 1997. Learning how these mammals fly is just one of the experiences available to all the family, alongside discovering how cities work, learning about health matters and more.

Map on page 164

Homes now museums

Some especially interesting old buildings around town are now museums. The **Austin Museum of Art at Laguna Gloria** (closed Mon; Sun pm only; entrance fee; tel: 512-458-8191; www.amoa.org) is located at 3809 W. 35th Street, on the banks of Lake Austin, on a site chosen by Stephen F. Austin for his own home. The downtown branch of AMOA (823 Congress Avenue; tel: 512-495-9224) is newer than the principal museum site.

The 1855, Greek Revival-style **Neill-Cochran House** Ⓔ (2310 San Gabriel Street; open Wed–Sun pm; entrance fee; tel: 512-478-2335) is now the Texas home of the grandly titled National Society of Colonial Dames of America and houses various historic documents.

The **O. Henry Home** Ⓕ (409 E. 5th Street; open Wed–Sun pm only; free; tel: 512-472-1903) was the residence of short-story writer William Sydney Porter (who used "O. Henry" as a pen name) from 1893 to 1895. The home features a display of Porter's desk and writing materials, as well as some period furniture.

Shiner beer, from the small town of the same name, southeast of Austin.

BELOW: evening flight of the Mexican free-tailed bat.

Maps:
Area 146
City 164

The Lyndon B. Johnson Library and Museum contains a replica of the Oval Office in the White House, as it looked when LBJ was president in the 1960s.

Historic sites

The oldest building in the city is probably the **French Legation Museum** G (802 San Marcos Street, east of I-35; open pm only; closed Mon; entrance fee; tel: 512-472-8180), a Creole-style mansion built in 1840 by Comte Alphonse Dubois de Saligny, French *chargé d'affaires*, who may never actually have lived in it. Saligny served under Maximilian I, the short-lived French-born emperor of Mexico who was executed in 1867, aged 35. It is a tradition in Normandy, where Saligny bought a château after making himself rich in America, for villagers to "dance on the old count's grave."

In the Maximilian Room of Austin's **Driskill Hotel** H (604 Brazos Street; tel: 800-252-9367), you can see mirrors ordered by the tragic Maximilian for his mad Empress Carlotta. The Driskill, whose second owner is said to have won it in a poker game and swapped it five years later for a California vineyard, has stood at the western corner of the historic 6th Street block, also known as Old Pecan Street since 1886, among other Victorian buildings now doing time as trendy bars and restaurants.

Further to the north, at 304 E. 44th Street, near the airport, is the former home of the German-born sculptress Elisabet Ney (closed Mon and Tue; Sun pm only; free; tel: 512-458-2255), who immigrated to the state in 1870 and whose marble busts and statues ordain many European palaces, as well as the Smithsonian in Washington, DC. The extensive collection in her studio here can be viewed.

BELOW: Lyndon B. Johnson library, Austin.
RIGHT: Austin's landmark Driskill Hotel.

Texan President

The most famous Texas-born president is memorialized in the grand **Lyndon B. Johnson Library and Museum** I (2313 Red River Street; open daily; free; tel: 512-721-0200) on the 357-acre (145-hectare) campus of the University of Texas. During his presidency (1963–69), Johnson was the recipient of hundreds of gifts from foreign heads of state and most of them seem to be here, along with his 1968 Lincoln limousine. There is also an interesting gift shop with authentic political memorabilia. Humanizing his life from boyhood onwards, the exhibitions include a 20-minute multimedia show, as well as a one-hour film of Lady Bird Johnson who is sometimes regarded with more affection than America's controversial 36th president.

For years Lady Bird devoted herself to getting the **Lady Bird Johnson Wildflower Center** 28 established on 60 acres (24 hectares) along the Colorado river. About 8 miles (13 km) southwest of Austin, at 4801 La Crosse Avenue (closed Mon; entrance fee; tel: 512-292-4100), it is a fine place for picnics among the flowers. There is also a visitor center, a library and "Ralph, the talking lawnmower."

Among the best places to see wildflowers, especially Texas bluebonnets blooming in the spring, is the region west of Austin where the Colorado river forms a series of lakes (one named for LBJ).

To the east and southeast of Austin the land is flat and fertile. Towns to look out for include **La Grange**, where the "Best Little Whorehouse in Texas" once stood, and **Shiner**, home of the Spoetzl Brewery, founded by German-Czech farmers in 1909. ❑

NO ALCOHOL
CONSUMPTION ON
PUBLIC STREETS
SIDEWALKS AND
PEDESTRIAN WAY
DESIGNATED AREA

LUCKENB
TEXA
BEER
JERRY JEFF WALKER
TICKETS
ON SALE NOW
IN THE BAR &
GEN. STORE FOR
WILLIE
NELSON'S
4TH OF JULY
PICNIC
WITH WILLIE,
NAYLOR & THE BOYS!
WILLIE
Grand Prize
SHAKE
Pop 4
POLICE
LUCKENBACH
T★E★X★A★S
LUCKENBACH

EST
1849
Luckenbach
BEER
TASTE OF TEXAS EDITION
IF YOU'RE
DRINKING
TO FORGET...
PAY IN ADVANCE
I CAN ONLY
PLEASE
ONE PERSON
AT A
TIME, AND
TODAY IS
NOT ANY
DAY!
SPECIALS
You Need Cash!
You don't need a Beer
You Need a Job
Signed
Joe the Wonder
34100-57222
Lite
BUD
LIGHT
24
Shiner
BOCK
4/6 PACK
Corona
BOTTLE LIGHTERS
Beer Bottle Lighters
TIPS
HOOCH

HILL COUNTRY

Map on page 172

The Hill Country is a Texas treasure, offering natural beauty, abundant wildlife, an intriguing slice of German culture and some of the friendliest towns in Texas

One of the most scenic towns in the Hill Country of Central Texas, a gentle area of sheep and cattle raising, is **Bandera** ❶ (the name is Spanish for "flag"), which describes itself as "the cowboy capital of the world." Bordered on three sides by the cypress-lined Medina river, its origins date to 1854 when a lumber mill was established. However, in the 1870s, it became a staging area for cattle drives through the Bandera Pass, where, in the 1840s, the Texas Rangers beat off a Comanche ambush.

Bandera is reputed to have once had a school operated by John Wilkes Booth under the name William J. Ryan. The old jail, one block north of the County Courthouse, is now the **Frontier Times Museum** (510 13th Street; open daily; Sun pm only; entrance fee; tel: 830-796-3864), which has 30,000 pieces from early Texas cultures and items of technology from the 19th and 20th centuries. Exhibits include a totem pole, a wooden idol from Easter Island and a 400-year-old pair of stirrups that once belonged to a conquistador. Bandera also has, on Main Street, two renowned honky-tonk dancehalls. Between May and Labor Day, there are rodeos twice a week, and in front of the Bandera Courthouse stands a bronze monument honoring the many national rodeo champions who lived in the town.

PRECEDING PAGES: Luckenbach sheriff, Marge Mueller, **LEFT:** the Texas bluebonnet in LBJ State Park. **BELOW:** the Admiral Nimitz Museum, Fredericksburg.

Pretend cowboys

Before the close of the 19th century, Bandera was already a popular vacation area for families from Houston. They would be entertained by hard-riding ranch-hands from nearby spreads who would ride in on weekends to show off, and gradually the concept of the "dude," or vacation cowboy, developed.

Today the Bandera area has dozens of dude ranches, with names like Silver Spur (tel: 830-460-3639); the Dixie (tel: 830-796-7771); Twin Elm Guest Ranch (tel: 830-796-3628); the Flying L (tel: 830-796-4592); the Running R (tel: 830-796-3984); and, on the Medina river, the Mayan (tel: 830-796-3312), nearly all offering comfortable accommodations, swimming pools, Western cuisine, cowboy-themed entertainment and horse-riding lessons. Some offer additional attractions such as golf and fishing.

Also of interest is a tour of the **LH7 Ranch** (entrance fee; tel: 830-796-4314), a 1,200-acre (485-hectare) ranch bought in 1982 by Maudeen Marks, whose family are dedicated to preserving the longhorn cattle. At **Mountain Home** ❷, near Kerrville, the **Y.O. Ranch** (tel: 877-967-3767) welcomes wildlife lovers, who can expect to see white-tail deer, antelope and a majestic longhorn or two.

At **Kerrville** ❸ itself, music plays a big part in everyday life, with a folk festival in the spring, a

Roadside welcome.

wine and music festival over the Labor Day weekend and a traditional festival of country and folk music in the fall (for information, tel: 830-257-3600; www.kerrville-music.com). The town's **Cowboy Artists of America Museum** (1550 Bandera Highway; open daily; Sun pm only; entrance fee; tel: 830-896-2553; www.caamuseum.com) is a treasure house of Western art, most of it executed by artists who have ridden the range, while the **Hill Country Museum** (226 Earl Garrett Street; closed Sun; entrance fee; tel: 830-896-8633), in a restored Victorian mansion, portrays the affluent life of the region's early days. In downtown Kerrville is Old Republic Square, with brick sidewalks, old stone walls, fountains and cedar-finished buildings shaded by pecan trees.

Wildlife

Near the Guadalupe river, at the Town Creek junction, is the **Riverside Nature Center** on Lemos Street (open daily; entrance fee; tel: 830-257-4837; www.riversidenaturecenter.org), incorporating a wildflower meadow and butterfly garden, surrounding a turn-of-the-20th-century house, which has exhibits and displays. It has an arboretum with over 140 species of tree.

The Texas Hill Country is a bird-watcher's paradise, home to such rare species as the golden-cheek warbler, the green kingfisher, and the zone-tail hawk. Near Kerrville, at **Ingram**, is the Exotic Wildlife Association (tel: 830-367-7761), which has helped introduce to the region such animals as the llama, the greater kudu, the Siberian ibex, the sable antelope, the ostrich, the zebra, and many varieties of deer. Completely out of context, on Farm Road 1340 in **Hunt**, near Ingram, is an inexact but intriguing replica of Stonehenge.

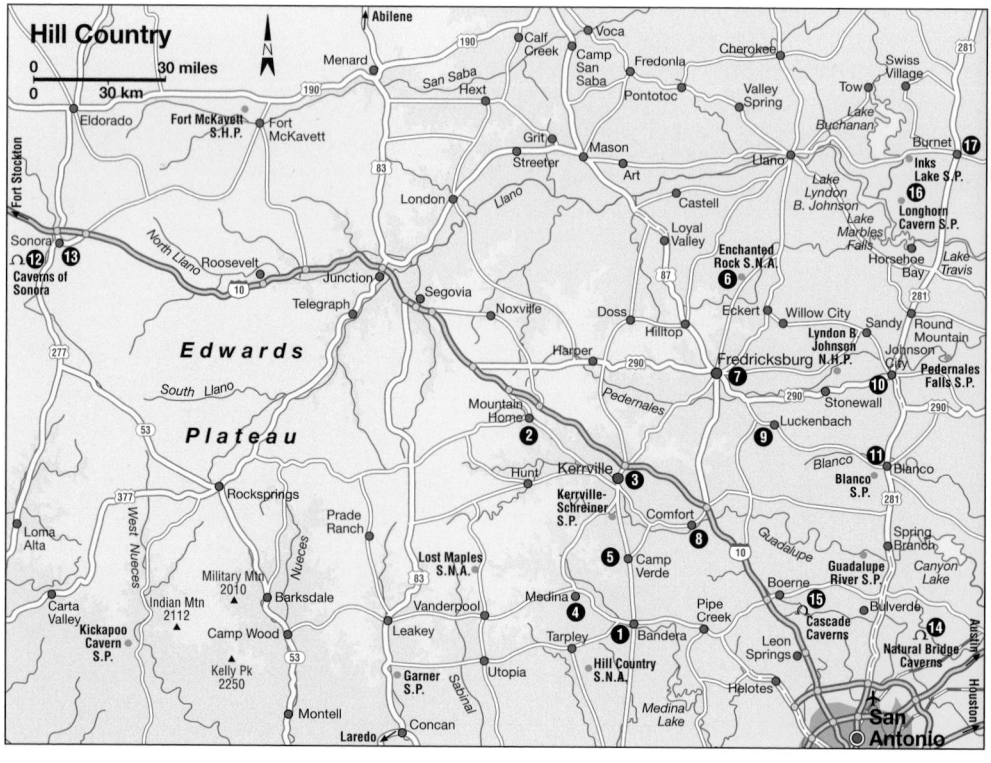

Apple capital

14 miles (22 km) upriver from Bandera is tiny **Medina** ❹, surrounded by apple orchards, from which it derives the title of "the apple capital of Texas." The Texas International Apple Festival is held here annually, on the last Saturday of July, with displays by bagpipers, balloon blowers and apple bobbers. Medina Lake (back south of Bandera) offers good fishing; local wildlife includes deer, antelope, boar and wild turkey; and the Medina river is lined with cypress trees, which were harvested from 1853 in a mill staffed by early Polish immigrants.

Medina Lake is also the scene every September of the Cajun Festival (held at Lakehills Civic Center in Lakehills), home of the Great Gumbo Cookoff. Cajun music and history are also celebrated.

Camel country

Camp Verde ❺, 60 miles (96 km) northwest of San Antonio, is where Jefferson Davis conceived the idea of training a US Camel Corps to operate in rough desert terrain during the Mexican War. Initially, 33 camels were imported, along with experienced handlers from North Africa and, although the sight and scent of the unfamiliar beasts frightened horses and mules, they proved capable of transporting loads up to 500 lbs (227 kg) without any trouble. The project ultimately failed, however, and, after the Civil War, the camels were sold to individuals and zoos, although a handful continued to roam the hills for many years.

Enchanted Rock

South of Llano and north of Fredericksburg is the **Enchanted Rock State Natural Area** ❻, centered around a huge pink granite dome rising 425 ft (131

Map on page 172

For a flavor of old Hill Country, check out the online *Enchanted Rock Archives* (www.texfiles.com/erarchives), which reprints the histories of people – settlers, adventurers and outlaws – who lived in the area in times past.

BELOW: Enchanted Rock.

TIP

Drive carefully when looking for Luckenbach. The little place is not easy to find. After the popularity of the song *Luckenbach, Texas*, so many road signs were stolen that the Texas Highway Department stopped erecting them.

meters) above the ground. Tonkawa Indians believed ghost fires flickered at the top and heard weird creakings and groanings, which geologists explain as the noise of the hot rock contracting in the cool of the night. It's a good, stiff vertical hike to the top.

Fredericksburg ❼ was founded in 1846 by German settlers and the town retains many traces of its ancestry in its architecture and in the German dialect heard on the streets. Large-scale German immigration continued right up until the Civil War. One notable characteristic is *Fachwerk* – a traditional German building technique consisting of heavy framing and diagonal bracing, with an infill of limestone. Early Germanic homes can be explored at the **Pioneer Museum Complex** (309 W. Main; open daily; Sun pm only; entrance fee; tel: 830-990-8441).

The town is popular with shoppers because of its antiques, gifts, ethnic foods and local wines, and its restaurants and bakeries offer a wide variety of cuisines. **Gish's Old West Museum** (502 N. Milam Street; call ahead; tel: 830-997-2794) is filled with saddles, lawmen's badges, guns and other relics. The **National Museum of the Pacific War** (340 E. Main Street; open daily; entrance fee; tel: 830-997-7269), which includes the Admiral Nimitz Museum, named for the naval officer born in the town, attracts visitors with an interest in World War II. Part of it is housed in a "ship-shape" old hostelry and includes a Garden of Peace, donated by the people of Japan.

Nearby **Comfort** ❽, another town settled by German immigrants, has, in addition to numerous century-old stores in the business district, a distinctive 1892 German church. Tiny **Luckenbach** ❾, southeast of Fredericksburg, is world-famous because of the Waylon Jennings song of the same name. On the

BELOW: "Booteek" and gift shop, Luckenbach.

banks of the Grape Creek, it was never much more than a store, a post office and a saloon, but people came from miles around for the impromptu Sunday music gatherings, which were often attended by major country and western stars. It still hosts live music gatherings, and the old bar is a classic.

Map on page 172

LBJ Town

Johnson City ⑩, at the intersection of US-290 and US-281, stages the Great Turkey Escape Festival at the end of October each year, when a hundred turkeys are driven through town, mimicking the turkey drives of the early 20th century. The town was named for the ancestors of 1960s President Lyndon Johnson, who was raised here. Tours of his restored **Boyhood Home** are given every half-hour (open daily; free; tel: 830-868-7128). Near Stonewall, between Fredericksburg and Johnson City, is the **Lyndon B. Johnson National Historical Park**, with buffalo, longhorns and white-tail deer in enclosures and a restored 1908 house on the site of a working farm. From the park, tours can be taken of the LBJ Ranch (open daily; free; tel: 830-868-7128).

Another of the Hill Country's little towns that retains some of the quiet style of a bygone era is **Blanco** ⑪. Beside the river of the same name, it promotes its friendly atmosphere and, from Thanksgiving to New Year stages a "Christmas Homecoming" around an immense oak tree on the Courthouse Square.

Country singer Jerry Jeff Walker has recorded two live albums in the dance hall at Luckenbach.

Untouched by civilization

What was once a 5,400-acre (2,180-hectare) ranch was donated to Texas Parks and Wildlife in 1976, with the stipulation that it "be kept far removed and untouched by modern civilization, where everything is preserved intact, yet put

BELOW: shoppers welcome here.

Map on page 172

Southwest of Bandera, Ney Cave was used during World War II for Project X-Ray, a plan to drop thousands of bats, carrying firebombs, on Japan. In a practice run, the bats returned to their home base, "dropping bombs" on US planes; the strategy was scrapped.

BELOW: Trinity Lutheran Church, Stonewall, attended by LBJ and his family.

to a useful purpose." Today it is the **Hill Country State Natural Area**, 45 miles (72 km) near Bandera northwest of San Antonio, a region of rocky limestone hills, flowing springs, oak groves, grasslands and canyons (for information, tel: 830-796-4413).

Five miles (8 km) north of Vanderpool, off State Route 187, is the **Lost Maples State Natural Area**, spectacularly colorful in November, but an attractive park the year round, offering camping and picnicking among rugged limestone canyons and bubbling springs (for information, tel: 830-966-3413).

Going underground

Over the centuries underground streams have carved out spectacular caverns all through this region. Among the best-known are the **Caverns of Sonora** ⓬ (open daily; entrance fee; tel: 325-387-3105), at exit 392 of I-10, 8 miles (13 km) south of the town of that name. With 8 miles (13 km) of passages lined with crystalline stalactites and stalagmites, it is one of Texas' longest caves. There is also a picnic area and a campground. From **Sonora** ⓭, between 1910 and 1921, a 250-ft (76-meter) wide, fenced track called Tillman's Lane ran 100 miles (160 km) northeast to Brady. Thousands of cattle were driven to the railroad on this track, which was equipped with holding pens, wells and windmills.

Natural Bridge Caverns ⓮ (I-35 exit 175; open daily; entrance fee; tel: 210-651-6101; www.naturalbridgecaverns.com) offer exotic sights carved over thousands of years out of the area's natural limestone. The tourist brochure describes the colors as resembling "35 flavors of ice cream," with rocks "nearly as translucent as china and rooms nearly as large as football fields." Nearby is the **Natural Bridge Wildlife Ranch** (open daily; entrance fee; tel: 830-438-7400; www.wildliferanchtexas.com), home to wallabies and camels, baboons and parrots. Similar to Natural Bridge Caverns are the **Cascade Caverns** ⓯ (on I-10 south of Boerne; open daily; entrance fee; tel: 830-755-8080; www.cascadecaverns.com), which include an interior, 100-ft (30-meter) waterfall.

One of the oldest commercial caves in Texas is Longhorn Cavern in the **Longhorn Cavern State Park** ⓰ (open daily; entrance fee; tel: 830-598-2283; www.longhorncaverns.com), near Burnet. This has seen a number of uses in the past 100 years but was opened as a tourist cave in 1938 by the Civilian Conservation Corporation. Camping is available in nearby Inks Lake State Park (tel: 512-793-2223).

Flying visit

For travelers seeking only a taste of Hill Country, a steam excursion train runs from Cedar Park City Hall, near US-183 and FM-1431, about 15 miles (24 km) northwest of Austin. The journey takes travelers through the Hill Country to **Burnet** ⓱, on US-281, once a frontier town from whose quarries marble for the State Capitol in Austin was mined. Running on weekends only, the 80-year-old Hill Country Flyer (tel: 512-477-8468) takes just over two hours each way, traveling through beautiful countryside and allowing a short stopover for shopping, museum browsing and refreshment. ❑

Texas Wines

Thanks to the Spanish, there was Texas wine at least 100 years before vineyards were planted in California. In the 19th century, Italian, German and Slavic immigrants to Texas also planted wine grapes and, when the root louse *phylloxera* destroyed millions of acres of European vineyards, it was Texas rootstock that saved the day. Thomas Volney Munson of Denison, whose rootstock was resistant to the *phylloxera*, sent over large amounts of it for grafting to French vines. In France there are at least three statues, and a *place* in Bordeaux, dedicated to Munson.

Since the 1960s, the revolution in wine making has swept into Texas, transforming the landscape, altering the agricultural economy and influencing Texans' choice of beverages to serve with barbecue or Tex-Mex dinners, as well as American or classic French cuisine.

Geology and geography in Texas are as complex as in any other wine-growing region of the world but the state's vineyards are generally concentrated in four basic areas: the limestone Hill Country to the west of Austin; the High Plains around Lubbock; the hilly plains west of Fort Worth; and the Davis Mountains in Far West Texas.

The rugged Davis Mountains are in the area of the state with the highest average elevation, a mile (1,600 meters) or more above sea level. The South Plains around Lubbock are around 3,000 ft (900 meters). Although daytime temperatures can go above 100°F (38°C) in summer, because of radiation cooling at these altitudes, temperatures at night fall to the 50s and 60s°F (10–20°C). In the Hill Country, which can also be very hot in summer, one of the vineyards is cooled by its proximity to a large lake.

On the whole, the climate is comparable to that of France and California, so that *vitis vinifera*, the grape variety that produces all their great wines, also thrives in Texas.

Soils in Texas are generally poor in organic matter. However, this is a condition wine grapes enjoy: the vines develop a widespread root system, with production of grapes limited – a necessity for fine wine.

Among red-wine grapes, Cabernet Sauvignon is a favorite with Texas wine makers. At least two wineries in the Lubbock region have produced fine Cabernets, as well as having considerable success with France's two greatest white-grape varieties, Chardonnay and Sauvignon Blanc. The Lubbock wineries also produce good Gewürztraminer, Johannisberg Riesling and Barbera.

Award-winning Sauvignon Blancs – complex, subtle and delicately herbaceous – are being produced near Austin, too. The University of Texas was even in the wine business for a while, collaborating with Cordier Vineyard. Texas' robust wine industry is celebrated every spring at the Hill Country Wine and Food Festival in Austin.

With Texas inhabiting the White House in recent years, Texas wines have been served there to dignitaries from all over the world. Texas wines have also turned up at famed Chef Wolfgang Puck's Spago restaurant in Los Angeles. And these days, it's hard to visit any part of Texas without running across a winery. ❑

RIGHT: taking in the grape harvest at Bryan, Central Texas.

TEXAS CUSTOMS AND FESTIVALS

Texas can't get enough of festivals, celebrating everything from watermelons to rattlesnakes: there's nothing that isn't a cause for a party

No matter when you arrive in Texas, there's always something going on – from the giant State Fair at Dallas, with Big Tex to greet the guests, right down to the small-town hoedown.

Texans are great party folk: they enjoy a celebration and they find plenty to celebrate. The pioneering past is a popular theme, seen in events like the Chisholm Trail Round-up in Fort Worth and Christmas at Old Fort Concho, which bring a taste of Old Texas back to life. The cowboy heritage is emphasized by the Texas Cowboy Reunion at Stamford and countless rodeos around the state, and historically important dates like Juneteenth (June 19), the day blacks in Texas were emancipated, are big occasions for fun and games. Regional specialties are highlighted in local happenings: the Tyler Rose Festival, the International Wine Classic at Lubbock – even the Great Texas Mosquito Festival, staged at Clute, on the Gulf.

All these events provide ample opportunity for good eating, but food fests, featuring anything from searingly hot chili and sizzling barbecue to Luckenbach's Big Picnic and Luling's Watermelon Thump, focus even more on the Texan appetite. And, like good food, good music is a Texan passion: Austin's South by SouthWest Music Conference and Fort Worth's Van Cliburn Piano Competition are huge draws, while the little town of Athens is home to the Old Fiddlers Reunion. In July, jazz takes over at Corpus Christi.

Texans are never shy about their heritage, achievements and individuality, but these festivals are the ultimate expression of that proud, strong Texan spirit.

▷ **ACTING IT OUT**
Dramatizing history keeps interest in Texas' past alive. The musical drama *Texas*, based around frontier settlers, is staged in the unrivaled setting of Palo Duro Canyon, with music in stereo echoing all around.

△ **TASTY COOK-OFFS**
Lubbock's Chuckwagon Cook-off complements events like Terlingua's chili contest, the Czech kolache bake-off in Caldwell and the Hill Country's *Wurstfest*.

△ **SCRAPING OUT A TUNE**
You're never far from a musical event in foot-tapping Texas, especially one featuring the fiddle, soul of much local music.

◁ **JUST FOR A LAUGH**
Most events are not meant to be taken too seriously. This clown entertains the crowds at the Funtier Days celebration, staged at Bandera in the Hill Country.

GOING BACK TO THEIR ROOTS

The ethnic diversity of the people of Texas expresses itself in numerous ways, but especially in the annual events that each population stages.

Fiesta Texas is San Antonio's celebration of its largely Hispanic past and takes the form of street parades, *mariachi* performances, fashion shows and general good, bustling fun. Mardi Gras is big in Galveston among the Cajun and Creole peoples, while Central Texas and the Hill Country commemorate their European roots: Little Ennis hosts the May Polka Festival, showcasing Czech food and entertainment, while Fredericksburg has its own German Oktoberfest and the colorful Easter Fires pageant.

Native Americans hold major Pow-Wows, which feature craft stalls as well as displays of dancing, in various locations throughout the state.

For details of all these events, *see Travel Tips.*

△ **A CHRISTMAS CAROL**
There's a distinctly British air to Galveston's Dickens on the Strand festival in December: plum puddings, roast chestnuts, bell ringers and Dickens' own works.

▽ **PLAYING DEAD**
Wild West re-enactments provide the core of numerous local events. Cattle round-ups, trail rides and shoot-outs are enjoyed by ordinary folk dolled up in the authentic attire.

▷ **RISING SUN/LONE STAR**
Not all Texas festivals are introspective. The Sun & Star festival held in Dallas was a three-month celebration of Japanese arts and crafts.

REPUBLIC
OF TEXAS

SAN ANTONIO

A cultural crossroads, San Antonio is where the United States and Mexico merge, with a splash of German tradition thrown in for good measure

Map on page 184

San Antonio (pop. 1.14 million), encompassing over 3,000 sq. miles (4,800 sq. km), is the seventh-largest city in the US and is sometimes called Mexico's northernmost city. Its majority Latino population is the largest of any city in the United States and the National Autonomous University of Mexico, the oldest institution of higher learning in this hemisphere, has maintained a campus in San Antonio since 1972.

Situated at the edge of the South Texas Plains – the brushy area leading to Mexico – as well as the edge of the pretty sheep and cattle-raising Hill Country, San Antonio has long been the principal city of both regions.

San Antonio hasn't always been slow-paced, but today that's exactly what attracts Texans and non-Texans alike to the city where tourism and the military are the major industries. The city's major delight is its 2½-mile (4-km) **River Walk** Ⓐ (open 24 hours; free). Here, 20 ft (6 meters) below street level, you will find a romantic sidewalk-lined river running through the heart of downtown, bordered by shops, restaurants, hotels, bars and museums.

For more than a century, the San Antonio river has been the scene of social clubs, carnivals, rodeos and circuses. There were private landings and wide lawns, children swam and the whole city picnicked on it, fished in it, and was baptized under it, sometimes en masse, as illustrated by photographs from earlier days.

PRECEDING PAGES: San Antonio's River Walk.
LEFT: the Tower Life building, illuminated for Christmas.
BELOW: local transport in San Antonio.

An early fan

The river was admired by one visitor as long ago as the 1850s. In his *A Journey Through Texas*, Frederick Law Olmsted noted: "Few cities have such a luxury… the streets are laid out in such a way that a great number of houses have a garden extending to the bank, and to a bathing-house, which is in constant use."

After the disastrous floods in 1921 and 1929, which left the business district under 8 ft (2.5 meters) of water, a three-block long river cut-off was created, joining the corners of the river where it bends around a 16-block area.

It is hard to believe today, but at one time there were plans to fill in the river, or run it underground so it would, in effect, be used as a sewer. Fortunately, the Conservation Society banded together to protect it and nearby landmarks, and, in 1938, aid was provided by the Works Progress Administration, a federal make-work scheme to cut unemployment. The river was dredged. Dams and rock retaining walls, the pleasant cobblestone and flagstone walks, and stairways from bridges were constructed. More than 11,000 trees were planted along the river's banks and, when it was complete, spotlights were deployed in the bushes. There are now 13 bridges crossing the River Walk.

During busy seasons, the sidewalks can become crowded with tourists, but the walk is still well worth the trouble. There is the choice of watching flat-bottomed *chalupa* boats drift by, or boarding the Yanaguana Cruises (daily tours; fee; tel: 210-244-5700) for a 45-minute round-trip boat ride. Tickets are available at the Rivercenter Mall. Private dinner cruises can also be arranged.

Mural along the River Walk.

Central area

The main river, which runs roughly north to south, makes an almost circular loop between College and Villita streets, with the vast majority of the city's attractions housed within those perimeters.

The most convenient starting point for tours of the city is at the **Alamo** Ⓑ (open daily; free; www.thealamo.org), originally known as the Mission San Antonio de Valero. Named after the viceroy at the time, it was built as the first of five missions in 1718, but its worldwide fame was established during 13 days in 1836, when the Alamo was besieged by 5,000 Mexican troops.

Early in the century it had served as a garrison for (and earned its name from) a cavalry unit from Alamo de Parras, but, by the time General Santa Anna seized the Mexican presidency, the Anglo settlers in San Antonio were claiming the city for their own and it was in the Alamo they chose to make a stand when Santa Anna came to reclaim it. Barricading himself with his small force within the Alamo's thick stone walls, the commander of the Texians on February 24 1836 sent out an appeal for reinforcements. The appeal read: "To the People of Texas and All Americans in the World – Fellow Citizens and Compatriots:

"I am besieged with a thousand or more of the Mexicans under Santa Anna. I have sustained a continual Bombardment and cannonade for 24 hours and

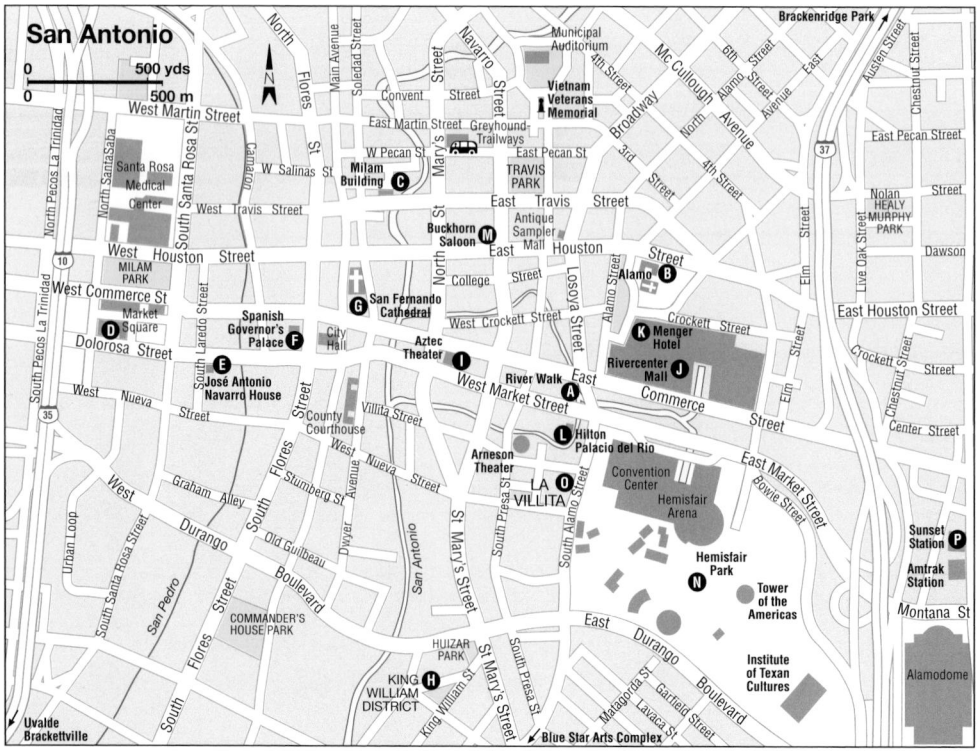

have not lost a man. The enemy has demanded surrender at discretion, otherwise, the garrison is to be put to the sword, if the fort is taken. I have answered the demand with a cannon shot, and our flag still waves proudly from the walls. I shall never surrender or retreat. Then, I call upon you in the name of Liberty, of Patriotism, and everything dear to the American character, to come to our aid with all dispatch. The enemy is receiving reinforcements daily and will no doubt increase to three or four thousand in four or five days. If this call is neglected, I am determined to sustain myself as long as possible and die like a soldier who never forgets what is due his honor and that of his country. VICTORY or DEATH."

– William Barret Travis Lt. Col. Comdt.

The roll call of "Heroes of the Battle of the Alamo" does not only list citizens of American states. Among the countries represented are Ireland, Scotland, Wales, England, Denmark and Germany.

A few volunteers

Thirty-two Texans, or "Texians," from Gonzales, the Lexington of Texas where the first shot of the Revolution was fired, joined Travis after he wrote his stirring letter. They were supported in their defense by some notable Tennesseeans. These included Colonel James Bowie, who had disobeyed General Sam Houston's order to destroy the fortress, and the now-famous Davy Crockett. However, early on the morning of March 6, Santa Anna's men attacked the Alamo, overran the fortress and killed all 189 of its defenders. It turned out to be a Pyhrric victory. Forty-six days later, the cry "Remember the Alamo" served as the inspiration for the Texans who surrounded and decisively beat Santa Anna's men at San Jacinto on April 21. (The date is still celebrated by the city of San Antonio with an annual fiesta.) Thus, the Republic of Texas was born.

The Alamo itself – preserved as a national monument, along with its library,

BELOW: Mission San Antonio de Valero (the Alamo).

Some historians complain about the presentation of the Alamo site today, that too much emphasis is placed on the famous battle, and not enough on the founding of the mission itself – effectively the founding of the city of San Antonio.

gift shop and its grounds – in conjuction with Fort Sam Houston, 2 miles (3 km) north, has become a symbol of the state's stubbornly independent spirit.

Preserved forever

In 1883, the State of Texas bought the familiar chapel with its bullet-riddled walls, but the convent, the surrounding area around it where the beautiful Alamo Gardens are planted, belonged to a liquor dealer and it is said plans were being made to build a hotel. Sam Johnson, the father of President Johnson, has been called the "Savior of the Alamo" because, while a State Senator in 1905, he arranged for the state to buy the Alamo convent.

Clara Driscoll (owner of Laguna Gloria, the lakeside mansion in Austin which later became that city's art museum) is also known as the Savior of the Alamo, since she advanced Sam Johnson $25,000 to buy it until the state was able to do so. Today, the Alamo is managed by the Daughters of the Republic of Texas, whose members trace their lineage to the original citizens of the republic.

On **Alamo Plaza** you will find the Visitor's Center (tel: 210-207-6748), offering friendly advice and discount coupons for San Antonio attractions. A bus or Texas Trolley Car (tel: 210-224-2288) tour provides an excellent history of the city in the shortest amount of time. For around $10, a horse-drawn carriage from the Yellow Rose Carriage Company (tel: 210-354-5077) can give you a 25-minute tour. Carriage stands are on either side of the Alamo.

A walking tour

Visitors preferring to get away from the crowds, at least for a while, can begin their stroll on the quieter stretch of the River Walk – at 4th Street, for example,

BELOW: Market Square.

Map on page 184

behind the Municipal Auditorium. The first major landmark on this route is at Travis Street, where the Art Deco **Milam Building** Ⓒ has been a landmark since the 1920s, when it housed the offices of early oil companies.

The next bridge – there are 35 within the city limits – is at Houston Street, from where a trolley can be taken to visit colorful **Market Square** Ⓓ (514 W Commerce), a few blocks to the west. A network of VIA streetcars continuously circles the most popular attractions and runs until late evening for around 25 cents per ride. There's music in Market Square, as well as many souvenir shops, myriad restaurants, weekend celebrations and full-scale festivals in summer and fall.

The huge Mi Tierra restaurant (218 Produce Row; tel: 210-225-1262) and bakery – open 24 hours – is a long-established landmark here and it's also where the mariachi bands gather. They will be happy to perform their music tableside, but this service is not free. And if you've brought your laptop, you can hook into wi-fi hotspots.

Mariachi musician.

Historic homes

Walking back to the river along Dolorosa Street, you'll pass the square, stuccoed limestone **José Antonio Navarro House** Ⓔ (Casa Navarro State Historical Park, 228 S. Laredo Street; open Wed–Sat; entrance fee; tel: 210-226-4801), home of one of the two native-born Texans who signed the Texas Declaration of Independence. Also here is the 18th-century **Spanish Governor's Palace** Ⓕ (105 Plaza de Armas; open daily; entrance fee; tel: 210-224-0601), restored between 1929 and 1930. It was never, in fact, the house of any governor, but served the captain of the presidio.

BELOW: more color on Market Square.

Overlooking Main Plaza is the limestone Gothic Revival **San Fernando Cathedral** Ⓖ (open daily; tel: 210-227-1297; www.sfcathedral.org), North America's oldest sanctuary, founded in 1731 and rebuilt in 1873. A plaque stating that the remains of the Alamo dead are located here may be inaccurate, as Santa Anna probably burned the bodies. Here, Graham Greene was reminded of Victorian albums and valentines by the *mantillas* worn by the Hispanic women. He wondered if the San Antonio river wound itself into a heart shape and, in fact, it very nearly does.

San Fernando Cathedral was founded by settlers from the Canary Islands.

In 1938, the pecan "shelleries," as Greene called them, still flourished on the West Side, where impoverished pecan shellers worked for a few cents a day. Greene attended a rally sponsored by Catholic Action, at which "pale and weak and self-conscious" Anglo girls mixed with the "dark sensual confident… half casters – who knew instinctively, you felt, all the beauty and the horror of the flesh."

The plaza fronting the cathedral is the earliest permanently settled spot (by European immigrants) in the state. After the Revolution, it became the liveliest place in town, featuring market stalls and feisty, flirtatious "chili queens," who were ordered to remove their chili stands when San Antonio's new City Hall and the red sandstone and granite Bexar County Courthouse, by James R. Gordon, were completed in the 1890s.

The German quarter

Soon after the Republic of Texas was established, a sizeable influx of German immigrants established themselves in the historic **King William District** Ⓗ – named after the Prussian king – between the river and S. St Mary's Street. Here,

BELOW: tombstone at D'Anis Cemetery, Castroville, west of San Antonio.
RIGHT: the Steves Homestead.

in this 25-block area, many refurbished Victorian homes can be admired on a walking tour conducted by the San Antonio Conservation Society (107 King William Street), which can supply a map of the neighborhood. At 509 King William Street is **The Steves Homestead** (open daily; entrance fee; tel: 210-225-5924), an impressive 1876 mansion filled with period antiques and surrounded by an exceptional garden and fountain.

Map on page 184

Across the river, at 1420 S. Alamo, is the **Blue Star Arts Complex** (tel: 210-227-6960; www.bluestarcomplex.com), a restored old warehouse district now rife with shops, contemporary art galleries and studios, as well as a brew pub.

The Blue Star Art Space is run by a non-profit making artists' collective and has a strong community-involvement ethic.

The San Antonio Conservation Society, organized in 1924, primarily to preserve and restore many of the Alamo buildings, later turned its attention to saving a trio of the city's Art Deco movie theaters. The facade is all that remains of the Texas (1926), while the Majestic (1929) is now a performing arts center. The third is the **Aztec Theater** I (1926), a movie theater on the River Walk whose architect gained his inspiration from studying Mexico's Mayan and Aztec ruins.

The colonnade at Mitla was the model for the foyer, and each column is decorated with a plaster mask of the Aztec moon goddess. A 2-ton (1.8-metric ton) chandelier is a replica of a sacrificial stone. On the fire curtain, the meeting of Cortez and Montezuma is depicted, and over the proscenium Quetzalcoatl, the plumed serpent god of the Aztecs, appears.

Hotels old and new

Behind the Alamo, another loop of the river is flanked by two Marriott Hotels (one of the many points you can board a boat for a sightseeing cruise). Here, too, is the **Rivercenter Mall** J (849 E. Commerce; open daily), with more than 100

BELOW: on the River Walk.

shops, and the city's huge Convention Center. The story of the hallowed Alamo is told in appropriately spectacular fashion on the six-story screen of the IMAX theater (tel: 210-247-4629) in the Rivercenter Mall, between the 1909 Crockett Hotel and the limestone and stucco **Menger Hotel** Ⓚ, the city's first deluxe hostelry, built in 1859.

In the 1850s, William Menger opened a brewery on the grounds of the Battle of the Alamo and, soon afterwards, he and his wife offered rooms to German farmers from Fredericksburg, Seguin, Comfort and New Braunfels, who rode into San Antonio every so often in ox carts.

Old German farmers gave way at the Menger to presidents, generals and writers, including Oscar Wilde and O. Henry, Jenny Lind, Sarah Bernhardt, and consumptive poet Sidney Lanier, who came to San Antonio for his health. At the Menger, people still use the old lobby (the "rotunda") and patio. It's a good place to savor the local's favorite cocktail, the margarita.

TIP

Save a visit to the Rivercenter Mall for a rainy day. As well as plenty of name shops, and the familiar food court, it has the benefit of an IMAX theater, where *The Alamo* movie is just one of a series of daily features.

A few good men

There is a theory that, just as the Menger had to send all the way to Boston for ice in those days, so Boston sent to Spanish Texas for horses. Accordingly, the horse Paul Revere chose for his famous midnight ride was obtained from a ranch 20 miles (32 km) southeast of San Antonio, where the Polish town of Cestohowa is now located.

In a similar vein, in 1898, during the Spanish-American War, Teddy Roosevelt recruited members of the U.S.Volunteer Cavalry ("Rough Riders") in the Menger Bar (now located at the other side of the hotel). "I need a few good men," he is reputed to have said, "who can ride a horse, shoot a gun, and want

BELOW: the "Blessing of the Animals" on January 17.
RIGHT: enjoying coffee on the River Walk.

to serve their country." This elite corps of cowboys and millionaires from the East generated a great deal of attention before they went on to Cuba.

In contrast, the 21-story **Hilton Palacio del Rio** Ⓛ, which overlooks the river a few blocks to the south, was built in record time in 1968. It was claimed to have been the world's first hotel put together from pre-constructed rooms produced on an "assembly line." As its honeycomb facade suggests, the rooms, completely furnished and ready to assign to guests, were lifted into place by a crane, and then nudged and straightened with the help of a helicopter.

Map on page 184

Fun and thrills

For some fun, next to the Visitor Information Center on Alamo Plaza you will find such attractions as **The Texas Adventure** (open daily; entrance fee; tel: 210-227-8224), a film history that, inevitably, includes yet another Alamo re-enactment, and the **Louis Tussaud's Plaza Wax Theater** (open daily; entrance fee; tel: 210-224-9299), which includes Ripley's Believe It or Not!

Another unusual attraction is the historic (1881) **Buckhorn Saloon and Museum** Ⓜ (318 E. Houston; open daily; entrance fee), which contains the world's largest collection of horns.

Riding in a charros rodeo.

Panoramic view

Further down Alamo, past the Convention Center, is **Hemisfair Park** Ⓝ – site of the 1968 World's Fair – dominated by the 750-ft (231-meter) Tower of the Americas (open daily; entrance fee), which has glass elevators to take you to an observation deck for a panoramic view of the city. Above the observation deck is a restaurant that rotates once each hour. Here also are the Institute of Texan

BELOW: the famous Menger Hotel.

Cultures (closed Mon; entrance fee; tel: 210-458-2300) and the Mexican Cultural Instititute (open daily; free; tel: 210-227-0123), both displaying interesting historical and contemporary exhibits.

TIP

The Tower of the Americas is open until 10pm (11pm on Friday and Saturday) and is worth a visit for a night-time view over the city.

Little Village

Opposite Hemisfair Park is **La Villita** **O** ("Little Village"), the old town of Béjar, now spelled "Bexar" and pronounced "bear," from which Santa Anna's troops set up their cannon line for the Alamo siege in 1836. The previous year, Santa Anna's brother-in-law, General Martin Perfecto de Cos, had stayed in a house here while in command of the Mexican forces sent to calm the Texans.

Despite its name, La Villita was not an exclusively Spanish neighborhood, for Germans and others moved here during the Republic. When it was restored, the intention was to honor San Antonio's Spanish, German, Mexican, French, American and Texan heritage, evidence of which is found in La Villita's architectural styles.

Today, the tiny limestone and adobe buildings contain craft shops, art galleries, restaurants and boutiques. Walk towards the river and you will find the grassy steps of the open-air **Arneson Theater** (tel: 210-207-8610), which often puts on dance and musical performances in summer and during Fiesta. Bring a blanket or a lawn chair.

To the east of I-37, close to the Alamodome sports and convention hall, is **Sunset Station** **P** (1174 E. Commerce), a strikingly distinctive 1902 railroad station that was refurbished in 1998 into an entertainment center. Where once the hoots and whistles of steam trains could be heard, today the noise and bustle come from live music events.

LEFT: Tower of the Americas.
RIGHT: the Polish settlement of Panna Maria, near San Antonio.

Annual Fiesta

San Antonio is invariably associated by most people with the mid-April Fiesta, but it looks festive most of the time. Fiesta is a 10-day, non-stop celebration revealing the heart and history of San Antonio. There are far too many parades, festivals and events to list here (over 100 of them), but check the Convention and Visitor's Bureau website for a schedule (www.sanantoniocvb.com).

San Antonio is the most Roman Catholic, and perhaps one of the most cosmopolitan, cities in America. European visitors feel at home here right away, especially if they are from Mediterranean countries, in a way they rarely do in the rest of the United States.

"Of distinctive Spanish cast," was the 1893 description in *Baedeker's Guide to the United States*, when, with its population of 40–50,000 "Americans, Mexicans, and Germans, with a few Coloured People," it was Texas' largest and best-known city.

Once less than law-abiding

Yet, in some ways, San Antonio is an atypical Texas city. There is not as much aggressive friendliness here as there is in other parts of the state where tourism is not a mainstay. And, in the past, San Antonio was often somewhat less than law-abiding.

"Hardly a day passes," wrote Frederick Law Olmsted in 1857, "without some noise… the street affrays are numerous and characteristic… More often than otherwise, the parties meet upon the plaza by chance, and each, on catching sight of his enemy, draws a revolver, and fires away. As the actors are under more or less excitement, their aim is not apt to be of the most careful and sure, consequently it is not seldom the passers-by who suffer. Sometimes it is a young man at a quiet dinner in a restaurant, who receives a ball in the head; sometimes an old Negro woman, returning from market, who gets winged.

After disposing of all their lead, the parties close, to try their steel, but as this species of metallic amusement is less popular, they generally contrive to be separated by friends before the wounds are mortal. If neither is seriously injured, they are brought to drink together on the following day, and the town waits for the next excitement."

As long as San Antonio lay at the beginning of the Chisholm Trail, there were murders, lynchings and gunfights by cowboys, according to the memoirs of Mary Maverick, the wife of Sam Maverick who lived by the Alamo, where so many of his friends died. And more than once it occurred to someone to call the city a frontier Venice.

When President Roosevelt toured San Antonio's red light district on East Commerce Street in 1936, with LBJ and the New Deal mayor Maury Maverick in tow, he exclaimed he had never seen so many taverns in one block. In fact, the taverns of San Antonio never closed, for the city totally ignored Prohibition. Later on, Governor W. Lee (Pappy) O'Daniel sent Texas Rangers here to enforce the state laws by smashing bars and gambling halls.

Pick up a copy of the city's own free weekly magazine, *San Antonio Current*, which lists all the local and nearby festivals, as well as music, theater, arts and nightlife.

BELOW: San Antonio's Visitor Information Center.

The Chisholm Trail

From 1867 to 1884, the major route north for cattle was the Chisholm Trail, named for Jesse Chisholm who had established regular trade with northern Indian camps.

At first the trail went by such names as the Kansas, or Abilene, Trail but "Chisholm" soon became the common term for its entire length, from the Rio Grande to Central Kansas. It became the most favored route after fears about Texas tick fever led six states to close off other trails. (The Texan longhorns had built up an immunity to the fever, but it had caused huge losses of cattle in other regions.)

Running from San Antonio through Austin, following what is, roughly speaking, today's I-35, and splitting up at Waco, the Chisholm Trail headed up to Fort Worth and turned eastward at Decatur, to the crossing at Red River Station, which marked the beginning of Indian Territory.

Author Wayne Gard, a former president of the Texas Historical Association, who wrote the definitive book on the Chisholm Trail, observed that it was like a tree, with the roots being the feeder trails from South Texas, the trunk the main route from San Antonio across Indian Territory, and the branches extending to the various railheads in Kansas.

In many places, such as Salado, the trail headed right up a town's main street. Only here, and at river crossings, were the cattle squeezed down to a group 50–60 ft (15–18 meters) across and confined to a specific trail: they were normally spread out across possibly half a mile (nearly 1 km) of prairie, grazing as they continued on their guided drift north.

Individual cattle tended to keep roughly the same position each day, but there was always an ambitious steer or two to take the lead, and usually a trail boss could rely on a favorite steer to give the herd a lead and be the first into the water at a river crossing.

Wayne Gard once told of a stampeding herd of 1,200 on a northbound trek, in the then small town of Dallas. The two steers that had led the drive stayed in place, remaining perfectly still, and eventually the frightened cattle returned to gather peacefully around them.

The writer J Frank Dobie stressed the importance of one's companions. Two sayings on the range, he wrote, best expressed the utmost in trustworthiness: "He will do to tie to" and "He will do to ride the river with."

When the railroads eventually penetrated the state and made the Chisholm Trail an anachronism, Texas had more cattle than there had been at the beginning and, although drives continued until the mid-1880s, they were on a reduced basis. In the quarter-century of its existence, the Chisholm Trail saw the passage of more than five million cattle, plus a million mustangs.

Jesse Chisholm himself died in 1838. "No one ever left his home cold or hungry," said the epitaph over his grave. Today's Highway 81 follows the route of the old Chisholm Trail from Fort Worth right through to Newton, Kansas. ❑

LEFT: giant mural commemorating the historic Chisholm Trail, Fort Worth.

Hispanics and Native Americans

The first Hispanic mayor of any major US city, San Antonio's Henry Cisneros, elected in 1981 and re-elected in 1985, was good for the self-esteem of young *Chicanos* – one of the many labels Hispanics have to choose from. (Texas Hispanics are called Mexican, Mejicano, Mexican American or Mexican-American, brown, Tejano, Tex-Mex, Hispanic, Hispano, Indio, Indio-Hispanic, Latino and La Raza. Each of these terms has a slightly different meaning: for example, Chicano and Indio acknowledge one's Native American heritage.)

Some of this early Native American history, as well as natural science exhibits and local flora and fauna, is documented in the Art Deco **Witte Museum** (3801 Broadway; open daily; Sun pm only; Tue till 9pm; entrance fee; tel: 210-357-1866; www.wittemuseum.org) in Brackenridge Park. Behind the museum is a complex of historic houses, including one owned by Francisco Ruiz, who was the uncle of José Antonio Navarro and the second of the two native-born Texans who signed the Texas Declaration of Independence. A new addition is the four-story Science Treehouse for kids of all ages.

The Witte Museum is a good place to take children. It depicts the ecology and wildlife of Texas through plenty of hands-on exhibits.

Park life

Brackenridge Park, which adjoins Fort Sam Houston, lies between US-281 and the Austin Highway, northeast of the city. In its 340 acres (138 hectares) can be found the well-stocked San Antonio Zoo (open daily; entrance fee; tel: 210-734-7184), the Japanese Tea Gardens, the Sunken Gardens Amphitheater, Brackenridge Golf Course, riding stables, a sky ride and a carousel, as well as a miniature train ride.

BELOW: acting out the Wild West at Alamo Village, Brackettville.

Map on page 184

Alamo Village was built between the years 1957 and 1959, specifically for the film The Alamo. *Other movies and TV dramas shot here include the classic* Lonesome Dove. *The set is housed on a working ranch.*

To the west, in a redesigned old brewery on Jones Avenue, is the **San Antonio Museum of Art** (closed Mon; Sun pm only; Tue till 9pm; entrance fee; tel: 210-978-8100; www.samuseum.org). Further north, before the airport, at 6000 N. New Braunfels, is the **McNay Art Museum** (closed Mon; Sun pm only; free; tel: 210-824-5368; www.mcnayart.org), housing the collection of an oil heiress, Marion Koogler McNay, who donated it to the state. Artists showcased include Gaugin, Picasso, Matisse and Cézanne.

On the trail of the Missions

The Witte now stands where, at the headwaters of the San Antonio river – named by the Spaniards for St Anthony of Padua – Spaniards and Native Americans may have encountered one another for the first time. It was here that Don Martin de Alcaron and Fra Antonio de San Buenaventura Olivares arrived with settlers, soldiers and Franciscans in 1718.

After the Mission San Antonio de Valero (now the Alamo) and the Villa de Béjar (now Bexar) were established, four more missions were founded. Today, these are part of the **San Antonio Missions National Historical Park** (open daily; free; tel: 210-932-1001), stretching over a 6-mile (10-km) route to the south, beside or close to the river *(see pages 198–9)*.

"Ol' San Antone"

San Antonio used to be the "Tin Pan Alley" of Texas. Like Austin today, the city attracted a variety of musicians, and many of them wrote songs about their new home. In many cases, the first time people outside of Texas heard about the city was through the music, and you will still find tourists today who are expecting to find the "ol' San Antone" made famous in song.

BELOW: stained-glass image of St Anthony in San Fernando Cathedral. **RIGHT:** San Fernando Cathedral at Christmas.

Out of town

Several thousand German settlers in the mid-1800s formed farming communities – **Gruene**, **Comfort** and **New Braunfels** – just northwest of San Antonio, where the German heritage survives in the form of *fachwerk* houses replete with gingerbread trimmings. Gruene is the most interesting historically and is home to the oldest dancehall in Texas, Gruene Hall (1878).

Heading out of San Antonio along US-90 will bring you to the border at Del Rio, around 150 miles (240 km) to the west. Along the way, sightseeing stops might include the **Garner Memorial Museum** at Uvalde (333 N. Park Street; closed Sat and Sun; tel: 830-278-5018), and the **Alamo Village Movie Location** (on Ranch Road 674, north of Brackettville; open daily; entrance fee; tel: 830-563-2580).

Uvalde was the home of John Nance Garner, or "Cactus Jack," controversial two-term vice-president to Franklin Roosevelt. Alamo Village was the first movie location built in Texas and has been the base for hundreds of television shows, commercials and films. Its reconstruction of an early Western village, adjoining the Alamo set, includes an Indian store, a saloon, cantina, gift shop and a museum dedicated to John Wayne. ❑

THE CRUCIAL ROLE OF THE SPANISH MISSIONS

Some of North America's oldest buildings survive in Texas, built by Spanish missionaries who sought to educate and "civilize" the local natives

Across Southern Texas lies a chain of early Spanish outposts. Established in the 18th century, these "missions" are evidence of the early efforts made by Spain to colonize the region, but the missions soon found a role in developing the Catholic faith among the local natives, bringing Indian communities under the Christian banner.

Many of the missions in the East became threatened by French incursions from Louisiana, and their communities relocated to San Antonio. The city is the mission heartland of Texas today, housing four separate complexes (five if you include the Alamo) within its boundaries. The four lie to the south, at 2-mile (3-km) intervals along the San Antonio river. The most beautiful is San José, dubbed "Queen of the Missions." Mission Concepción *(above)* is noted for its handsome twin towers, while Missions San Juan and Espada have distinctive three-bell towers. All can be explored using the San Antonio Missions Trail, with literature from the tourist office.

Each complex presents a different theme about mission life for the visitor. Concepción deals with the religious role of the mission; San José handles the defense and social functions; San Juan focuses on the economic importance; and Espada looks after the educational angle.

▷ MISSION UNDER SIEGE
The most famous mission of them all, though not universally known as such, is the bullet-riddled Alamo – or Mission San Antonio de Valero – founded in 1718 and now surrounded by city-center structures.

△ ATTENTION TO DETAIL
The craftsmanship of the builders working on the missions is demonstrated by the Rose Window at San José Mission, San Antonio.

▷ ENLIGHTENMENT
Inside, the mission churches are calm and mysterious, lit mostly by feeble window light and the glow of votive candles, such as these at Mission San José.

◁ QUIET SIMPLICITY
Mission church decor is simple: bare walls and beams, the occasional fresco and a dotting of religious icons.

◁ **THE TRAIL OUT WEST**
Socorro Mission, one of the three missions on the El Paso Trail. The original building was destroyed by flooding in 1829.

▷ **COMMUNITY CENTER**
The mission was more than a church: it was the base for a community, its grounds housing animals, gardens, workshops, granaries, kilns and sleeping quarters.

◁ **OUR DAILY BREAD**
Links between the old El Paso missions and the local Native Americans remain strong. This traditional Indian *(horno)* oven forms part of the Ysleta Mission.

▷ **RECONSTRUCTION**
The wooden Mission of San Francisco de los Tejas, the first mission in East Texas, was founded in 1690. It has now been fully rebuilt.

NATIVE AMERICAN INFLUENCES

In addition to the one in and around San Antonio, Texas has another mission trail beginning in El Paso. Stretching some 8 miles (13 km) out to the east of the city, it covers three historic sites: Ysleta Mission, Socorro Mission and San Elizario Presidio.

These centers differ from the San Antonio missions in that they were established by the Spanish together with the local Indian communities. The Native American influence is apparent. The oldest is Ysleta *(above)*, which stands next to the Tigua Indian Cultural Center; it was rebuilt in 1908. Socorro, like Ysleta, dates originally from the late 1600s, though the current structure was completed in 1840. Its foundation by Piro Indians is reflected in the Indian traits in the architecture. San Elizario is the chapel of a former fort and was rebuilt in 1877. All three sites can be visited independently or as part of a trolley-bus tour, departing 10.30am daily from El Paso's Civic Center.

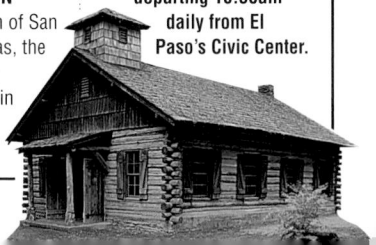

SLOANE

HOUSTON

Map on page 204

Bustling port, financial hub and the gateway to the stars, Houston is an eccentric boomtown: an enjoyable, fast-changing metropolis, with a wealth of attractions

Houston is without a doubt the weirdest, most entertaining city in Texas, a combination of subtropical funk, life in the fast lane, cowboys, a layer of oil, and spacemen: "Houston" was the first word spoken from the moon when the astronauts made contact with home base. Virtually a small town as recently as the late 1950s, Houston's population of over 4 million now makes it the largest city in Texas and the fourth-largest in the US, most of it recently built. One must really search in Houston to find buildings erected before 1960.

Houston is a success in spite of itself. The freeway traffic is as thick as Tokyo's, and the hot humid summers as bad as Calcutta's, once inspiring President George Bush, now the city's most famous retiree, to install air conditioners on outdoor sidewalks to cool G-7 delegates. The lack of initial planning has created a sprawl: an unchecked, wide open city overlaid with intersecting highways, creating a score of separate and distinct neighborhoods.

Surreal scale and proportion result from the lack of zoning: a small boutique may stand next to a 60-story office building, adjoining a house next to a heliport. Houston, more than anywhere else in Texas, operates according to the wildcatter's philosophy: "Dig a little deeper where others have given up, and maybe you'll bring something in."

PRECEDING PAGES: Houston skyline. **LEFT:** the Galleria shopping center. **BELOW:** Houston skyscraper.

Risk-taking wildcatters

Its economy is based on black gold, on an oil and gas industry notorious for the eccentrics and risk-takers it spawns. Because of the oil price fluctuation in the 1970s, Houston's fortunes rose more quickly than those of any other Texas city. After the drop in world oil prices and demand for energy supplies, its growth slowed to merely brisk. However, the boom that had shaped the city for three decades faltered following Enron's spectacular plunge into bankruptcy in 2001. The collapse of the Houston-based energy company left thousands unemployed, accelerating the city's dip into recession.

But Houston's listless economy has picked up, and there is still plenty of room here for personal and professional growth. Another legacy of the 1970s is the rich ethnic mix – Hispanics, Blacks, Native Americans, Indians, Iranians, Chinese, Thai and Vietnamese. The ethnic mix contributes to Houston's resilience, and is undoubtedly part of the reason that it is so tolerant of individuality – and eccentricity.

Near this utterly flat city are low hills and pine forests, salt marshes, swamps and steamy "bayous" (marshy inlets), some of which are infested with alligators. Far to the west, but no more than a day's drive, are real hills, then cactus and the desert. And it is only an hour's drive to the Gulf of Mexico beaches.

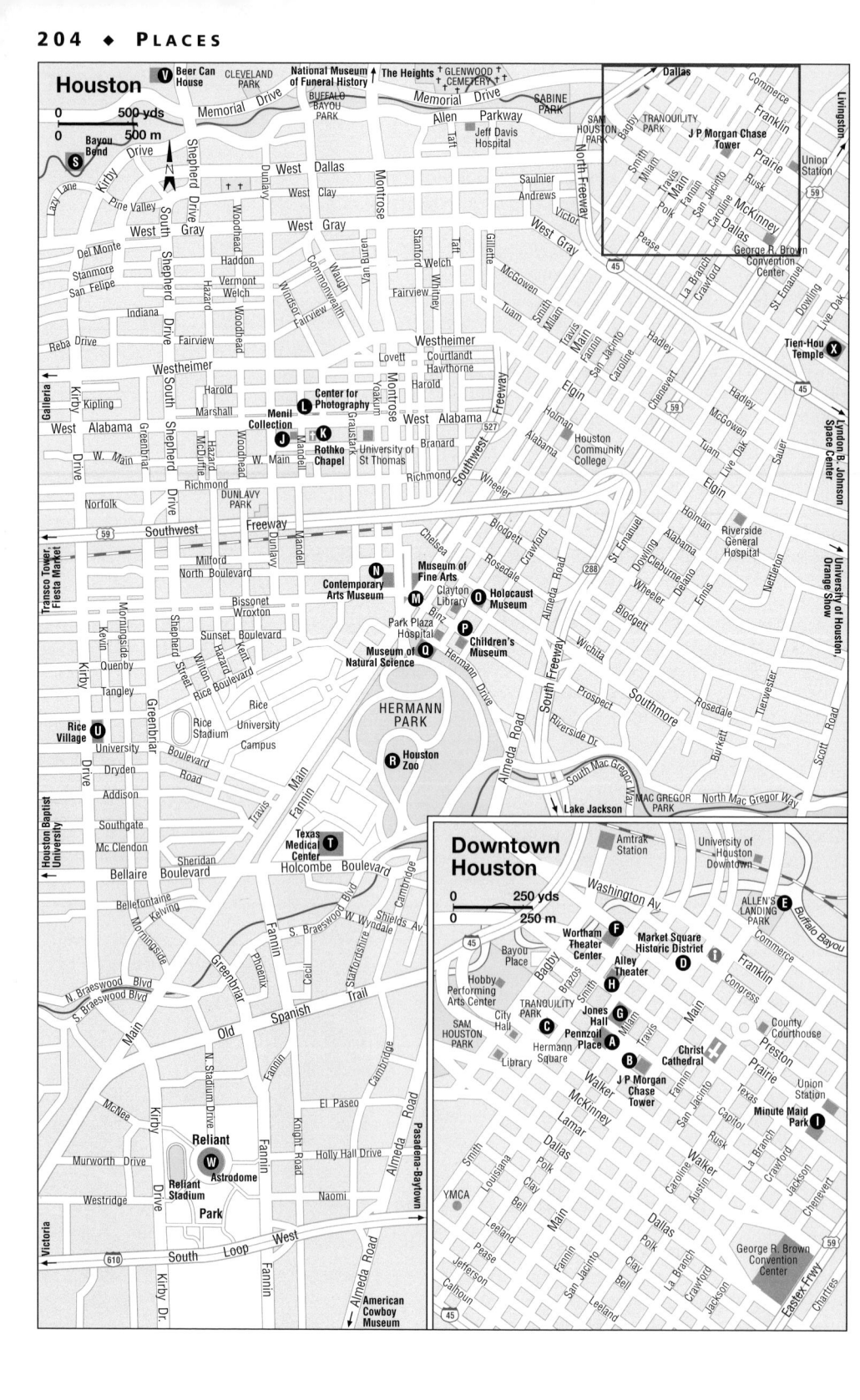
Houston
0 500 yds
0 500 m
Beer Can House
CLEVELAND PARK
National Museum of Funeral History
The Heights
GLENWOOD CEMETERY
BUFFALO BAYOU PARK
SABINE PARK
Memorial Drive
Allen Parkway
Jeff Davis Hospital
Bayou Bend
Kirby Drive
Shepherd Drive
West Dallas
West Clay
Montrose
Saulnier
Andrews
North Freeway
Victor
West Gray
Del Monte
Stanmore
San Felipe
Haddon
Vermont
Welch
Indiana
Fairview
Reba Drive
Westheimer
Lovett
Courtlandt
Hawthorne
Harold
Marshall
Kipling
Galleria
West Alabama
Center for Photography
Menil Collection
Rothko Chapel
University of St Thomas
Branard
Richmond
Houston Community College
Norfolk
DUNLAVY PARK
Southwest Freeway
Milford
North Boulevard
Transco Tower Fiesta Market
Contemporary Arts Museum
Museum of Fine Arts
Clayton Library
Holocaust Museum
Bissonet
Wroxton
Sunset Boulevard
Park Plaza Hospital
Children's Museum
Museum of Natural Science
Quenby
Tangley
Rice Village
Rice Stadium
Rice University
Campus
HERMANN PARK
Houston Zoo
Dryden
Addison
Southgate
Mc Clendon
Sheridan
Bellaire Boulevard
Bellefontaine
Kelwing
Texas Medical Center
Holcombe Boulevard
Houston Baptist University
Shields Av.
S. Braeswood Blvd
W. Wyndale
N. Braeswood Blvd
Spanish Trail
Old Main
N. Stadium Drive
El Paseo
McNee
Reliant Astrodome
Reliant Stadium
Park
Murworth Drive
Holly Hall Drive
Knight Road
Naomi
Westridge
Victoria
South Loop West
Almeda Road
Pasadena-Baytown
American Cowboy Museum
Almeda Road
South Mac Gregor Way
MAC GREGOR PARK
North Mac Gregor Way
Lake Jackson
Dallas
Commerce
Franklin
Prairie
Livingston
SAM HOUSTON PARK
TRANQUILITY PARK
J P Morgan Chase Tower
Union Station
McKinney
George R. Brown Convention Center
Tien-Hou Temple
Lyndon B. Johnson Space Center
University of Houston, Orange Show
Riverside General Hospital
Downtown Houston
Amtrak Station
University of Houston Downtown
Washington Av.
ALLEN'S LANDING PARK
Buffalo Bayou
Wortham Theater Center
Market Square Historic District
Alley Theater
Bayou Place
Hobby Performing Arts Center
City Hall
Jones Hall
Pennzoil Place
Hermann Square
Library
Christ Cathedral
J P Morgan Chase Tower
County Courthouse
Minute Maid Park
YMCA
George R. Brown Convention Center
Eastex Frwy

Freeway life

Because of its size, the only logical way to tour Houston is by car, in which many Houstonians spend more time than at home, just as they spend more on car payments than on rent. The downtown area is enclosed by I-45 on the west and, some way to the east, US-59, with two other much-visited areas – the Museum District and the Texas Medical Center – to the southwest. The city sprawls between a vast network of busy highways, as a result of which buildings are consciously designed as "freeway architecture." Since there are no changes in elevation, tall buildings function as the only landmarks for the driver.

The I-610 loop that garlands the city also divides it as surely as the Wall once separated Berlin. Snobbery on the part of those who live inside the Loop, where all the desirable neighborhoods and almost all of the tourist attractions are located, is an accepted feature of local life. Perhaps the best-known downtown structure is Philip Johnson's **Pennzoil Place** Ⓐ, with its two towers that appear to separate and then come together as one drives around the city. One block from Pennzoil Place is I.M. Pei's distinctive **JPMorgan Chase Tower** Ⓑ, formerly the Texas Commerce Bank Tower, a cool, gray slab nicknamed "the Texas Tombstone."

Tranquility Park Ⓒ, near Sam Houston Park and its restored century-old structures, including an 1878 general store, is named for the moon base Tranquility. Five gold towers in the park resemble space rockets. The oldest part of the original city is **Market Square** Ⓓ, opposite the Visitor Information Center (801 Congress Street; tel: 800-365-7575), but more significant is **Allen's Landing Park** Ⓔ, a few blocks north, beside the bayou. Here is where Houston's founders, Augustus and John Allen, first came ashore in 1836.

A 6-mile (10-km) system of **underground tunnels** connects 55 buildings with three hotels in Houston's downtown area, making it possible to visit more than 100 shops and some small restaurants without surfacing into the heat. This subterranean city is open from 7am to 6pm weekdays and maps are available at banks along the route.

Entertainment areas

Downtown Houston is also the upscale entertainment district, home of the **Wortham Theater Center** Ⓕ, (501 Texas Street; tel: 713-237-1439), hosting both the city's Grand Opera and Ballet companies. The Houston Symphony bunks down in **Jones Hall** Ⓖ (615 Louisiana Street; tel: 713-227-3974), and drama has its main home at the acclaimed **Alley Theater** Ⓗ (615 Texas Avenue; tel: 713-228-9341).

A new ballpark was built downtown in 2000 for the Houston Astros baseball team. Originally called Enron Field, the ballpark became **Minute Maid Park** Ⓘ after Enron's corporate scandal. It features a full-size vintage locomotive along one side and has a retractable roof to cater for all aspects of the Texan climate. Tours are available daily (closed Sun; entrance fee; call in advance 713-259-8000).

Heading south on Montrose Boulevard, west of downtown, brings you to the **Montrose** district, a major entertainment area whose center is the inter-

Map on page 204

Statue of General Sam Houston, the Texan hero who gave his name to the city.

BELOW: canoeing on Buffalo Bayou.

TIP

To get a feel for the diversity of lifestyles in the Montrose area, grab a drink at one of the sidewalk cafés and watch a colorful parade of punks, college kids, trendy singles and transvestites cruise by on foot and in cars.

section of Westheimer and Montrose. Driving from downtown along Gray Street takes you through the old Fourth Ward, a tough neighborhood of single-corridor houses. Montrose is the home of the largest gay community in Texas, as well as of artists, designers, museum personnel and trendy young singles.

In its back streets, gay bars cater to every taste; on the main drag, Westheimer, entertainment is directed to a broader spectrum and boutiques display vintage clothing, erotic birthday cakes, neon hair ornaments and punk garb. In the 5000–6000 blocks are elegant shops such as Fendi and Barney's New York. East of the intersection is a string of restaurants and bars, characterized by Tex-Mex cuisine, lasers, videos and neon.

Art and interfaith

As Montrose Boulevard heads south, it becomes more elegant prior to crossing US-59 and heading into the grassy purlieus of the Museum District. A few blocks west, at 1515 Sul Ross, in a specially designed building, is the vast **Menil Collection** **J** (open Wed–Sun; free; tel: 713-525-9400), a legacy of the de Menil family, with exhibits ranging from medieval and Byzantine art to contemporary works, including the world's largest private collection of surrealist art.

Across the street is a Greek Orthodox church offering a collection of icons for public viewing, and facing it, at the corner of Yupon, is the **Rothko Chapel** **K**, commissioned by John and Dominique de Menil to house 14 paintings by the abstract expressionist Mark Rothko. This interfaith chapel, its entrance flanked by the Broken Obelisk – a memorial to Dr Martin Luther King – is open every day (free; tel: 713-524-9839). Near here can be found the **Houston**

BELOW: the Cockrell Butterfly Center.

Center for Photography Ⓛ (1441 W. Alabama; closed Mon and Tue; Sat and Sun pm only; free; tel: 713-529-4755), a worthwhile visit for those with an interest in the subject.

Where Montrose Boulevard crosses Bissonnet Street, heavy culture sets in: the **Museum of Fine Arts** Ⓜ (MFA; 1001 Bissonnet; closed Mon; Sun pm only; free Thur; tel: 713-639-7300; www.mfah.org) and the **Contemporary Arts Museum** Ⓝ (CAM; 5201 Bayard Lane; closed Mon; Sun pm only; free; tel: 713-284-8250; www.camh.org) sit across the street from one other. The MFA, whose modern addition was the work of the renowned architect Ludwig Mies Van der Rohe, houses a large permanent collection from all periods, with strong holdings of French Impressionists and 20th-century Americans. Across the street, the museum's Cullen Sculpture Garden is open until 10pm. The CAM does not have a permanent collection, but is a stainless-steel *kunsthalle* staging nine exhibitions each year, featuring the latest wrinkles in new art.

A more sombre experience is offered at the **Holocaust Museum** Ⓞ (5401 Caroline Street; open daily; Sat and Sun pm only; free; tel: 713-942-8000; www.hmh.org; tours available), an educational facility aimed at eliminating prejudice and hatred through poignant permanent and visiting exhibitions.

Hermann Park covers some 455 acres (185 hectares) of wooded land and, as well as museums and gardens, includes facilities for sports such as golf, tennis, cycling and hiking.

Science and nature

Four blocks down Binz Street is the **Children's Museum** Ⓟ (closed Mon; Sun pm only; entrance fee; tel: 713-522-1138; www.cmhouston.org), with hands-on exhibits. In nearby Hermann Park there is the **Museum of Natural Science** Ⓠ, home to a Space Age Museum and a planetarium (both open daily; entrance fee; tel: 713-639-4629; www.hmns.org). Part of the complex houses the **Lillie and Roy Cullen Gallery of Earth Science**, containing more minerals and gemstone varieties than you knew existed, and the **Wortham IMAX Theater**, which projects movies hourly onto a six-story screen (tel: 713-639-4629 for schedule). As you enter the park you might want to take a few moments to smell the roses at the Garden Center (open daily; free).

There are other attractions in the park. A six-story glass cone houses the recently renovated and expanded **Cockrell Butterfly Center** (open daily; entrance fee; tel: 713-639-4600), in which thousands of brightly colored lepidoptera flutter around a waterfall in a tropical garden, while the **Houston Zoo** Ⓡ (open daily; entrance fee; tel: 713-533-6500; www.houstonzoo.org) has a Tropical Bird House, which takes the form of an Asian jungle.

BELOW: Jean DeBuffet sculpture.

More museums

There are more museums and art galleries in Houston than in any other Texas city. The Museum of Fine Arts, for example, also owns **Bayou Bend** Ⓢ (1 Westcott Street; open Tue–Fri pm, plus Sat am; entrance fee; tel: 713-639-7750), just before Memorial Park. This stunning 24-room mansion, designed by Houston architect John F. Staub, is filled with renowned American art from Colonial times to the early part of the 20th century. The collection was left to the museum by the philanthropist Ima Hogg (it was her real name),

daughter of the state's first Texas-born Governor, James Stephen Hogg. The 14 acres (6 hectares) of landscaped grounds are open to the public every day except Sunday and Monday (entrance fee). Also not to be overlooked is the **Blaffer Gallery** (closed Mon; Sat and Sun pm only; free; tel: 713-743-9530) – described as a "laboratory for the visual arts and contemporary culture" – at the University of Houston. Echoes of the old West are preserved in the **American Cowboy Museum** (11822 Almeda; open by appointment; tel: 713-433-4441), and the **National Museum of Funeral History** (415 Barren Springs Drive; open daily; Sat and Sun pm only; entrance fee; tel: 281-876-3063; www.nmfh.org), with a collection of hearses, sarcophagi and coffins, always evokes curiosity from macabre-minded visitors.

Exhibit at Houston's Museum of Medical Science, another attraction in the Museum District.

Oak-shaded campus

The gentle Victorian Romanesque campus of **Rice University**, surrounded by giant oaks, abuts Hermann Park to the west. **Rice University Art Gallery**, displaying contemporary art, is open to the public (closed Mon; Sun pm only; free; tel: 713-348-6069). Beyond is the immense and highly regarded **Texas Medical Center** Ⓣ, whose 700-acre (283-hectare) complex is home to celebrity surgeons. Rice, a pleasant retreat from the sterile towers of the Medical Center, has set up a monumental sculpture by Michael Heizer – three 70-ton (63.5-metric ton) blocks of pink Texas granite.

BELOW: glistening Houston skyscraper.

Eccentric architecture

The area around Rice is the most beautiful in Houston. **Rice Village** Ⓤ, at Kirby and University, was Houston's first upscale shopping center and its 325 stores are still a major attraction today. Two stately streets, North and South Boulevard, set the local standard for majestic oak tree canopies, and, behind Georgian Revival facades live the old moneyed classes of Houston eccentricity, as seen in a totally pink house at the corner of Hazard and Sunset streets. Everything, including the fence and garage, is painted tropical flamingo pink.

A comprehensive tour of Houston architecture would also have to include the unbelievable **Beer Can House** Ⓥ (222 Malone Street, off Memorial Drive), constructed from 50,000 cans, near the extensive and lovely Memorial Park. Equally unbelievable is the **Orange Show** (2402 Munger Street; open Sat and Sun pm and Wed–Fri am in summer; entrance fee; tel: 713-926-6368), a labyrinth of passages, murals, antiques and a tiny museum, otherwise impossible to describe. The life's work of retired postal worker Jeff McKissack, who built it over 26 years out of junkyard scraps, it promotes the life-giving qualities of the orange. "Be smart; eat oranges" is spelled out in mosaic tiles.

Art Deco tower

Heading out from the city center, US-59, also called the Southwest Freeway, carries a river of commuters every day, with rush hours lasting 6–9am and 2–8pm. At the point where it intersects with Loop 610 stands

the ultimate in freeway architecture, the **Williams Tower**, formerly the Transco Tower, designed by Philip Johnson and John Burgee. The facade, inspired in part by the San Jacinto Monument, is the same on all four sides, in order to be admired from any direction, and its Art Deco lines can easily be taken in while driving at 55 mph (88 kmph). A beautiful nearby fountain rewards those who see it on foot.

Upscale shopping

A byproduct of Houston's geographical fragmentation has been the emergence of a galaxy of shopping malls. The best-known is the **Galleria** area, centered around Post Oak Road and Westheimer Road near the West Loop (I-610), not far from the Williams Tower. Here can be found a *Who's Who* of retailing – Neiman Marcus, Saks Fifth Avenue, Gucci, Tiffany, Cartier and Versace, to name but a few. The area is marked by glamorous buildings designed by Cesar Pelli and Johnson and Burgee, and the enclosed Galleria itself is modeled on Milan's Galleria, but blown up to immense size. Every luxury store under the sun is represented, as well as an ice-skating rink and a jogging track around the roof.

The Galleria is home to around 250 stores, in three sections and on three levels. Deluxe department stores like Neiman Marcus grab the headlines but even the cheapest goods can be bought in the center.

Who shops at the famous Houston Galleria? Well, everyone does now, but in its early years it was supported by the well-heeled from sections like **River Oaks**, west of downtown. Kirby Drive and River Oaks Boulevard are the main streets of River Oaks, Houston's Monument Valley of money and conspicuous consumption. The mansions along streets like River Oaks Boulevard, Lazy Lane and Inwood belong to captains of industry, oil and cattle barons, their descendants and a few Arab sheiks. First-run foreign and independent movies can be seen at the 1939 vintage **River Oaks Theatre** (2009 W. Gray Street, near Shepherd; tel: 713-866-8881).

BELOW: Rice University.

Restaurant row

Further west, the stretch of Richmond Avenue between Chimney Rock and Hillcroft emulates a Parisian-style boulevard, lined with art galleries and sidewalk cafés. Many of the city's best restaurants are found around here, some offering entertainment nightly – blues at **Magnolia Bar and Grill** (tel: 713-781-6207), and bowling and electronic games at **Dave & Buster's** (tel: 713-952-2233), both on Richmond near Fountainview. Houstonians are said to eat out more than residents of any other US community and there are over 6,000 restaurants in the Houston area from which to choose.

With its increased Asian population, Houston is no longer just known for its Cajun or Tex-Mex cooking. Here you can eat Chinese, Vietnamese, Thai, Japanese, Indian and many other exotic cuisines.

Fiesta Market

If you exit the Southwest Freeway at Hillcroft and head south toward the Bellaire intersection, you will come to the **Fiesta Market**, the ultimate ethnic grocery store. Advertising is in Spanish, Vietnamese, Chinese, Hindi and English. Fiesta sells everything from cowboy boots to goat's milk. It is always jammed with shoppers, and the interior is ablaze with huge neon signs. It is an astonishing and hilarious store, now replicated at other locations. In another display of pure Texas culture – the culture of bigness – a huge piano on the Southwest Freeway alerts drivers to the presence of a piano store. Alas, the gigantic neon cockroach that once graced that same freeway (advertising an exterminator shop) no longer exists.

Heading north

Just north of the center of the city, and slightly west, is a mixed residential and industrial neighborhood called **The Heights**. The houses are older and more

BELOW: Hermann Park.

graceful, but one of the highlights of The Heights is the grave of Texas billionaire Howard Hughes in **Glenwood Cemetery**, off Washington Boulevard. Hughes' grave is as simply marked as those of his parents nearby. All three are completely overshadowed by the dramatic figure of a weeping angel embellishing an adjacent grave. This flamboyant monument was prepared by a local interior designer in advance for himself.

Map on page 204

Down south

In the southern part of the city is **Reliant Park** Ⓦ (tel: 713-667-1400), which includes the Reliant Astrodome. The Astrodome has to be seen to be believed. It is vast – large enough to fit an 18-story building inside – and everything that takes place there is a Texas-sized spectacle. Reliant Park can be toured (entrance fee) every day at 11am. In addition to the Astrodome, Reliant Park includes Reliant Stadium, home of the NFL American football team the Houston Texans, along with Reliant Center (with 706,000 sq. ft/7,061 sq. meters of exhibit space) and Reliant Arena, another event center. Reliant Stadium has a retractable roof and seats nearly 70,000 spectators. Reliant Park is the host of the huge Houston Livestock Show and Rodeo, the world's largest event of its kind, featuring Western contests from bronco-busting to chuckwagon-racing.

The Harris County domed stadium, or Reliant Astrodome, is 218 ft (67 meters) tall at its highest point and can seat up to 65,000 spectators.

Houston's Orient

Many of Houston's attractions are to the east of town, beginning, on the other side of US-59, with **Old Chinatown**, whose major landmark is the **Tien-Hou Taoist Temple** Ⓧ (1507 Delano Street; tel: 713-236-1015). Here visitors can determine their fortune by shaking out numbered reeds. Be sure to visit the

BELOW: Super Bowl at Reliant Stadium.

nearby **Kim Son** (2001 Jefferson Street; tel: 713-222-2461), a Vietnamese landmark and the largest Oriental restaurant in the state. Across town there's a burgeoning Vietnamese community operating other restaurants on Milam Street, just south of downtown, while Chinese immigrants and their descendants shop and eat in **New Chinatown**, located in Southwest Houston along Bellaire Boulevard, between Gessner and Wilcrest. New Chinatown is sometimes referred to as the Bellaire Corridor, or the Diho Area, after the **Diho Supermarket**, a large, Chinese food mart.

At the base of the San Jacinto Monument is a free museum dedicated to the history of the region, covering events from the Native American period through to the Civil War and beyond.

Ships and spaceships

The wealth Houston enjoys today derives not only from oil discovered elsewhere but the 50-mile (80-km) **Ship Channel** that turned it into an inland port. Houston businessmen persuaded the government to pay for the Channel, which developed their city into one of the three busiest ports in the US, stealing the glory (and the trade) from coastal Galveston, after an apocalyptic storm wrecked the latter city's harbor in 1900. The Channel's turning basin, off US-90A near Navigation Boulevard, is the site of free harbor tours, but a more rewarding trip is to visit the other end of the Channel, where it enters Burnett Bay and ends its journey to the sea.

The way there, however, takes one through the **Pasadena–Baytown Industrial Corridor**, a district filled with every kind of petrochemical processing plant. The air smells like floor cleaner and plays havoc with the sinuses, although at night the industrial landscape assumes a beautiful, otherworldly quality. Pasadena also has a landmark: the vast **Armand Bayou Nature Center** (8500 Bay Area Blvd; closed Mon; Sun pm only; entrance fee; tel: 281-474-2551; www.abnc.org). You can visit the center's Martyn Farm, which will take you back to farm life in the late 1800s.

BELOW: David Adickes' *Virtuoso,* in downtown Houston. **RIGHT:** San Jacinto Monument.

There are two attractions at this end of the Channel: the World War I dreadnought **Battleship *Texas*** (open daily; entrance fee; tel: 713-827-9620), which served as General Eisenhower's flagship during the 1944 D-Day invasion, and the **San Jacinto Monument**. The latter commemorates the Battle of San Jacinto on April 21 1836, making it arguably the most significant monument in the state, as it marks the date on which Texas won its freedom from Mexico with General Sam Houston's defeat of Mexico's Santa Anna. Only weeks after the ignominy of the Alamo, revenge must have been sweet. The Art Deco monument (3523 Highway 134; open daily; entrance fee; tel: 713-453-7114), offers an elevator ride 570 ft (174 meters) to the top for a view of downtown Houston on one side and a spaghetti bowl of pipelines on the other.

Notwithstanding its varied other attractions, what has brought Houston to worldwide attention in recent decades has been the **Lyndon B. Johnson Space Center** *(see pages 214–215)*, 25 miles (40 km) southeast of downtown (take I-45, then NASA Road 1; open daily; entrance fee; tel: 281-244-2100). Thanks to this facility, the name "Houston" has now taken on universal significance. ❑

CITIZENS
SOLDIE
SAN
BAMA
ILLIN
ANA,
MICH
HAM
TEXAS AND
THE ARMY OF IMMIGRANT
WERE NATIVES TEXAS AT
SAS, CONNECTICUT, OF ALA-
IANA, KENTUCKY, GEORGIA,
MARYLAND, MASSACHUSETTS, LOUISI-
SIPPI, MISSOURI, NEW
ORK, NORTH CAROLINA,
RHODE ISLAND, SOUTH
E, TEXAS, VERMONT
CANADA, ENGLAND,
NY, IRELAND, ITALY,
ORTUGAL AND SCOTLAND.

HOUSTON: THE EARTH'S SPACE CAPITAL

Houston, as home base for NASA's Apollo lunar missions, can claim to be the Earth's most important city in these early days of space travel

In the future, should aliens look back on man's first tentative steps beyond his home planet, the name Houston will be on the tips of their tongues, tentacles or whatever it is they use for speaking.

Texas' biggest city has never actually launched a man into orbit, but US-manned space flights have relied upon ground staff here to guide them on their way. Houston is the home of Mission Control, the focus of all earthly activity when an astronaut is up there in the deep blue yonder. But, as well as guiding space craft during their missions, Houston is also the selection and training base for NASA astronauts. It is here that they go through their paces, physically and mentally, before being allowed into orbit.

The Manned Space Center, later re-named the Johnson Space Center, was opened by NASA (National Aeronautics and Space Administration) in 1962, part of a plan to fulfil President Kennedy's declared intention for America to land a man on the moon and return him safely to earth before the decade was out. The Center played its part to perfection, and "Houston" was the first word spoken from the surface of the moon, by Apollo XI commander Neil Armstrong.

In 1981, NASA launched the Space Shuttle, the first re-usable space exploration vehicle, and Houston was again central to its success. Much of NASA's work now revolves around the International Space Station, a co-operative venture between the US and Russia.

▷ GIANT LEAP
The men who made history – the crew of Apollo XI, the first mission to land on the moon: Neil Armstrong, Michael Collins and Edwin "Buzz" Aldrin.

△ SPACE SHUTTLE
The Space Shuttle, like earlier rockets, blasts off from Florida but is guided by Houston.

▷ ASTRONAUT'S VIEW
From the air, the enormity of the Space Center's 1,625-acre (660-hectare) site is immediately apparent.

◁ **ROCKET POWER**
One of the Center's biggest attractions is the 363-ft (110-meter) long Saturn V rocket. The most powerful rocket of its day, it lifted the Apollo craft into space.

△ **GALACTIC HONOR**
Originally known as the Manned Space Center, NASA's Houston site was later renamed to honor Texan-born President Lyndon B. Johnson.

▽ **MISSION CONTROL**
In 1995, NASA opened a new Mission Control Center at the site. Costing around $250 million, it replaced the old Mission Control, which had monitored the Apollo and Space Shuttle crews.

SPACE-AGE FUN FOR ALL

NASA was established in 1958 as a US Government agency for research into aeronautics and space flight. Throughout the 1960s, it enjoyed substantial funding and plenty of glory, but times have become harder since, with both politicians and the public losing interest in the agency's work.

The fatal 2003 space-shuttle explosion cast further doubt on NASA, which now needs to publicly justify every mission.

Part of the PR exercise has been the opening up to the general public of bases like the Kennedy Space Center in Florida and the Johnson Space Center in Houston.

With the help of the Walt Disney Corporation's creative genius, NASA has developed a fascinating entertainment and educational exhibit. Now 1½ million visitors a year drop by to see IMAX films, moon rocks, spacecraft and other memorabilia, and to take tram tours of previously off-limits areas. Interactive exhibits allow them to land a space shuttle or retrieve a satellite.

EAST TEXAS

Map on page 220

Unparalleled woodland, stunning lakes and historic towns make this often ignored part of Texas a discovery; even the oil-producing cities of the "Cajun Triangle" have much to interest the traveler

There's a whole section of the state larger than New England – and containing more trees – that is certain to confuse most newcomers with its "unTexan" topography. It's the **Piney Woods**, the timber country between Louisiana and Central Texas, the region which was the state's economic launching pad. It was here that industrial interests first wrestled with Mother Nature, raking timber off the land and squeezing oil from below it. A lot of scars remain, but it is known as much for its natural beauty as for its oil and timber industries.

The economic significance of the Gulf and the salt dome geological formations along the relatively unsettled coast mean that the region's largest metropolitan area is found at its southeastern corner, specifically around Beaumont, Port Arthur and Orange. Practically located in Louisiana, the three cities – often called the "Cajun Triangle" – flanking I-10, together have a metropolitan population approaching 200,000.

PRECEDING PAGES: East Texas farming. **LEFT:** Kilgore Rangerette. **BELOW:** East Texas pines.

Good guess

Founded in 1835, **Beaumont** ❶, the state's first oil boomtown, sits 21 miles (32 km) up from the Gulf on a deep-water ship channel dredged from the Neches river. Geologists of the late-19th century had scoffed at the theory that oil reservoirs might be tucked inside the salt domes but a local real-estate developer, Patillo Higgins, suspected the gaseous vapors and sulfurous water at nearby Spindletop Hill indicated a pool of the valuable liquid. Along with an Austrian immigrant, Anthony F. Lucas, he drilled several unsuccessful wells in 1900 before hitting the Lucas Gusher. After the Spindletop oil discovery on January 10 1901, Texas was transformed from an agriculturally dominated economy into one that could tap very fast-flowing pockets of wealth.

In the space of two years, Beaumont's population swelled from 9,000 to 50,000 as East Texas became a kind of get-rich-quick magnet. Oil derricks sprouted here as thick as the pines, and their furious pumping of the salt domes took its toll.

At the appropriately named **Sour Lake** ❷, about 20 miles (32 km) west of Beaumont on State Route 105, visitors can still survey the damage in the form of a 10-acre (4-hectare) sinkhole created in 1929 by three decades of drilling.

Among the many museums devoted to the industry's fascinating history are Beaumont's reconstructed **Spindletop-Gladys City Boomtown Museum** (closed Mon; Sun pm only; entrance fee; tel: 409-835-0823; www.spindletop.org) on the Lamar University campus, and the **Texas Energy Museum**, on Main Street (closed Mon; Sun pm only; entrance fee tel: 409-833-5100; www.texasenergymuseum.org).

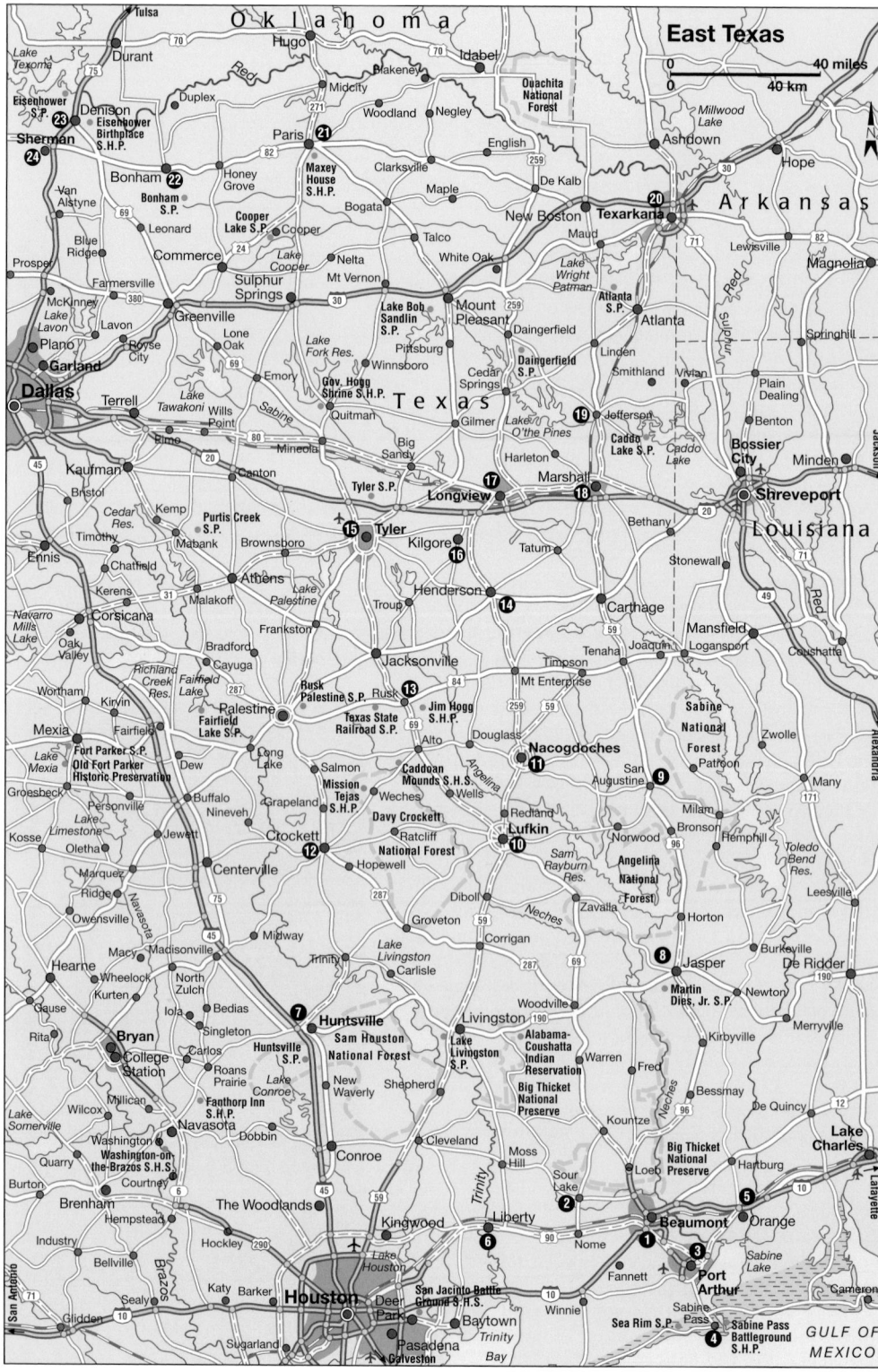
East Texas
0 40 miles
0 40 km
Oklahoma
Arkansas
Texas
Louisiana
GULF OF MEXICO
Tulsa
Durant
Hugo
Idabel
Lake Texoma
Red
Blakeney
Midcity
Ouachita National Forest
Millwood Lake
Ashdown
Hope
Eisenhower S.P.
Denison
Eisenhower Birthplace S.H.P.
Sherman
Duplex
Woodland
Negley
Paris
English
Bonham
Bonham S.P.
Honey Grove
Maxey House S.H.P.
Clarksville
De Kalb
Van Alstyne
Leonard
Cooper Lake S.P.
Cooper
Bogata
Maple
New Boston
Texarkana
Blue Ridge
Talco
Maud
Lewisville
Magnolia
Prosper
Commerce
Lake Cooper
Nelta
White Oak
Lake Wright Patman
Farmersville
Sulphur Springs
Mt Vernon
McKinney
Lake Lavon
Lavon
Greenville
Lake Bob Sandlin S.P.
Mount Pleasant
Atlanta S.P.
Atlanta
Sulphur
Springhill
Plano
Boyce City
Lone Oak
Lake Fork Res.
Pittsburg
Daingerfield
Daingerfield S.P.
Linden
Garland
Winnsboro
Cedar Springs
Smithland
Vivian
Plain Dealing
Dallas
Emory
Gov. Hogg Shrine S.H.P.
Terrell
Lake Tawakoni
Wills Point
Sabine
Quitman
Gilmer
Lake O'the Pines
Jefferson
Benton
Elmo
Mineola
Big Sandy
Caddo Lake S.P.
Caddo Lake
Bossier City
Jackson
Kaufman
Canton
Harleton
Minden
Bristol
Tyler S.P.
Longview
Marshall
Shreveport
Cedar Res.
Kemp
Purtis Creek S.P.
Timothy
Mabank
Tyler
Kilgore
Tatum
Bethany
Ennis
Chatfield
Brownsboro
Stonewall
Athens
Lake Palestine
Henderson
Kerens
Malakoff
Troup
Carthage
Navarro Mills Lake
Corsicana
Frankston
Mansfield
Oak Valley
Bradford
Tenaha
Joaquin
Logansport
Cayuga
Jacksonville
Timpson
Coushatta
Richland Creek Res.
Fairfield Lake
Wortham
Kirvin
Rusk Palestine S.P.
Rusk
Mt Enterprise
Palestine
Jim Hogg S.H.P.
Texas State Railroad S.P.
Sabine National Forest
Mexia
Fairfield
Fairfield Lake S.P.
Alto
Douglass
Zwolle
Lake Mexia
Fort Parker S.P.
Old Fort Parker Historic Preservation
Dew
Long Lake
Salmon
Caddoan Mounds S.H.S.
Nacogdoches
San Augustine
Patroon
Groesbeck
Buffalo
Mission Tejas S.H.P.
Weches
Wells
Angelina
Many
Personville
Nineveh
Grapeland
Davy Crockett National Forest
Redland
Milam
Lake Limestone
Kosse
Jewett
Ratcliff
Lufkin
Bronson
Norwood
Hemphill
Oletha
Crockett
Hopewell
Sam Rayburn Res.
Angelina National Forest
Toledo Bend Res.
Marquez
Centerville
Leesville
Ridge
Navasota
Owensville
Diboll
Zavalla
Neches
Groveton
Horton
Corrigan
Midway
Macy
Madisonville
Trinity
Lake Livingston
Carlisle
Jasper
Burkeville
Hearne
Wheelock
North Zulch
Kurten
Martin Dies, Jr. S.P.
De Ridder
Newton
Gause
Iola
Bedias
Huntsville
Woodville
Livingston
Merryville
Rita
Bryan
Singleton
Sam Houston National Forest
Lake Livingston S.P.
Alabama-Coushatta Indian Reservation
Kirbyville
College Station
Carlos
Huntsville S.P.
Roans Prairie
Lake Conroe
New Waverly
Shepherd
Warren
Fred
Big Thicket National Preserve
Bessmay
Millican
Fanthorp Inn S.H.P.
Wilcox
Lake Somerville
Navasota
Dobbin
Kountze
De Quincy
Washington
Washington-on-the-Brazos S.H.S.
Cleveland
Moss Hill
Big Thicket National Preserve
Lake Charles
Quarry
Conroe
Loeb
Hartburg
Burton
Courtney
Trinity
Sour Lake
Lafayette
Brenham
The Woodlands
Beaumont
Orange
Hempstead
Kingwood
Liberty
Industry
Hockley
Nome
Sabine Lake
Bellville
Lake Houston
Port Arthur
Brazos
Fannett
Cameron
San Antonio
Katy
Barker
Houston
San Jacinto Battle Ground S.H.S.
Winnie
Sabine Pass
Sealy
Glidden
Deer Park
Baytown
Sea Rim S.P.
Sabine Pass Battleground S.H.S.
Sugarland
Pasadena
Trinity Bay
Galveston
1
2
3
4
5
6
7
8
9
10
11
12
13
14
15
16
17
18
19
20
21
22
23
24

The city's oldest home, the **John Jay French Historic House Museum** (3025 French Road; closed Sun and Mon; entrance fee; tel: 409-898-0348; www.jjfrench.com), depicts the life of the Connecticut-born trader who settled here in 1845, while the elegant **McFaddin-Ward House** (1906 Calder Avenue; closed Mon; Sun pm only; entrance fee; tel: 409-832-2134; www.mcfaddin-ward.org) is a 17-room mansion owned by an early 20th-century oilman. Among the city's other sights are the **Edison Plaza Museum** (350 Pine Street; open Mon–Fri pm; free; tel: 409-981-3089; www.edisonmuseum.org), housed, appropriately, in a converted power station and devoted to the life of the great inventor; the **Fire Museum of Texas** (400 Walnut Street; closed Sat and Sun; tel: 409-880-3927; free), and a memorial (open daily; tel: 409-833-4622; free) on I-10 to the state's most famous athlete, Babe Didrickson Zaharias, the Beaumont-born triple winner of track and field events at the 1932 Los Angeles Olympics.

The marshy areas of East Texas are alligator country – beware!

Lively Cajuns

Beaumont's sister city to the southeast is **Port Arthur** ❸. Home of the world's largest petrochemical complex, it is noted for its fleet of shrimp boats, its superlative seafood and its Cajun nightclubs with their fiddle music and rowdy atmosphere. "*Les le Bon Ton Roule!*" – Let the good times roll! – is a much-quoted Cajun saying, which the tourist board never tires of pointing out.

Port Arthur was the home of the late rock singer Janis Joplin, whose birthday is celebrated every January 19, and is the kind of place where tourists can attend a genuine, music-filled Cajun wedding – of two alligators.

The city was founded in 1895 as the seaport terminus of his Gulf Coast Railroad by Arthur Stilwell, who ran out of money and lost ownership to a famous speculator, John "Bet-a-Million" Gates. But the glamorous mansions of what was once "Stilwells' Dream City" still remain along the white sandy shores of **Lake Sabine**, some 9 miles (14 km) long and 7½ miles (12 km) across, and joined to the ocean by the Sabine–Neches Ship Channel, which flows right through the city.

BELOW: East Texas lakes.

The little town of **Sabine Pass** ❹, laid out by Sam Houston himself in 1836, was the site of a famous 1863 Civil War battle. About 40 Confederates, led by a barkeeper named Dick Dowling, deployed half a dozen cannons to drive off a Federal force at least a hundred times as large. Today, Sabine Pass, long ago annexed by its larger neighbor, is famous for fishing and a seafood restaurant, the Channel Inn (5157 S. Gulfway; tel: 409-971-2400), which boasts "if it were any fresher, it would be swimming."

The most famous house in Port Arthur is **Pompeiian Villa** (1953 Lakeshore Drive; closed Sat and Sun; entrance fee; tel: 409-983-5977), an historical site built in 1900 for the barbed-wire inventor Isaac Ellwood. He sold it to a fellow tycoon, Diamond Match Company president James Hopkins. When Hopkins' wife arrived to discover Port Arthur's oppressive heat, mosquitoes and muddy streets she turned right round and returned to St Louis, so Hopkins traded the mansion to banker George Craig for 10 percent of the stock in the

newly formed Texas Oil Company (which became Texaco). When chivvied later about why he'd given up his stock for what became known as "the billion dollar house," Craig replied: "Oil companies were a dime a dozen then. How did I know the Texas Oil Company would survive?"

Two other old Lakeshore mansions are worth visiting: **Rose Hill Manor** (100 Woodworth Street; tel: 409-985-7292) and **White Haven** (2545 Lakeshore Drive; tel: 409-982-3068) – both of which are open for guided tours (Mon, Wed and Fri am; fee) – and Port Arthur's heritage is further displayed in its **Museum of the Gulf Coast** (700 Procter Street; open daily; Sun pm only; entrance fee; tel: 409-982-7000), where such celebrated locals as Janis Joplin, the Big Bopper, Harry James, Babe Didrickson Zaharias and artist Robert Rauschenberg are honored. One-hour hard-hat tours can also be made of the oil refineries (tel: 800-235-7822 for appointments).

Over the Rainbow

Rainbow Bridge, a 1½-mile (2.5-km) graceful arc over the Neches river, at a clearance height of 177 ft (56 meters), is the tallest on the coast and joins Port Arthur with the city of **Orange** ❺. Here Farmer's Mercantile on Division Street, a funky store that opened in 1928, is not only still in business but carries some of the same items as when it began.

On Green Avenue, the **Stark Museum of Art** (closed Sun and Mon; free; tel: 409-883-6661) and nearby **W.H. Stark House** (guided tours Tue–Sat; entrance fee; reservations requested; tel: 409-883-0871; www.starkmuseum.org) are eye-popping structures whose exteriors are almost as interesting as the furniture and artworks that they contain. From Orange, fascinating airboat tours can be taken (tel: 409-883-7725) of the alligator-infested swamps, salt marshes and bayous that surround the area. The rice fields and marshlands, with their moss-laden trees and tropical palms, are a refuge for hundreds of thousands of migrating waterfowl, attractive alike to the birdwatcher and, alas, the hunter.

BELOW: the late Janis Joplin grew up in East Texas.

Further north

Liberty ❻, on US-90 near the Trinity River, between Beaumont and Houston, traces its history back to the Spanish mission erected nearby and its downtown area created by the Mexican government in 1831. **Huntsville** ❼, 70 miles (113 km) north of Houston, on US-75 and I-45 – which marks the western boundary of the East Texas pioneer region – was founded in 1830 by settlers from Huntsville, Alabama. It has the state prison and Sam Houston State University, and claims added significance as the town where Sam Houston lived his later life. The site of Houston's grave is also here. **Jasper** ❽, 100 miles (160 km) to the east, where US-190 meets US-96 (which runs part of the way alongside Sabine National Forest), offers visitors another chance to view historic sites. Founded in 1824 beside the Angelina river, Jasper was the home of the **Tavern Oak**, a 250-year-old giant pine oak (connected to a tavern there in 1839 but unfortunately destroyed by a tornado in 1996). Several old historic houses, from around the middle of the 19th century, do, however, exist.

Almost in Louisiana, **San Augustine** ❾ is a town where, at one time or another, nearly every famous Texan in those early days walked the streets, including Davy Crockett who was given a feast here on the way to the Alamo. Historic places include the 1839 house of the famous Texas judge Ezekiel W. Cullen (open Mon–Sat pm; Congress and Market streets); the site of the 18th-century Mission Señora de los Dolores de los Ais; and the Old Town Well, dug to a depth of 27 ft (8 meters) by slaves in 1860 to serve travelers.

The Mission Señora de los Dolores Ais (also known as the Dolores Mission) was founded in 1716 and abandoned in 1773. Nothing remains of the historic structure but its site is marked.

Wood wealth

After the political turmoil of the early 1800s had been quelled, a new wave of boomtowns grew up in East Texas, built on another economic base: timber. **Lufkin** ❿, on US-69, southeast of San Augustine, was founded in 1882 and was the home of the South's first paper mill. It remains the center of the state's timber industry. One main attraction in this city of 38,000 people is the newly expanded **Texas Forestry Museum** (open daily; Sun pm only; 1905 Atkinson Drive; free; tel: 936-632-9535; www.treetexas.com), built in a grove of Texas pines, with large glass windows bringing the forest right inside. A moonshiner's still and a blacksmith's forge are among the exhibits. Lufkin also stages an annual Forest Festival every September.

Nacogdoches ⓫, 20 miles (32 km) further north on US-259, was originally settled by Native Americans several thousand years ago and claims to be the first incorporated town in Texas. Now a modern city of 34,000, with a solid economic base of manufacturing, agriculture, retail trade and tourism, Nacogdoches, almost midway between Houston and Texarkana, makes a fine base for exploring the rest of East Texas.

BELOW: Rainbow Bridge.

The town of Nacogdoches has one further claim to fame: it was here that Texas' first newspaper, the Gaceta de Tejas, *was published.*

Nacogdoches has numerous historic sites, of which the most interesting, just north of town, is possibly **Millard's Crossing** (6020 North Street; open daily, Sun pm only; entrance fee; tel: 936-564-6631). It comprises a dozen or more structures, including a church and schoolhouse, some dating back as far as 1820 and many stocked with original artifacts. **La Calle del Norte** (presently North Street) once linked the original Native American settlement to villages in the north, and is said to be the oldest public thoroughfare in the United States.

At Pilar and Lanana streets is the **Sterne-Hoya Home** (closed Sun; free; tel: 936-560-5426), built in 1828 by a pioneer merchant who helped found the state, and now occupied by a library. Here too, is the **Old Stone Fort Museum** (closed Mon; Sun pm only; free; tel: 936-468-2408), a 1779 Spanish trading post reconstructed on the campus of Stephen F. Austin State University. The fort marks the site of four unsuccessful rebellions, and the museum features tribal artifacts alongside memorabilia from the eras of the eight flags that have flown above the fort – Spain, Magee-Gutierrez Expedition, Long Republic, Fredonian Republic, Mexico, Republic of Texas, Confederacy and US.

El Camino Real

Nacogdoches is on one of the most historic routes in America: **El Camino Real**, blazed by the Spanish as "The King's Highway," or the Old San Antonio Road. Travelers can follow that path today by taking US-21 out of Nacogdoches in either direction. El Camino Real linked colonial Mexico with Spanish settlements in Texas and Louisiana by following Native American trails, shallow fords or rivers. Incorporated into the state highway system in 1929 as Highway 21, El Camino Real connects innumerable other historical sites. Not

BELOW: Texas State Railroad, Rusk Station.

far to the west, for example, is **Crockett** ⓬, founded in 1837 on the spot where Davy Crockett camped en route to his martyrdom at the Alamo. Historical markers note the location of Davy Crockett Memorial Park, 35 wooded acres (15 hectares) that are ideal for picnics and relaxing.

Map on page 220

Trains and Confederate guns

Rusk ⓭, at the intersection of US-84 and US-69, between Lufkin and Tyler, was founded in 1846 and is home of the **Texas State Railroad Historic Site** (trains depart 11am Sat and Sun mid-Mar–mid-Nov plus Thur and Fri in summer; fee; tel: 903-683-2561), a train track which forms the nation's longest and narrowest state park. Visitors can climb aboard for an enjoyable 50-mile (80-km) round-trip journey through the Piney Woods and across 30 bridges, one a 1,000-ft (300-meter) crossing of the Neches river.

Historic Fifth Street features old homes and what is claimed to be the nation's longest footbridge, a 547-ft (168-meter) span built in 1861, separating the business district from the old residential area. As an important Confederate Army conscription center, Rusk figured prominently in the Civil War. Look for the historical marker that denotes the Confederate Gun Factory. Two miles (3 km) west of town is the Jim Hogg State Historical Park, 178 acres (72 hectares) dedicated as the birthplace of Texas' first native-born governor (1891–95).

Henderson ⓮, on US-259 in the center of Rusk County, is another find for visitors in search of old houses, with 44 historic properties on the National Register. Founded in 1843 on land owned by the Cherokee Indians, Henderson's attractions include The Depot (514 N. High Street; closed Sun; Sat am only; entrance fee; tel: 903-657-4303), an old railroad depot restored as a museum and children's learning center.

Tyler roses.

BELOW: Sam Rayburn Library, Bonham.

Metropolitan centers

Three other metropolitan centers – Tyler, Longview and Marshall – are located well within East Texas and are the most representative of purely East Texan urban life, with their oil and timber economic foundations.

Tyler ⓯ (pop. 80,000), the largest, is located about 100 miles (160 km) east of Dallas on I-20 and is a petroleum production center. Also known as the "Rose Capital of America," the town markets more than 50 percent of the nation's rose bushes, maintaining a 14-acre (6-hectare) **Municipal Rose Garden** (420 Rose Park Drive; open daily; free; tel: 903-531-1212), containing over 30,000 bushes and more than 400 varieties. The garden is at its best from May through October.

The oil boom of 1900 at Beaumont proved a harbinger of things to come for the entire region, as wildcatters scattered throughout the Piney Woods prospecting for oil. The frenzy peaked in 1930 with the discovery of the biggest well of all, in Rusk County. This well, known as the Great East Texas Oil Field, was a discovery that held the state's economic spotlight until the fields of West Texas surfaced after World War II.

The boom town associated more than any other with the 1930 strike is **Kilgore** ⓰, just off US-259,

TIP

Auto travel remains the best way to explore the scattered East Texas cities and towns, and the Longview Visitors Bureau can suggest several routes.

25 miles (40 km) east of Tyler. It lies in the center of the field, with more than 1,000 oil-producing wells. The "world's richest acre" was the description for a downtown block of Kilgore, where 24 oil wells once produced simultaneously. The town's **East Texas Oil Museum** (US-259 and Ross Street; closed Mon; Sun pm only; entrance fee; tel: 903-983-8295) tells the story. Another attraction is the **Rangerette Showcase** (closed Sun; Sat pm only; free; tel: 903-983-8265) at Kilgore College, which pays tribute to the college's high-kicking precision dance team, formed in 1940 to provide half-time entertainment at football games.

On I-20 is **Longview** ⓱ (pop. 72,000), 10 miles (16 km) northeast of Kilgore, which enjoyed explosive growth in the oil-crazed 1930s. Thanks to a dynamic industrialization program begun after World War II, Longview considers its location – among the tall pines, near several well-stocked bass lakes – a magnet for industry as well as recreation. The town's **R.G. Le Tourneau Museum** (2100 S. Mobberly Avenue; open Mon–Fri; free; tel: 903-233-3675, ext. 314), on the university campus, displays patents and objects related to the man who became the world's foremost inventor of heavy earth-moving equipment.

Confederate base

Continuing east on I-20, next comes **Marshall** ⓲ (pop. 26,000), a once-wealthy city that supplied gunpowder and ammunition to the Confederacy, for which it became an administrative center. Originally a stagecoach stop, it achieved its prosperity after the arrival of the Texas and Pacific Railroad. A reminder of those early days is provided by the venerable **Ginocchio Hotel** (1896), which anchors the town's three-block historic district.

BELOW: French trading post.

Historic homes

When experts on East Texas gather to swap yarns, there's always debate about which town reigns as the best place to see old homes. San Augustine usually wins great praise, but **Jefferson** ⓳ (pop. 2,200) on US-59, just 58 miles (93 km) south of Texarkana, must be considered a required stop. It is a living museum of antebellum houses.

Laid out in 1842 as a river landing on Big Cypress Bayou, Jefferson boomed into early Texas' primary river port, as steamboats from New Orleans brought settlers westward. With them came the plantation culture and architecture of the Old South. But decline began when the city refused a rail depot.

Many of the city's fine old homes are open during the Annual Historical Pilgrimage on the first weekend in May. Highlights include **The Freeman Plantation** (State Route 49; tours pm daily, except Wed; entrance fee; tel: 903-665-2320), built in 1850 in Greek Revival style and embodying the grandeur of Louisiana plantation life.

Famous patrons

Jefferson's **Excelsior House Hotel** (211 W. Austin; tours daily at 1pm and 2pm; entrance fee; tel: 903-665-2513), dating from 1858, is the second-oldest hotel in Texas, a place patronized by presidents Rutherford B. Hayes and Ulysses S. Grant, as well as Irish playwright and novelist Oscar Wilde and the famous 19th-century industrialist Jay Gould. Still in operation today, it offers guests a chance to relax amid period furnishings, many of them acquired when the hotel first opened more than a century ago – and rumor has it some of the rooms are haunted.

For an easy insight into Jefferson's past, board one of the City Trolley Tours (tel: 903-665-1665). The trolleys run three times a day from Historic Jefferson Tour HQ (222 E. Austin) and take in all the town's historic buildings.

BELOW: Caddo Lake cypress trees, draped with Spanish moss.

Nearby is Jay Gould's well-preserved luxury railroad car, named the *Atalanta* (open daily; entrance fee). From **Jefferson Landing**, across the bridge from downtown Jefferson, visitors have the chance to take a 45-minute river tour along the old steamboat channel in 20-ft (6-meter) handcrafted river boats.

Twice as nice

Sign on the state border.

In the northeastern corner of the region is **Texarkana** ⓴ (pop. 33,000), perched on the Texas-Arkansas state line and thus half in each state. Texarkana is an agribusiness center for farming, livestock and timber interests in Arkansas, Louisiana and Texas. Its slogan is "Twice as Nice," a phrase to describe the city's unique status, which is best illustrated by one of its most unusual landmarks – the Post Office Building, which straddles the state line.

In addition to the town's **Museum of Regional History** (219 State Line Avenue; closed Sun and Mon; entrance fee; tel: 903-793-4831), depicting 19th-century life in the region, there is the multi-faceted **Ace of Clubs House** (420 Pine Street; closed Sun and Mon; entrance fee; tel: 903-793-4831), built over a century ago by the winner of a poker game and still containing the original furnishings.

Pioneer towns

Another notable pioneer town is **Paris** ㉑ (pop. 25,000), on US-82 near the Oklahoma border. Founded in 1839, Paris became home to a notorious list of frontiersmen, including retired outlaw Frank James (brother of Jesse James) and bandit queen Belle Starr. Here (by appointment) visitors can tour the **Maxey House State Historical Park** (812 S. Church Street; closed Mon–Thur;

BELOW: jet skiing on Lake Texoma.

Fri and Sun pm only; entrance fee; tel: 903-785-5716), an exquisite Victorian home built in 1868 by a Confederate general. A lesser-known victim of the Alamo siege in 1836, James B. Bonham, had a town named after him the following year. It can be found on US-82 in the northern part of the state. **Bonham** ㉒ (pop. 9,000) was the home of Sam Rayburn, the Texas politician who served as Speaker of the US House of Representatives for longer than anyone else. The **Sam Rayburn House Museum** (closed Mon; Sun pm only free; US-82; tel: 903-583-5558; www.friendsofsamrayburn.org), with the nearby Library, contains papers of the farmer's son from Fannin County who was Speaker from 1940 until his death in 1961, apart from two brief interludes.

The **Fannin County Museum of History** (1 Main Street; open Tues–Sat, pm only in winter; free; tel: 903-583-8042), in a restored railroad depot, is an absorbing collection of pioneer artifacts, ranging from ancient costumes to railroad tools. **Fort Inglish Park** (W. Sam Rayburn Drive; closed Mon and Sept–Apr; free; tel: 903-583-3943) displays replicas of the blockhouse and stockade built by Bailey Inglish in 1837.

When visiting any of the East Texas natural areas, don't forget your insect repellent. The mosquitoes can be ferocious!

Eisenhower country

Denison ㉓ and **Sherman** ㉔ on the Oklahoma border near Lake Texoma – an impoundment of the Red River – are rich from farming and livestock industries. While it is well known that Texas produced President Lyndon Johnson, another president also came from the Lone Star State, and Denison takes pride in honoring that favorite son, Dwight D. Eisenhower. The **Eisenhower Birthplace** (609 S. Lamar Avenue; closed Mon; Sun pm only; entrance fee; tel: 903-465-8908; www.eisenhowerbirthplace.org), a two-story frame house, has been restored to its appearance in 1890, the year Ike was born. The adjoining visitor center depicts life during the years when he was president.

BELOW: Native American at the Alabama-Coushatta Reservation.

Green preserves

Despite the development of East Texas – and the disregard of its ecological system – there have been some attempts at conservation. The four national forests offer visitors the opportunity to sample the Piney Woods in their most primitive form, while the **Alabama-Coushatta Indian Reservation** has existed since 1854. Sam Houston established it as a reward to this tribe for their courageous neutrality during the war for Texan independence.

The **Big Thicket National Preserve**, with an information station 7 miles (11 km) north of Kountze (open daily; tel: 420-246-2337; free; www.nps.gov/bith), is a dense and mysterious forest that blankets much of the southeast. It was established during the Depression, when the Federal government bought the area from hard-pressed timber companies. A botanist's and ornithologist's delight, the Big Thicket withstood challenges from the oil and timber industries for decades, until environmentalists, in 1974, finally persuaded the US government to establish the Preserve. Its 97,000 acres (39,260 hectares) attract tourists with hiking trails, seminars and guided walks conducted by Park Rangers. ❑

THE
CAND

ATHERBE FISHING
N'S DREA

THE GULF COAST

The sea border of Texas runs from Louisiana in the east to Mexico in the south. Its sweeping arc encompasses countless unspoiled beaches, several wildlife sanctuaries and two historic cities

It's been called a lot of different things – "funky," "scruffy," oddly even "Byzantine" – but one label has rarely been pinned on the Texas Gulf Coast: "chic" just does not fit. It's not the Riviera, and it isn't Rio. Even Daytona and Malibu are very distant American cousins. But, from South Padre Island north to the Bolivar Peninsula, the Gulf Coast ranks as one of Texas' most powerful magnets for travelers. It exudes history.

When the European explorers arrived, its shores were home to beachcombing Native Americans, some of them with a reputation for cannibalism. In keeping with its faded, once rather barbaric image, the coast actually sheltered early 19th-century pirates seeking refuge from the young United States Navy, which established strongholds on the Gulf. From such a heritage sprang a prosperous trading culture in the late 19th century. The inheritors of that legacy are the present-day developers who have ventured cautiously on to its shores in order to build condominiums and professional buildings. They tread lightly with good reason because, within that legacy, lies a pattern of destruction which visits with clockwork regularity.

PRECEDING PAGES: beach chairs, Padre Island.
LEFT: king mackerel catch on the Gulf Coast.
BELOW: Gulf Coast seafood restaurant.

Nature's fury

Here on the Texas coast, nature has demonstrated its powers as it has nowhere else. Galveston is the site of the most celebrated catastrophe in US history – the 1900 hurricane, which destroyed the city and killed thousands of people.

Whether or not the wind and rain are pounding from above, the Gulf of Mexico is always pulling from below, eating at the shoreline and claiming the land. Engineers have predicted the eventual reclamation of beach homes at many points during the 21st century.

The great escape

Still, developers take their risks and beach visitors continue to seek that special relationship with the sea. Between storms, and in spite of their fears, coastal Texans have created an enchanting domain. The Gulf of Mexico in summertime is as warm as bath water, and the hour's drive from the urban monster, Houston, to nearby tranquil Galveston provides a contrast that can literally be felt as well as seen.

Less cluttered by neon and glitz than most modern coastlines, Texas' Gulf shore is a welcome escape hatch for city refugees. Visitors won't find the world's best surf, but they will find isolated beaches and sleepy villages with a lifestyle that is as surprising as it is charming.

The Texas coastline runs 367 miles (590 km) in a great arc that forms the southeastern corner of the

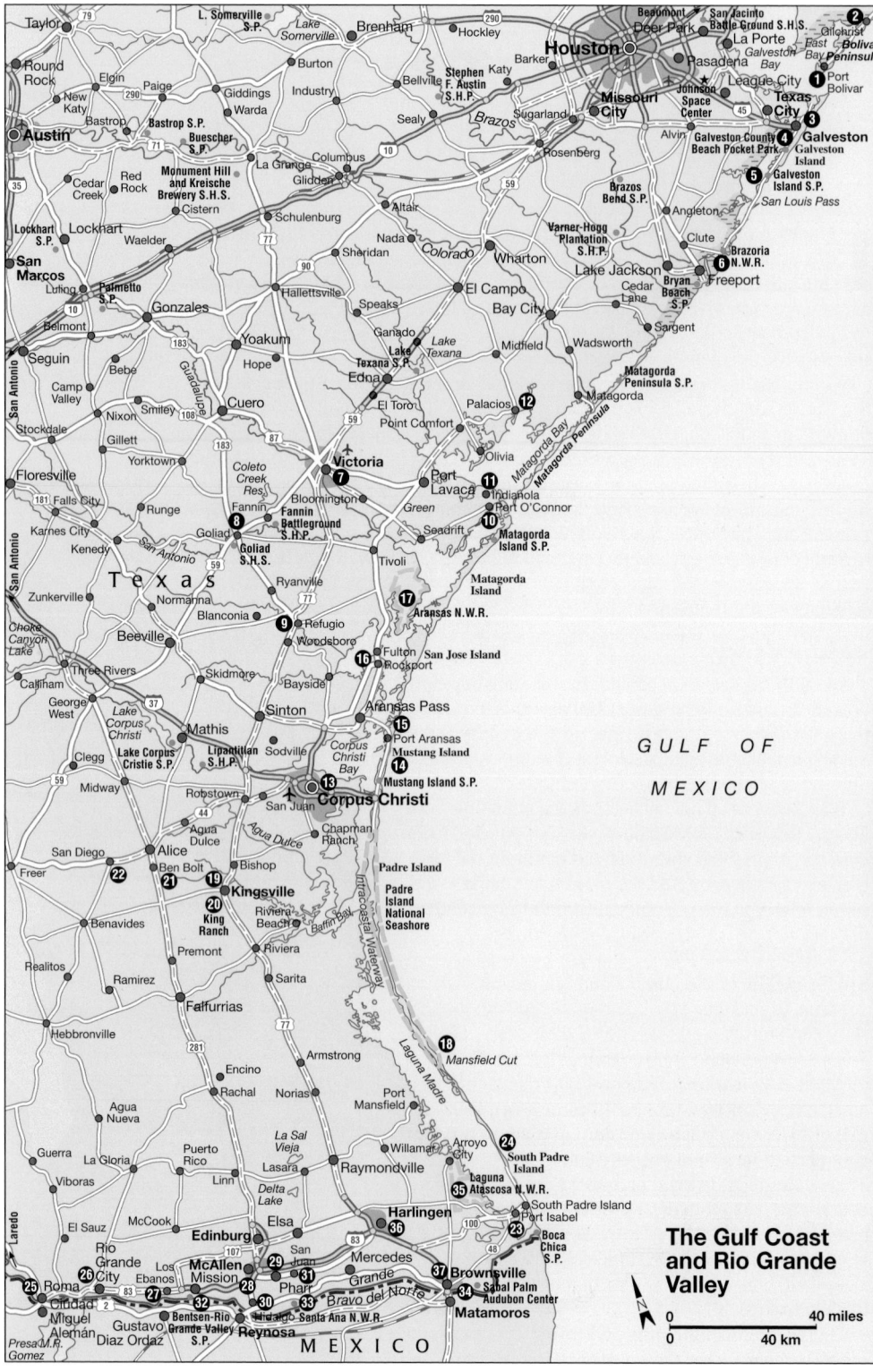
The Gulf Coast and Rio Grande Valley
GULF OF MEXICO
MEXICO
Texas
Taylor
L. Somerville S.P.
Lake Somerville
Brenham
Hockley
Houston
Beaumont
Deer Park
San Jacinto Battle Ground S.H.S.
La Porte
Galveston Bay
Pasadena
Gilchrist
East Bay
Bolivar Peninsula
Port Bolivar
League City
Texas City
Round Rock
Elgin
Paige
Giddings
Industry
Bellville
Stephen F. Austin S.H.P.
Katy
Barker
Missouri City
Johnson Space Center
Galveston County Beach Pocket Park
Galveston
Galveston Island
Galveston Island S.P.
San Louis Pass
New Katy
Bastrop
Bastrop S.P.
Buescher S.P.
Warda
Sealy
Brazos
Sugarland
Alvin
Austin
Monument Hill and Kreische Brewery S.H.S.
La Grange
Columbus
Glidden
Rosenberg
Cedar Creek
Red Rock
Cistern
Schulenburg
Altair
Brazos Bend S.P.
Angleton
Lockhart S.P.
Lockhart
Waelder
Nada
Colorado
Varner-Hogg Plantation S.H.P.
Clute
Brazoria N.W.R.
San Marcos
Luling
Palmetto S.P.
Gonzales
Hallettsville
Sheridan
Wharton
Lake Jackson
Freeport
El Campo
Bay City
Cedar Lake
Bryan Beach S.P.
Belmont
Speaks
Sargent
Seguin
Yoakum
Hope
Ganado
Lake Texana
Midfield
Wadsworth
Bebe
Lake Texana S.P.
Edna
Matagorda Peninsula S.P.
Camp Valley
Nixon
Smiley
Cuero
El Toro
Palacios
Matagorda
Stockdale
Gillett
Point Comfort
Olivia
Yorktown
Coleto Creek Res.
Victoria
Port Lavaca
Matagorda Bay
Matagorda Peninsula
Floresville
Falls City
Runge
Fannin
Bloomington
Fannin Battleground S.H.P.
Green
Indianola
Port O'Connor
Karnes City
Goliad
Goliad S.H.S.
Seadrift
Matagorda Island S.P.
Kenedy
San Antonio
Tivoli
Matagorda Island
Zunkerville
Ryanville
Normanna
Aransas N.W.R.
Blanconia
Refugio
Choke Canyon Lake
Beeville
Woodsboro
Fulton
San Jose Island
Rockport
Three Rivers
Skidmore
Bayside
Callihan
George West
Lake Corpus Christi
Sinton
Aransas Pass
Mathis
Port Aransas
Mustang Island
Clegg
Lake Corpus Cristie S.P.
Lipantitlan S.H.P.
Sodville
Corpus Christi Bay
Mustang Island S.P.
Midway
Robstown
San Juan
Corpus Christi
Agua Dulce
Chapman Ranch
San Diego
Alice
Ben Bolt
Bishop
Padre Island
Freer
Kingsville
Padre Island National Seashore
Benavides
King Ranch
Riviera Beach
Baffin Bay
Intracoastal Waterway
Premont
Riviera
Realitos
Ramirez
Sarita
Falfurrias
Hebbronville
Mansfield Cut
Laguna Madre
Encino
Armstrong
Rachal
Norias
Port Mansfield
Agua Nueva
La Sal Vieja
Willamar
Arroyo City
South Padre Island
Guerra
La Gloria
Puerto Rico
Lasara
Raymondville
Laguna Atascosa N.W.R.
Viboras
Linn
Delta Lake
Harlingen
South Padre Island
Port Isabel
El Sauz
McCook
Elsa
Boca Chica S.P.
Laredo
Edinburg
San Juan
Mercedes
Rio Grande City
McAllen
Los Ebanos
Mission
Brownsville
Sabal Palm Audubon Center
Roma
Phar
Bravo del Norte
Ciudad Miguel Alemán
Gustavo Diaz Ordaz
Bentsen-Rio Grande Valley S.P.
Hidalgo
Santa Ana N.W.R.
Reynosa
Matamoros
Presa M.R. Gomez
0 40 miles
0 40 km
N

state. The land here does not end in the abrupt cliffs and rocky shores to be found in other parts of America. In Texas, the land surrenders gradually to the water, drifting from the region of rolling hills and pine forests known as the Coastal Plains into a grassy marshland called the Coastal Prairie. The Coastal Plains includes East Texas and the Rio Grande Valley; the Coastal Prairie is, more precisely, the Texas coast.

Starting at Bolivar Peninsula, just north of Galveston, the Texas shore forms the world's longest chain of barrier islands as it slips towards Mexico: 624 miles (1,000 km) of tidewater coast, when you add the bays, lagoons, and swamps between the bayou marshland in the north and coastal brush in the south. The region includes two cities – Galveston to the north and Corpus Christi to the south.

Anyone looking for something fancy will be disappointed with Bolivar Peninsula. But it is its simplicity that many find most appealing, and it still stands as one of the best reasons to venture anywhere on the Texas Gulf Coast.

Diamond in the rough

Unspoiled South Padre Island, to the south, is generally considered the tourist's best chance for a Caribbean resort-style vacation in this state. Compared with South Padre, **Bolivar** ❶, to the far north, is a diamond in the rough. But it can be a true gem for those who appreciate a holiday uncluttered with glitz.

Extending like a long finger down the Texas Coast from Louisiana, the peninsula was named in 1815 to honor the Latin American revolutionary Simon Bolivar, during an era when the Gulf Coast and the Caribbean were aflame with anti-Spanish sentiment. A free ferry carries cars and their passengers from Galveston's east end to State Route 87 on the peninsula, and provides the only convenient access to Bolivar's beaches. But this very remoteness has guaranteed splendid isolation for Bolivar's beach-goers, who go birding (334 species), crabbing, and camping near the surf.

The **Bolivar Point Lighthouse** poses for pictures at Port Bolivar. Constructed in 1852, it was dismantled by Confederates in the "War Between the States" and rebuilt in 1872. Ramshackle beach houses can be rented, but reservations should be made in advance through one of Galveston's real estate companies.

Gilchrist ❷ is a small town about 20 miles (32 km) north on State Route 87, and its main attraction is **Rollover Pass**, a channel that slices through the center of town, serving up some of the best bankside fishing in the state. Elsewhere along the peninsula, visitors will find a montage of honky-tonk taverns, hamburger joints and convenience stores.

BELOW: the historic Strand district, Galveston.

Galveston

This island city of 65,000 residents has been described as the only part of the coast you'd want to visit on a rainy day. Visitors who head directly for the beach will miss plenty, because, in addition to the sea, recreational attractions and good shopping, **Galveston** ❸ offers a unique historical perspective.

But for that 1900 hurricane, Galveston might have been today *the* industrial heavyweight, instead of its neighbor, Houston. After a roguish beginning as a seaport haven for the pirate clan of Jean Lafitte, Galveston was one of the South's most significant cities by the end of the 19th century.

The French-born Jean Lafitte and his brother,

Juneteenth, or Emancipation Day, is celebrated in cities all over Texas, with marching bands, music (especially gospel) and dance.

Pierre, were already legendary smugglers in nearby New Orleans, when, in 1817, they founded a town called Campeachy on Galveston Island. Their fort, Maison Rouge, attracted a "navy" of over 1,000 men, who continually disrupted Spanish shipping in the Gulf of Mexico. Lafitte's pirate "den," as it has been called, was a wicked place: slaving, gaming, drunkenness and whoring abounded. He sold all the blacks of Galveston, including freed slaves, in New Orleans. To some a romantic figure, Lafitte was the last of the pirates on the Gulf – until the US Navy forced him out of the area in the early 1820s. He sailed away to Mujeres Island off Yucatan.

Galveston was then developed as a seaport during the Republic, and soon became the state's largest city. Blockaded during the Civil War, the city remained in Confederate hands, except for a few months in 1862. The Union Navy entered the harbor in October, landed on Christmas morning and was expelled on New Year's Day 1863. They were back on June 19, 1865, to take over the city and proclaim the freedom of the slaves. "Juneteenth" has been celebrated by blacks in Texas ever since.

Sulfurous harbor

Galveston continued to grow, but its population was eventually surpassed by San Antonio and Houston. Much of Texas' cotton was exported through the city – ancient cotton warehouses and grain elevators survive today – and the water of the bay is still yellow from the shipping of sulfur. A hub of commercial activity between the 1870s and 1900, Galveston had Texas' first telegraph, electric lights, brewery and medical college. Splendid mansions were erected, paid for with the profits from all the city's commerce.

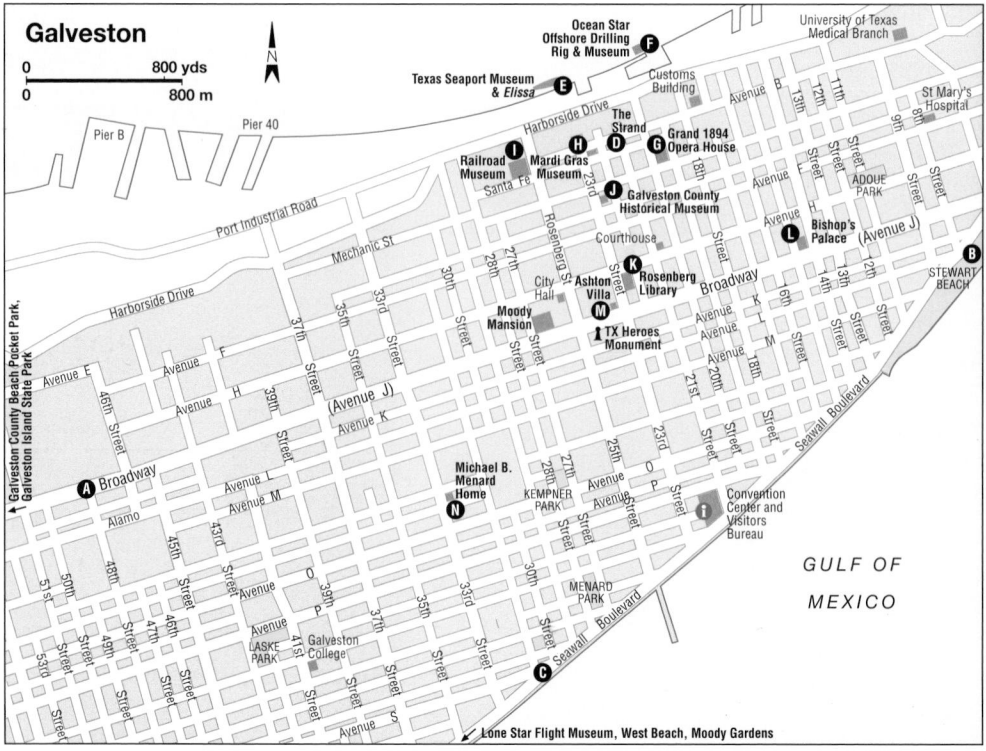

The 1900 hurricane on September 8 and 9 dimmed Galveston's glow in a matter of hours. Winds sometimes in excess of 100 mph (160 km/h) swept tides of 4–6 ft (1–2 meters) across the island to produce one of the nation's worst natural disasters. There was nothing to break the hurricane's force: Galveston's highest elevation was a mere 8 ft (2.5 meters). At one point the water rose 4 ft (just over a meter) in four seconds: 1,500 acres (600 hectares) of houses were completely destroyed. Death estimates have ranged from 5,000 to 8,000. So complete was the devastation that many wanted to abandon the place, but, stubbornly, Galveston refused to surrender. The people resurrected their demolished homes and constructed a 17-ft (5-meter) seawall, protection against future ravaging by the waters of the Gulf. The present seawall is 10 miles (16 km) long, 16 ft (5 meters) wide at its base and 5 ft (1.5 meters) wide at the top.

Meanwhile, its big rival, Houston, with more people and better rail connections, seized its opportunity and, with Federal money, began dredging a ship channel in the Buffalo Bayou to the San Jacinto river and, from there, into the Gulf. So, Houston – 50 miles (80 km) inland – became a port city while Galveston, although remaining a port, became less important and was frequently referred to as "that island city south of Houston."

Maps: Area 234 City 236

"Galveston" is an anglicized version of "Galvez," the original Spanish name for the island settlement. It was named for Bernardo de Galvez, the Spanish Governor of Louisiana.

Onto the island

Primary access to the island city is via I-45, a freeway which stretches from Dallas, through Houston, and over a bridge into Galveston. Once on the island, it becomes **Broadway** Ⓐ, Galveston's main street, which carries you through the oldest part of the city to **Stewart Beach** Ⓑ. A right turn on to 61st Street, before I-45 becomes Broadway, bypasses the central city and takes you to the island's

BELOW: Galveston shrimp fleet.

most popular beach district, **West Beach**, on the south shore. In Galveston, all other roads seem to lead eventually to **Seawall Boulevard** Ⓒ, a broad avenue along the waterline above the city's dramatic seawall, with an array of shops, restaurants, motels, bicycle rentals, arcades and other amusements lining one side, and the Gulf of Mexico pleasantly filling the horizon on the other. The tourist office is at 2027 61st Street (tel: 888-425-4753). Popular seafood restaurants on Seawall include Gaido's, founded in 1911, and the adjoining Casey's. The Flagship Hotel is built on a pier out over the Gulf. The Boulevard has several fishing piers where visitors can rent equipment and try their luck at catching redfish, trout and other Gulf game fish, depending on the season.

The Elissa *at sea.*

Buildings restored

Visitors should start with a walk in **The Strand** Ⓓ, a 12-block area that parallels Broadway between 20th and 25th streets, which was once part of the city's warehouse district. The solid, iron-fronted Victorian structures have been refurbished with more than 90 shops and restaurants. An old-style trolley (tel: 409-797-3900 for schedule) operates around here.

Some highlights in the area include Colonel Bubbie's Surplus Store, possibly the world's best army-navy surplus center, stocking more than 10,000 items from 100 different countries; La King's Confectionery, home of old-fashioned ice-cream; Hendley Market (Victorian clothing, antique postcards); and the restored square-rigged tall ship *Elissa* at the **Texas Seaport Museum** Ⓔ (Pier 21; daily 10am–5pm; entrance fee; tel: 409-763-1877). The museum also offers harbor tours with dolphin watching, a documentary of the 1900 hurricane, and a database of immigrants who debarked in Galveston between 1846 and 1948.

BELOW: fun in the sun at Galveston Pier.

On board the **Ocean Star Offshore Drilling Rig and Museum** Ⓕ (10am–5pm; Pier 21; entrance fee; tel: 409-766-7827) three decks of equipment, exhibits and interactive displays detail offshore oil and gas exploration, drilling and production. Housed in a retired jackup drilling rig, the museum offers the rare opportunity to explore the rig floor and pipe deck of a massive, sea-going structure.

Another historic structure is the spectacular **Grand 1894 Opera House** Ⓖ (Mon–Sat 9am–5pm, Sun noon–5pm; 2020 Postoffice; entrance fee; tel: 409-763-7173) where contemporary Broadway musicals are performed.

Map on page 236

The stage of the Grand 1894 Opera House has, in its time, played host to the likes of actress Sarah Bernhardt, singer Al Jolson and the Marx Brothers.

Mardi Gras

The Strand's ambiance is reminiscent of New Orleans' Bourbon Street and, like that colorful Louisiana city, Galveston makes a big thing of the Mardi Gras. The entire city turns out for the parade that marks Fat Tuesday. Beads and token coins fill the air as the Strand celebrates and rejoices. The **Mardi Gras Museum** Ⓗ is devoted to the subject (Mon–Sat 10am–8pm, Sun 10am–6pm; The Strand at 23rd Street; tel: 409-765-5930), displaying costumes and other historic memorabilia. The **Railroad Museum** Ⓘ (daily 10am–4pm; 25th Street and The Strand; entrance fee; tel: 409-765-5700), with audiovisual displays and a collection of 35 old rail cars, is situated in the wonderfully restored Santa Fe Railroad Depot on Shearn Moody Plaza. Sculptured life-like figures sit optimistically in the waiting room.

The **Galveston County Historical Museum** Ⓙ (summer Mon–Sat 10am–5pm, Sun noon–5pm; winter Mon–Sat 10am–4pm, Sun noon–4pm; 2219 Market Street; donation; tel: 409-766-2340) contains exhibits about Jean Lafitte, the 1900 hurricane and other important local events and characters.

BELOW: Galveston's colorful Strand.

More history is exhibited at the **Rosenberg Library** Ⓚ (closed Sun; 23rd and Sealy streets), opened in 1902 as the first library in the state.

Historic homes

The city is rich in old mansions and these include the pink granite **Bishop's Palace** Ⓛ (1402 Broadway; open daily; Sun pm only; entrance fee), the only building in Texas on the American Institute of Architecture's list of 100 outstanding structures. Owned since 1923 by the Galveston-Houston diocese of the Roman Catholic Church, it served as the bishop's official residence. The 148-year-old **Ashton Villa** Ⓜ (Broadway at 24th Street; summer Mon–Sat 10am–4pm, Sun noon–4pm; winter daily noon–4pm; entrance fee), with its wide wrought-iron balcony, is now a museum containing 19th-century treasures, as is the **Moody Mansion** (2618 Broadway; daily, summer Mon–Sat 10am–4pm, Sun noon–4pm, winter daily noon–4pm; entrance fee). The oldest mansion is the **Michael B. Menard Home** Ⓝ (1605 33rd Street; Fri–Sun noon–4pm; entrance fee; tel: 409-762-3933), built in 1838. Michael B. Menard was the founder of Galveston in the time of the Republic of Texas. His mansion has now been restored and houses remarkable period furnishings and other antiques.

Coastal mix

Between Galveston and Houston is the Kemah-Seabrook area, a region where visitors are certain to find a real mixture of Texas coastal dwellers, ranging from space scientists on their day off from NASA to old seadogs and fishermen swapping yarns at popular hangouts like Jimmy Walker's and Maribelle's. In the west, **Galveston County Beach Pocket Park** ❹ and **Galveston Island State**

BELOW: Corpus Christi sand armadillos.

Park ❺ provide beach access with parking, for picnics, swimming and sunbathing. Out here, just south of I-45, you will also find the **Moody Gardens** (open daily; various entrance fees; tel: 800-582-4673), Galveston's major tourist attraction. Among highlights is a 10-story glass rainforest pyramid packed with exotic flora and fauna, which thrive among waterfalls, cliffs, caverns and forests. There's also a Bat Cave, an IMAX 3-D theater, an authentic reproduction of an 1800s paddlewheel, which offers cruises along the bayou, and an aquarium. Other attractions are a discovery pyramid and an IMAX Ride film theater, developed in conjunction with NASA's Johnson Space Center. There is also a 300-room convention hotel. Not far from Moody Gardens, at Galveston International Airport, is the **Lone Star Flight Museum** (2002 Terminal Drive; daily 9am–5pm; entrance fee; tel: 409-740-7722), a magnet for fans of vintage aircraft, with more than 40 restored planes on display.

Maps: Area 234 City 236

Make a point of visiting Goliad State Park, just south of Goliad, off US-183. The huge park includes the reconstructed Mission Espiritu Santo, which was established in 1749. You can also camp, picnic and fish.

Down the coast

Just down the coast, at the point where the Brazos river empties into the Gulf, is the **Brazoria National Wildlife Refuge** ❻. It was near here that Stephen F. Austin and his colonists first landed and also where the new government of the Republic of Texas held its first session.

Between the cities of Galveston and Corpus Christi, on US-59, the **Texas Zoo** (daily 9am–5pm; Riverside Park; entrance fee) at **Victoria** ❼ features 150 species found in Texas, plus lions, tigers and Texas black bears.

Another place of interest is historic **Goliad** ❽, at the crossroads of Highways 59 and 77. Here, not far from the Fannin Battlefield, are the graves of Col. James Fannin and the 342 men who, in 1836, were massacred after sur-

BELOW: Gulf Coast beach homes on stilts.

rendering to Mexican general Santa Anna. "Remember Goliad!" became a battlecry of the Texas Revolution. At **Refugio** ❾,visitors can take haywagon rides and watch cowboys at work at the Dos Vaqueros ranch (tel: 361-543-4905).

The "Wind in the Sails" statue, on Corpus Christi's Shoreline Drive.

Seashore towns

There are a number of relatively unspoiled little seashore towns close to State Route 35, among them **Port O'Connor** ❿, a focal point for serious fishermen and duck hunters. **Indianola** ⓫, now reduced to just a few fishing families living among stone foundations at the water's edge, rivaled Galveston as the top Texas port until September 17 1875, when a hurricane literally blew the place away. Further up the coast, **Palacios** ⓬, with its ancient, family-style Luther Hotel, is worthy of note, as are Freeport and Surfside.

Corpus Christi

For fans of sparkling seaside development, **Corpus Christi** ⓭ has the flavor of a young Miami Beach. With a population of 278,000, it is the state's eighth-largest city, yet its semitropical climate and reputation as a recreation capital have created the image of tranquility. "The isles of Texas" is the tourist department's description, and those visitors who experience the offshore beaches, deep-sea fishing, catamaran trips and the sailboarding and jetskiing might well remember it that way.

Corpus Christi's 2-mile (3-km) **Seawall** Ⓐ, 14 ft (4 meters) high and 20 ft (6 meters) wide, is an attraction in itself, having been designed by the famous sculptor Gutzon Borglum, who went on to carve the presidential heads on Mount Rushmore. Steps from the seawall down to the beach provide a popular resting place, while joggers, strollers and cyclists populate the top.

RIGHT: taking a rest on a Gulf Coast beach.

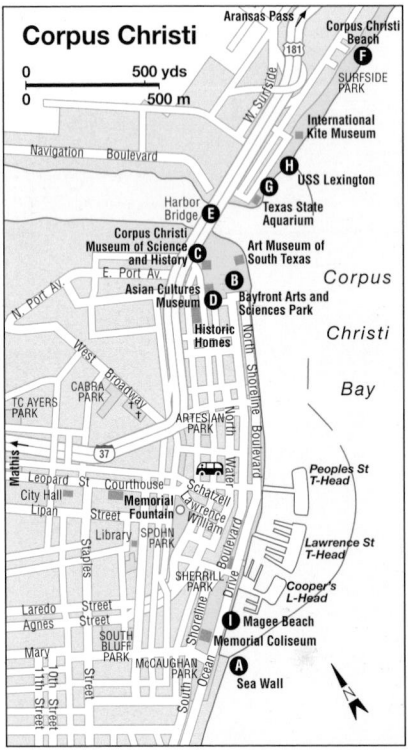

Driving in Corpus Christi requires a good map. Because it follows the curve of the bay, few of its streets run straight. The focal point for activity is the **Bayfront Arts and Sciences Park** Ⓑ, at the north end of Shoreline Drive. In addition to a convention center and auditorium, the complex contains the **Art Museum of South Texas** (1902 N. Shoreline; Tues–Sat 10am–5pm, Sun 1–5pm; entrance fee; tel: 361-825-3500), designed by Philip Johnson; the Marina; and the Harbor Playhouse – all built right beside the water. Near here is the **Corpus Christi Museum of Science and History** Ⓒ (1900 N. Chaparral; Tues–Sat 10am–5pm, Sun noon–5pm; entrance fee; tel: 361-826-4650), which includes a fascinating display of shipwreck artifacts.

Another site worth viewing is the surprising **Asian Cultures Museum** Ⓓ (1809 N. Chaparral; Tues–Sat 10am–5pm; entrance fee; tel: 361-882-2641), home of a prize collection of treasures from Japan acquired by a Corpus native, Billie Trimble Chandler, during her 17 years as a teacher there.

Maps: Area 234 City 242

The USS Lexington *was the longest-serving carrier in the US Navy. It saw action in the waters around Japan during World War II. Self-guided tours take in most areas of the ship, including the massive flight deck. There is also a new MEGA-Screen film theater.*

North Beach

Corpus Christi first came to life as a tent city and shipping point for the US Army, when the annexation of Texas sparked a war with Mexico. In the 1920s, the US government sent in the dredgers to create what became the deepest port on the coast and one that has retained its military ties, with half of the US Navy's air training bases located in the area.

Just across the 620-ft (191-meter) **Harbor Bridge** Ⓔ – at 250 ft (77 meters) above the water, the state's second highest – is **Corpus Christi Beach** Ⓕ. This area was famous for its casinos and amusement parks in the 1930s, but fell out of favor until a revival in the 1970s. Natives call it "North Beach," and it offers

BELOW: Municipal Marina, Corpus Christi.

the city's most challenging surf. Also here are the **Texas State Aquarium** Ⓖ (2710 N. Shoreline Boulevard; daily 9am–5pm; entrance fee; tel: 361-881-1200), and the WWII aircraft carrier USS ***Lexington*** Ⓗ (daily 9am–5pm; entrance fee; tel: 361-888-4873). About a mile (1.5 km) to the south is the much shorter **Magee Beach** Ⓘ, a popular attraction for families with small children, on account of its calm and shallow bay waters.

Making the most of Spring Break week on South Padre Island.

Wild horses

From the crook of Corpus Christi Bay, the city allows excellent access northeast to Mustang Island, Port Aransas and Aransas Pass, known as the "Shrimp Capital of Texas." **Mustang Island** ⓮, earning its name from the wild mustang ponies left behind by the Spaniards several hundred years ago, is a barrier between the bay and the Gulf of Mexico. It protects the city to some extent from hurricanes. Visitors will find one of the state's finest beaches located at Mustang Island State Park, and, at the northern end of the island, they'll find one of the state's best fishing ports.

A (free) 24-hour ferry runs across from where US-361 ends to **Port Aransas** ⓯, home for hundreds of shrimp boats moored in Conn Brown Harbor. Among numerous places offering accommodation is the landmark Tarpon Inn (200 E Cotter) – an old hotel once favored by President Franklin Roosevelt. Its lobby walls are covered with tarpon scales autographed by successful fishermen.

Whooping cranes

BELOW: surf shop, South Padre Island.

This whole seashore is a big draw to bird-watchers. The **Rockport-Fulton** ⓰ area attracts thousands of hummingbirds, which rest over to gain weight for

their 500-mile (800-km) flight across the Gulf of Mexico. Nearby, famous for the November migration of whooping cranes, is the **Aransas National Wildlife Refuge** ⓱ (open sunrise–sunset; entrance fee; tel: 361-286-3559). These protected birds arrive from Canada for the winter and evoke admiration in thousands of tourists with their 7-ft (2-meter) wingspans, long black legs and voracious appetites. The rescue of the whooping cranes from near extinction is a real success story: in 1941 there were only 16 known whoopers; now as many as 237 birds turn up at Aransas. They can be viewed through binoculars from an observation tower, or seen closer up on one of the frequent boat tours, many of which feature talks by professional ornithologists.

Maps: Area 234 City 242

The first 9 miles (14 km) of Padre Island have a paved roadway and another 5 miles (8 km) can be driven by car. But the 55 rugged miles (90 km) to Mansfield Cut demand four-wheeling. For beachcombers and shell collectors, however, this trip is

Padre Island

Further south, **Padre Island National Seashore**, divided from South Padre Island by **Mansfield Cut** ⓲, and preserved from developers, is the finest stretch of natural beach in America. It was named for Padre Nicolas Balli, who bought it from the Spanish Crown for 400 pesos. In 1844, the last of the Balli family moved away and three years later John Singer and his family were shipwrecked on the island. They chose to build a home and stay here. Singer became rich from his shares in his brother's sewing machine company and reputedly buried treasure on the island before leaving. It has never been found and, after a century of storms disrupting the island's landscape, it is doubtful if it ever will be.

Ranch country

Inland, the closest you can get to the coast is along US-77 through ranch country and **Kingsville** ⓳. From here, a diversion should be made westwards

BELOW: Memorial Day crowds on South Padre beach.

Map on page 234

Whooping crane at Aransas N.W.R.

along US-141 to the headquarters of the famous **King Ranch** ⓴ (Mon–Sat 9am–4pm, Sun 1–5pm; entrance fee; tel: 361-592-8055). Visitors can watch a video and then take a guided tour along a 12-mile (19-km) loop of the immense ranch known for its wealth – worldwide holdings once covered almost 11 million acres (over 4 million hectares) in seven countries. It also developed a stable of Kentucky Derby winners and its own breed of Santa Gertrudis cattle.

Nearby, on State Route 281, is **Ben Bolt** ㉑ (a tiny place with about 100 inhabitants), where a legendary Headless Horseman is buried. This phantom-like figure, who terrorized the region in the mid-1800s with a head dangling from his saddlehorn, was actually a rustler who had been killed by a Texas Ranger, his head tied to a wild mustang as a warning to others.

Northwest of Kingsville, the town of **San Diego** ㉒, on State Route 44, was an important cattle shipping center that grew to be so rowdy that a special detachment of Texas Rangers was stationed there. Their task was to deal with the bands of rustlers which infested the back country.

South to the border

Between the coast and Padre Island, the Intracoastal Waterway continues all the way down to **Port Isabel** ㉓. The Port Isabel Lighthouse (open daily; entrance fee), irresistible to photographers, was built in 1852 on a site used by General Zachary Taylor's army in the Mexican War.

The most unusual wildlife refuge around is **Sea Turtle, Inc.** (Tues–Sun 10am–4pm; entrance fee; 6617 Padre Boulevard, South Padre Island; tel: 956-761-1720), a non-profit organization that is helping restore the population of the endangered Kemp's Ridley turtle by protecting their nests and hatchlings on South Padre Island beaches. Through rehabilitation, research and education, the group is actively involved in the survival of all sea turtle species threatened by harvest of their eggs and by hunting. Baby and adult sea turtles, in rehabilitation or non-releasable, are on view in large tanks.

BELOW: Port Isabel lighthouse.
RIGHT: a peaceful South Padre day.

South Padre Island ㉔, a 34-mile (54-km) section of what is really just a 100-mile (160-km) sandbar, is nowhere more than half a mile (0.8 km) wide, yet it has become the state's premier beach resort, thanks to its windswept dunes, gorgeous beaches and balmy tropical temperatures. Discovered by Spanish explorers in 1519, it was first named *Isla Blanca* for its white sands, whose purity has been preserved despite extensive development.

Only one paved road, Padre Boulevard, running up the center of the island, carries on beyond the city limits, but it peters out after a few miles amidst sand dunes, marshes and birdlife.

Even after the island was joined to the mainland by a causeway in 1974, development barely took off, but, later, a real estate boom began when the causeway was widened and the Texas legislature passed laws forcing the insurance industry to provide coverage to coastal areas.The nearest airports are at Harlingen and the border town of Brownsville. ❑

RIO GRANDE VALLEY

Map on page 234

Drab and downbeat to some, a warm winter haven for others, the Rio Grande Valley looks set to diversify from its citrus-growing past and may well become the new Florida

Along the river, from the dusty Tex-Mex town of Roma to the sultry fishing village of Port Isabel, lies the Rio Grande Valley, a region packed with the history of border wars, steamboat navigation and nomadic Indians who have long since disappeared. There are 38 communities scattered along 110 miles (177 km) of alluvial plain, but most of the towns situated between Falcon Lake and the lower Rio Grande Valley are nothing but caution lights and an extra lane along the highway.

Roma ㉕, founded in 1765, might be considered the beginning of the Valley. Marlon Brando came to Roma in the early 1950s to film several scenes for *Viva Zapata*, a movie about the most romantic hero of the Mexican Revolution, Emiliano Zapata. (Much of the film was also shot in the sleepy (and more picturesque) village of **San Ygnacio** further up the river. The 1830 Jose Trevino house here was chosen because of its typical Mexican design.)

Roma is a border town in economic and architectural decline. There is some interesting old architecture, but the place is so dreary that one South Texas newspaperman declared sarcastically after Falcon Dam was built that a real opportunity had been passed up when Roma wasn't relocated to its middle. The 5-mile (8-km) long dam, constructed in 1953 to control irrigation, was built jointly by the US and Mexico and bears the seals of both countries at the international border line.

LEFT: a *resaca* (oxbow lake) in Rio Grande Valley. **BELOW:** Rio Grande Valley wild turkeys.

Joined by a suspension bridge across the river from Roma is **Ciudad Miguel Alemán** *(ciudad* means city), a clean, modern and uninteresting Mexican town named after a former president. Eleven miles (18 km) northwest of Ciudad Alemán is the forgettable Mexican town of **Mier**. Mier was the site of the capture, in 1842, of the renegade Republic of Texas soldiers involved in the "black bean incident." After capturing Mier, the Texans had to surrender to the Mexican army. They were marched farther into Mexico to Saltillo where 17 of the 176 were executed. A lottery determined who was to die; those who drew one of the black beans from a pot were shot by a firing squad.

Roman hills

Along this stretch of the Rio Grande there are some tenuous connections with continental culture. Until the 1830s, Roma was called Garcia's Ranch. A visiting priest convinced himself, and the locals, that the hills here were like those of Rome. It still looks like Garcia's Ranch. In **Rio Grande City** ㉖, a Catholic priest built a replica of the Grotto at Lourdes in France, while, in the same town, a nostalgic François La Borde, in 1899, commissioned a Paris architect to design the family residence. Now the **La Borde House** (601 E. Main Street), it has been restored as an inn.

Until the arrival of the railroads, the river was the Valley's principal avenue of commerce, and Rio Grande City, complete with Victorian-era buildings, was an important riverboat terminal. The buildings are still there but the river has retreated to the south, leaving the town high and dry.

Americans fleeing the bitter winters of the North are known familiarly here as "Winter Texans." But their economic contribution to the Valley is never underestimated.

The Magic Valley

The region was nicknamed the "Magic Valley" by land developers in the early 1900s to entice farmers to the fertile irrigated fields capable of producing two or three crops a year. The Magic Valley also lures about 130,000 "Winter Texans" annually. These fugitives from the mid-continental weather of Minnesota, Michigan, Canada and Ohio head south in recreational vehicles to bask in the sun and eat just-picked oranges. Years ago, it was not uncommon to see citrus orchards doubling as seasonal trailer parks, but catering to Winter Texans is now big business. Citrus growers, like other farmers, experience boom and bust years. While citrus acreage is shrinking, farm stands still sell fresh, fragrant fruit.

Rich soils

Centuries of flooding have deposited layers of rich alluvial soil along the Rio Grande's banks, helping to make Hidalgo County one of the state's richest agricultural regions, with sugar cane, cotton and vegetables – especially onions – grown the year-round. The land produces numerous varieties of fruit and vegetables and most of the aloe vera grown in the US. But a series of unprecedented cold snaps has occasionally frozen not only the winter citrus crops but many of the trees themselves. Some of the growers of the famous Texas Ruby Red grapefruit have sold out rather than replant.

BELOW LEFT: Ruby Red Grapefruits.
BELOW RIGHT: hand-drawn ferry at Los Ebanos.

The Valley's disastrous lockstep with the Mexican economy and peso has loosened in recent years. While more and more Valley companies are supplying components and logistics for the dozens of brand-name automotive, electronic and appliance manufacturers just across the border, the region's economic base has diversified. The healthcare, tourism, agriculture and service industries have expanded enough to bring unemployment levels down. The University of Texas campuses in Brownsville and Edinburg, each with more than 10,000 students, are graduating educated adults; a lack of education in older generations has meant about 25 percent of Valley residents have incomes below the poverty level.

The Rio Grande Valley now ranks among the fastest-growing regions in the nation with a construction boom seen in new houses, businesses and roads, propelled by a relatively young population and a lower than average cost of living. The overwhelming majority of the population is ethnically hispanic. Although a significant number of the people whose families have lived here for generations do not speak Spanish at all, first-generation immigrants tend to speak only Spanish. But, like the three-car, hand-drawn ferry at **Los Ebanos** ㉗ – the last of its kind, running since 1954 – some things still move at a slow pace.

Map on page 234

White prickly poppy in the Bentsen-Rio Grande Valley State Park.

Bigger and better

Many consider **McAllen** ㉘ one of the livelier places in the Valley. It is bigger (pop. 106,000), tidier and a little more upbeat than most surrounding cities. There are adequate hotels and restaurants, though these are usually full during the September white-wing dove-hunting season. The city also has large shopping centers and chain restaurants. The ancient **Oblate Mission** is where the fathers planted the region's first citrus orchards, but the Valley's vast citrus

BELOW: dancing at the Palmer Pavilion, McAllen.

For detailed advice about crossing the border into Mexico – even just for a few hours – and all the formalities involved, see *Travel Tips* at the back of this book.

industry began with the McAllen estate of John Shary. Although his estate is still privately owned, the lush orchards can be observed from the road, and, in spring, the air is heavy with the fragrance of orange and grapefruit blossoms.

East of McAllen, the little town of **Pharr** ㉙ is home to **Ye Olde Clock Museum** (929 E. Preston; Mon–Fri 1–5pm; free; tel: 956-787-1923), some of whose 2,000 exhibits are more than 200 years old. For music machines, visit **Smitty's Juke Box Museum** (116 W. State; Mon–Fri 9.30am–4pm; tel: 956-787-0131). Used clothing shops *(ropa usada)* are plentiful in Pharr and it's easy to find a bargain.

Hot spot

The Mexican border is a political hot spot. Farm workers and growers here will continue to square off across picket lines. Mexicans and Central Americans will continue to slip across the river to work in a country where the streets may not be paved with gold, but are at least paved.

The river is 8 miles (13 km) to the south and here the International Bridge connects the American "town" of **Hidalgo** ㉚ – a cluster of freight-forwarding houses – with **Reynosa**, a rapidly expanding Mexican city of 750,000. Parking is available on the American side of the bridge.

Within walking distance of the bridge is Reynosa's Plaza Hidalgo and an open shopping mall in the town's *zona rosa* ("pink zone"). In addition to housing tourist-oriented stalls, shops and restaurants, the zone features bars, discos and hotels. Most of the men in khaki uniforms are not policemen, but *cuidadores*, public parking attendants who, for a reasonable fee, will watch your car and attend to the parking meter while you roam.

BELOW: Rio Grande City from the Mexican side.

Border trouble

This muddy stretch of the Rio Grande, called the Río Bravo by Mexicans, is shallow enough that undocumented immigrants can tie their belongings around their necks and hazard an illegal entry into the US. Sometimes they hire a "mule," who will carry passengers on his back. When the river is high, inner tubes or small boats shuttle the illegal immigrants – usually young men, hoping to find work – to the American side. US Immigration and Customs Enforcement officers – *la Migra* – each year apprehend nearly half a million undocumented aliens in Texas, most of whom crossed here. What discourages illegals from crossing further north is the brutal, unforgiving desert, but, from here, Corpus Christi, San Antonio or Austin can be reached within days. And once within a large American community, Mexicans easily disappear into the largely Hispanic population.

Map on page 234

The Rio Grande is the 21st longest river in the world, traveling 1,885 miles (3,030 km) from its source in Colorado to its estuary on the Gulf of Mexico.

Miraculous medicine

East of McAllen at **San Juan** ㉛, on I-83, the reconstructed Basilica of Our Lady of San Juan houses a replica of a Mexican statue of the *Virgen de Los Lagos*. This local statue won an identity of its own in 1970 when it survived a plane crash that destroyed the original. *Curanderas*, or religious faith-healers, often invoke the Virgin to work healings and offer some competition to the more legitimate medical practitioners here. On the Mexican side of the river, Mexican doctors have established clinics that offer treatments the Food and Drug Administration refuses to approve. Even more popular are Mexican dentists and pharmacists with goods and services at a fraction of US prices. Tiny Nuevo Progreso, south of Weslaco, has over 300 dentists.

BELOW: San Ygnacio, between Laredo and Roma.

Map on page 234

Wildlife

The Rio Grande Valley is a bird-lover's paradise. Some 274 species are sighted in the **Bentsen-Rio Grande Valley State Park** ㉜. The subtropical woodland near Mission has been preserved as a wildlife habitat. Other wildlife can be observed at **Santa Ana National Wildlife Refuge** ㉝, south of Alamo, which includes over 380 bird species, plus bobcats, coyotes, ocelots and jaguarundis. Nature trails run through the preserve and a tram takes visitors on tours with a skilled guide (daily Thanksgiving–April; entrance fee.)

Green jay in the Santa Ana Wildlife Refuge.

On FM 1419, south of Brownsville, is the **Sabal Palm Audubon Center and Wildlife Sanctuary** ㉞ (daily 7am–5pm; entrance fee; tel: 956-541-8034), an attractive preserve with self-guided trails. Also open to the public is the **Laguna Atascosa National Wildlife Refuge** ㉟ (open daily; entrance fee; tel: 956-748-3607). The refuge of open water, marshes, coastal prairie, cropland and brushland is a sanctuary for deer, bobcat and migrating birds, located on the coast south of Port Mansfield. Half an hour's drive west of the refuge is **Harlingen** ㊱, noted for its original working model of the famous Iwo Jima War Memorial (320 Iwo Jima Boulevard; daily 10am–4pm; free) at Arlington National Cemetery. It depicts the raising of the flag in World War II. At **Ramsey Nature Park**, native plants have transformed a former landfill into a refuge for animals and people.

Brownsville

BELOW: Boca Chica Beach. **RIGHT:** barbecue Texas-style.

To the south, **Brownsville** ㊲, connected to the Gulf of Mexico by a 17-mile (27-km) ship canal, is the largest American city on the lower border. Here, the **Gladys Porter Zoo** (500 Ringgold Street; open daily; entrance fee; tel: 956-546-2177) is a cageless habitat allowing endangered and other species to reside on mini islands; visitors can wander along ingenious water-fringed walkways. Nearby, the museum **Costumes of the Americas** displays an extensive collection of native garb of North and South American tribes and settlers (Dean Porter Park; Tues–Sat 9am–5pm, Sun noon–4pm; entrance fee; tel: 956-547-6890).

North of Brownsville, near the intersection of FM 1847 and 511, is where an artillery duel opened the Mexican War on May 8, 1846. At the Palmito Ranch, south of the city, on May 12–13, 1865, the last battle of the American Civil War took place, although Lee had surrendered at Appomatox a month earlier. Photographs of such battles can be inspected in the **Historic Brownsville Museum** (641 E. Madison Street; Mon–Sat 10am–4pm; entrance fee; tel: 956-548-1313) in the old Southern Pacific Railroad Depot, and at **Brownsville Heritage Complex** (1305 E. Washington; Tues–Sat 10am–4pm; entrance fee; tel: 956-541-5560).

Crossing the border

Thousands of people cross every day over the border between Brownsville and Matamoros on the Mexican side. Because of the need for Mexican automobile insurance, many visitors choose to park their cars near the Brownsville Civic Center on International Boulevard, or across from the Chamber of Commerce on Elizabeth Street, both of which are close to the Gateway International Bridge. ❑

DEL RIO TO LAREDO

Map on page 260

This well-watered stretch of the Rio Grande Valley has long been a magnet for colorful characters, attracted by the ease of crossing into Mexico and the trade the border region encourages

Water has been the moving force in Del Rio's history, as in the history of all the Texas border towns. Around 1870, there was considerable development of San Felipe Springs, whose 90 million gallons (over 340 million liters) of water a day attracted farmers and ranchers, and provided agricultural and drinking water for the region. In more recent times, the damming of the Rio Grande and the Devils and Pecos rivers has created a massive lake with huge recreational potential.

Friendship Lake

Lake Amistad ❶ ("friendship" in Spanish), a reservoir with more than 1,000 miles (1,600 km) of shoreline, was created in 1969. Boat rentals and scuba diving are available here in what is reputedly the state's best lake for bass fishing and also good for underwater visibility. Hunting licenses for deer, turkey, dove, quail and the more exotic game found in this National Recreational Area are available on a daily or seasonal basis. Native American cave paintings, some dating back 8,000 years, are also found along the shores of Lake Amistad and, although many are inaccessible, others such as Panther Cave can be reached by boat if lake levels are high enough. Sadly, hundreds of caves were inundated when the Amistad Dam was built, and many of the more accessible ones have been defaced by vandals. However, some of the better paintings are now protected by the State of Texas at **Seminole Canyon State Park** ❷ (open daily; entrance fee), on the northern extension of the lake. Camping is permitted in the park. All 400 or so archeological sites on the lake shore are owned jointly by the United States and Mexico.

PRECEDING PAGES: cacti grow all over Texas.
LEFT: Rio Grande River, Big Bend National Park.
BELOW: barber shop in Del Rio.

Wine maker

Del Rio ❸ (pop. 35,000), 13 miles (21 km) south of the lake, remains free of the herds of tourists that frequent the towns of the Lower Rio Grande valley. San Felipe Springs feeds the Horseshoe Park swimming hole and has kept the Qualia family prospering at the **Val Verde Winery**, along Qualia Drive, for more than 100 years. Texas' oldest vintner offers free tours and wine-tasting every day (tel: 830-775-9714).

Del Rio's downtown area has a fine variety of 19th-century architecture. A taste of the cowboy past appears at the **George Paul Museum** (entrance fee; tel: 830-775-9595), saluting a champion bull rider from Del Rio with exhibits of rodeo gear and hosting the nation's largest bull-riding event in April.

Across the river from Del Rio is the city named after the romantic, but ultimately suicidal, Manuel Acuña (1849–73), one of Mexico's most widely read poets. In order to reach **Ciudad Acuña** (pop. 85,000), drive out

of Hudson or Las Vacas to the International Bridge. There is ample parking on the American side and most of the shops offering typical souvenirs are clustered together on Hidalgo Street near the bridge.

Actress Lily Langtry, for whom Judge Roy Bean named the town of Langtry.

Radio healing

Driving at night, you may hear – even as far away as the Canadian border – the broadcast from **XERF**, one of the last Mexican border-blaster radio stations. In the 1950s, Wolfman Jack worked at a border-blaster and introduced a generation of Americans to rock 'n' roll. Nowadays, the standard fare is medicine commercials and cassette-tape Christianity. These airwave evangelists suggest that to be saved and healed (via the US Postal Service and 200,000 watts of Christianity), just put your hand on the radio and a check in the mail.

The American Medical Association had its reservations about the authenticity of the pills and elixir marketed by one early Del Rio citizen. The proximity of the Mexican border probably made Del Rio seem a favorable business climate to Dr Johnny Brinkley of Kansas, who made a career of peddling exotic cures. In 1933, Brinkley used his own border radio station – on which he cranked the power up to 1 million watts – to sell goat-gland pills and extended virility to thousands of Americans. He became wealthy, spent some time in jail, and built **The Dr John R. Brinkley Mansion**, which still stands at 512 Qualia Drive.

The city's **Whitehead Memorial Museum** (1308 S. Main Street; Tues–Sat 9am–4.30pm, Sun 1–5pm; entrance fee; tel: 830-774-7568) houses a collection of reconstructed pioneer buildings put together by a local ranching family. Exhibits include a replica of the famous saloon and courtroom of the notorious Judge Roy Bean who, along with his son, is buried in the grounds.

LEFT: Judge Roy Bean.

Langtry

Map on page 260

Bean's original Jersey Lilly Saloon, named after Lily Langtry, the English actress whom he admired from a distance, still stands in tiny **Langtry** ❹ (pop. 30), northwest on US-90, near the Pecos river. Proclaiming himself "Law West of the Pecos," the illiterate Judge Bean doffed his bar apron in favor of a waistcoat whenever court was in session, drafting a jury from drinkers at the bar. One example of his unconventional justice came during an inquest, when $40 and a pistol were found on the corpse. Fining the corpse $40 for having a concealed weapon, Bean pocketed the money.

Strangers from the east would drop off the train to drink beer at the saloon and buy a round for the judge's pet bear, Bruno. In 1904, the year after the 78-year-old Bean died after a drunken outing, Lily Langtry made her first visit to the town, admired her portrait (which still hangs in the saloon) and was given one of Bean's six-shooters. Today, 85,000 visitors a year call in on the Judge Roy Bean Visitor Center in the tiny hamlet to watch a video about the old judge.

Further downstream is the small town of **Comstock**, before the river runs into Lake Amistad and joins the Rio Grande.

A humble storekeeper by profession, Roy Bean was created a Justice of the Peace by the Texas Rangers when the new town, which Bean named Langtry, was founded in 1880. His novel law-keeping methods have been described as "creative," but suitable for the times.

Military times

56 miles (90 km) south of Del Rio is **Eagle Pass** ❺ (pop. 27,000) and its Mexican neighbor, Piedras Negras (pop. 122,000). Other than Mexican political unrest that closed the International Bridge on several occasions in 1985, not much has happened here since **Fort Duncan** was closed for the second and last time after World War I. It had been established by the US Army in 1849, and a detachment of mixed-race Native American scouts, descended from runaway

BELOW: Judge Roy Bean's Jersey Lilly saloon in Langtry.

black slaves, served there after the Civil War. Many of the original buildings, now restored, comprise the **Fort Duncan Museum** (Bliss Street; Tues–Sun 1–5pm; entrance fee; tel: 830-758-1445), featuring military memorabilia and relics of mid-19th-century Texas.

The town of Piedras Negras (or "Black Rocks") was named for a seam of coal which had been made visible by the effect of erosion.

Military history buffs may also want to hazard a guess as to the precise spot along the Rio Grande from which Confederate General Joseph O. Shelby, on July 4, 1865, ordered his Confederate flag weighted and lowered into the river. Shelby, in the romantic tradition of the South, also tore the plume from his hat and cast it into the water.

Black rocks and nachos

Eagle Pass is the seat of Maverick County, named after early rancher and signer of the Texas Declaration of Independence Samuel Maverick *(see page 42)*. In October each year, the town organizes a nacho cook-off, attracting over 3,000 hungry visitors. Piedras Negras ("black rocks") and Eagle Pass *(paso de águila)* are regular stops for Kickapoo Indians who, under a US-Mexican agreement, are free to reside in either country. The Kickapoo sell handcrafted goods at the border, and at the **Kickapoo Lucky Eagle Casino** (7777 Lucky Eagle Drive; tel: 830-758-1936), Texas' only casino. The flashing lights and bells of slot machines vie for attention with games of Texas hold 'em poker and roulette.

Piedras Negras remains a stop-and-shop Mexican town with a few good restaurants. Indeed, the most famous building in the area is probably the **Restaurant Bar Moderno** (Allende 407 Oriente; tel: 878-782-0684), which, in its former guise of the Victory Club, claims to have invented nachos.

BELOW: prickly pear cacti.

Twin Laredos

Map on page 260

Laredo ❻ and its Mexican neighbor, Nuevo Laredo, together form a city of some 480,000, with 90 percent of the residents on the Texas side Hispanic. The cities were outposts in what was once the backwater of Spain's American colony, and retain little of what colonial charm they may once have had. Most of the culture here is commercial. Residents from each side of the border once lined for bargains on the other. Nuevo Laredo's current reputation for violence, reflecting drug gangs' heavy presence in the city, has destroyed its appeal for visitors unwilling to be targets of kidnapping or stray bullets.

Downtown Laredo caters to Mexican shoppers buying inexpensive clothing, various electrical items – often made in Asia – and some processed foods. This seedy area has been abandoned by many American shoppers, but competition for the Mexican buyer has lowered prices on portable TVs, stereos, and other electronic goods, and a variety of other appliances and clothing unavailable in Mexico. Away from the bridge, the downtown area improves. Riverdrive Mall, on Water Street, includes outlets of national chains.

San Agustín Plaza, where the Texas city began as a Spanish settlement in the 1750s, is flanked by the cathedral (built 1872), La Posada Hotel and the former Capitol of the Republic of the Rio Grande, now a museum (Tues–Sat 9am–4pm, Sun 1–4pm; entrance fee; tel: 956-727-3480). The Republic was a short-lived revolt led by disenchanted Mexican federalists who met in convention in what was still a Mexican city in 1840. Somewhere between the rapidly expanding Manifest Destiny of the United States and the rapidly receding border of Mexico, the Republic of the Rio Grande was lost. The museum's exhibits explain some of this history.

Laredo was often seen as a "no man's land," abandoned between Texas and Mexico. Only when the Rio Grande was formally recognized as the international frontier in 1848 did Laredo finally settle north of the border.

BELOW: campers at Seminole Canyon State Park.

Summer can be blisteringly hot in these parts and the ideal month to visit Laredo is February when many festivals, including the 10-day celebration of George Washington's birthday, take place.

Two blocks north, at San Bernardo and Washington streets, is Bruni Plaza, named for Antonio Mateo Bruni, an Italian immigrant who died a politician and wealthy rancher in 1931. Engraved on a plaque here is part of his philosophy: "God has given us political power to be used for the welfare of the people."

San Bernardo Street shops overflow with Mexican pottery, clothing, leatherwork, colonial-style furniture and curios mixed with the work of artisans. The TAMIU **Planetarium** (5201 University Blvd; Fri and Sat evenings; entrance fee; tel: 956-326-2463 for information on shows and times) brings the wide Texas skies into focus at sky shows and telescope nights.

The Rio Grande watershed's native plants and animals (alligators, cactus, wildflowers) tend to be prickly for protection in an arid setting like the **Lamar Bruni Vergara Environmental Science Center** at Laredo Community College (Mon–Fri 8am–5pm; tel: 956-764-5701).

About two-thirds of the US trade with Mexico crosses the border here, a volume that has only increased since the passage of the NAFTA agreements. Laredo is now the nation's largest inland port. Immigration and Customs Enforcement offices are open 24 hours daily. On the US side, customs agents collect hundreds of millions of dollars in duties each year. *Casas de cambio,* or currency exchange houses, on both sides of the bridge, usually offer a fair exchange rate for pesos and dollars, and they are convenient. Check the banks (Mexican banks are generally open weekdays 9am–1.30pm) before changing large amounts.

Across the border

Nuevo Laredo, a short walk across the old International Bridge, is something of a Texas Tijuana, with the usual plethora of tacky tourist souvenir shops. Nuevo ("new") Laredo is old, but not attractive. It is also very dangerous as drug cartels fight for power with shootouts on city streets, day and night. You may want to consider visiting other border towns rather than this one.

BELOW: ocotillo plant.

Surrounding Laredo are miles of the Texas one sees in movies. Ranches are enormous, since making a living on arid scrubland requires a "Ponderosa"-sized spread. When oil and gas were discovered, most of the region's wealth, although greatly increased, remained concentrated in the hands of a few people. Poverty is still the norm here and many of the streets of Laredo remain unpaved.

Lake Casa Blanca State Park ❼ (off Highway 59, at the eastern edge of Laredo; entrance fee) offers swimming, boating, fishing and camping (tel: 800-792-1112 for reservations). There is abundant wildlife with whitetail deer and ground squirrels. 78 miles (125 km) south of Laredo is **Falcon Lake** ❽, a jointly owned American-Mexican impoundment (State Park open daily; entrance fee; tel: 956-848-5327).

Falcon, a massive reservoir covering 87,210 acres (35,293 hectares), has an international reputation for black bass and catfish, as well as deer and dove hunting in the surrounding countryside. Downriver, the landscape gradually changes from semi-arid, scrubby hills to the lush delta of the Lower Rio Grande Valley. ❑

Tex-Mex Food

Visitors to Texas are guaranteed to encounter Mexican food – and plenty of it. But it's not exactly Mexican. What you will find is a Texan version of it called "Tex-Mex." These dishes are quite a bit hotter than California-Mex or Arizona-Mex, so keep plenty of yoghurt or rice handy.

Visitors to Texas will discover that discussing what precisely constitutes Tex-Mex is a state pastime – so don't expect to discover any definitive answers. Most Texans would probably agree that, in its most elemental form, Tex-Mex food consists of some preparation of flat cornmeal tortillas, beans, and tomatoes, onions and chili peppers, frequently chopped together in a picante (hot) sauce. They'd possibly also accept in the definition cheese and chili meat sauce, but beyond that they're likely to disagree.

Texans are more unified in their definition of what Tex-Mex isn't. Any part of the States with a Mexican heritage will have its own related version of "Mex" cooking, but the cuisine of Mexico is not Tex-Mex. Neither is New Mexico-Mex, with its refined green *tomatillo* sauces and blue cornmeal; neither is California-Mex, rich with sour cream and lavish produce. Tex-Mex food is not fancy. What little meat it includes is usually inexpensive and tough, chopped or marinated into submission. Tex-Mex food is home fare, the food of the common people. But, most importantly, it is the supreme expression of the noble chili pepper, and as such it must be as hot as the hinges of Hell's Front Door.

Where to find the best Tex-Mex is a bigger debate than what it contains. Serious devotees contend that real Tex-Mex food can't be found north of Waco (mid-state) but all Texans agree it doesn't exist outside Texas.

Most Tex-Mex is eaten as Mexican restaurant fare. The menu traditionally consists of the following: baskets of fried tortilla chips and bowls of *salsa picante*, accompanied by beer or iced tea, are offered while the order is prepared. Shortly afterwards, a hot plate of several different specialties arrives.

These might include *enchiladas* – tortillas wrapped around cheese and onions and covered with meat or a spicy tomato sauce; *tacos* – tortillas folded, fried and stuffed with ground meat, beans, cheese and the abovementioned vegetables; a guacamole salad of mashed avocados; and *fajitas* – marinated and grilled bits of steak. The meal is served with rice and beans, hot tortillas, and, of course, several more bowls of *salsa picante* to spoon over everything. Dessert may be a token scoop of sherbet, or a praline candy purchased at the cash register counter.

Tex-Mex cooking has recently absorbed some refinements – in the preparation of better cuts of meat than its beloved *cabrito* (roast kid) and *menudo* (tripe stew) for example; and the "Tex-Mex cuisine" gaining popularity in the eastern US and Europe is a considerably cooled down version of it. The more accessible it becomes, the less it resembles real Tex-Mex. To a certain extent this is necessary: every ethnic food has ingredients that appeal only to those who have been raised on them. ❑

RIGHT: colorful, spicy, authentic Tex-Mex dishes can only be truly savored in Texas itself.

RESE

EN MI PU

EL PASO

Maps: Area 278 City 270

Thanks to its Indian roots, its proximity to Mexico and its distance from other major towns, El Paso – the former haunt of Wild West outlaws – is quite unlike any other Texas city

For some 1,200 miles (1,930 km), the Rio Grande twists and turns, widens, then roars through tight places, all the while uniting Texas with the Mexican states of Chihuahua, Coahuila, Nuevo León and Tamaulipas. In Spanish it is described best, as a region, as *la frontera* – the border. La Frontera is a place apart, where you will find neither the best of Texas nor Mexico, being, in a sense, one of the few places where the First World meets the Third World. On the Mexican side, *maquiladoras* – American-owned assembly plants – enjoy proximity to the border, combined with Third World operating costs. American retail businesses sell Mexicans what their country can't or won't manufacture: TVs, stereos, medical instruments and designer jeans. They capitalize on a widely held Mexican belief: *Lo gringo es lo mejor* – American-made is best.

The differences in lifestyle and economic status are striking. Outside a Zenith assembly plant in Reynosa, a 40-year-old man scratches out an existence selling salted pumpkin seeds. *"Semillas, semillas, semillas,"* he sings to passing workers. Mostly, he is ignored. A University of Texas professor in El Paso writes poetry describing the "trenchant sadness" of the Mexico framed in the window of his office. In the lower Rio Grande Valley, a Border Patrol officer quietly delivers three Salvadoran refugees, who were apprehended an hour earlier, to a church-sponsored sanctuary house.

PRECEDING PAGES: migrant children at a shelter in El Paso. **LEFT:** Tigua Indian baking bread. **BELOW:** Eagle Dancer statue outside the Speaking Rock Casino.

The final barrier

For the Central Americans, the Rio Grande river represents the last geographical obstacle in their struggle toward a better life, here in *el Norte*. Most are only a few weeks away from a country ravaged by war and poverty. And most of them enter the US illegally. For the fortunate few who find their way to the sanctuary houses, the chances of remaining in the country usually improve. Nevertheless, many will spend their first, and last, night in *América* in one of the border detention facilities operated by the US Immigration and Customs Enforcement.

Despite the Rio Grande's length, fewer than 10 international cities straddle the river. In and around them has gathered a unique mixture of Texans and Mexicans, including a motley crew of international hucksters of low culture and high commerce. If you're looking for the cosmopolitan culture of Mexico City, or the quiet charm of San Antonio, it's unlikely that you'll find it here. But this place is worth a closer look: *la frontera*, if nothing else, is unique.

Much of what this border is about is people queueing up on one side to cross over for something on the other. Border regulars start lining up before dawn:

Virgin Mary icon at Socorro Mission.

Mexican agricultural laborers wait for the contractor's bus to take them to their day's work. By seven it's too late; they've missed their ride. By 11, the lines are on the other side. The American day trippers are here – stereotypical tourists, out for an afternoon in the market, and dinner. Almost all will be home before dark, with a bottle of José Cuervo tequila, crepe flowers and something for the kids. And so it goes. Dollars to pesos, pesos to dollars. You can usually spend both on either side. Money is the motor that moves this place.

Cash flow

Much of the recent history of this border can be read in the rate of exchange of two currencies. For some 30 years, the peso was tied to the dollar at an exchange rate of 12.5 to one. Most border towns seemed to be slouching toward prosperity. But with the first devaluation in 1976, and then another devaluation in the early 1990s, the value of the peso fell precipitously and the economic climate on both sides of the river has been, at best, cloudy.

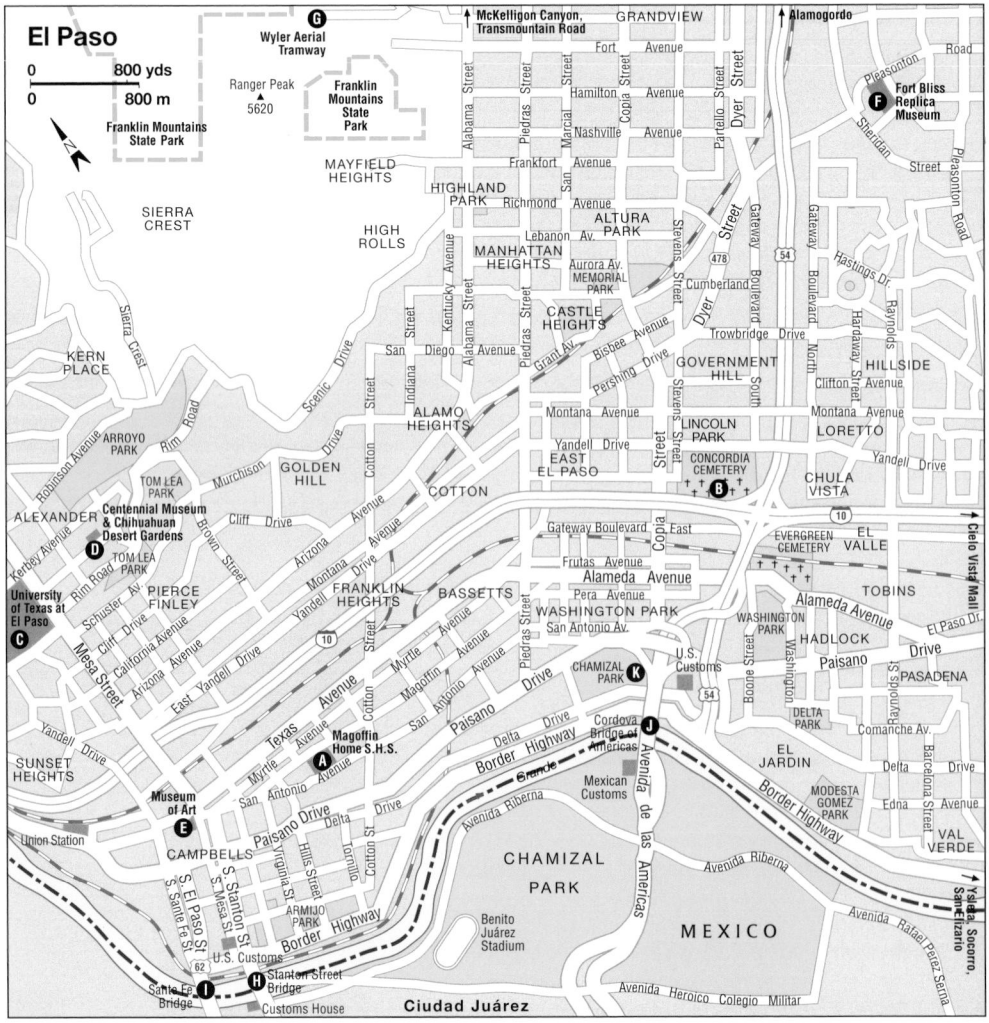
El Paso
0 800 yds
0 800 m
Wyler Aerial Tramway
Ranger Peak 5620
Franklin Mountains State Park
Franklin Mountains State Park
McKelligon Canyon, Transmountain Road
GRANDVIEW
Alamogordo
Fort Bliss Replica Museum
MAYFIELD HEIGHTS
SIERRA CREST
HIGH ROLLS
HIGHLAND PARK
ALTURA PARK
MANHATTAN HEIGHTS
MEMORIAL PARK
CASTLE HEIGHTS
GOVERNMENT HILL
HILLSIDE
KERN PLACE
ALAMO HEIGHTS
LINCOLN PARK
LORETTO
EAST EL PASO
CONCORDIA CEMETERY
CHULA VISTA
GOLDEN HILL
COTTON
ARROYO PARK
TOM LEA PARK
ALEXANDER
Centennial Museum & Chihuahuan Desert Gardens
University of Texas at El Paso
PIERCE FINLEY
FRANKLIN HEIGHTS
BASSETTS
WASHINGTON PARK
EVERGREEN CEMETERY
EL VALLE
TOBINS
HADLOCK
PASADENA
CHAMIZAL PARK
U.S. Customs
DELTA PARK
EL JARDIN
MODESTA GOMEZ PARK
VAL VERDE
Cordova Bridge of the Americas
Mexican Customs
Magoffin Home S.H.S.
Museum of Art
SUNSET HEIGHTS
CAMPBELLS
Union Station
ARMIJO PARK
Benito Juárez Stadium
CHAMIZAL PARK
MEXICO
Ciudad Juárez
Stanton Street Bridge
Santa Fe Bridge
Customs House
Cielo Vista Mall
Ysleta, Socorro, Sanfizario
Avenida de las Americas
Avenida Riberna
Avenida Rafael Pérez Serna
Avenida Heroico Colegio Militar
Border Highway
Paisano Drive
Alameda Avenue
Mesa Street
Texas Avenue
Yandell Drive
Montana Avenue
Gateway Boulevard East
Frutas Avenue
Pera Avenue
San Antonio Av.
Cumberland
Trowbridge Drive
Pershing Drive
Bisbee Avenue
Grant Av.
Lebanon Av.
Aurora Av.
Fort Avenue
Hamilton Avenue
Nashville Avenue
Frankfort Avenue
Richmond Avenue
San Diego Avenue
Cotton Street
Magoffin Avenue
Myrtle Avenue
Delta Drive
Edna Avenue
Comanche Av.
Barcelona Street
Hastings Dr.
Pleasonton Road
Sheridan Street
Clifton Avenue
Hardaway Street
Raynolds Street
Boone Street
Washington
Copia
Dyer Street
Stevens Street
Piedras Street
Kentucky Avenue
Alabama Street
Indiana Street
Scenic Drive
Sierra Crest
Rim Road
Robinson Avenue
Murchison
Cliff Drive
Brown Street
Arizona Avenue
California Avenue
Schuster Av.
Kenley Avenue
Hills Street
Virginia St.
Tornillo
S. Stanton St.
S. El Paso St.
S. Santa Fe St.
S. Mesa St.
Gateway Boulevard
Boulevard
Gateway
Sheridan
Pleasonton
Road
Street
Dyer
Copia
Piedras
Marcial
San
Partello
Alabama
Cotton
Magoffin
San Antonio
Paisano
Delta
Texas
Myrtle
Yandell
Montana
Arizona
Mesa
Cliff
California
Schuster
Rim Road
Robinson
Murchison
Brown
Kenley
Sierra Crest
Scenic
Indiana
San Diego
Grant
Bisbee
Pershing
Trowbridge
Cumberland
Lebanon
Fort
Hamilton
Nashville
Frankfort
Richmond
Frutas
Pera
Gateway East
Montana
Yandell
Delta
Edna
Comanche
Hastings
Clifton
Hardaway
Raynolds
Pleasonton
Sheridan
Boone
Washington
Copia
Dyer
Stevens
Piedras
Kentucky
Alabama
Indiana
Cotton
Magoffin
Myrtle
Hills
Virginia
Tornillo
Cotton
S. Stanton
S. El Paso
S. Santa Fe
S. Mesa
Avenida Riberna
Avenida Rafael Pérez Serna
Avenida Heroico Colegio Militar
Avenida de las Americas
Rio Grande

Part of what the diminished peso means is longer lines on both sides. Mexican workers, with or without papers, find the lure of the dollar irresistible. And why shouldn't they? The federally fixed *daily* wage on the Mexican side is usually about the same as the *hourly* rate on the American side. For the American tourist, the lure is undervalued Mexican goods and accommodations.

Consider **El Paso** ❶. To get there from most Texas cities requires driving from dawn to sundown. Politicians and cartographers claim that El Paso is part of Texas. Most Texans know better. About halfway between Houston and San Diego, California, El Paso's heart belongs to New Mexico.

Maps: Area 278 City 270

The pictographs at Hueco Tanks are sacred to the Tigua Indians. One of the most revered sites is Speaking Rock – hence the name of the tribe's gambling center at Ysleta.

Indian foundations

Sprawling across the Valley of El Paso del Norte, **El Paso-Juárez** is an international city of 2 million people, regarded by some as the most diverse city on the border, with its mix of three cultures. The Tigua (or Tiwa) Indians were here first, followed by Norteño Mexicans and Southwestern Americans. Related to the Pueblo Indians of New Mexico, the Tiguas moved to the Spanish mission of San Antonio (later San Augustín) de la Isleta del Sur in the 1680s, when the Pueblos went to war with the Spanish. They claim to be the oldest continuously occupied Native American community in the country.

Today, the Tiguas still reside on the reservation at **Ysleta** ❷ (an archaic Spanish spelling of "little island"), the oldest community in Texas (1681). This is a large agricultural community, and there is a tourist-oriented reservation – fine breads but lethally hot chili. The Tiguas operate the 850-seat Speaking Rock Casino (tel: 915-860-7777), just behind the mission.

There are a few other Native American communities around the city but the major legacy of early Native Americans can be found in **Hueco Tanks State Historic Site** ❸ (open daily; entrance fee; tel: 915-857-1135), 32 miles (51 km) to the northeast, with its thousands of colorful and engaging pictographs of human, animal and mythological figures.

BELOW: Tigua Indians.

Early missions

The mission at Ysleta is still in use, as is the Socorro Mission in **Socorro** ❹ (tel: 915-851-1682), which was built in the same decade, the 1680s, and is the oldest continuously active parish in the US. Across the border in Juárez, the even older (1668) Guadalupe Mission is famous for the legend that its shadows point to the Lost Padre Mine – in the nearby Franklin Mountains, a 24,000-acre (9,700-hectare) state park within city limits – where Spanish gold is said to be hidden. The famous El Camino Real, once a royal highway but today a quiet farm road, connects the Ysleta and Socorro missions with the San Elizario Presidio Church in **San Elizario** ❺, built in 1789 in a mixture of Spanish colonial and native architectural styles, as a fortified base for the army and reconstructed in 1877.

Ever since the Spanish explorer Juan de Oñate laid claim to El Paso del Rio Grande del Norte – a self-explanatory name – this city has been Hispanic, as are most of its residents. Far removed from the

John Wesley Hardin is buried in the "Boot Hill" section of Concordia Cemetery near the west entrance to the walled Chinese section.

events of the Texas Revolution, El Paso for a long time shared a common religion, language and history with Juárez, becoming a part of Texas a full five years after Texas itself became a state.

There are few historic buildings in the city, the main one being the **Magoffin Home State Historic Site** Ⓐ (1120 Magoffin Avenue; daily 9am–4pm; entrance fee; tel: 915-533-5147), an 1875 adobe mansion containing many of the original family furnishings and paintings, and walls 2½-ft (76-cm) thick.

El Paso, whose 800,000 population makes it Texas' fourth-largest city, nevertheless retains something of the ambiance of the slap-leather town that it was in 1896, when gunman John Wesley Hardin was shot dead in the Acme Saloon. Hardin had been pardoned, reformed, and was practising law in El Paso when a local constable ended his life. Along with other notorious gunslingers, he is buried in **Concordia Cemetery** Ⓑ, east of downtown. Years after his death, the city remained a convenient place for outlaws to cross the river.

El Paso also has a small Chinese community, descendants of the "Chinamen" who laid the tracks for the railroad that reached here in 1881. It grew with Mexican revolutionary Pancho Villa's 1910 attacks on the Chinese living in the neighboring Mexican states of Chihuahua and Coahuila.

Tibetan revival

An unrelated Oriental feature is the Tibetan architecture on the **University of Texas at El Paso** Ⓒ (UTEP) campus. Katherine Worrell, the wife of the Dean when UTEP was known as the Texas State School of Mines and Metallurgy, lifted the design from *National Geographic* after a 1916 fire destroyed almost half of the campus. The three oldest buildings are pure "Bhutanese eclectic,"

BELOW: the historic Socorro Mission in El Paso.

copied from a Tibetan monastery and fortress at Grag-Gye-Jong, in the Himalayas. Most later buildings are variations on this style. Also on the campus is the **Centennial Museum and Chihuahuan Desert Gardens** Ⓓ (Tues–Sat 10am–4.30pm; free; tel: 915-747-5565), where displays include ancient pottery, dinosaur bones and relics from the Ice Age.

Texas-El Paso, in the foothills of the Franklin Mountains, is a large state university that began life in 1914. Its stadium hosts college football on weekends during the season and is the site of the **Sun Bowl**, an annual football classic, second only in age to Pasadena's Rose Bowl. The game is usually played in late December, but the weather is invariably fine: El Paso has more sunny days than almost every other city in the country. Occasional music events are also staged at the stadium. North of UTEP, **McKelligon Canyon**, popular with hikers, is the site of the summer-long outdoor dance extravaganza *¡Viva El Paso!* (for information tel: 915-534-0062) in a 1,500-seat amphitheater.

A unique feature of El Paso is "The Star on the Mountain" – a 460 by 280-ft (140 by 85-meter) star erected by the local electrical utility in 1940. Illuminated by 459 white light bulbs, it can be dedicated by anybody to a friend or relative by the night, week or month. The El Paso Times publishes the dedications daily, and sponsors get a star-shaped pin and certificate.

Downtown

San Jacinto Plaza marks the original city square and is the starting point for bus routes. Around here is what remains of the El Paso that has been documented, along with downtown Juárez, by Elroy Bode, the city's master of the *bosquejo*, or literary sketch. Until the 1960s, alligators were kept in the plaza.

Maps: Area 278 City 270

If you can't acquire tickets for the Sun Bowl, pack your binoculars and drag a blanket up the side of the mountain along with the locals and students.

BELOW: El Paso from the hills.

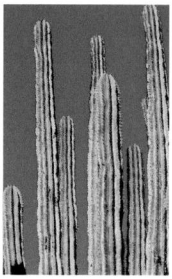

Trans-Pecos cactus.

The El Paso Chamber of Commerce on Civic Center Plaza publishes a free guidebook that includes walking and driving tours, and focuses on points of interest and border crossings. Also on the plaza is the visitors' bureau. Nearby is the **Museum of Art** Ⓔ (Tues–Sat 9am–5pm, Sun noon–5pm; free; tel: 915-532-1707), which, in addition to its European collection and contemporary American works, possesses an unusually impressive collection of Mexican Colonial art. Also interesting, northeast of the city, off US-54, are **Fort Bliss Replica Museum** Ⓕ (open daily; free; tel: 915-568-4518), where history buffs can wander through the adobe pre-Civil War army outpost. It is a re-creation of what a frontier fort of the late 1800s would have looked like. The **Wilderness Park Museum** (4301 Transmountain Road; Tues–Sun 9am–5pm; entrance fee; tel: 915-755-4332), highlights lifestyles of the local Native Americans, and the **Border Patrol Museum** (4315 Transmountain Road; Tues–Sat 9am–5pm; free), chronicles the heritage of the Border Patrol force since its inception in 1924.

All of El Paso can be seen from the **Wyler Aerial Tramway** Ⓖ to Ranger Peak (5,632 ft/1,716 meters), with views of Mexico and New Mexico (Thur–Mon; fee; tel: 915-566-6622). Northwest of the city, scenic drives across the Franklin Mountains, and especially along **Transmountain Road** (exit off I-10 West), provide spectacular views.

Across the border

Back in 1911, El Pasoans were able to gather on the flat roofs of their houses for "battle teas" and watch the Mexican Revolution unfold in **Ciudad Juárez** across the Rio Grande. For a while, Pancho Villa took refuge north of the

BELOW: cars waiting in Ciudad Juárez to go through US Immigration and Customs at El Paso.

border, acquiring a taste for ice cream and learning to ride a motorcycle here.

Political geography, as well as climate, shaped the character of this Mexican city. It was named for Benito Juárez, who fled here in the 1860s when Napoleon III made the Austrian Archduke Maximilian the Emperor of Mexico. Juárez, a Zapotecan Indian, fought as President to make Mexico a secular state.

Maps: Area 278 City 270

Mexican bargains

Like most border towns, Juárez offers something for almost everyone. The **Museo de Arte e Historia**, on Avenida Lincoln, exhibits Mexican art by period, from pre-Hispanic to the present. The building's design is modern, unique and certainly worth a look. The museum is situated in a tourist-oriented commercial center that includes the government-sponsored FONART artisans' market. This is not as fecund as the *mercado central*, and there is no haggling with vendors, but it is interesting nonetheless. Along Lincoln, between FONART and the intersection of Avenida de las Americas, are a number of artisans' and curio shops, providing a good walking tour for shoppers.

Benito Juárez.

Shopping is a popular pastime on both sides of the border. In El Paso, the fly-and-buy tourist will find the boutiques of La Placita conveniently located near the airport, and, at I-10 and Hawkins is the Cielo Vista Mall.

Around El Paso, great bargains can be found at factory outlets for cowboy boots and Western wear. On the other side of the river, in the central *mercado*, Avenida 16 de Septiembre, you'll discover a variety of regionally manufactured goods – generally leather and textiles – and local produce.

Pedestrians can enter Mexico over the downtown **Stanton Street Bridge** Ⓗ, which is the closest approach to the Mexican Tourist Center, and walk back across the river by the **Santa Fe Bridge** Ⓘ. Most automobile traffic crosses via the **Cordova Bridge of Americas** Ⓙ, off I-10, the largest bridge – and best avoided at rush hours. Close to the bridge terminals, on both sides, are parks named **Chamizal** Ⓚ, which memorialize the victims of the border war of a century ago and mark its peaceful settlement. Here the **Chamizal Memorial** (800 South San Marcial; open daily; free; tel: 915-532-7273) records how the border has been surveyed over the centuries. Park entertainments – which take place in an art gallery, an indoor theater and an al fresco amphitheater – vary from displays of local artworks and musical performances to films and temporary exhibitions. A fourth bridge, the **Zaragosa Bridge**, can be found on the far eastern side of El Paso.

BELOW: US Border Patrol officer guarding the frontier.

Much of Juárez can be seen on foot and most cab drivers speak English (but you should agree on a price before closing the door). Spanish and English are spoken in both towns.

The atmosphere in Juárez is a little more *picante* – spicy – than in El Paso. There are lots of good and bad bars, and equally good and bad restaurants. Women are discouraged from visiting – and in some cases turned away from – *cantinas*, the traditional "men's bars." In fact, several working-class *cantinas* in downtown Juárez are best avoided by all tourists: size things up before you decide to hang around. ❑

THE TRANS-PECOS

Map on page 278

This arid region is as tough as it gets, a land dominated by unforgiving desert and a lack of drinkable water, but a land rich in minerals and natural beauty, with the highest peaks in the state

West *of the Pecos* was the title of Zane Grey's classic novel, which described an area as "desolate, gray and lonely, an utter solitude uninhabited even by beasts of the hills or fowls of the air." The Spanish conquistadors who discovered it in the 16th century named the region *el despoblado*, the uninhabited place, and 300 years later a pioneer cattleman, Charles Goodnight, cursed it as "the graveyard of the cowman's hopes." General Sheridan summed up his impressions by saying that, if he owned Texas, he would "rent it out and live in hell."

The Pecos river

Beginning as a clear stream in the Sangre del Cristo mountains north of Santa Fe, the Pecos flows 900 miles (1,440 km) southwards to the Rio Grande, entering "a flat, hellish desert of mesquite and greasewood" even before it reaches Texas. "Buzzards soar above the flat, torrid land," wrote Bryan Wooley in the *Dallas Morning News* about the Pecos region, "Dust devils dance across the plain like small brown tornadoes. Oil well pump jacks dot the landscape, many of them leaking. Quicksand forms below the river's banks and its water turns too salty for man or beast to drink." It was a major hazard to all who had to cross it, from the Indian fighters marching to their West Texas forts to the early 1850s immigrants on their way to search for gold in California.

The mythical Pecos Bill, legendarily reared by coyotes and who fed his horse barbed wire, stems from this region of tall tales and great accomplishments. Such an accomplishment was featured in Larry McMurtry's *Lonesome Dove*, which was inspired by the way that Goodnight and Oliver Loving expanded the range of the longhorn hundreds of miles north, driving a quarter of a million cattle across the Pecos. In that era – the 1860s – the river was 50–100 ft (15–30 meters) wide, spreading to a mile (1.5 km) after floods and leaving deadly lakes of poisonous alkaline water behind when the floods receded.

Spanish gold is said to be buried in the desert, though it would take unimaginable endurance to search for it. In the 1930s, Hollywood struck a rich vein of its own with a raft of titles such as *The Pecos Kid*, *The Stranger from Pecos*, *King of the Pecos* (starring John Wayne) and *Robin Hood of the Pecos* (Roy Rogers). "The Pecos river holds a fascination for people," Paul Patterson, a 90-year-old cowboy who has lived along the river most of his life, told the *Dallas Morning News*, "unless they have to stop and camp and drink the water." A local joke maintains that when a coyote drinks the water he immediately licks his behind to get the bad taste out of his mouth.

LEFT: McDonald Observatory.
BELOW: Sul Ross State University, Alpine.

The fossil clock

Perhaps nowhere else in the United States can the history of the earth be read so clearly as in dry Far West Texas, where vegetation has not scrawled its graffiti of decay. Nature's first attempts at complex creatures can still be seen in the 600-million-year-old remains of algal colonies in pre-Cambrian limestone, 2½ miles (4 km) north of Allamoore, which is 10 miles (16 km) northwest of **Van Horn** ❻ (pop. 3,000). Van Horn is an historic crossroads of the old Bankhead Highway and the Old Spanish Trail, 150 miles (240 km) southeast of El Paso. US-90 and I-10 cross here today. Petroglyph tours are conducted from the town, most of whose income comes from tourism.

Heading west, I-10 crosses the foothills of the Sierra Diablo Mountains before passing through **Sierra Blanca** ❼, with dramatic views of 6,950-ft (2,120-meter) Sierra Blanca mountain and "forests" of Spanish dagger yucca plants. This is where Chinese railroad workers from the west met Irish laborers from the east to complete the second transcontinental railroad.

View from Presidio County Courthouse, Marfa.

Marfa

Beginning life in 1883 as a water stop and freight headquarters for the Galveston, Harrisburg and San Antonio Railway, **Marfa** ❽ (pop. 2,100), 75 miles (120 km) south of Van Horn, was named for a character in Feodor Dostoevski's *The Brothers Karamazov*. The book was being read at the time by the wife of the chief railroad engineer. By 1885, when the impressive courthouse was built, poker bets in the saloons were being made with town lots. At 4,688 ft (1,428 meters), in a semi-arid region, Marfa boasts a superb climate and, in summer, is one of the coolest places in Texas. It has the highest golf course in the state

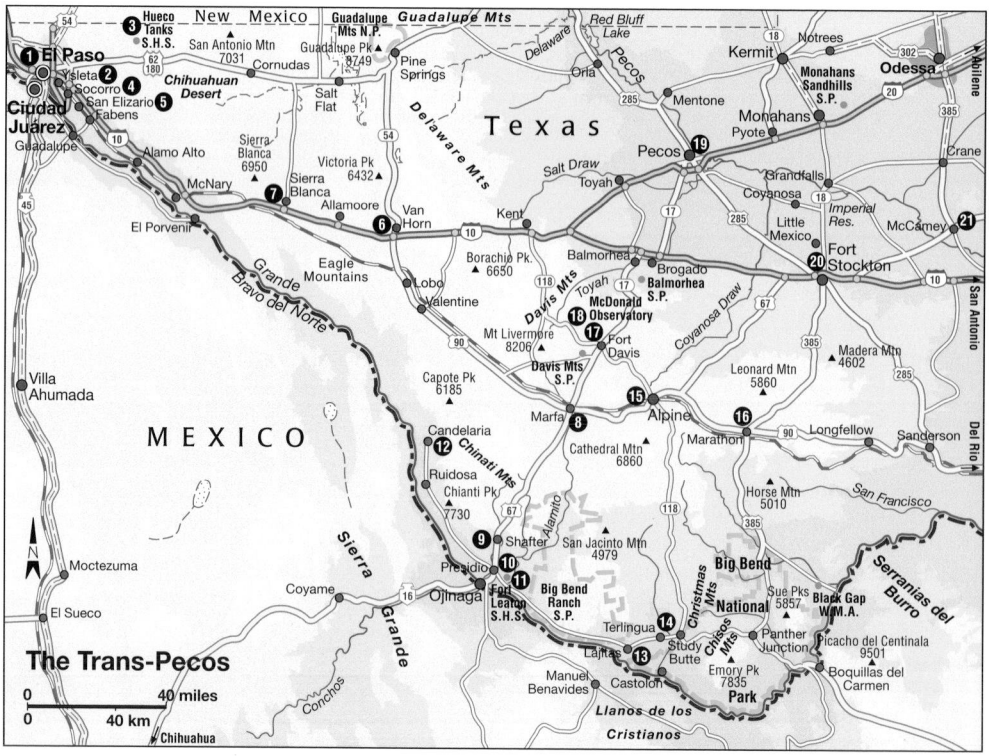

and holds the championships for sailplane soaring. Mike's Place on W. San Antonio advertises "Seven days without a Mike's Burger makes one weak." Among movies shot in the town are *Giant* (1956), starring Rock Hudson, Elizabeth Taylor and James Dean, and *The Andromeda Strain* (1971). A major tourist attraction are the mysterious lights *(see page 287)* that, for more than a century, have been observed to the southwest in the Chinati Mountains. Here, fluorite is found in the igneous rocks of **Chinati Peak**. Its phosphorescent glow and its fluorescence in ultra-violet light make it particularly worth looking for.

Map on page 278

James Dean, star of Giant, *which was filmed at Marfa.*

Fort Russell

Spain had practically abandoned Far West Texas by the time it became a part of independent Mexico in 1821. As the Anglo frontier moved westward, the fierce mounted Comanche war parties began to prey on wagon trains and Mexican and Anglo settlements along the Comanche War Trail, especially during the late summer and early fall harvest season. To counter these depredations, a line of cavalry forts was established soon after the Republic of Texas joined the United States in 1846. Near Marfa, **Fort Russell**, the army's last horse-mounted cavalry post, has now been transformed into the Chinati Foundation, a monumental space for the permanent installation of modern sculpture (tours Wed–Sat 10am and 2pm; entrance fee; tel: 432-729-4362).

The New York sculptor Don Judd fathered the $4 million project, with Houston oil heiress Philippa de Menil Pelizzi Friedrich as reluctant mother. Judd needed isolation for himself and open spaces for his work, both of which Marfa offers in abundance. His variously permutated groups of large rectangular concrete structures are rhythmically arranged in an endless progression toward the

BELOW: desert art installation near Valentine.

far horizon; some 100 aluminum pieces are housed in a glass-walled gun shed. There are also works by other prominent contemporary artists on display in the fort, such as the crushed auto-body sculptures of John Chamberlain and the fluorescent sculptures of Dan Flavin.

The Big Bend Ranch State Natural Area should not be confused with Big Bend National Park, although it is equally stunning in many ways. The land was acquired by Texas Parks and Wildlife Department in 1988.

Down to the border

From Marfa, US-67 heads southwest through the mountains to **Shafter** ❾, a ghost town in the Chinati Mountains, where millions of dollars of silver were mined and where stories persist about treasure buried in caves. Further south, on the banks of the Rio Grande, is **Presidio** ❿ (pop. 4,100), described in the WPA guidebook to Texas in 1940 as "an old town of sunbaked adobe houses, squatting like an ancient *hombre* in the shade of giant cottonwoods." The town, which was founded by Franciscan missionaries in 1683, hosts an annual onion festival (May). **Fort Leaton State Historic Site** ⓫ (daily 8am–4.30pm; entrance fee; tel: 432-229-3416), an interesting example of native adobe construction, southeast of town, was not a military outpost but a trading post operated in the mid-19th century by a certain Ben Leaton. Leaton had been among the first "Anglo" settlers to arrive in Presidio. In their fortified trading post, he and his wife outfitted and accommodated travelers who were somehow drawn to this backwater of civilization. The Texas Rangers had a base here when Pancho Villa was rampaging south of the border, but the post was abandoned in 1926. Most of the old outpost has now been restored.

Across the river from Presidio is **Ojinaga** ("o-hee-NAH-ga"). Since Presidio gets few visitors, Ojinaga lacks the touristy feel of most border towns. There are a few good restaurants, and at least one good hotel.

BELOW RIGHT: Terlingua ghost town and cemetery.

THE LAW WEST OF THE PECOS – RULES FOR SURVIVAL

The Trans Pecos region is a tough country. It has bred the toughest of men who have had to fight for everything they have gained. The region has not traditionally taken kindly to strangers. Since, it is claimed, there is still damned little "law west of the Pecos," the celebrated Judge Roy Bean's legacy notwithstanding, here in writing is the unwritten code of conduct for these parts:

1. Never go on a man's land without his permission.
2. Don't ask a man how much land he has.
3. Never step over a man sleeping on the floor.
4. Don't mess with a man's hat.
5. Never throw a hat on a bed.
6. Never rope another man's cow that wanders onto your land.
7. Never take a man's last chaw of tobacco.

Adherence to these rules allows a man to leave Texas with as many enemies as he came with.

The highest waterfall in Texas is located on a private ranch near the tiny settlement of **Candelaria** ⓬, northwest of Presidio. Capote Falls crashes 175 ft (54 meters) on to the rocks below. Inquire locally about making a visit.

El Camino del Rio (Farm Road 170) follows the Rio Grande southeast from Presidio down to the tiny village of **Lajitas** ⓭, a spectacular drive with sharp curves, steep grades and occasional wandering livestock. The village owes its origins to the 1915 US Army base established to protect settlers against Pancho Villa's border raids, and is a useful base from which to explore the area. The Cavalry Post, one of three motels in town, is built on the site of the trading post established by General Jack Pershing before he mounted his "punitive expedition" against Villa. This unsuccessful foray demonstrated the army's lack of experience in fighting on foreign terrain. A young lieutenant by the name of George Patton saw his first action here, as a member of Pershing's expedition, and killed two men and a horse. The hotels in Lajitas are part of a large conference center which has a variety of recreational activities including a nine hole golf course, a pool and a saloon/dance hall.

Several companies licensed by the National Park Service offer raft trips of one to nine days' duration on the Rio Grande river, through narrow 1,500-ft (460-meter) deep canyons, or farther down in challenging rapids. Among them is Farflung Adventures (tel: 800-839-7238). Just east of Lajitas, on FM 170, is the Barton Warnock Environmental Educational Center (daily 8am–5pm; entrance fee), named after a local botanist and acting as a gateway to the Big Bend Ranch State Park.

Map on page 278

If you're a fan of hot food, Terlingua is the place to make for on the first Saturday in November. Since 1967, the desolate town has been the venue for the International Chili Cookoff. Expect the few hotels to be full.

Gem hunting

FM 170 continues onwards to **Terlingua** ⓮ (pop. 250), now a collection of mostly abandoned stone and adobe ruins, but, at the turn of the 20th century, a prosperous mining town of 2,000 inhabitants. Here red cinnabar ore was mined and cooked to yield millions of dollars' worth of mercury. The 27 miles (43 km) of tunnels and shafts – some as much as 900 ft (275 meters) deep – of the abandoned mercury mines have yielded a treasure trove of rocks, fossils and mineral specimens cast aside by miners, as well as abundant specimens of cinnabar. This looks much like lipstick smears on the fissured surfaces of igneous rocks.

Views of the nearby peaks of the Chisos Mountains in Big Bend National Park *(see pages 289–292)*, and multicolored badlands on every side, form a surreal backdrop for rock hounds and cactus collectors, who can run amok here. Amber, the hard golden resin of prehistoric plants, is occasionally collected from cretaceous coal outcrops along **Terlingua Creek**, just west of Big Bend.

On the banks of Terlingua Creek, mysterious lights of uncertain source illuminate the walls of La Kiva Restaurant and Bar. Here, furniture is made from redwood stumps and cowhide. The mountains in this region were once the hideout of outlaws, renegades and the like – especially the little settlement of **Valentine** (pop. 260) on US-90, northwest of Marfa. They now attract rock hunters, on account of the numerous

BELOW: minding the store in Marathon.

Desert Plantlife

The flowering plants of the Chihuahuan Desert perform a spectacular, although brief, extravaganza after the spring rains; but most of the rest of the year they are occupied with vegetative survival rather than reproductive exhibitionism. If you see a *lechuguilla* plant, you'll know where you are, since the habitat of this member of the amarillis family coincides perfectly with the boundaries of the Chihuahuan Desert. *Lechuguilla*, which means "little lettuce" in Spanish, is easily recognized by its rosette of succulent bluish-green, spine-tipped leaves about 2 ft (67 cm) long and 1½ inches (4 cm) wide. In true desert plant fashion, it can inflict a painful wound on the unwary.

The yucca species are somewhat similar to agave but are actually members of the lily family. They have narrower, more flexible and less succulent leaves, and flower annually. The torrey yucca grows almost to the height of a tree north and west of Van Horn, forming the only "forest" in the desert lowlands.

The cactus family, that classic form of desert life, originated in the southwestern US and Mexico and has attained its greatest diversity there. Over 100 species of cactus are Texas residents.

Ocotillo is a cactus prevalent in the Far West. It looks like a naked spider on its back and its long 6–20-ft (2–6-meter) legs, protected by stiff spines, are used as living fences by goat raisers. This cautious species puts out leaves only after rainfall and discards them as soon as drought returns.

Greasewood, or the creosote bush, is, along with cactus, almost ubiquitous in North American deserts, taking its name from the thick resin on its small yellowish-green paired leaflets. Usually only around a meter in height, it has been used as fuel by the desert cultures for thousands of years. Its wide, even spacing and the general absence of competing species are the result of special adaptation to the limited availability of water, for greasewood secretes a poison that kills even its own seedlings.

Another plant particularly common on mesas and hillsides is sotol, called "bear grass" for its 4-ft (1.25-meter) long, arching, narrow leaves with small claw-like spines along the margins. Its slender, 4–15-ft (1.25–4.5-meter) brush-like, flowering stalk may persist for several seasons.

All of these large plants were important to the Native Americans who inhabited the area. Their leaves provided fiber for clothing and utensils, as well as soap, and the thick basal stems were baked in stone-lined fireplaces, of which the scattered remains can be seen.

The pea family is also well represented by thorny shrubs like the infamous cat claw acacia, or "wait-a-minute bush," from the automatic cry of "Wait a minute!" as hikers try to extricate themselves from this vegetable's clutches.

Devil's head cactus is an interesting plant about a foot (31cm) in diameter which lurks partially buried, ready to snare a hoof, paw or tennis shoe with its four-pronged spines. On the whole, desert plants are best admired from a safe distance. ❑

LEFT: flowering eagles claw cactus, in Big Bend National Park.

minerals and gems they yield. An outstanding example is the famous Texas plumed agate, in which red flames and black feather shapes are captured in a translucent white matrix. It is most easily found near Marfa and Alpine.

Map on page 278

Alpine

Alpine ⓯ (pop. 5,800) is the main center of activity in this mountain region of Texas, and it must be noted that, to someone arriving from the broiling flatlands, the town's 4,500-ft (1,370-meter) altitude can seem alpine. In the heart of cattle country, Alpine is a stop on AMTRAK's Sunset Limited, between Chicago and Los Angeles. Many people choose the town for their vacation headquarters and enjoy summer theater productions and museums at **Sul Ross State University**, which stages the annual Cowboy Poetry Gathering every March for a week-long celebration of culture and art.

Wheeled longhorn cow outside of Marathon.

Marathon

Less than one hour to the south of Alpine, at the junction of US-385 and US-90, **Marathon** ⓰ (pop. 800) is centrally isolated in a desolate area of interest only to naturalists. Geologists are delighted by the diversity of rocks and minerals in the vicinity, while rugged nature photographers use Marathon as a jumping-off point for trips to **Black Gap Wildlife Management Area**, 58 miles (93 km) away. Though 80 miles (129 km) distant, Big Bend National Park is the next sign of civilization toward the south.

The town's 1920s Gage Hotel has been well renovated and furnished with antiques, Native American artifacts and Mexican furniture, in keeping with its role as a desert way-station. The restaurant is an oasis in a culinary wasteland.

BELOW: mural in downtown Alpine.

Fort Davis

To the north of Alpine, at the intersection of highways 17 and 118, is **Fort Davis** ⓱, named after the much-honored Jefferson Davis, who was President of the Confederate States of America but is remembered locally as the man who, as Secretary of War, introduced camels to West Texas. The fort stands dramatically with its back to a wall of volcanic rock named Sleeping Lion Mountain. At 5,000 ft (1,540 meters), the community is the highest in Texas and boasts of not possessing a single shopping mall.

The world's largest roadrunner, Fort Stockton.

In the **Fort Davis National Historic Site** (daily 8am–5pm; entrance fee; tel: 432-426-3224), the life of the late 19th-century frontier soldier has been recreated. Actual buildings survive from the days when such soldiers mounted up to escort wagon trains on the Chihuahuan Trail, or stage coaches on the Butterfield Overland Mail Route.

The **Chihuahuan Desert Research Institute** (Mon–Sat 9am–5pm; free; tel: 915-364-2499), on Highway 118 a few miles south of Fort Davis, is a popular port of call for those fascinated by native desert plants. Among its attractions is a cactus greenhouse. Visitors can also, in two hours, drive a scenic loop on highways 166 and 118 through the Davis Mountains, whose gentle, weathered slopes belie their violent volcanic origins. From Wild Rose Pass on, one has the same view of Limpia Brook, as it runs between high cliffs, that the Apache and Comanche raiding parties had as they lay in ambush.

In this area, the **McDonald Observatory** ⓲, perched atop Mount Lock, houses one of the largest astronomical telescopes in the world, the giant 433-inch (9.2-meter) HET optical telescope (daily 10am–5.30pm; entrance fee; tel: 432-426-3640).

BELOW: Loving County sheriff, Billy Burt Hopper.

The mountains

Interstate roads I-10 (which runs through Fort Stockton) and I-20 (through Pecos) meet to the west, on the edge of the Davis Mountains. This vast range (under different names) runs from the New Mexico border – apart from a gap between Fort Davis and Alpine – all the way south to the Big Bend National Park on the Rio Grande. Islands of green – the forests and meadows of the high mountains – rise in the sea of brown.

Six of them soar to over 8,000 ft (2,400 meters), including **Mount Livermore** at 8,206 ft (2,525 meters). In these enclaves of pine, fir, maple and oak, there are small populations of elk, black bear, bighorn sheep and mountain lions, the reminders of better, wetter grazing times. There has been a drying trend over the past 100 years and livestock has been allowed to overgraze the land. The grass has not returned, so the steppe has become a desert hell.

The youngest ranges are the Franklin Mountains at El Paso and the Delaware Mountains north of Kent, which are part of the Rocky Mountain system and still rise at an average rate of more than ¼ inch (0.65 cm) per year. Many of the ranges in the mountain and basin area of Texas were formed during the tumultuous Tertiary period approximately 60 million years ago. Massive uplifting and faulting led to intrusions of molten rock, like those in the Chisos Mountains of Big Bend National Park, and extensive lava flows which created the Davis Mountains.

These volcanic formations cover mountains from earlier periods, as well as marine sediments and coral reefs. Folding and overthrust faulting have left young rock strata covered by a layer 150 million years older in places – a picture puzzle complex enough to delight the most jaded structural geologist.

The Davis Mountains State Park attracts more than 150,000 visitors each year. Facilities include camping sites, hiking trails and fishing.

BELOW: roadside shrine in Reeves County.

Map on page 278

Texas' highest and most majestic mountains, the Guadalupes, at the New Mexico border, began as a massive coral reef, some 250 million years ago. Two periods of uplifting have raised these marine remains to an altitude of over 8,000 ft (2,440 meters). The dominant feature here is the 8,749-ft (2,667-meter) **Guadalupe Peak**, the highest point in Texas. Approached from the west on US-62/180, this giant wedge of limestone resembles an enormous ship moving over the desert. The cliffs of El Capitan Peak form the prow, towering above a white sea of salt.

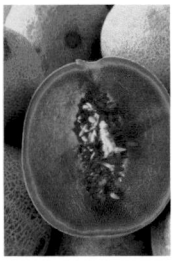

Cantaloupes are a popular fruit in Pecos.

Cantaloupes and rodeos

Pecos ⑲ (pop. 9,500) is the biggest town along the river of the same name. Gourmets take note: Pecos is to cantaloupe what Smithfield, Virginia, is to ham. Here, in 1883, the world's first rodeo took place. The boys from the Hashknife outfit challenged boys from other ranches to horse-racing, bronc busting, and calf-roping contests. The tradition is carried on by holding a major rodeo here around July 4 each year. The **West-of-the-Pecos Museum and Park** (120 E. First Street; June–Sept Mon–Sat 9am–5pm, Sun 1–5pm; Sept–May Tues–Sat 9am–5pm; entrance fee; tel: 432-445-5076) displays a century-old saloon in one of its 50 rooms.

North of Pecos, bordering New Mexico, is **Loving**, the most sparsely populated county in the US – 67 people with an average 10 sq. miles (26 sq. km) each. So despite the name and with such a sparsely spread population, not a whole lot of loving goes on. Four hundred oil leases have been registered here, but there is no water – it has to be trucked in.

The only reservoir in Texas along the Pecos river is Red Bluff in Loving County, but it has only once been full in the past 60 years. New Mexico defended itself in court for 16 years against Texan charges that it was taking too much water out of the river. Finally, in 1988, the US Supreme Court ruled in Texas' favor and its neighbor was forced to pay $14 million in damages.

BELOW: white sand dunes near Guadalupe Mountains National Park.

The first place of any size along the river south of Pecos is **Fort Stockton** ⑳ (pop. 7,800). By the mid-1880s, with no enemies left to fight, the fort was abandoned but it has been restored to its earlier appearance. Four of the original fort's buildings, built in 1867, can be visited and a museum (Mon–Sat 10am–8pm, Sun noon–6pm; tel: 432-336-8421) has been established in the old barracks. Burrowing owls pop out of the earth of the parade grounds during the day. Other interesting local sights, including the world's largest roadrunner, are included on the self-guided tour map (tel: 800-336-2166).

Forty miles (64 km) east of Fort Stockton, at the junction of US-67 and US-385, is **McCamey** ㉑, an "instant town" on November 16 1925, when the No. 1 Baker oil well blew in. Within months, there were 10,000 people in town and the solitary Texas Ranger – lacking a jail – was obliged to chain prisoners to a post. One group of tethered roughnecks uprooted the pole and took it to the nearest saloon. In 1936, McCamey was the scene of the world's first Rattlesnake Derby, with a $200 purse for the winner. ❑

The Marfa Lights

Robert Reed Ellison, a young cowhand, was the first to report the Marfa Lights. Looking across to the Chinati Mountains in West Texas he saw them twinkling in the night and figured they must have been the campfires of Apache Indians. But when he went searching the next day he found no Indians – nor even the ashes of any fires. This was 114 years ago and people have been watching the lights ever since, but still without being able to explain what they are and where they're coming from. As elusive as rainbows, they disappear as soon as you think you're getting up close.

According to one guidebook the lights "move about, split apart, melt together, disappear and reappear." In recent years they have become such a tourist attraction that the Texas State Highways Department has built a special parking area from which to view them along US-90, about 10 miles (16 km) east of town. And at the Apache Trading Post, just west of Alpine, there's now a Screening Room where visitors can view films and videotape of the lights.

During World War II, pilots training at the nearby army base conducted an aerial search but were no more successful than previous investigators: the lights remained a mystery. Superstitious locals tend to reflect the views of a Mrs W.T. Giddings who claims they are a friendly source that once saved her father from a blizzard by leading him to a cave. Other explanations have included: electrostatic discharge; St Elmo's Fire; swamp gas or other natural gases igniting; moonlight reflecting on veins of mica; and even the ghosts of conquistadors in search of gold.

A New Handbook of Texas says the most likely explanation is that the lights are a mirage caused by atmospheric conditions, produced by the interaction of cold and warm layers of air that bend light so that it can be seen from a distance but not up close.

The Desert Candle, the local newspaper, has run numerous reports of sightings, some of which were compiled in a book by editor Judith M. Brueske, who suggests that the spaciousness of the Big Bend region and "the relatively low light contaminant," compared to more heavily populated areas, might make such lights easier to see. In *The Marfa Lights*, she offers several explanations, ranging from the phenomenon known as *ignis fatuus* (the spontaneous combustion of natural gases) or static electricity to the combination of moisture with bat guano phosphates (there are many bat caves in the mountains). And she, too, brings up the possibility that many of the sightings could be mirages, pointing out that, especially at sea, people have conjured up the vision of islands or villages.

What argues against this theory is the sheer ubiquity of the sightings. Usually they are small and seen at a distance but occasionally lights as big as footballs have come close to people's cars. Nobody has ever reported being harmed.

Marfa Lights are visible every clear night between Marfa and Paisano Pass as one faces Chinati Mountains. ❑

RIGHT: Marfa Lights viewing shelter erected by the Texas Department of Transportation.

BIG BEND NATIONAL PARK

Beautiful Big Bend, where the Rio Grande lurches to the northeast, has canyons, waterfalls and hiking trails galore, but with far fewer visitors than you'll find at Yosemite or the Grand Canyon

The state's largest park, Big Bend National Park, is most challenging to backpackers and nature lovers. The Chisos Mountains, the wide desert, the Rio Grande river and the magnificent canyons combine to form a true wilderness, sections of which are still relatively unexplored.

Big Bend (open daily; entrance fee; tel: 432-477-2251) is one of those places you have to be going to in order to get there. The closest town is Alpine, about 65 miles (105 km) to the northwest of the northernmost tip. The park encompasses a vast area of 801,163 acres (324,230 hectares) and varies in altitude from 1,850 ft (570 meters) all the way up to 7,835 ft (2,410 meters). There are hundreds of trails, 100 miles (160 km) of paved roads and 170 miles (272 km) of dirt roads. There is a trailer park, a post office and a gas station. **Panther Junction** ❶ is the park headquarters and home of the visitors' center (open daily 8am–6pm), while, open year-round, the Chisos Mountains Lodge (tel: 432-447-2291), at **Chisos Basin** ❷, provides camping and motel accommodations. Trailer and tent camping areas are also available at **Rio Grande Village** ❸, near Boquillas, and at Cottonwood, near Castolon. Permits (free) are required for back-country camping.

LEFT: Boot Canyon in the Chisos Mountains.
BELOW: exploring Big Bend.

Wild country

"In 1902, the Big Bend was pretty wild country. The stage brought mail and passengers once a week from Marfa and that was the only connection there was… the area at the time was a favorite hangout for cattle rustlers," wrote topographical surveyor Stuart T. Penick. "It was easy to run cattle from one side of the Rio Grande to the other. Texas Rangers were scarce and didn't get to that part of the country very often." Big Bend's first cattleman, Don Milton Faver, had a herd of longhorns and burro-riding cowboys. Many were unbranded and were stolen. His cattle drives were the subject of TV's *Rawhide* series.

King of the air around here is the endangered peregrine falcon, whose concentration of eyries is the largest in the contiguous 48 states. Golden eagles are frequently seen in winter, near the mountains and over the high grasslands, but, as the clouds move across this desolate land, you may be reminded of the gargantuan pterosaur whose 51-ft (15.5-meter) reptilian wings cast terrifying shadows on the lesser dinosaurs below. The remains of these cretaceous creatures, the largest animals ever to fly, were found in the Big Bend area in the early 1970s.

The great outdoors

The real Big Bend is best seen from its hiking trails, or from a canoe expedition on the Rio Grande river.

TIP

Water can be a real problem on both long and short hikes. Dehydration comes on quickly in the Big Bend's dry air, and springs and streams are not reliable for drinking. Make sure you always take your own water and drink some frequently.

Extensive information about getting the best out of your visit through hiking, camping, canoeing, scenic hikes and river trips is available from the National Park Service. But Big Bend is wild country, and should be respected as such.

Hit the trail

Some of the 36 marked hiking trails are strenuous and treacherous; others are easy. Many are interpreted by self-guiding leaflets and trail signs. A number of trails take off from near Chisos Basin.

During the summer, a hike down the easy, 1½-mile (2.5-km) **Chisos Basin Trail** is guided by a park naturalist. At the overlook about halfway along the trail, the major features of the Chisos Basin stand out against the sky: towering Emory Peak, at 7,825 ft (2,400 meters) the highest in the park; Ward Mountain; Carter Peak and The Window; Vernon Bailey Peak and Pulliam Ridge; Casa Grande and Toll Mountain. This trail provides a good introduction to the major features of the Big Bend park.

Halfway between The Basin and Panther Junction, the **Pine Canyon Trail** explores a wooded canyon for 4 miles (6.5 km). At trail's end, a waterfall pours down the 200-ft (60-meter) cliff after a heavy rain.

Map on page 290

Just north of The Basin, the moderately difficult 5-mile (8-km) **Lost Mine Trail** follows the north slope of Casa Grande and leads to a point high on the west side of Lost Mine Peak. It affords beautiful views of the surrounding mountains and canyons. A very difficult trek up the 7,500-ft (2,300-meter) Casa Grande Peak takes off from the Juniper Canyon Overlook along the Lost Mine Trail.

The 5-mile (8-km) **Chimneys Trail** lies southwest of The Basin and leads to a group of high rock outcroppings, or "chimneys," the southernmost of which contains ancient Native American pictographs.

Two groups of trails into the Chisos lie south of The Basin: the High Chisos Complex trails and the Outer Mountain Loop trails. The High Chisos trails are some of the most beautiful, but they require serious hiking and climbing. The panorama from the **South Rim Trail** includes Santa Elena Canyon 20 miles (30 km) to the west, Emory Peak to the north, and the mountains in Mexico to the south. Various trails branch off from this one and, for instance, lead up Emory Peak into Boot Canyon – the summer home of the Colima Warbler, found nowhere else in the United States.

While the High Chisos trails are strenuous, they are, at least, well-marked. The **Outer Mountain Loop** trails, on the other hand, are not so well-marked and hardly flat at all. Among these, **Blue Creek Trail** is known for its colorful balanced rocks and pinnacles. However, these two series of trails can be combined for a lengthier expedition into the Big Bend wilderness.

White-tailed deer roam in Big Bend National Park.

BELOW: Santa Elena Canyon, Big Bend.

Map on page 290

TIP

If you're planning to drive out and explore Big Bend for yourself, check the condition of all roads within the park beforehand with the Park Rangers.

Spectacular canyons

Another popular trailhead is the Rio Grande Village area, near the river in the eastern part of the park. The very easy **Rio Grande Village Nature Trail**, ¾ mile (1 km) long, interprets several plant habitats, including the lush river plain-flood and the arid desert. An overlook at trail's end gives breathtaking views of Mexico, the river, the Chisos Mountains and Boquillas Canyon.

Boquillas, the longest canyon in the park, is also accessible along the 1½-mile (2.5-km) **Boquillas Canyon Trail**. For the more adventurous, a three-day trip covering 17 miles (27 km) in the canyon and 8 miles (13 km) on the Rio Grande can be a wonderful experience, with all the side canyons there are to explore on both banks, in Texas and Mexico.

Santa Elena Canyon

The most spectacular of the Big Bend canyons, **Santa Elena**, can be seen on an easy 1½-mile (2.5-km) trail that crosses Terlingua Creek and wanders through the magnificent 17-mile (27-km) canyon to the river.

If you decide to run the waters of this most spectacular of canyons, bear in mind that the river is very tricky, especially in high or low water. Eleven miles (18 km) of scenic river precede the canyon entrance, but watch for strong currents over hidden rocks. The most dangerous part of the canyon is the rockslide about a mile (1.5 km) beyond the entrance. Running the slide is always difficult, and downright dangerous at high and low water levels. Portaging it is socially acceptable and no blemish whatsoever on anyone's manhood. After the slide, navigation is more tranquil and boaters can enjoy colorful canyon walls and also explore the jewel-like Fern Canyon.

Mariscal Canyon, the most isolated of the three major canyons, is accessible on a strenuous, unshaded 6½-mile (10-km) hike. The rim affords a wide view of the canyon 1,500 ft (460 meters) below, to reward the persevering hiker.

RIGHT: relaxing in the Hot Springs bathing pool, along the Rio Grande in the south part of the park.

By car

Even from a car the Big Bend visitor can see the wild country. The River Road traverses the 51 miles (82 km) between the Boquillas-Rio Grande Village road and Castolon. The road can be traveled by most high-clearance vehicles, but its side roads usually require four-wheel-drive. Old ranches and fishing camps occasionally appear along the road, and it passes the ruins of Mariscal Mine, an old mercury working at the foot of Mariscal Mountain. The ruins are fun to explore, but beware of open, unmarked mine shafts. Further west lie the remains of the Johnson Ranch House, probably the largest adobe ruin in the park. The road ends at **Castolon** ❹, a 19th-century farming settlement and early 20th-century US Cavalry and Texas Ranger post.

Big Bend has facilities and adventures to offer everyone – from automobile tours to rugged mountain trails and river running, in moderate mountain temperatures or hot-as-Texas sun. But the visitor does well to remember that it's still wild country and must be enjoyed on its own terms. ❑

THE WONDERFUL WILDLIFE OF TEXAS

You don't need to venture deep into the Texas countryside to discover the state's weird and wonderful wildlife. But, if you do, take care

They're big; they're small. They run, they fly and they crawl. They enchant you with their beauty; they make you reel with horror. *They* are the wild animals of Texas.

IT'S A JUNGLE OUT THERE

As you wander the civilized streets of Dallas or Houston, catching your reflection in a glass skyscraper, it's easy to forget that this is still the Wild West. "Wild" in the sense that the animals that call Texas their home remain as unfazed by progress as they were in the days of the frontier pioneers. The scurrying armadillo is a familiar sight in many parts of the state. Other creatures are more regionalized, preferring the marshy wetness of the East, or the unrelenting dryness and heat of the Far West. Some Texas wildlife is continually on the move, winging, crawling or grubbing its way into new corners of the state.

However, the comical antics of the prairie dog, the elegance of deer grazing in the Hill Country or the smiling dolphins off the Gulf Coast should not lead visitors into a false sense of security. Like the prickly desert plants, native Texan beasts must be met on their own terms, if met at all. They can bite, they can sting. They can annoy, they can maim. The key rule is: Don't mess. If you leave the animals to themselves, the chances are they'll keep well away from you. Be sensible. Follow all warning signs and don't tempt danger. But, for all the cougars, black bears, rattlesnakes, alligators and coyotes, there are also stunning birds, majestic buffalo, thriving longhorns, languid sea turtles and exotic fish you won't find anywhere else.

And with scores of natural refuges for "safe" viewing, the beautiful creatures of Texas can still charm and enthrall.

△ **SNAP SHOT**
In the marshy bayous of East Texas lurk some 200,000 alligators, the state's largest reptile. They feed on fish and other small animals, and seldom attack humans – but don't push it!

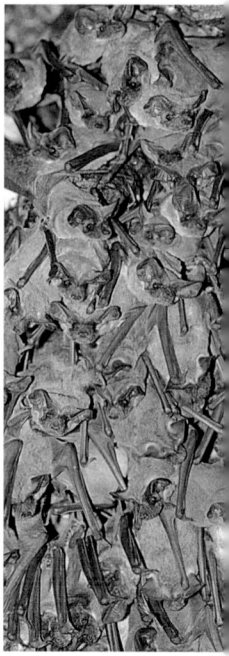

▷ **BATTY BEHAVIOR**
The caves of Central Texas are the breeding grounds for a variety of bat species. The adults here are all female, the males being left in South America.

◁ **PRAIRIE DOG**
This burrowing member of the squirrel family lives in colonies of thousands. Its name is derived from its cry, or "bark."

SNAKES IN THE GRASS

The statistics tell the truth: there is more chance of being killed by a lightning strike in Texas than from a snake bite. Nevertheless, the thought of a venomous rattler is enough to panic many Texas visitors.

The state is home to more than 100 species of snake, but less than 10 percent are a danger to humans. The rattlesnake (actually 11 varieties) is the most feared. It can be found in most parts of Texas, but is prevalent in the Trans-Pecos region. The coral snake *(above)* is also a nasty little wriggler and may be encountered in areas from Central Texas south. The same territory is inhabited by the copperhead, equally dangerous if provoked, while the cottonmouth is semi-aquatic and lives mostly around rivers in Central and East Texas.

▷ **JAVELINA**
Despite being armed with tusks and musk, the near-sighted javelina, a cousin of the South American tapir, is not dangerous.

▽ **BLOODSHOT EYES**
The prickly looking horned lizard, often mistakenly referred to as the "horny toad," can shoot a stream of blood from its eyes.

▷ **THE LION'S SHARE**
Cougars are found in the mountains of the Trans-Pecos. As this warning notice confirms, they should not be approached. Smaller cats live elsewhere in the state: lynx-like bobcats in East Texas and ocelots in South Texas. Look out for wild dogs, too, particularly coyotes and wolves.

THE WEST

Map on page 298

West Texas, a hard land to colonize, has changed its complexion with every industrial advance – from coal mining to oil extraction – yet it buzzes with the spirit of self-reliance imprinted on its citizens

The people of southern North Central Texas call themselves "West" Texans, not out of geographical ignorance, but out of a sense of history and place. After the Civil War, their ancestors from Southern states, knowing no place else to go to begin a new life, headed west, where they encountered a foe more relentless than General Sherman: the slow-yielding, tightfisted land itself, ruled by distance, drought and the most ferocious aboriginal army ever to ride horseback. Thus, mile after uncertain mile was conquered by people who were not searching for wealth, but for a place to survive. They did survive, and left their descendants with the knowledge that anything is possible if one is self-reliant and looks toward the horizon. Travel in this relatively featureless landscape can become an agonizingly slow unfolding of geography, if you expect to be constantly entertained by the fluff and fanfare of tourist extravaganzas. However, if you adopt the easy-going friendliness of its people, and attune yourself to the voices of its heroic past, West Texas will be an unforgettable experience.

LEFT: a Texas icon: the oil pump. **BELOW:** Wild West cowboy on the range.

Fort Worth to El Paso

West of Fort Worth, where I-20 drops down from rough-cut juniper and oak-covered hills on to the fitful beginning of the plains, are the ruins of **Thurber** ❶, a coal-mining town better suited to northeastern Pennsylvania or the Ruhr Valley than post-frontier Texas. Where 10,000 people from 17 countries lived between 1880 and 1922 there now exist only a tall brick smoke stack, a restaurant-museum, the remains of a great brick factory and a service station. The rest of the town has been sold brick by brick, down to the last utility pole. As one looks across the now empty valley to the conical piles of black coal spoil and "red dog" cinders, it is difficult to imagine the wealthy, cosmopolitan city that stood here on the near side of frontier times. Thurber is where the Metropolitan Opera of New York performed, where Miss Wallis "Wildcat" Warfield, later the Duchess of Windsor, grew up in one of the mansions along Silk Stocking Road on New York Hill, and where a World War I clothing drive netted no fewer than four dozen mink coats.

In 1895, Thurber was one of the first completely electrified cities in the world. After a long, bitter strike presided over by Texas Rangers, Thurber became the first and perhaps the only 100 percent unionized town in America. The 100 million tonnes of coal mined here powered the belching locomotives of Jay Gould's Texas & Pacific (T&P) Railway as they trundled across the prairie. In 1881, the last 595 miles (958 km) of the T&P mainline were completed between Fort Worth and Sierra Blanca in a phenomenal 11 months, by a crew of 300 hard-drinking Irishmen.

Decorated pump jacks brighten fields.

The railroad's role in the rapid demise of the frontier is dramatically demonstrated by the almost simultaneous founding of Abilene, Big Spring, Midland, Odessa and the other major cities of the region. They were shipping points for cattle, eliminating the long trail drives to Dodge City and Abilene in Kansas. The change from coal- to oil-powered locomotives led to the dismantling of Thurber and helped set the stage for the meteoric emergence of **Ranger** ❷, 13 miles (21 km) to the west and the most rip-snorting boomtown of all.

Oil boom doom

Derricks and pump jacks are still in evidence, but the quiet streets of modern Ranger fail to suggest the frenzy of the weeks in 1917, after oil rig McClesky No. 1 blew in with 1,700 barrels a day. At World War I prices, a good well yielded $250,000 a week. The 10 trains that rolled into Ranger every day were filled with speculators, jacklegs, riffraff and ruffians, ambitious men and loose women. The town exploded from a village of 1,000 to a seething city of 40,000 in a mat-

ter of months. Streets turned into a sea of mud, traversed on sleds or the backs of men in hip boots. Guests in those days paid luxury hotel rates to sleep in armchairs. The evangelist Billy Sunday went in search of souls to saloons called the Grizzly Bear, the Blue Moose and Oklahoma, where as many as five people a day met their oil boom doom. Small wonder there was violence when, for example, one lease changed hands three times on a Friday, increasing in value from $150 to $15,000. Everyone in the trade but the middle man must have felt taken. Talk to some of the old-timers for more details of the years when Ranger's oil produced more wealth than the California gold rush at its peak.

Horny toads like Rip, an Eastland celebrity, are not actually amphibians, but lizards. Although the little critters are unable to cause warts, they do shoot a thin stream of blood out of the corners of their eyes, to a distance of up to 4 ft (1.2 meters).

Rest In Peace

A few miles west lies **Eastland** ❸, another boomtown gone bust. Today its principal claims to fame are the Post Office mural, a montage of 11,217 stamps, which depicts the history of the communications service; the restored 1920s Majestic Theatre; Outdoor Art's reproductions of 41 masterpieces such as Andy Warhol's Campbell's soup can on a round building; and a horned toad named Rip (Rest in Peace), which was sealed into the cornerstone of the old courthouse in 1897 and found to be alive when the new courthouse was built some 28 years later. The creature died a year later, after achieving national fame. His stuffed body was then placed in a glass case in the new building. In his miniature coffin, he resembles a rather flat and very prickly pin-cushion, about the size of a child's hand.

Today, one approaches **Albany** ❹, northwest of Cisco, over the same rolling red plains the cowboys covered on the trail to Dodge City in the 1870s. Due to overgrazing, however, the lush prairie grasses they found here are gone. There

BELOW: barbed wire and tumbleweed in West Texas.

In spite of all its agricultural and culinary benefits, Texas ranchers hate mesquite and hire "wetbacks," illegal immigrants from Mexico, to remove it from time to time.

is only the eroded soil and lacy-leaved mesquite trees. Although mesquite steals precious moisture from the soil, it puts back nitrogen, since it is a leguminous plant. Its beans were ground into a flour by the nomadic Plains Indians and are still eaten by cattle in times of drought. Its wood is considered by many Texans to be without parallel for cooking barbecue.

Only in Albany

At first sight, Albany is as unimposing as the mesquite "forests" that surround it, but this prairie town of 2,000 possesses an exceptional collection of 20th-century art, displayed in **The Old Jail Art Center** (201 S. Second Street; Tues–Sat 10am–5pm, Sun 2–5pm; free; tel: 325-762-2269), a place where drunken cowboys and assorted desperados were once detained. The limestone building itself (*circa* 1878) is a good example of frontier architecture, with its decoratively routed and scored casements and cistern out front. Alongside pre-Columbian displays, among the many artists represented in the large permanent collection are Matisse, Rouault, Picasso, Modigliani, Miró, Henry Moore and Giacometti.

Albany's Fort Griffin "Fandangle" is an outdoor historical pageant staged during the last two weeks in June. The roles of Native Americans, cowboys, buffalo hunters, soldiers, bandits and settlers are sung and acted, as they have been since 1938, by the descendants of those who originally occupied the Texas frontier (tel: 915-762-3838). Before leaving Albany, head for the **Ledbetter Picket House Museum** (24 S. Main Street; hours vary; free), a restored frontier ranch house with many authentic furnishings. A similar ranch house served as the commandant's headquarters in the early days of what is now **Fort Griffin State Historic Site** ❺ (daily 8am–5pm; entrance fee; tel: 325-762-3592), 15 miles (24

BELOW: roadside cowboy.

km) north of Albany on US-283. Established in 1867, Fort Griffin belonged to the outer line of frontier defense. The first line, which swung in a wide arc southwest from Fort Worth to San Antonio, was established in the late 1840s on the edge of Comanche territory. Its line of forts was a buffer between the Plains Indians and white colonies.

Map on page 298

The roughest town in Texas

From its hilltop, the stone ruins and partially reconstructed wooden remains of the fort look down on what was possibly the roughest, most brawling and iniquitous town in the history of Texas: "The Flats." Never has a lustier mixture of manhood been stirred in one pot. Imagine them bellied up to the same bar: bitter, defeated Southern veterans of the Civil War alongside the blue-jacketed conquerors and the "buffalo soldiers," as the Native Americans called freed slaves who were part of the army. As if they were not enough, add buffalo hunters flush from selling hides, plus the professional gamblers and bandits who preyed on them, and the bounty hunters who preyed in turn on them. Ironically, one of the few original buildings remaining in "The Flats" was far more respectable: it served as the church, school and Masonic lodge.

The Texas longhorn, protected at Fort Griffin State Park.

Herds of the once-threatened longhorn cattle are found in increasing numbers again across the state, but they are particularly accessible to the public at Fort Griffin State Park. Cowboys still exist, too, and you can find them at the Texas Cowboy Reunion at **Stamford** ❻, around July 4. This is no slick, professional production in an air-conditioned coliseum. This is where "good ol' boys" risk their necks, not for love of money, but for love of their favorite roping horses or even the love of their girls who perch on the top rail of the arena fence.

BELOW: the Sierra del Carmen.

Fort Phantom Hill is housed on private land. You can visit the site for no charge, but bear in mind that there are no special visitor facilities.

Further west, 14 miles (22 km) north of Abilene, is **Fort Phantom Hill** ❼. The very name has the chill of desolation to it. Loneliness still lingers about the tall, solitary chimneys, the empty commissary, guardhouse and powder magazine, especially in the dim red light of dusk. From its founding in 1850, to protect the region from hostile Indians, there were frequent desertions from this post, where boredom alternated with Comanche raids. After its abandonment in 1854, the hated fort was burned by one of the withdrawing soldiers. Later it became an overnight stop for mail coaches on the Butterfield Trail.

In making your way through the scrub oak and mesquite to Abilene, you will probably see the silver and salmon flash of the scissor-tailed flycatcher. In excited flight, the graceful tails, which are twice as long as the bodies, almost seem to flitter like a carnival bird on a stick.

God's glorious city

Abilene ❽ (pop. 116,000) likes to promote its slogan "A Whole Lotta Texas Goin On," but might more aptly be described as the "Glorious City of God," being the home of three religiously affiliated institutions of learning – McMurry University, Abilene Christian University and the Southern Baptists' Hardin-Simmons. Round-the-clock prayer meetings for rain didn't bring an end to the drought of the early 1950s, but they must have made an impression: the region has been blessed with oil discoveries ever since. A rig was set up on the **Taylor County Exposition Center** (Highway 36 at 11th Street) grounds here for demonstration and, of course, it struck oil. Rodeos are held here each spring and fall.

Abilene's **Historical Museum** (part of the Grace Museum, 102 Cypress Street; Tues–Sat 10am–5pm; entrance fee; tel: 325-673-4587) has exhibits relat-

BELOW: West Texas on the right track.

ing to Camp Barkeley, the World War II army base and prison camp, whose ruins can still be seen on US-277, south of town. There are other museums in this complex devoted to children and fine arts.

Buffalo Gap

An authentic taste of the Old West is to be had 10 miles (16 km) southwest of town, where the low, dark juniper-covered hills of the Calahan Divide are broken abruptly at **Buffalo Gap Historic Village** ❾ (June–Sept Mon–Sat 10am–6pm, Sun noon–6pm; Sept–May Mon–Sat 10am–5pm, Sun noon–5pm; entrance fee; tel: 325-572-3365). A mix of authentic frontier buildings and new tourist attractions is found here. An old courthouse, jail and log cabins are among the old buildings. A doctor's office, a barber shop and a print shop are modern reconstructions. Twice a year, in the 19th century, buffalo passed through the mountain gap here, indelibly etching a permanent trail. When this brown, woolly group flowed between these ancient hills, Tonkawa and Comanche Indians still camped in the cool shade of the native pecan groves and made arrowheads, traces of which can still be found. Charles Goodnight, one of the most celebrated of early longhorn ranchers out west, described the main buffalo herd as being 125 miles (200 km) long and 25 miles (40 km) wide. The trail they blazed was later the one he used to drive his own cattle to the Kansas railheads. When the area was settled by whites in the 1870s, this natural funnel through the hills continued to be a focus for the region. Today, 19 of the original buildings have been restored, including the limestone courthouse and jail. Gravestones, of Civil War veterans and others, in the Buffalo Gap Cemetery, tell the history of the settling of West Texas in a few poignant words. **Frontier**

The Texan town of Abilene, founded by cattlemen in 1881, was named for Abilene in Kansas, which was the final stop on the Chisholm Trail.

BELOW: crop dusting in West Texas.

Texas (625 N. First; Mon–Sat 9am–6pm, Sun 1–5pm; entrance fee; tel: 325-437-2800) is a multi-media immersion in early Texas with buffalo stampedes and saloon shootouts.

It was the sheer abundance of rattlesnakes, which were troubling local ranchers and farmers, that led the town of Sweetwater to organize the first rattlesnake roundup.

Gypsum deposits

The town of **Sweetwater** ⑩, 40 miles (64 km) west of Abilene on I-20, was well-named in this area where many of the streams are tainted with gypsum. Gypsum, otherwise known as Epsom salts, is fine for soaking tired feet but, as a drink, keeps one on the run. The rich local gypsum deposits have been put to constructive use in the manufacture of wallboard by two large factories.

One of the few towns in West Texas to predate the coming of the railroad, Sweetwater began in 1877 as a general store for buffalo hunters, dug into the banks of Sweetwater Creek. The world's largest rattlesnake roundup is held here during the second weekend in March, at the Nolan County Coliseum (for information, tel: 325-658-6757). It is a bring-em-back-alive affair in which the snakes are milked for their venom and prizes are given for the longest, shortest and heaviest (by the pound). A record 14,000 lbs (6,350 kg) were delivered in 1985. If you have ever had a hankering to eat a fried 6-ft (2-meter) long western diamondback, or buy a transparent toilet seat with a rattler coiled in it, here is such an opportunity.

A few moments on the weed-broken tarmac of the Old Sweetwater Army Airfield will resurrect memories of the 1940s, when the Women's Airforce Service Pilots (WASPs) received their flight training here. Further west, past Colorado City (locally pronounced *Cahla Rayda Cidy*), is the town of **Big Spring** ⑪, a site important in another war. This natural oasis was occupied by

BELOW: Lake Colorado City State Park.

Native Americans as long as 10,000 years ago and served as a major rest stop for the tribes on the Comanche War Trail, halfway between their home on the High Plains to the north and the white settlements in Texas and Mexico to the south. The Native Americans shared its precious water with antelope, buffalo and wild mustang horses. The appeal of this ancient oasis is still felt in the cool late afternoon among the trees of Comanche Trail Park, while the **Big Spring State Park** (open daily; entrance fee) provides a view of the entire area from a 200-ft (60-meter) mesa within the city limits.

Southbound travelers along US-87 from Big Spring will pass through **San Angelo** ⓬, a modern city of lakes and rivers on the edge of the Texas Hill Country. Like San Antonio, it has a River Walk, winding its way past landscaped gardens, parks and beautiful homes by the Concho river. **Fort Concho**, the best-preserved of the Indian War stockades, is filled with exhibits from frontier times (630 S. Oakes Street; Tues–Sat 10am–5pm, Sun 1–5pm; entrance fee; tel: 325-481-2646).

For a taste of old fort life, visit Fort Concho on the first weekend in December, when an 1880s-style celebration is held, re-enacting a Christmas holiday from that era.

The Permian Basin oil field

At the midway point of the 600-mile (965-km) drive from Fort Worth to El Paso, a mirage of civilization rises out of the endless illusion of water over the highway ahead. The small city of **Midland** ⓭ (pop. 95,000), the hometown of President George W. Bush, is dominated by glass and steel towers, containing the offices of more than 650 firms dedicated to coaxing crude oil from the bottom of a 250-million-year-old sea, now buried tens of thousands of feet below the desert sand. The city is a vibrant, modern haven with an active cultural scene. It has weathered the roughest historic and economic storms. The city was in the thick of battles between Commanches and settlers. When the oil boom arrived, prosperity flooded the region. Consequently, when Texas oil went bad, the city faced rough times. The **Permian Basin Oil Field** is the second-largest in the world, and the price of a barrel of Texas Permian Intermediate Weight Crude is the standard against which the prices of all other US oils are determined. The nodding, hobbyhorse-like pump jacks seem to repeat as they suck at the earth: "Fiftydollars, fiftydollars, fiftydollars..." Not only have their rhythms enriched many a slouch-hatted rancher, but the University of Texas as well. In the 19th century, having virtually no funds to offer the fledgling institution, the state legislature apologetically proffered 2.2 million acres (890,000 hectares) of sand and desert scrubland. That these holdings coincide with the outlines of the Permian Basin is a happy coincidence that has bequeathed the University around $2.5 billion.

BELOW: prairie dog.

The science and technology of oil are brilliantly explained in the **Petroleum Museum** (1500 I-20 West, exit 136; daily 9am–5pm; Sun 2–5pm; entrance fee; tel: 432-683-4403), where visitors can stroll along the bottom of the sea. Another educational site is the **American Airpower Heritage Museum of the Commemorative Air Force**, near the airport (9600 Wright Drive; Mon–Sat 9am–5pm, Sun noon–5pm; entrance fee; tel: 432-563-1100) with a collection of World War II aircraft and a new Aviation Art Gallery.

Midland's other claim to fame is that it is the "Tumbleweed Capital of the World." In the scorching 100+°F (38+°C) days of summer, when all else turns brown, legions of prickly green tumbleweeds crowd the roadside and abandoned fields. These tumbleweeds resist the heat as they grow up to 8 ft (2.5 meters) tall, awaiting the moment in the fall when they break free of the earth to rush pell-mell down the road. Since Bob Nolan and the Sons of the Pioneers immortalized this common nuisance in the song *Tumbling Tumbleweed*, the plant has become a symbol for the spirit of movement that led to the development of the West Texas frontier, especially in the person of the drifting cowboy.

The Presidential Museum recalls past election campaigns.

BELOW: historic oil derrick and pump jack in Reagan County.
RIGHT: Highway 54 in West Texas.

Odessa

Traveling on to **Odessa** ⓮, one finds the authentic West Texas "redneck." Midland is the business center of the Permian Basin, and Odessa is the home of the oil field worker or "roughneck." "Oil field trash and proud of it," say bumper stickers often seen on pickup trucks with loaded rifles hung in the back window. No need to search further for the modern counterpart of the frontier cowboy.

Odessa does hold a few surprises though. For example, the Globe of the Great Southwest Theater, a replica of Shakespeare's Globe Theatre in London, plus a replica of Anne Hathaway's Cottage, complete with a Shakespeare library, can be found on the local college campus (tours available, call in advance; tel: 432-332-1586). A professional repertory company produces the classics plus an annual Shakespeare Festival. There is also a Permian Playhouse Theater and a symphony orchestra. At 622 N. Lee Street is the **Presidential Museum** (Tues–Sat 10am–5pm; entrance fee; tel: 432-363-7737), an intriguing exhibit dedicated to the US Presidency, including campaigning memorabilia and First Lady dolls.

For a natural wonder, inspect the **Odessa Meteor Crater** ⓯, just west of town, off Farm Road 1936. The nation's second largest, it has a diameter of 500 ft (152 meters). The crater was formed when some 2 million lbs (907,200 kg) of extraterrestrial iron crashed into the earth during the last Ice Age.

West of Odessa, at the western edge of "West Texas," the great Chihuahuan Desert begins and continues across the Trans-Pecos region into Mexico. The best vantage point for an eyeful of sandy "desertscape" is **Monahans Sandhills State Park** ⓰, 24 miles (38 km) west of Odessa on I-20, exit Park Road 41 (open daily; camel treks available; entrance fee; tel: 800-792-1112), where naked dunes tower up to 70 ft (21 meters) high and stretch north and south for 200 miles (320 km).

America's most bizarre forest grows along the margin of this desolation. The Havard oak forms a dense, at times almost impenetrable, growth which is easily overlooked, because the mature trees stand only about 3 ft (1 meter) tall. West Texans call the trees shin oak and the forest the "shinnery." These plants are marvelously well-adapted to drought, with roots that can reach a depth of 90 ft (27 meters). But, even when transplanted to moist conditions, the Havard oak remains dwarfed – obviously as suspicious of easy times as the hardy humans who settled in the region. ❑

54
TEXAS
334

the BIG
TEXAN
STEAK RANCH

AMARILLO TO LUBBOCK

Arid high plains give way to the dramatic natural beauty of Palo Duro Canyon, while the cattle city of Amarillo and Buddy Holly's home town of Lubbock have more to offer than at first glance

The Panhandle, Permian Basin and South Plains of Texas are collectively referred to as West Texas. The landscape stretches in an unbroken line, with perhaps an occasional pump jack or farmhouse on the horizon. The sunsets can be breathtaking: with nothing to obscure the view, the sky blazes with oranges, yellows and reds, and fades to soft pinks and purples. Driving at night, you can see the lights of many small towns in all directions. Because of the relatively high altitude, the air is very clear and dry. And, after the sun sets in the summer, the evening brings cool breezes.

Amarillo

In the northern Panhandle is **Amarillo** ⓱ (pop. 180,380), which means "yellow" in Spanish. It is a major center for cattle distribution; Amarillo claims to have the world's largest private cattle auction. The Amarillo Livestock Auction (100 Manhattan Street; tours daily; auctions Tues; free; tel: 806-373-7464) sells over 100,000 head a year. At the American Quarter Horse Hall of Fame and Museum (2601 E. I-40; open daily; Sun pm only; entrance fee; tel: 806-376-5181), visitors learn why this particular breed was the cowboy's favorite mount. Amarillo is headquarters for the Working Ranch Cowboys Association, which organizes the World Championship Ranch Rodeo every November.

Visitors to the Don Harrington Discovery Center (1200 Streit Drive; closed Mon; Sun pm only; entrance fee; tel: 806-355-9547) can enjoy the experience of an interactive science and technology attraction, as well as laser and planetarium shows (open daily; entrance fee). Suburban **Old San Jacinto**, with antique and gift stores along a section of historic Route 66, calls itself "the heart of Amarillo."

Finally, test your beef-eating mettle at the kitschty **Big Texan Steak Ranch** (7701 E. I-40; daily; tel: 806-657-7177), where the famous 72-ounce (2-kg) steak is free if eaten (with all the trimmings) in an hour.

LEFT: the Big Texan Steak Ranch, Amarillo, home of the "free" 72-oz steak.
BELOW: chaps come in all sizes.

O'Keeffe's country

Further south is the town of **Canyon** ⓲, home of West Texas A&M University and the sprawling **Panhandle-Plains Historical Museum** (2503 4th Avenue; open daily; Sun pm only; entrance fee; tel: 806-651-2244). This state history museum contains an art collection, geological exhibits and a reconstructed pioneer town of a century ago. One wing is devoted to the oil-boom years of the Texas Panhandle during the 1920s and 1930s, displaying equipment from that period. One exhibit, People of the Plains, relates 14,000 years of man's occupation of the South-

ern Great Plains. Canyon is also notable for the tenure from 1912 to 1918 of Georgia O'Keeffe. As a young woman, the celebrated artist came to teach art in Amarillo and then at West Texas State Normal College in Canyon. While there, she produced a striking series of watercolors of the plains, sunrises and night skies. She said: "Texas is my spiritual home."

Rusty Spur Outpost, Palo Duro Canyon.

Search for gold

Here at Canyon, 16 miles (29 km) south of Amarillo, the flat plains come to a dead halt. What lies ahead is a vast chasm – the **Palo Duro Canyon** ⓴. The multicolored canyon is 60 miles (96 km) long, up to 20 miles (32 km) wide, and has 800-ft (245-meter) walls. In summertime, there are nightly (except Sundays) performances of the spectacular, rousing musical drama *Texas* (reservations tel: 806-655-2181). With a canyon wall as a backdrop, a cast of 60 brings to life Pulitzer Prize-winner Paul Green's play about the settling of West Texas. Geologists say over 240 million years of erosion by creeks and streams, abetted by incessant wind, formed this majestic canyon. *Palo duro* means "hard wood" in Spanish, and refers to the juniper trees found in the area.

A Spanish explorer, Francisco Vasquez de Coronado, is believed to have come upon Palo Duro in 1541 while searching for Quivira, the richest of the mythical cities of gold. In the 19th century, the canyon became a stronghold of the Comanche Indians who suffered their final defeat in 1874. They were surprised by a cavalry force commanded by General Ranald Mackenzie, who drove 1,500 horses and mules out of Palo Duro and slaughtered them. Without their horses, the Native Americans were helpless. The Comanches were removed to reservations in Oklahoma. Today, **Palo Duro State Park** (11450

BELOW RIGHT: the famous Cadillac Ranch.

CADILLAC RANCH

Millionaire rancher Stanley Marsh 3 (never III) once said that he envisioned art as "a series of unanticipated rewards." If so, then his **Cadillac Ranch** ⓳, alongside I-40 west of Amarillo, is art of the highest order. Who, after all, could anticipate a row of ten long-finned luxury cars (from the years 1949–63) buried nose down in a field in the plains at, it is said, the exact same angle as the Great Pyramid of Cheops? A San Francisco art collective called The Ant Farm, which specialized in art as public spectacle, built the 1974 creation at Marsh's behest. Marsh, the proverbial eccentric Texas tycoon, made his money in television stations and decided to spend it having some fun. The much-photographed and repainted Cadillac Ranch is his love letter to the promise of the open road. Cadillac Ranch is located along eastbound I-40, between exits 60 and 62 (open daily during daylight hours; free).

Park Road 5; open daily; entrance fee; tel: 806-488-2227) comprises more than 16,400 acres (6,600 hectares). Hiking and camping are possible, along with horseback riding in season.

Map on page 298

The great ranches

The legendary figure of Charles Goodnight, the first rancher to move into the Panhandle in 1876, is closely associated with Palo Duro Canyon and with the beginning of the cattle drives. Goodnight designed the first chuckwagon. Backed by the British financier John Adair (their cattle were branded with "JA" and the ranch was christened "The JA"), Goodnight built up his herd to as many as 100,000 head in 1889. For a while in the 1880s, theirs was the largest ranch in Texas – more than 1,325,000 acres (over 536,210 hectares). Then in 1885, the XIT Ranch was established in the far northern Panhandle on over 3 million acres (1.25 million hectares), which the State of Texas had traded for the new State Capitol building in Austin. In order to stock the XIT Ranch, British and Midwestern investors were again brought in. An XIT reunion is held at **Dalhart**, 80 miles (130 km) north of Amarillo every year, in the first full week of August. The amateur rodeo and enormous barbecue attract thousands.

Cowboy Morning (April–Oct daily except Mon; entrance fee; reservations required; tel: 806-488-2100; guided jeep tours available) on the Elkins ranch always draws plenty of guests. It begins with a chuckwagon breakfast on the rim of Palo Duro, to which visitors are carried in a horse-drawn wagon from the Elkins Ranch near Claude, off US-217 east of Canyon, next to the Palo Duro Scenic State Park entrance. Another popular attraction is the nightly **Old West Show** at the **Creekwood Ranch** (tel: 806-356-9256/1-800-658-

Take advantage of the fact that Palo Duro is one of America's more accessible canyons. A spectacular 10-mile (16-km) drive by car can be made year-round across the canyon floor.

BELOW: statue of Will Rogers at Texas Tech University, Lubbock.

Buddy Holly

Charles Hardin Holley, better known as Buddy Holly (his name was misspelled on his first recording contract), was born at Lubbock, Texas, on September 7, 1936, into a loving, musical family. As a child he played piano, then accompanied himself with guitar on favorite country songs, particularly those of Hank Williams who, along with Bill Monroe was to influence his early singing style. But seeing Elvis Presley perform changed Buddy's style forever, prompting him to distill a blend of pop, blues and country.

It's hard to overstate Holly's and the Crickets' importance to the development of rock 'n' roll. Holly was among the first – if not the first – to use his own band in the studio. They were among the first to generate their own material for release as singles; among the first to work outside the established studio system and to use overdubbing and other soon-to-be-common effects in their recordings. Holly cast a long shadow over the Beatles, the Rolling Stones, Bob Dylan, Bruce Springsteen and generations of other rock performers.

In 1955 a Nashville recording agent saw Buddy and his group and, the following year, invited him to Nashville, where he recorded "Blue Days, Black Nights", his first single release. With a country melody, but a blues inflection, the track was difficult for some reviewers to categorize.

In February 1957, Buddy, along with Jerry Allison, Niki Sullivan and Larry Welborn as The Crickets, recorded "That'll Be the Day" at Norman Petty's studios in Clovis, New Mexico. This was the beginning of the Crickets, a name chosen by flipping through an encyclopedia (and providing the inspiration for a British foursome naming themselves The Beatles). "That'll Be the Day" topped the charts in September 1957 and was followed by "Peggy Sue". Its innovative "Holly sound" included steady guitar strumming, rapid, accented drumming and his famous vocal "hiccup." With "Words of Love" (also recorded in 1957) Buddy introduced another innovation – overdubbing.

The same year, the Crickets released "Not Fade Away" and "Oh Boy!". 1958 saw the release of "Rave On" (many believing it was the most exciting record the Crickets ever made), "Think It Over" and "It's So Easy".

Also in 1958, Buddy and the Crickets toured widely and appeared for the second time on the top-rated *Ed Sullivan Show*. They also toured Britain – where their records were even more successful than in the US – and visited Australia.

On February 3, 1959, a few weeks into a tour with singers Ritchie Valens and J.P. Richardson (the "Big Bopper"), Buddy was killed when their plane crashed in a snowstorm near Clear Lake, Iowa.

Although his dream was cut short, Buddy Holly left a stylistic legacy to generations of musicians. His statue stands outside Lubbock's Civic Center and visitors from all over the world pay homage at his grave in the City of Lubbock Cemetery on East 34th Street, near Quirt. The city also has a museum in his honor. ❑

LEFT: Not Fade Away: the Buddy Holly statue and Walk of Fame Memorial, Lubbock.

6673; dinner and performances Thur–Sat at 6pm), which begins with a wagon ride to the camp site, where supper is cooked over an open campfire.

Map on page 298

Lubbock

Even though the singer Mac Davis claims "happiness is Lubbock, Texas, in my rear-view mirror," most residents of **Lubbock** ㉑ (pop. 212,365) would live nowhere else. Even Mac concedes at the end of his song that now "happiness is Lubbock, Texas, getting nearer and dearer." Lubbock, a center for cotton growing, and which also ships grain and livestock, is situated on the South Plains at one of the southermost tips of the Llano Estacado, or "Staked Plains." This is the name for the immense Great Plains that sweep for 1,600 miles (2,560 km) through America's center, all the way up to Canada, and produce a substantial proportion of the country's grain, meat and fiber. A plaque marking the Llano Estacado's eastern boundary sits on US-84 southeast of town.

Texas Tech University, at 4th Street and Indiana Avenue, is one of Lubbock's main attractions. Its full sports agenda entices enthusiastic crowds. The university's teams are known as Red Raiders and are members of the Big 12 Conference. The university has established the Texas Tech Museum (closed Mon; Sun pm only; free; tel: 806-742-2490) and the National Ranching Heritage Center (3121 4th Street; open daily; Sun pm only; free; tel: 806-742-0498), a 30-acre (12-hectare) area through which winds a trail past more than 38 buildings (schoolhouse, blacksmith's shop, homes, barns, windmills) representing ranching's early days. The museum offers a mixed bag of paintings of the American West, along with European art, sculpture, ceramics and lithographs. Changing exhibitions narrate the story of the region from prehistoric times through the

For somewhere to eat in Lubbock, check out the Historic Depot District. This collection of restaurants and clubs is housed in the old Fort Worth to Denver Railroad Depot in the downtown area. It is also the home of the Buddy Holly Center.

BELOW: working cowboys at Goodnight Stables, Palo Duro Canyon.

Spanish explorations and the settling of the region by ranchers and farmers. The museum also contains the **Moody Planetarium** (entrance fee), and operates an archeological site beside Lubbock Lake Landmark (northwest of the city, near US-84 and Loop 289; closed Mon; Sun pm only; free; tel: 806-742-1116). This has yielded artifacts and tools from all known cultural groups who once lived in the Southwest, from the mammoth-hunters 20,000 years ago to the Comanches of the 19th century. No other New World site houses such a complete chronological record (guided tours Sat 10am and 1pm, and Sun 2pm; tel: 806-742-2456). A museum dedicated to Lubbock's most celebrated musical son is housed in the Historic Depot District. The **Buddy Holly Center** (1801 Crickets Avenue; open daily, Sun pm only; entrance fee; tel: 806-767-2686) honors the rock 'n' roll pioneer.

Cask at the Llano Estacado Winery.

An offbeat monument to another Lubbock musical icon lies on East Broadway across from the South Plains Fair grounds. A larger-than-life bronze of the late C.B. Stubblefield stands on the site of his former Stubb's BBQ restaurant and club. "Stubbs" was a mentor and friend of many of the 1970s generation of Lubbock musicians, including Terry Allen, Joe Ely and Butch Hancock.

Off University Avenue, 3 miles (5 km) south of town, is **Science Spectrum** (2579 S. Loop 289; open daily; Sun pm only; closed Mon in winter; entrance fee; tel: 806-745-2525), a hands-on science, nature and technology museum, along with an OMNI theater and a cinema with a 58-ft (18-meter) domed screen (shows daily; tel: 806-745-6299; entrance fee).

BELOW: ranch gate ornamentation. **RIGHT:** a wooden eclipse windmill.

The Canyon Lakes Project is a string of five lakes in Lubbock's **Yellowhouse Canyon**, where man-made waterfalls, fishing piers, camping and picnicking areas, and hike and bike trails, attract fans of the outdoors. Part of the canyon is devoted to **Mackenzie State Park**, where one of the few remaining colonies of prairie dogs resides. These amusing, squirrel-like creatures proved such a pest at one time that farmers did their best to exterminate them. Living in giant underground colonies, their "towns" covered thousands of square miles under the prairie grass before civilization overtook them.

The region's soil and climatic conditions have proved to be excellent for most of the California-type wines. There are several vineyards, among them the **Llano Estacado Winery** ㉒, 3 miles (5 km) east of US-87, on FM 1585. Here, free daily tours and wine tastings are offered (tel: 806-745-2258).

Post

Fifteen miles (24 km) southeast of Lubbock, at the foot of the dramatic Caprock escarpment on US-84, is **Post** ㉓ (pop. 3,900), named for cereal magnate Charles W. Post. He founded it in 1907, after an extended stay in the Kellogg brothers' Battle Creek sanitarium for his health. Noting that the Kelloggs had devised for their patients food substitutes made from grain, Post blended wheat, bran and molasses to create a coffee substitute called Postum. In the decade beginning in 1902, he spent $60 million to advertise Postum and such other products as grape nuts and post toasties. Long after his death in 1914, the Postum cereal company became General Foods Corporation. ❑

TEXAS PARKS

Map on pages 320–21

Camping, fishing and watersports are major attractions in the state's many parks, but these well-tended sites also provide fascinating lessons in geography, history and natural science

Parks in Texas are as varied as the people and the landscape. There are very large areas, like the massive Big Bend National Park *(see pages 289–292)*, while, at the opposite extreme, the most intimate one is probably the grave of Davy Crockett's wife in **Acton State Historic Site** ❶, near Granbury, in the heart of the Cross Timbers region. Parks planned around lakes and rivers are especially plentiful, testifying to the Texans' love affair with water, historically a rare and even a mystical commodity in much of the state.

Tent and trailer camping, hiking, picnicking, birdwatching, horse-riding, golf and all manner of zoos are found in parks throughout the state. Best of all, Texas parks showcase the natural features of their region, whether they are the moss-laden cypresses of Caddo Lake in East Texas, the cliffs of Palo Duro Canyon in the Panhandle or the lonely shell-strewn beaches of Padre Island.

Some 13 parks are operated by the National Park Service, 131 are state-owned, and there are countless roadside parks. At least one park is found in every Texas town or county and beside every lake. Facilities and standards of maintenance vary, but all these parks exist because of Texans' strong attachment to the outdoors. Many were developed by the Civilian Conservation Corps (CCC), established as part of Roosevelt's New Deal program.

Many Texas parks are built around water. Large lakes are found in various parts of the state. Although mainly for power generation and flood and drought control, they are the basis of some of the best park fun in the Lone Star State, and especially sports such as waterskiing, boating and fishing. While most lakes are man-made, the parks on Texas rivers are notable for their natural scenery and features. And the many miles of Texas beaches are just plain fun-in-the-sun.

PRECEDING PAGES: Guadalupe Mountains National Park. **LEFT:** Indian pictograph, Hueco Tanks State Historic Site. **BELOW:** grave of Davy Crockett's wife in Acton.

National Forests

Angelina National Forest, one of the four national forests in Texas, lies on both sides of the Sam Rayburn Reservoir, a 115,000-acre (47,000-hectare) lake east of Lufkin, 160 miles (256 km) northeast of Houston. This is Texas' largest reservoir and its surrounding recreation areas provide a wide variety of boating, hiking and camping activities in the towering pine forest and along the lake branches. Backpacking and primitive camping are permitted throughout the 153,000-acre (62,000-hectare) forest, unless otherwise posted.

West of Angelina, the **Davy Crockett National Forest** covers more than 160,000 acres (65,000 hectares) along the Neches river. A second-growth forest, it has made a remarkable comeback since logging stopped in the 1920s. The 4-C Trail, a scenic 20-mile (32-km) trek, connects Ratcliff Lake Recreation Area with the Neches Bluff Recreation Area. It

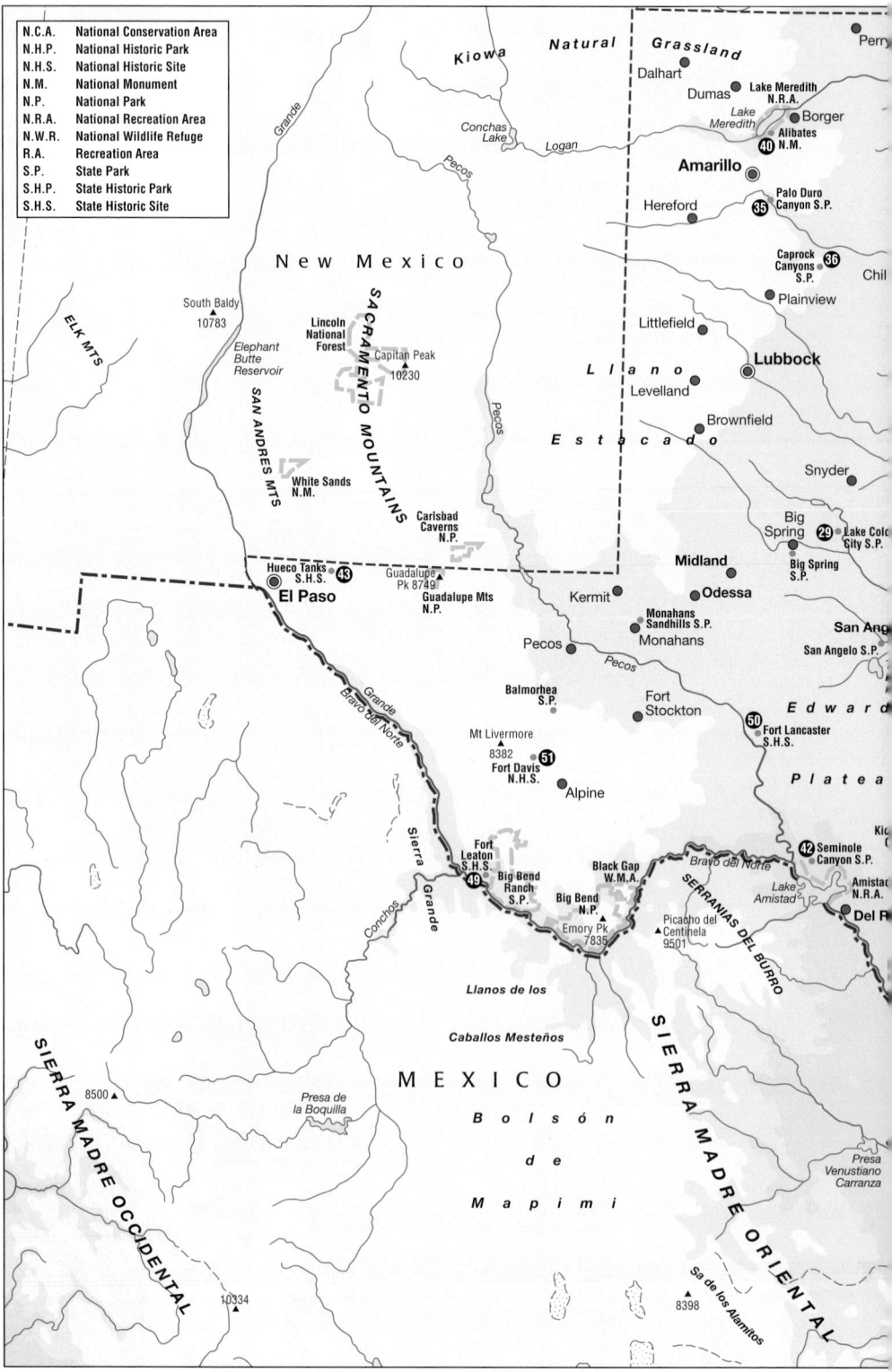
N.C.A. National Conservation Area
N.H.P. National Historic Park
N.H.S. National Historic Site
N.M. National Monument
N.P. National Park
N.R.A. National Recreation Area
N.W.R. National Wildlife Refuge
R.A. Recreation Area
S.P. State Park
S.H.P. State Historic Park
S.H.S. State Historic Site
Kiowa Natural Grassland
Perry
Dalhart
Dumas
Lake Meredith N.R.A.
Lake Meredith
Borger
Alibates N.M.
40
Amarillo
Palo Duro Canyon S.P.
35
Hereford
Caprock Canyons S.P.
36
Chil
Plainview
Conchas Lake
Logan
Pecos
Grande
New Mexico
South Baldy 10783
ELK MTS
Lincoln National Forest
Capitan Peak 10230
Elephant Butte Reservoir
SACRAMENTO MOUNTAINS
SAN ANDRES MTS
White Sands N.M.
Carlsbad Caverns N.P.
Littlefield
Lubbock
Llano Estacado
Levelland
Brownfield
Snyder
Big Spring
29
Lake Colo City S.P.
Big Spring S.P.
Midland
Odessa
Hueco Tanks S.H.S.
43
El Paso
Guadalupe Pk 8749
Guadalupe Mts N.P.
Kermit
Monahans Sandhills S.P.
Monahans
San Ang
San Angelo S.P.
Pecos
Balmorhea S.P.
Fort Stockton
Edward
50
Fort Lancaster S.H.S.
Mt Livermore 8382
51
Fort Davis N.H.S.
Alpine
Platea
Bravo del Norte
Sierra Grande
Fort Leaton S.H.S.
49
Big Bend Ranch S.P.
Black Gap W.M.A.
Big Bend N.P.
Emory Pk 7835
Conchos
42
Seminole Canyon S.P.
Lake Amistad
Amistad N.R.A.
Del R
Picacho del Centinela 9501
SERRANIAS DEL BURRO
Llanos de los Caballos Mesteños
MEXICO
Bolsón de Mapimi
Presa de la Boquilla
8500
SIERRA MADRE OCCIDENTAL
SIERRA MADRE ORIENTAL
Presa Venustiano Carranza
10334
8398
Sa de los Alamitos

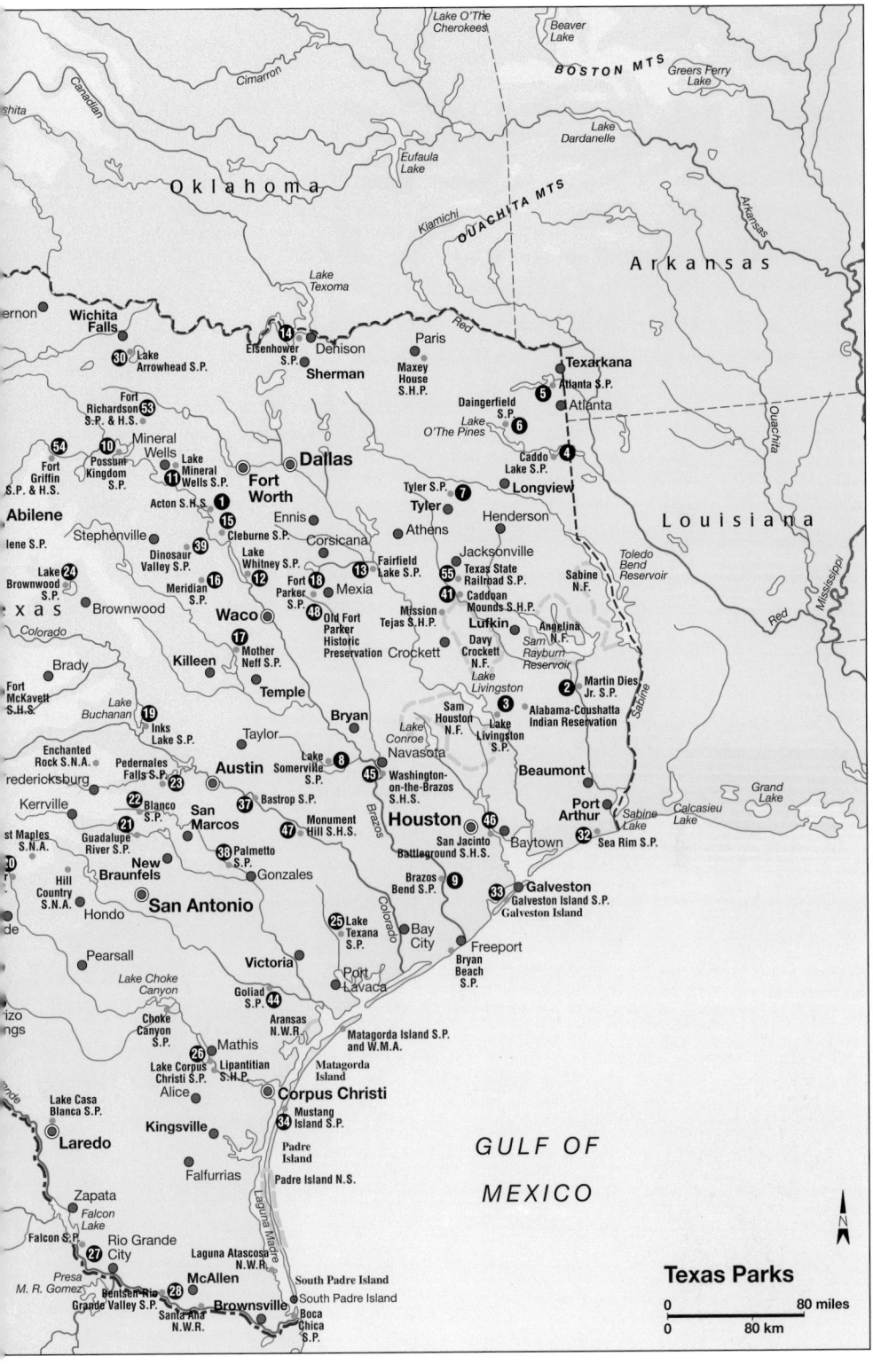
Texas Parks
0 80 miles
0 80 km
N
Oklahoma
Arkansas
Louisiana
GULF OF MEXICO
Lake O'The Cherokees
Beaver Lake
BOSTON MTS
Greers Ferry Lake
Cimarron
Canadian
Lake Dardanelle
Eufaula Lake
OUACHITA MTS
Kiamichi
Arkansas
Lake Texoma
Red
Ouachita
Mississippi
Sabine
Toledo Bend Reservoir
Sam Rayburn Reservoir
Lake Livingston
Lake Conroe
Brazos
Colorado
Laguna Madre
Wichita Falls
Lake Arrowhead S.P.
Eisenhower S.P.
Denison
Sherman
Paris
Maxey House S.H.P.
Texarkana
Atlanta S.P.
Atlanta
Daingerfield S.P.
Lake O'The Pines
Caddo Lake S.P.
Longview
Tyler S.P.
Tyler
Henderson
Fort Richardson S.P. & H.S.
Mineral Wells
Possum Kingdom S.P.
Lake Mineral Wells S.P.
Fort Griffin S.P. & H.S.
Dallas
Fort Worth
Acton S.H.S.
Abilene
Ennis
Athens
Cleburne S.P.
Corsicana
Stephenville
Dinosaur Valley S.P.
Lake Whitney S.P.
Jacksonville
Texas State Railroad S.P.
Fairfield Lake S.P.
Lake Brownwood S.P.
Meridian S.P.
Fort Parker S.P.
Mexia
Caddoan Mounds S.H.P.
Brownwood
Waco
Old Fort Parker Historic Preservation
Mission Tejas S.H.P.
Lufkin
Angelina N.F.
Davy Crockett N.F.
Crockett
Mother Neff S.P.
Killeen
Brady
Fort McKavett S.H.S.
Temple
Lake Buchanan
Inks Lake S.P.
Bryan
Sam Houston N.F.
Lake Livingston S.P.
Martin Dies Jr. S.P.
Alabama-Coushatta Indian Reservation
Taylor
Navasota
Enchanted Rock S.N.A.
Pedernales Falls S.P.
Austin
Lake Somerville S.P.
Washington-on-the-Brazos S.H.S.
Beaumont
Fredericksburg
Kerrville
Blanco S.P.
San Marcos
Bastrop S.P.
Monument Hill S.H.S.
Houston
Port Arthur
Sabine Lake
Calcasieu Lake
Grand Lake
Fort Maples S.N.A.
Guadalupe River S.P.
Palmetto S.P.
San Jacinto Battleground S.H.S.
Baytown
Sea Rim S.P.
New Braunfels
Gonzales
Hill Country S.N.A.
Hondo
San Antonio
Brazos Bend S.P.
Galveston
Galveston Island S.P.
Galveston Island
Lake Texana S.P.
Bay City
Freeport
Bryan Beach S.P.
Pearsall
Victoria
Port Lavaca
Lake Choke Canyon
Goliad S.P.
Choke Canyon S.P.
Aransas N.W.R.
Matagorda Island S.P. and W.M.A.
Mathis
Lake Corpus Christi S.P.
Lipantitian S.H.P.
Matagorda Island
Alice
Corpus Christi
Lake Casa Blanca S.P.
Mustang Island S.P.
Laredo
Kingsville
Padre Island
Falfurrias
Padre Island N.S.
Zapata
Falcon Lake
Falcon S.P.
Rio Grande City
Laguna Atascosa N.W.R.
Presa M. R. Gomez
McAllen
South Padre Island
Bentsen-Rio Grande Valley S.P.
Brownsville
Santa Ana N.W.R.
Boca Chica S.P.

Spring and fall are the prettiest times of the year to visit parks in East Texas; summertime, as in the deep South, is hot, humid and bug-ridden. Remember to bring a good insect repellent.

is best to travel along it in the fall, winter or spring, when the climate is more hospitable and the bugs are less numerous. Basic camping is allowed along the 4-C Trail, but be suspicious of the water. Carry your own or use water purifiers.

Sabine National Forest, with 160,000 acres (65,000 hectares), stretches along the Texas side of the Toledo Bend Reservoir on the Louisiana border. It includes a historic battleground where a 47-strong band of Confederates prevented a Union invasion of Texas. There are facilities for hikers, campers, boaters and anglers. Catfish, bass and crappie are the major fish to be found in the smaller lakes, but be sure to have a current fishing license and observe all bag limits.

Hiking in the east

In East Texas, the **Sam Houston National Forest** offers excellent hiking and camping between Huntsville and Lake Livingston. Its highlight is the **Lone Star Trail**, the longest developed hiking route in the state, at 129 miles (208 km). The forest's Double Lake and Stubblefield Recreation areas have extensive camping and picnicking, and serve well as trailheads. Camping is also permitted along the trail and in designated areas. Hikers are advised to tote their own water in and garbage out. But beware: from mid-November until January 1, hiking can be dangerous, because the hunting season is open.

On the water

Martin Dies, Jr. State Park ❷, on Steinhagen Reservoir, lies 15 miles (24 km) east of the town of Woodville. The trees are gorgeous in the fall and, in addition to water sports, there is a wide variety of birdlife along its trail.

BELOW: Fort Concho, National Historic Site, San Angelo.

Lake Livingston State Park ❸, 75 miles (120 km) northeast of Houston, occupies the east shore of the 85,000-acre (34,000-hectare) lake. Ninety-eight species of birds have been spotted along its 4 miles (6 km) of trails.

Just 15 miles (24 km) east is the **Alabama-Coushatta Indian Reservation**, established in 1854, when the state legislature gave 1,280 acres (520 hectares) to the Alabama Indians, who had settled in East Texas 40 years before. Additional land has since been added to this densely forested region known as the Big Thicket. Gourd dancing predominates at the annual tribal powwow held the first weekend in June.

About 550 Native Americans still live on the Alabama-Coushatta Reservation. Their homes are now made of brick, or are wood-framed, they only wear traditional dress for ceremonies, and many work in the timber industry.

Mossy cypresses

Further north, **Caddo Lake State Park** ❹, near Marshall, is the largest natural lake in the state. Spanish moss drapes its ancient cypress trees. Waterskiing is possible on sections of the lake, but drifting along in a canoe is better suited to its peaceful nature.

In the northeast corner of Texas, **Atlanta State Park** ❺ sits on the banks of Lake Wright Patman, in a forest of oak, pine and dogwood. Near the town of Daingerfield, 30 miles (50 km) to the southeast, **Daingerfield State Park** ❻ surrounds a small lake often filled with blooming water lilies. Its trails reward hikers with glimpses of wildlife, including deer and raccoons.

Tyler State Park ❼, just north of the city of Tyler, is a large park where swimming areas and a good fishing lake can be found. When the dogwood blooms in spring, Tyler Park is at its best.

Lake Somerville State Parks and Trailway ❽, on the western edge of East Texas near Brenham, 85 miles (135 km) northwest of Houston, consists of two

BELOW: fishing in an East Texas park.

If you plan to visit several Texas State Parks, invest $50 in an annual Gold Texas Conservation Passport, which allows unlimited admission to the parks and to some areas closed to the general public, for all the passengers in your vehicle. Contact Texas Parks and Wildlife Department on (800) 792-1112.

units on either side of the lake. They are connected by a 13-mile (21-km) trail, along which some of the campgrounds are especially for equestrians. There is also a wildlife management area in the park.

On the Brazos river less than 70 miles (110 km) south of Houston, **Brazos Bend State Park** ❾ has 3¼ miles (5 km) of river frontage. The alligator and hundreds of bird species are stars here, and migrating waterfowl lure so many visitors in the fall that reservations are necessary for its overnight facilities.

New lakes

Drought and flood control projects of the 1950s and 1960s created a multitude of new lakes in the central and western parts of Texas. There are no pine forests surrounding these lakes, but they often have their own special appeal.

About 100 miles (160 km) west of Fort Worth is **Possum Kingdom State Park** ❿, its 10 miles (16 km) of shoreline shaded by deciduous oaks and the juniper trees which many Texans call "cedar." Waterskiing and scuba diving are popular here. About 55 miles (89 km) southeast, **Lake Mineral Wells State Park** ⓫ sits in a pretty valley with an equestrian trail and small boats for rent.

Down the road, **Lake Whitney State Park** ⓬, 75 miles (120 km) south of Fort Worth, is excellent for waterskiing and bass fishing. Its numerous facilities include an airfield for campers who fly in with the herons and geese.

Anglers in search of a good fishing lake with a lot of variety will enjoy **Fairfield Lake State Park** ⓭, 90 miles (145 km) southeast of Dallas, noted for redfish, large-mouth bass, crappie, catfish, bluegill and drum.

On the Red River border separating Texas and Oklahoma, Lake Texoma is popular with sail-and ski-boaters. Anglers go after the native Red River white bass, and

BELOW: Highway Department rest area on the Rio Grande river road.

the black and striped bass. **Eisenhower State Park** ⓮ lies on the cliffs above Lake Texoma, offering plenty of room for campers, fishermen and boaters, and even a protected cove for swimmers. There are campgrounds along the lake's 15-mile (24-km) Cross Timbers Trail but water is not available, except in the developed areas, and the presence of snakes requires caution. Five miles (8 km) southeast in Denison is the restored two-story birthplace of President Dwight D. Eisenhower.

Map on pages 320–21

Less crowded

Four parks in North Central Texas, more or less along the Fort Worth–Waco corridor, are very pleasant, have good facilities and are not often crowded. **Cleburne State Park** ⓯, near the town of the same name, was built around a small lake, while **Meridian State Park** ⓰, 70 miles (110 km) southwest of Fort Worth, also has a small lake with a hiking trail around.

Mother Neff State Park ⓱, 128 miles (206 km) south of Fort Worth, was the first Texas state park, the first 6 acres (2.5 hectares) being donated by Governor Pat Neff's mother. The governor gave an additional 250 acres (100 hectares) in 1933. Developed by the CCC in the 1930s, it is a fitting tribute to early park pioneers. **Fort Parker State Park** ⓲ on Fort Parker Lake, near Mexia, provides waterskiing and fishing; the grounds incorporate the now-dead town of Springfield – only its cemetery remains.

Denison's most famous son, Dwight D. Eisenhower, who has a State Park named after him.

Hill Country

Large lakes and cypress-shaded rivers in the Texas Hill Country host a wide array of water activities. There are six large lakes on the lower Colorado river alone, all dotted with informal camping and fishing areas, and with private

BELOW: space wins in Texas State Parks.

On the Guadalupe and other rivers in the state, the water levels are unpredictable and are subject to rapid rises and falls. Be forewarned.

marinas and resorts, while the Guadalupe river feeds Canyon Lake, about 40 miles (65 km) southwest of Austin, and six smaller lakes. The most popular lake park is probably **Inks Lake State Park** ⑲, near Burnet, offering water-skiing, scuba diving and fishing, as well as a nine-hole golf course and a 7-mile (11-km) hiking trail. Reservations are essential.

Garner State Park ⑳, on the Frio river, 30 miles (50 km) north of Uvalde, although now enlarged, still tends to be crowded, with reservations necessary year-round for the picturesque cabins. *Frio* means cold in Spanish, and this river usually is. The scenery is at its best when the spring wild flowers make their show. One of the best ways to see the beautiful river canyon is from a rented pedal boat or inner tube.

Guadalupe River State Park ㉑ is a favorite spot for canoeing, which is a growing sport in Texas. Thirty miles (50 km) north of San Antonio, the park's four rapids have excited enthusiasts of all skill levels. Deer, coyotes, raccoons and gray foxes can often be spied directly from the hiking trails, and bird watching enthusiasts will find golden-cheeked warblers nesting in a stand of Ashe juniper from March to late summer.

Within an hour's drive north of San Antonio, **Blanco State Park** ㉒ straddles 1½ miles (2.5 km) of the Blanco river, near its namesake town. Its small size seems to discourage crowds. The park's main activities are swimming, fishing and watching the river go by.

The diversity of the Hill Country is especially evident at **Pedernales Falls State Park** ㉓, about 45 miles (70 km) west of Austin. Along parts of the Pedernales river, one finds lush vegetation and armadillos among the scrub cedar. The Pedernales, like a lot of Texas rivers, floods when it rains, but is otherwise a peaceful stream running over a rock bed into calm pools. Watch out for flash floods and an occasional treacherous waterfall or whirlpool, especially when the river is rising. The 7-mile (11-km) Wolf Mountain Trail is rewarding to skilled backpackers and hardy novices alike.

BELOW: end of the day in one of the parks.

Lake Brownwood State Park ㉔ is 22 miles (35 km) west of Brownwood, where the Texas Hill Country segues into West Texas. Its many facilities include picturesquely situated stone cabins. The 7,300-acre (3,000-hectare) lake imposes no limit on boat size.

Keeping cool

Perhaps nowhere in the state are watersports more appreciated than in South Texas, often a pretty dry place which can get very hot in the summer. Spring and fall are the most enjoyable seasons for both locals and visitors. **Lake Texana State Park** ㉕ is well-stocked with catfish, large-mouth bass and striped bass, with early spring being the best time for fishing. Additional campsites are available at the nearby Lavaca-Navidad River Authority's Brackenridge Campground.

Although **Lake Corpus Christi State Park** ㉖ was developed by the CCC in the 1930s, most of its facilities are more modern. Fishing, especially for catfish, is good. Because of its mild climate and proximity to Corpus Christi, 35 miles (55 km) to the south, the park is popular all year round and can be crowded.

Up the Rio Grande, near Del Rio, **Amistad National Recreation Area** provides facilities all along the American side of Lake Amistad for watersports. Scuba diving is especially good because the water is so clear. Deer (with bow and arrow only) and bird hunting are allowed in certain areas during the season.

One of the largest lakes in Texas, Falcon Lake, is also on the US-Mexican border. **Falcon State Park** ㉗, 15 miles (24 km) north of the historic border town of Roma, has comfortable accommodations. Birders here are rewarded with a variety of rare species, including the green kingfisher.

Bentsen-Rio Grande Valley State Park ㉘, on the river near Mission, is most popular in the winter, when its subtropical climate attracts many wintering tourists. Its nature trail interprets the hundreds of rare birds, animals and plants in the area.

Hunting and boating

As in South Texas, where large lakes make summer more acceptable, way up in the Panhandle, 35 miles (56 km) east of Amarillo, **Lake Meredith National Recreation Area** cools the arid Llano Estacado. Deer and bird hunting is permitted in certain parts of this park during the season. There is usually a good wind for sailing, but storms are unpredictable and boaters of all types should always be very cautious on this stretch of water.

Not as heavily developed as Lake Meredith, other West Texas lakes still give welcome recreational relief to many Texans and tourists. **Lake Colorado City State Park** ㉙, between Big Spring and Abilene, and **Lake Arrowhead State Park** ㉚, near Wichita Falls, are both on good-sized lakes and are popular with motor boaters and waterskiers.

Map on pages 320–21

Nature lovers should make plans to stay overnight at Bentsen-Rio Grande Valley State Park, in order to observe the park's nocturnal inhabitants, as well as those normally seen in the daytime.

BELOW: whooping crane at Aransas National Wildlife Refuge.

Remember that hiking is taxing on soft beaches, and even the most experienced trekkers should be thoroughly prepared before setting out on any extended hike along the seashore.

Abilene State Park ㉛, about 20 miles (30 km) southwest of town, is just across the road from Lake Abilene, and not far from an area once rife with wild buffalo. The park's campgrounds and swimming pool are set in a historic pecan tree grove.

At the beach

The beaches of the Gulf of Mexico are the site of some of the state's best-developed and most popular parks. **Sea Rim State Park** ㉜, on the coast near the Louisiana border, is one of the more tranquil. The greater part of the large park is an extensive marsh inhabited by a multitude of alligators, nutria, mink, raccoons and wintering waterfowl.

Galveston Island State Park ㉝, on the west end of the island, has well-situated beach campgrounds and picnicking areas. Occupying 5½ miles (9 km) of Gulf beach, down the coast, is **Mustang Island State Park** ㉞, with hundreds of campsites and picnic sites. About half of the beach front is undeveloped. At both parks, reservations are advisable, especially in the summer.

Fourteen miles (23 km) further south is **Padre Island National Seashore**, America's largest designated national seashore whose camping facilities stretch along a 66-mile (106-km) white sand beach – probably the prettiest white sand beach in Texas.

The most remote beach park has to be **Matagorda Island State Park and Wildlife Management Area**. Accessible only by ferry across Aransas Bay or private boat, the park has no drinking water, no electricity and no telephones. Whooping cranes winter on the island. Make sure you contact the park headquarters in Port O'Connor prior to a visit.

BELOW: Padre Island beach.

To the mountains

Guadalupe Mountains National Park straddles the New Mexico-Texas border, about 100 miles (160 km) due east of El Paso. These mountains, which range in both states, are probably the largest fossil reef in the world and contain the Carlsbad Caverns, as well as the highest point in Texas, Guadalupe Peak, at 8,749 ft (2,667 meters). The landscapes of the park are the most varied in the whole state. Here, the Chihuahuan Desert rises to spectacular evergreen forests, likelier to be located in the Colorado mountains than in Texas. The sheer cliffs of El Capitán tower 2,000 ft (610 meters). Greasewood and lechuguilla give way to lush ferns in the protected canyons, and more than 170 species of bird and over 50 different reptiles and amphibians live in the Guadalupe Park, as well as elk, mule deer, coyotes and a mountain lion and black bear or two.

McKittrick Canyon is one of the highlights. The canyon displays a rare and varied collection of vegetation. High sheltering walls and year-round streams ensure the right conditions for ferns, big-tooth maples and little-leaf walnuts to grow. The marked trail into it is not difficult, but stay on the trail to avoid disturbing the fragile ecological system. Permits are required for camping.

Rugged landscapes also characterize **Palo Duro Canyon State Park** 35, in the Panhandle, spectacular from every angle. Smaller canyons can be found at **Caprock Canyons State Park** 36, 60 miles (100 km) southeast of Palo Duro.

Central Texas

Central Texas has its share of natural and scenic attractions, too, although the scale is less awesome. **Enchanted Rock State Natural Area**, 18 miles (30 km) north of Fredericksburg, centers around a billion-year-old granite mountain.

Map on pages 320–21

Lifeguard station, Galveston Island.

BELOW: El Capitán.

Its prominence in the landscape made it a source of Native American ghost tales and a traveler's landmark. While most trails around the rock are taxing, one trail to the top is manageable by most healthy hikers.

A large stand of big-tooth maples, 35 miles (55 km) southwest of Kerrville, is the focus of **Lost Maples State Natural Area**. One of the few remnants of the large maple forests of a less arid time in Texas, these trees provide glorious color in October. Most of the trails here are challenging, but a short one along the Sabinal river is easy. The park is pleasant at all times and is particularly popular with birders. Golden and bald eagles can often be seen in winter.

TIP

The most popular time to visit Lost Maples is late October/early November, when the leaves turn stunning colors. If you want to visit at this time, make it a weekday, when the crowds aren't so pervasive.

In a relic pine forest less than 30 miles (45 km) southeast of Austin, rustic **Bastrop State Park** 37 gives another glimpse of an earlier Texas. Its picturesque cabins were built by the CCC. Reservations are necessary for these and for the park's campgrounds.

Palmetto State Park 38, 60 miles (95 km) east of San Antonio, near Gonzales, has hiking trails that show off the plant and animal life and the extensive bird population. Its Ottine Swamp contains a tropical forest of palmettos (low-growing palms native to Texas) and other exotic flora. Spring and fall are the best times to visit: summer can be humid and stifling.

Wildlife refuges

Aransas National Wildlife Refuge, on San Antonio Bay near Rockport, has a visitors' center and miles of trails for viewing the refuge wildlife, including the rare and endangered whooping cranes which winter here. Sixteen miles (26 km) of roads give glimpses of the many deer, alligators and javelinas, as well as the multitude of other birds who live here year-round. Prob-

BELOW: Padre Island National Seashore.

LOCAL HERITAGE

Like much of the rest of the United States, Texas has gradually become more aware of its cultural heritage over the past 30 years.

Almost every city and town has at least one historic house museum that local folks point to with pride. Some are large groupings of houses with a paid staff and long opening hours, like **Sam Houston Park** in Huntsville, which has gathered together buildings associated with the Texas hero, including two homes, a gazebo and a blacksmith's shop.

Others are smaller, often the work of dedicated volunteers, like **French's Trading Post**, now the **John Jay French Museum**, in Beaumont, the city's first two-story house. In the same vein are the **Annie Riggs Hotel**, a museum in Fort Stockton which once accommodated passengers on the Butterfield Overland Mail coaches, the **Bishop's Palace** in Galveston (his official, not actual residence), and the **Charles Stillman House** in Brownsville, built in 1851 by Charles Stillman, founder of the city, himself.

The majority of these fine historic sites and structures date from the 19th century. Individually and collectively, they skillfully illustrate life during that colorful era.

ably the surest way to see the whoopers is to take the boat that goes out from the Sea Gun Inn, near Fulton from October to early April. Campgrounds are handy at nearby **Goose Island State Park**.

The **Laguna Atascosa National Wildlife Refuge** is just north of Port Isabel on the Laguna Madre. When ducks and geese fly south for the winter, this is where many of them come. Camping is not allowed, but there are auto and walking trails.

Santa Ana National Wildlife Refuge, on the Rio Grande near McAllen, has 12 miles (19 km) of hiking trails through its 2,000-acre (800-hectare) sub-tropical forest. It is the northern limit of many Mexican birds' migration. Furthermore, one of the forest's ebony trees may be the oldest and largest in the United States.

Map on pages 320–21

The Alibates flint, found in the quarries of Alibates National Monument, was named for Ali Bates, a one-time local cowboy.

Cultural past

A large and growing class of parks protect and display the cultural heritage of the state. The historical and recreational are often combined in these parks, providing fun flavored with a little education.

Dinosaur Valley State Park 39 exhibits the tracks made by the Pleurocoelus and Acrocanthosaurus dinosaurs, prehistoric reptiles which walked around this swamp millions of years ago. The interpretive center explains the tracks, and a trail leads right to them. Camping, hiking and picnicking are also provided in this park, which is centered 60 miles (95 km) southwest of Fort Worth, near Glen Rose.

Remnants of other prehistoric Texas cultures are preserved in several parks. **Alibates National Monument** 40, in the Panhandle, was the source of a particular flint. **Caddoan Mounds State Historic Park** 41, clear across the state in East Texas, 30 miles (50 km) west of Nacogdoches, was the home of a group

BELOW: Dinosaur Valley State Park, Glen Rose.

of agricultural Texans from the 8th to the 14th centuries. A sedentary people who may have had some association with the pyramid builders in Mexico, they left behind three large earthen mounds, filled with religious and other artifacts. Interpretive exhibits and a self-guided tour explain as much as is known about these ancient people. During summer, archeological digs sometimes take place, and visitors are invited to watch.

Recreational and camping facilities are convenient at **Mission Tejas State Park**, 8 miles (13 km) down the road.

Indian pictograph at Hueco Tanks State Historic Site.

Pictographs

Close to Del Rio, on the border, is another site with striking evidence of inhabitants 2,000–8,000 years ago. These ancient nomadic people painted the walls and ceilings of their cave dwellings, in what is today **Seminole Canyon State Park and Historical Site** ㊷, with fanciful animals and other images whose meaning is now lost. One pictograph-covered shelter is open to visitors on a guided tour. The trail leading to it takes stamina, particularly in the summer heat. An award-winning exhibit at the Visitors' Center interprets the prehistory and history of the park. Campsites with water are available.

Rock art is also found at **Hueco Tanks State Historic Site** ㊸, 32 miles (51 km) northeast of El Paso. Tribes may have come through the area as long as 10,000 years ago. Water held in the depressions of the rocks made it a popular place for travelers in the surrounding desert. There is Pueblo rock art dating from AD 1000 and Mescalero Apache images from the 18th century. The artworks can be seen on a self-guiding tour. Bird- and animal-watching is also fruitful here, and campsites and picnic areas are both available.

BELOW: Goliad State Park.

Spanish colonial

The first colonizers of Texas, the Spanish, have left substantial reminders of their presence. The **San Antonio Missions National Historical Park** *(see pages 198–9)* includes five 18th-century mission churches, a dam and an aqueduct. The Spanish mission of Nuestra Señora Espiritu Santo de Zuniga is the centerpiece of **Goliad State Park** 44, just south of the historic town of Goliad. The mission was reconstructed by the CCC on the ruins of the 1749 church. The park has a scenic campground on the river and exhibits in the church and granary. The nearby Presidio La Bahia gained notoriety in 1836 when it was the site of Santa Anna's execution of Fannin's men during the Texas Revolution – hence "Remember Goliad!" The old *presidio* has been reconstructed and is open to the public.

Map on pages 320–21

It's hard to believe that the little village of Washington-on-the-Brazos was once capital of the independent Republic of Texas. Today, it has only around 250 inhabitants.

Independent Texas

Washington-on-the-Brazos State Historic Site 45 is the site of the proclamation of the Texas Declaration of Independence on March 2, 1836. Nothing much remains of the bustling 1850s town, but a replica of Texas' Independence Hall and the home of the Republic's last president have been reconstructed. Re-enactors bring 19th-century life to present-day visitors. The Star of the Republic Museum, operated by Brenham's Blinn College, sits in the park grounds and has a number of good exhibits about life in early Texas. The park's riverside picnic area is on a bluff above the Brazos.

Six weeks after the declaration of Texas' Independence, Sam Houston's small band of Texans routed Santa Anna in the marshes of Buffalo Bayou, now commemorated by the **San Jacinto Battleground State Historic Site** 46. In La Porte, just east of Houston, the San Jacinto Monument rises in the midst of the battleground and houses a museum. The park provides picnic areas, but no campgrounds.

Although the Texas Republic was established by the April 1836 battle at San Jacinto, it struggled against continued Mexican incursions for the next 10 years. **Monument Hill State Historic Site** 47, in La Grange, 70 miles (115 km) east of Austin, honors the Texans who died in two responses to such attacks, the Dawson and Mier expeditions. The **Kreische Brewery State Historic Site** is contiguous and contains the ruins of a mid-19th-century brewery, at one time the third-largest in the state. The sites share a well-developed picnic area and grand views of the Colorado river. No camping is available.

BELOW: Washington-on-the-Brazos State Historic Site.

Frontier forts

Fortifications of many types are scattered around the state and represent battles of various sorts fought on Texas soil. The most famous of all, of course, is the Alamo in San Antonio. **Old Fort Parker Historic Preseveration** 48, about 35 miles (55 km) east of Waco and now owned by the City of Groesbeck, commemorates another famous battle of 1836, the Native American attack on Parker's Fort and the capture of little Cynthia Ann Parker. The "Fall of Fort Ceremony" each May vividly recounts the story of this family fort and the lives and deaths of its inhabitants.

The Texas frontier, after annexation by the United

Map on pages 320–21

States in 1845, stretched long and wide, and was almost unprotected. Settlers in the most remote areas had to create their own defense systems against hostile Native Americans and outlaws. **Fort Leaton State Historic Site** 49, on the Rio Grande near present-day Presidio, was built by a border trader (some called him a smuggler), Ben Leaton. The Federal government also built forts to cope with Native American threats to the advancing settlers, and a group of fort parks represents the 40- year struggle. **Fort Lancaster State Historic Site** 50, **Fort Davis National Historic Site** 51 and **Fort McKavett State Historic Site** 52 were all forts built before the Civil War.

Fort Lancaster's adobe ruins lie about 70 miles (115 km) east of Fort Stockton, and are interpreted in the visitors' center and via a self-guided tour of the old parade field. At Fort McKavett, about 40 miles (65 km) northwest of Junction, and Fort Davis, in the Davis Mountains 25 miles (40 km) north of Alpine, little is left of their earliest incarnations, but they have been restored to their post-Civil War state. More forts were built after the war, when Native American hostilities reached their height. **Fort Richardson State Park and Historic Site** 53 in Jacksboro, 100 miles (160 km) northwest of Fort Worth, and **Fort Griffin State Park and Historic Site** 54, 50 miles (80 km) north of Abilene, have been developed with pleasant camping and picnicking adjuncts. Highlights of visits to all the forts are occasional military re-enactments: check individual parks for details.

Steaming along the Texas State Railroad State Historic Park.

BELOW: McKittrick Canyon, Guadalupe Mountains National Park.
RIGHT: Monahans Sandhills State Park.

Parks of another kind

Some parks defy the usual categories. **Texas State Railroad State Park** 55 runs for 25 miles (40 km) between Rusk and Palestine, and is one of the most popular parks in East Texas. The turn-of-the-20th-century rolling stock gives an authentic flavor to the scenic ride along the historic route. The round trip takes three hours. There are picnic sites at both ends to round off the journey.

The **Battleship *Texas* State Historic Site**, a memorial to Texans who fought in World War II, is moored at San Jacinto Battleground State Historic Site in La Porte. Commissioned in 1914, it is the only surviving Navy ship that served in both wars, notably in D-Day operations off the coast of Normandy in 1944 and in the Pacific at Iwo Jima and Okinawa in 1945. Open to the public seven days a week, the ship features a self-guided tour and interesting displays about ship life.

It is not the only warship to be named after Texas. More recently a nuclear submarine was named after the city of Corpus Christi, which is the home of a naval air station. The name had to be changed when complaints about the implications of its Latin meaning (Body of Christ) were voiced.

Beyond words and pictures

There are, of course, many excellent parks in the state that have not been mentioned here, through lack of space. But the list is also incomplete in that no words or pictures can ever fully capture the beauty and spirit of the Texas landscape like a campout in the East Texas Piney Woods, a hike through a dusty, rugged canyon, or a quiet afternoon's sailing on a placid lake on a late fall afternoon. ❑

INSIGHT GUIDES

TRAVEL TIPS

TEXAS

The Guides That Are Streets Ahead

INSIGHT GUIDES
LONDON
CITY GUIDE
UNDERGROUND
KNOW THE CITY LIKE A LOCAL

PARIS
METRO
KNOW THE CITY LIKE A LOCAL

INSIGHT GUIDES

www.insightguides.com

Insight Guides to every major country are also available.

Travel Tips

Transportation

Getting There 340
By Air 340
By Train 340
By Bus.....340
Down Mexico Way.....340

Getting Around 341
On Arrival 341
Public Transportation..... 341
Driving 341
Car Rental 342
Driving Times 342

Accommodations

Choosing a Hotel 343
Campgrounds..... 343
Accommodations Listings .. 344
Dallas/Fort Worth and Environs 344
Central Texas 345
San Antonio and Environs 347
Houston and East Texas 348
The Gulf Coast 350
Rio Grande Valley 351
Del Rio to Laredo 351
El Paso, the Trans-Pecos and Big Bend 351
Amarillo, Lubbock and Environs..... 353
The West 353

Eating Out

What to Eat 355
Restaurant Listings 355
Dallas/Fort Worth and Environs 355
Central Texas 357
San Antonio and Environs 359
Houston and East Texas 359
The Gulf Coast 361
Rio Grande Valley 361
Del Rio to Laredo 361
El Paso, The Trans-Pecos and Big Bend 362
Amarillo, Lubbock and Environs..... 363
The West 363

Activities

Festivals 364
The Arts 365
Art 365
Music and Dance.....365
Theater.....366
Activities for Children.....366
Nightlife 366
Dallas/Fort Worth 366
Houston 366
San Antonio 366
Austin.....367
Shopping 367
Where to Shop 367
Clothing Chart.....367
Shop Listings 368
Sports 369
Participant Sports 369
Who Plays Where.....369
Spectator Sports 369
Stock Shows and Rodeos 369

A – Z

Admission Charges 370
Budgeting for your Trip 370
Business Hours.....370
Climate 370
Crime and Security 371
Customs Regulations 371
Disabled Travelers.....371
Embassies and Consulates 371
Emergency Numbers 371
Entry Requirements.....371
Etiquette.....371
Gay and Lesbian Travelers ..372
Health and Medical Care 372
Internet 373
Lost Property 373
Maps 373
Media.....373
Money Matters 373
Postal System.....373
Public Holidays 374
Public Restrooms 374
Religious Services.....374
Taxes 374
Telecommunications 374
Local Dialing Codes 374
Time Zones.....374
Tipping 374
Tourist Information 374
Tour Operators 375
Websites 375
What to Bring 375

Further Reading

General 376
History and Current Affairs..376
Art and Architecture.....376
Natural History 376
Armchair Travel 377
Other Insight Guides 377

TRANSPORTATION

GETTING THERE AND GETTING AROUND

GETTING THERE

By Air

There are three airports in Texas classified as international: Dallas-Fort Worth, George Bush Intercontinental in Houston, and San Antonio. Air passengers to Texas usually arrive at Dallas–Fort Worth Airport or George Bush Intercontinental Airport in Houston, although many flights touch down in El Paso for passengers to board or change planes.

A network of smaller airports serves the state with scheduled flights to over 30 cities. Connections are easy to arrange, even between different carriers, and there are frequent shuttles between major cities all day.

Airline Companies

More than two dozen airlines fly in and out of Texas airports, including major carriers such as Fort Worth-based American Airlines (and its regional off-shoot, American Eagle), as well as United, Continental, and Delta.

Air fares change frequently, as do schedules and special bargain rates. It is wise to arrange your trip through a travel consultant, who has the most current information. However, all airlines can be contacted directly by telephone for information and reservations. Local or toll-free central numbers can be obtained either from directory assistance (in Texas, dial 1-411) or the *Yellow Pages* of the local telephone directory.

Airlines

American	800-433-7300
British Airways	800-247-9297
Continental	800-231-0856
Delta	800-241-4141
Express Jet	800-958-9538
Qantas	800-227-4500
Southwest	800-435-9792
United	800-241-6522
US Airways	800-428-4322

Down Mexico Way

Many visitors to Texas proceed onwards into or visit Mexico. This can be done at several border points, of which the main ones are El Paso, Eagle Pass, Laredo and Brownsville. US citizens require a passport to visit Mexico and to re-enter the US by air or by sea. From January 1 2008, they will also require a passport to re-enter the US at a land crossing. Citizens of some countries, including Australia, Canada, New Zealand and the UK, do not need a visa but must carry proof of citizenship. If you're traveling deeper into the country or staying for longer than 72 hours, a Mexican tourist card is required. These cards, called the ***forma migratoria turista*** (FMT), are free from immigration officials at the border and also from Mexican consulates, Mexican government tourist offices and travel agents.

Drivers must obtain automobile permits, valid for 180 days, when venturing beyond the border region. These cost $30 from Mexican immigration officials on production of a tourist card.

It is mandatory to obtain Mexican insurance and highly advisable because in the event of an accident vehicles are usually impounded, regardless of fault. **Sanborn's** Mexican Insurance is a reliable company that specializes in this insurance. They have offices in most large border towns and also in San Antonio. At the border you will be given a temporary import permit after you show proof of ownership (photocopy of title will do) and the insurance policy. Keep these handy, as 12 miles (19 km) into Mexico, every car without Mexico tags is stopped at the border checkpoints.

Further information is available on 800-44-MEXICO or www.visitmexico.com

By Train

Two **Amtrak** lines run through Texas: the Eagle from Chicago to San Antonio, with a Dallas to Houston connection; and the Sunset from Los Angeles to Orlando. The trains stop at 19 passenger terminals in the state: Alpine, Austin, Beaumont, Cleburne, Dallas, Del Rio, El Paso, Fort Worth, Houston, Longview, Marshall, McGregor, Mineola, San Antonio, Sanderson, San Marcos, Taylor, Temple and Texarkana. Accommodations include coach and sleeping facilities. There are lounge and dining cars. Outside North America, you can purchase a USA Rail Pass from travel agencies, which allows unlimited rail travel within specified dates.

For reservations and information inside the US, call 1-800-USA-RAIL or 1-800-872-7245 toll-free or visit www.amtrak.com

By Bus

Greyhound buses, tel: 800-229-9424; www.greyhound.com, connect Texas with all major US cities. Buses are always

air-conditioned and there are toilets on board. Outside North America, contact your travel agent for an Ameripass, which allows unlimited bus travel within specified dates.

GETTING AROUND

On Arrival

Dallas–Fort Worth Airport

The airport is 18 miles (29 km) northwest of Dallas and within four hours of most cities in the US. The third busiest airport in the world, it handles approximately 2,000 domestic flights per day and 500 international flights per week. Tel: 972-574-8888.

The **Trinity Railway Express** (TRE), train system that connects Fort Worth to Dallas, stops near the airport (you must take a Remote South bus to reach it) at least once an hour, Mon–Sat, and costs $2.25. Allow at least an hour's travel time. A taxi ride downtown takes around 35 minutes and costs about $50. **SuperShuttle**, which transports passengers to all areas by van or minibus, is cheaper at $25, but can take up to 90 minutes, depending on destination. Tel: 800-258-3826.

Love Field Airport

The hub for Southwest Airlines is 7 miles (11 km) northwest of downtown Dallas, but within the city limits. Tel: 214-670-6073. A bus stop outside the terminal runs at least once an hour for a 40-minute ride to the **West Transfer Center** in downtown Dallas and costs $1.50. A taxi takes about 20 minutes to get downtown and costs about $15. SuperShuttle shared-van service (tel: 800-258-3826) is approximately $20 and can take over an hour, depending on destination.

George Bush Intercontinental

Located 23 miles (37 km) north of downtown Houston, this airport has daily services to 119 US cities and 65 international destinations, and is a hub for Continental Airlines. Tel: 281-230-3100.

Houston's **METRO bus system** has a route that runs from Intercontinental Airport to downtown Houston every 15 minutes, from 6am to midnight Mon–Fri, and once an hour on weekends for $1.50. Taxis to downtown cost about $50 and take around 30 minutes. SuperShuttle shared-van service is approximately $25 and can take 90 minutes, depending on destination.

ABOVE: home on the road, West Texas.

William P. Hobby Airport

Serving as a hub for Southwest Airlines, the airport is 8 miles (13 km) southeast of downtown Houston. Tel: 713-643-3000.

METRO bus system goes from Hobby to downtown Houston every 15 minutes from 6am to midnight Mon-Fri and at least once an hour on weekends for $1.50. Taxis downtown cost about $30 and take around 20 minutes. SuperShuttle shared-van service (tel: 800-258-3826) is approximately $20 but takes an hour or more, depending on destination.

Public Transportation

By Air

Within Texas, Southwest Airlines has the largest number of flights and usually the lowest fares; Express Jet offers discount-rate flights between Austin and Houston.

By Bus

All cities and most towns have some form of local bus service at very low rates. Contact the local tourist office for listings *(see pages 374–5)* or call the main office of the bus company listed in the telephone directory. Major cities like Dallas, Fort Worth, Austin, San Antonio, and Houston offer other bus services well suited to visitors, such as the 'Dillo (armadillo) "trolleys" in Austin and CITRAN (City Transit Service) in Fort Worth.

By Train

There are 43 stations on the popular light-rail **DART** system (Dallas Area Rapid Transit) (tel: 214-979-1111, www.dart.org). Each station has ticket machines with clear instructions for use. There are also special services for the disabled. For further information, tel: 214-515-7272.

DART stops at Union Station from which **Amtrak** trains connect Dallas with Chicago and Houston. The station is connected by pedestrian tunnel to the Hyatt Regency Hotel (beside Reunion Tower). For **Amtrak information** *(see page 340)*.

Dallas is a huge, sprawling area most of which cannot be reached by public transport. Despite the addition of DART, renting a car is considered essential.

Houston's **METRORail** connects downtown, midtown, the Museum District, the Texas Medical Center, Reliant Park and the South Fannin Park & Ride lot (tel: 713-635-4000 or visit www.ridemetro.org).

By Taxi

Taxis can be a convenient way to get around cities. However, unlike those in major cities like New York and London, Texas taxis do not cruise around looking for people hailing them from the curb. To get a taxi, you must call the cab company (*see companies listed below* or look under Taxicabs in the *Yellow Pages* of the local telephone directory). Ask what the rates are, as they vary from city to city (but not from cab to cab). A 15 percent tip is appreciated if you are satisfied with the service provided, and especially if you need help with luggage.

Taxi Companies in Dallas
Executive Taxi Service: 972-554-1212
Terminal Taxi Corp: 214-678-9951
Yellow Cab: 214-426-6262

Taxi Companies in Houston
Fiesta Cab: 713-225-2666
Liberty Cab: 713-695-6700
Square Deal Cab: 713-659-7236
United Cab: 713-699-0000
Yellow Cab: 713-236-1111

Driving

The size and climate of Texas are good reasons to drive, since walking between attractions, even in a city, requires more time than most people have for vacations and, much of the year, it is too hot to walk for pleasure.

US (Interstate) Highways 10, 20, 27, 30, 35, 37, 40 and 45

crisscross Texas, providing direct and relatively hazard-free routes to major cities. For anyone interested in a closer look, however, there are a variety of state highways and back roads (marked on the maps as FM or "Farm to Market", RM or "Ranch to Market", and RR or "Ranch Road") intertwined between all the major cities, smaller communities, and even ghost towns. Buy a map and plan a tour, but allow plenty of time to reach your destination since some of these Texas roads get quite winding and pot-holed.

Be aware, as well, that leaving the main track means fewer gas stations and convenience stores. However, if you remember to fill the tank and allow plenty of time to get where you're going, especially after dark, these secondary roads may prove the most enjoyable way to travel since you'll be able to enjoy the countryside without having to worry about heavy traffic.

The Texas Department of Transportation runs 12 information centers offering advice on trip planning, road conditions and other travel matters. For information call 800-452-9292.

Car Rental

Cars can be rented in most cities. This is usually done at the local airport since much of the rental business is with customers who have arrived by air. Choose the best rate available from one of the side-by-side booths.

You must be at least 21 to rent a car. Credit cards are accepted, and by several companies they are required. Some agencies expect the car to be returned to them. If you want to drive to another city and fly on from there, be sure to inform the rental agent at the time you arrange the terms. There may be a charge to drop the car at their branch in another city.

Alamo	1-800-327 9633
Avis	1-800-331 1212
Budget	1-800-527 0700
Dollar	1-800-800 4000
Enterprise	1-800-325 8007
Hertz	1-800-654 3131
National	1-800-227 7368
Thrifty	1-800-847 4389

Interstate Highways

Interstate highways are planned to bypass most towns, and they do get you to your destination fast, but when you are driving from Austin to Dallas or from San Antonio to El Paso, even fast can mean 4 to 10 hours. Along the interstates there are restrooms and roadside picnic areas, as well as food and petrol.

Highway Patrol and Hitchhiking

The Highway Patrol cruises these highways, not just monitoring speed limits but also looking for drivers in trouble. If you have any emergency that won't allow you to continue the trip, signal your distress by raising the hood. Be sure to keep a current driver's license and a certificate proving you have liability insurance with you at all times because you will be required to show them to the law enforcement officer who stops your car for any reason. It is illegal to drive in Texas without these items.

Motorists are often warned that they are safer staying in the car with the doors locked until a patrol car stops to help, rather than leaving it and trying to hitchhike. Hitchhiking is not considered safe, whether you are on the giving or the receiving end. In some places in the US it is illegal.

Rules of the Road

Speed limits for roads and highways are posted on white signs to the right, as are all other **road signs**. Some roads are for one-way traffic only and are identified by a black and white sign with an arrow pointing in the permitted direction of travel. At an intersection where each corner has a red stop sign with a smaller sign below it which says "4-Way" or "All-Way," motorists must completely stop and then proceed across the intersection following the order in which they arrived at the stop.

The official highway **speed limit** is 70 mph (112 kph). Although everyone passes you, resist the temptation to accelerate. If caught in a "speed trap" by the Highway Patrol, whose black-and-white cruisers have radar, you will get a speeding ticket that has to be paid in a nearby (or sometimes not so near) town before continuing your trip.

The same advice should be followed when driving through towns and cities. Be sure to notice the white signs warning that, upon entering the town, you will be in a different "Speed Zone Ahead." Be prepared to slow to the lower speed you will soon see posted on upcoming white signs. Some very small Texas towns are notorious for catching and fining drivers who have not slowed down quickly enough from the highway speed to the in-town 30 mph (48 kph) speed limit. You may not notice the local (variously colored and lettered) police car parked surreptitiously in an alley until it is too late.

Pay attention to other drivers flashing their lights at you; probably either an accident or speed trap is ahead. Some Texas motorists ask the gas station attendants if there are Highway Patrol cars ahead but they cannot always be relied upon.

Parking fees vary from town to town, with rates higher in larger cities and nonexistent in smaller towns.

A state law requires every passenger in a car to use a **seatbelt** and there are also requirements that small children and babies be secured in youth or infant seats which have been fitted into the car seat. In Texas, a traffic ticket is a criminal offense.

Texas state law requires that all drivers carry **auto insurance** policies, Auto rental companies offer insurance that runs from $10 to $25 per day, depending on coverage,

In Texas a traffic ticket is a criminal offense. **Penalties** run from $75 for an expired registration all the way up to $1,085 for passing a school bus.

Driving Times

Texas is a vast state: approximately 800 miles (1,287 km) across from west to east, and 900 miles (1,448 km) from north to south. The following will give you a rough idea of driving times between destinations.

Austin to: Amarillo: 478 miles (769 km) or 7 hours; Brownsville: 325 miles (523 km) or 5½ hours; Dallas/Fort Worth: 190 miles (305 km) or 3½ hours; El Paso: 573 miles (922 km) or nearly 10 hours; Galveston: 206 miles (476 km) or 3½ hours; Houston: 160 miles (257 km) or a little over 2 hours; San Antonio: 80 miles (128 km) or just over 1 hour.

Dallas/Fort Worth to: Amarillo: 413 miles (664 km) or 7 hours; Brownsville: 550 miles (885 km) or nearly 10 hours; El Paso: 640 miles (1,030 km) or 11 hours; Galveston: 270 miles (434 km) or 4½ hours; Houston: 225 miles (362 km) or nearly 4 hours; San Antonio: 252 miles (405 km) or just over 4 hours.

Houston to: Amarillo: 530 miles (853 km) or 9 hours; Brownsville: 355 miles (571 km) or 4 hours; El Paso: 745 miles (1,199 km) or 12 to 13 hours; Galveston: 48 miles (77 km) or 45 minutes; San Antonio: 189 miles (304 km) or 3 hours.

San Antonio to: Amarillo: 510 miles (820 km) or 8½ hours; Brownsville: 275 miles (442 km) or 4.25 hours; El Paso: 555 miles (893 km) or just over 9 hours.

ACCOMMODATIONS

HOTELS, YOUTH HOSTELS, BED & BREAKFAST

Choosing a Hotel

Whatever your budget, you should be able to find a suitable place to spend the night in Texas. In addition to independently owned hotels and motels in every price range, even the many chains operating in Texas reach into some of its smallest towns.

At the expensive end of the scale there are Sheratons, Hiltons, Marriotts and Hyatt Regencies. A more moderately priced choice would be the Holiday Inns, La Quintas and Ramada Inns. Quality Inns, Howard Johnsons and Best Western motels are reasonable; the Motel 6, Days Inn, Rodeway Inn and Travelodge chains are relatively inexpensive.

Historic inns and other lodgings are the specialty of an association called **Hospitality Accommodations of Texas**, P.O. Box 203, Vanderpool, TX 78885, tel: 800-428-0368, www.hat.org. A free brochure lists the statewide membership.

Bed & Breakfast

Bed and breakfast rates in Texas are generally very reasonable. In historic districts or towns there is not much of a distinction made between "bed and breakfast" and "historic inn," since they are much the same.

Useful Contacts

For information and bookings at many of Texas' B&Bs, you can contact:

Bed & Breakfast Texas Style, 6374 Ivanhoe Lane, Beaumont, TX 77706, tel: 409-860-9100/800-899-4538/800-899-4538, e-mail: info@bnbtexasstyle.com

Campgrounds

There are more than 200 state, federal, or privately owned campgrounds throughout Texas.

For information on camping in national parks, recreation areas, forests and the 20-plus lakes administered by the US Army Corps of Engineers contact: **The National Park Service**, Southwest Region, PO Box 728, Santa Fe, New Mexico 87504.

Around 70 Texas parks and recreation areas managed by the state allow camping within their grounds. **Central Reservations**, tel: 512-389-8900, www.tpwd.state.tx.us can make bookings for anywhere within the state park system. A useful free booklet, called *Texas Public Campgrounds*, is available from the **Travel and Information Division, State Department of Transportation**, P.O. Box 5064, Austin, 78763.

RV and Camping Guide to Texas, the best list available of private campgrounds, which include about half the total number of campgrounds in Texas, is available free of charge from the **Texas Association of Campground Owners**, 4621 S. Cooper #131–104, Arlington 76017, www.campingfriend.com/taco. In addition, **The Texas KOA Kampground Owners Association**, www.koa.com, can provide a list of 20 member campgrounds around the state.

Holiday Apartments

Condominiums and beachfront/bay front homes are available to rent in some areas, particularly on Galveston and South Padre islands. Check the *Yellow Pages* under "Realtors," or contact:

- **Century 21 Bay Reef Realty** 12200 FM 3005 Rd, Galveston, 77554, tel: 800-527-7333; www.bayreef.com
- **Sand 'N Sea Pirates Beach** 13706 FM 3005 Rd, Galveston, 77554, tel: 409-737-2556 or 800-880-2554, www.sandnsea.com
- **Island Services** 1700 Padre Blvd, South Padre Island, 78597, tel: 956-761-2649 or 800-527-0294, www.island-services.com
- **Padre Island Rentals** 3100 Padre Blvd, South Padre Island, 78597, tel: 956-761-5512 or 800-926-6926, www.pirentals.com

Chain Hotels

Best Western: tel: 800-528-1234 www.bestwestern.com
Comfort Inn: tel: 800-228 5150 www.comfortinn.com
Days Inns of America: tel: 800-325-2525 www.texasdaysinn.com
Embassy: tel: 800-362 2779 www.embassysuites1.hilton.com
Holiday Inn: tel: 800-HOLIDAY www.holidayinn.miami.ichotelsgroup.com
Hyatt: tel: 800-228-9000 www.hyatt.com
La Quinta: tel: 800-642-4271 www.lq.com
Marriott: tel: 800-228-9290 www.marriott.com
Sheraton: tel: 800-325-3535 www.sheraton.com
Motel 6: tel: 800-466 8356 www.motel6.com
Ramada: tel: 800-272 6232 www.ramada.com
Red Roof Inn: tel: 800-733 7663 www.redroof.com
Super 8: tel: 800-800 8000 www.super8.com
Travelodge: tel: 800-578 7878 www.travelodge.com

DALLAS/FORT WORTH AND ENVIRONS

Dallas

The Bingham House
800 S. Chestnut St, McKinney, 75069
Tel/Fax: 972-529-1883
www.binghamhouse.com
Friendly hosts Bill and Karen Lynch, history buffs, have decorated their 1883 home in charming period style. **$$**

Crescent Court
400 Crescent Court, 75201
Tel: 214-871-3200
Fax: 214-871-3272
www.crescentcourt.com.
Elegantly furnished hotel with gardens, pool, spa, exercise room, renowned restaurants. **$$$$**

Doubletree Market Center
2015 Market Center Blvd, 75207
Tel: 214-741-7481
Fax: 214-747-6191
www.doubletree.com
Handy for business and leisure; work-out facilities, 228 units. **$$$**

Dowell House
1104 S. Tennessee St, McKinney, 75069
Tel: 972-562-2456, 800-373-0551
www.dowellhouse.com
This 1870 home doubled as a haunted house in the 1973 movie *Benji*. **$$$**

Embassy Suites – Airport South
4650 W. Airport Freeway, Irving, 75062
Tel: 972-790-0093
Fax: 972-790-4768
www.esdfwsouth.com
Free transport to and from the airport. Restaurants, pool, sauna and free breakfast. **$$**

Fairmont Hotel
1717 N. Akard, 75201
Tel: 214-720-2020
Fax: 214-720-5269
www.fairmont.com
Lavish hotel in Arts District. Pool; 550 rooms. **$$$$**

Four Seasons Hotel and Resort
4150 N. MacArthur Blvd, Irving, 75038
Tel: 972-717-0700
Fax: 972-717-2550
www.fourseasons.com/dallas
Raquetball and squash courts. Pools and sauna; 357 rooms. **$$$$**

Harvey Suites
4550 W. Carpenter Freeway, Irving 75063
Tel: 972-929-4499/0774
www.harveyhotels.com
Facilities for the disabled. With 313 units, whirlpool/spa, work-out facilities. Just 5 minutes from Galleria mall. **$$**

Hilton Anatole Hotel
2201 Stemmons Freeway, 75207
Tel: 214-748-1200
Fax: 214-761-7520
www.hiltonanatole.com
27-floor hotel with 1,600 rooms. Pool, seven restaurants, valuable art on loan from Trammell Crow. **$$$**

Hotel Indigo
1933 Main St, 75201
Tel: 214-741-7700
Fax: 214-939-3639
www.hotelindigo.com
A national landmark with period charm, dating from 1925; 172 rooms. **$$$**

Hotel InterContinental
15201 Dallas Parkway, Addison, 75001
Tel: 972-386-6000
Fax: 972-991-6937
www.interconti.com
Located in north Dallas. With 530 rooms and a whirlpool/spa. **$$$**

Hotel Palomar
5300 E. Mockingbird Lane, 75206
Tel: 214-520-7969, 888-253-9030
Fax: 214-520-8025
www.hotelpalomar-dallas.com
Chic Kimpton remodel with fitness center and spa. Central location. Hip, kitschy Polynesian restaurant-bar. **$$$**

Hotel St Germain
2516 Maple Ave., 75201
Tel: 214-871-2516
Fax: 214-871-0740.
www.hotelstgermain.com
Luxurious, in a former Victorian home. Champagne bar. **$$$$**

Hyatt Regency DFW Airport
International Parkway, 75261
Tel: 972-453-1234
Fax: 972-456-8668
www.dfwairport.hyatt.com
Pool, sauna, racquetball, tennis, golf, restaurants. **$$$$**

Magnolia Hotel
1401 Commercial St, 75201
Tel: 214-915-6500, 888-915-1110
Fax: 214-253-0053
www.magnoliahoteldallas.com
Renovated historical building downtown with free breakfast and milk and cookies at night. Periodical room, high-speed Internet access, billiards and on-site Starbucks. **$$**

The Mansion on Turtle Creek
2821 Turtle Creek Blvd, 75219
Tel: 214-559-2100
Fax: 214-528-4187
www.mansiononturtlecreek.com
Famously luxurious, hill-top haven for the affluent. Pool, sauna, health club, expensive restaurant. **$$$$**

Melrose Hotel
3015 Oak Lawn Ave., 75219
Tel: 214-521-5151
Fax: 214-521-2470
www.melrosehoteldallas.com
Classy, 75-year-old landmark built in 1924, 3 miles (5 km) from Love Field airport. **$$$**

The Ritz-Carlton
2121 McKinney Ave., 75210
Tel: 800-241-3333
www.ritzcarlton.com
Luxury reaches new heights at the newly opened Ritz-Carlton Hotel. Eat in style at Fearing's Restaurant, and relax in the spa with a Texas Eight-Hand massage. **$$$$**

Sheraton Grand at DFW
4440 W. John Carpenter Freeway, Irving, 75063
Tel: 972-929-8400
Fax: 972-929-4885
www.sheratongranddfw.com
Whirlpool/spa and work-out facilities. Interpreters. **$$$**

Stoneleigh Hotel
2927 Maple Ave., 75201
Tel: 214-871-7111, 800-678-8946
Fax: 214-871-9379

BELOW: cool cocktails at the Hyatt Regency DFW Hotel bar.

www.stoneleighhotel.com
European-style hotel. Pool, choice of restaurants, 153 units. **$$$**
W Dallas Victory
2440 Victory Park Lane, 75219
Tel: 214-397-4100
Fax: 214-397-4105
www.starwoodhotels.com/whotels
Opulent high-rise with spa, fitness center, "infinity" pool, 24-hour room service, restaurant and rooftop bar. **$$$–$$$$**

Fort Worth

Green Oaks Hotel
6901 W. Freeway, 76116
Tel: 817-738-7311
Fax: 817-737-4486
www.greenoakshotel.com
284 units, pools, sauna, spa, tennis courts. **$$**
Hilton Arlington
2401 E. Lamar Blvd, 76006
Tel: 817-640-3322
Fax: 817-633-1430
www.hilton.com
Close to all local attractions. **$$**
Hilton Hotel
815 Main St, 76102
Tel: 817-870-2100
Fax: 817-335-3408
www.hilton.com
National historic landmark, fresh from a $10-million renovation. Located in the heart of downtown, adjacent to Convention Center. **$$$**
La Quinta Inn and Suites
4900 Bryant Irvin Rd, 76132
Tel: 817-370-2700
Fax: 817-370-2733
www.lq.com
Complimentary breakfast; spacious rooms. **$$**
Renaissance Worthington Hotel
200 Main St, 76102
Tel: 817-870-1000
Fax: 817-338-9176
www.renaissancehotels.com
This imposing, modern, downtown hotel dominates Sundance Square, with adjoining mall, athletic club, pool, restaurants and sauna. There are 504 units. **$$$**
Residence Inn by Marriott
1701 S. University Dr., 76107
Tel: 817-870-1011
Fax: 817-877-5500
www.marriott.com
All large suites with kitchens; and the zoo is close by. **$$**
Stockyards Hotel
109 E. Exchange Ave., 76106
Tel: 817-625-6427, 800-423-8471
Fax: 817-624-2571
www.stockyardshotel.com
Choice of four decors – Victorian, Mountain Man, Cowboy or Native American. **$$**

Denton

The Heritage Inn
815 N. Locust St, 76201
Tel: 940-565-6414
Fax: 940-565-6515.
This pleasant inn, as well as Magnolia House next door and Pecan House, are under the same ownership of Heritage Inns. **$$**
Holiday Inn Hotel & Suites
1434 Centre Place Dr., 76205
Tel: 940-383-4100, 888-465-4329
Fax: 940-383-4110
www.holidayinn.com
Conveniently located, 1 mile from both Texas Women's University and the University of North Texas, as well as historic downtown Denton. Amenities include outdoor patios, high-speed wireless Internet access, flat panel TVs, pool, whirlpool, fitness center. **$$**

Grapevine

AmeriSuites
2220 Grapevine Mills Circle W., 76051
Tel: 972-691-1199, 877-774-6467
Fax: 972-691-3596
www.amerisuites.com
Spacious rooms with refrigerators and microwaves. **$**
Gaylord Texan Resort
1501 Gaylord Trail, 76051
Tel: 817-877-7788, 866-782-7987
Fax: 817-778-1001
www.gaylordhotels.com/gaylordtexan
Huge glassed-in complex with gardens, shops and restaurants on site. Numerous amenities including high-speed Internet access, spa, fitness center, pool. **$$$–$$$$.**

CENTRAL TEXAS

Austin

Austin Motel
1220 S. Congress Ave., 78704
Tel: 512-441-1157
www.austinmotel.com
Award-winning 1938 motel is conveniently located a few blocks south of Town Lake. Restaurant and laundromat, pool, whirlpool/spa, and video rental library. Weekly rates can be arranged; 41 units. **$$**
Brava House
1108 Blanco St, 78703
Tel: 512-478-5034
www.bravahouse.com
Classy, period bed-and-breakfast suites, centrally located. **$$**
Days Inn
820 E. Anderson Lane, 78752
Tel: 512-835-4311
Fax: 512-835-1740
www.daysinn.com
146 rooms, with a pool, and a golf course nearby. **$**
Doubletree Guest Suites
303 W. 15th St, 78701
Tel: 512-478-7000
Fax: 512-478-5103
www.doubletreehotelaustin.com
All-suite hotel with 189 units. **$$$$**
Driskill Hotel
604 Brazos St, 78701
Tel: 512-474-5911, 800-252-9367
Fax: 512-474-2214
www.driskillhotel.com
Historic hotel in a great downtown location. Workout facilities, bar and internet-wired TVs, 176 rooms and 12 suites. **$$$$**
Embassy Suites Downtown
300 S. Congress Ave., 78704
Tel: 512-469-9000
or 800-362-2779
Fax: 512-480-9164.
www.embassysuites.com
Cooked-to-order breakfasts, and workout facilities. **$$–$$$$**
Four Seasons Hotel
98 San Jacinto Blvd, 78701
Tel: 512-478-4500, 800-819-5053
Fax: 512-478-3117
www.fourseasons.com/austin
This four-star hotel has a restaurant with outdoor dining overlooking Town Lake. Most rooms have a lake view. On hike-and-bike trail. **$$$$**
Hyatt Regency on Town Lake
208 Barton Springs Rd, 78704
Tel: 512-477-1234
Fax: 512-480-2069
www.austin.hyatt.com
Excellent location on Town Lake's hike-and-bike trail. **$$$**
Lake Austin Spa Resort
1705 S. Quinlan Park Rd, 78732
Tel: 800-847-5637
Fax: 512-266-1572
www.lakeaustin.com
All amenities, including facilities for the disabled.Interesting package deals. **$$$$**
Radisson Hotel
6000 Middle Fiskville Rd, 78752
Tel: 512-451-5757, 888-201-1718
Fax: 512-467-7644.
www.radisson.com
Fitness club; facilities for the disabled. **$$$**
Renaissance Hotel
9721 Arboretum Blvd, 78759
Tel: 512-343-2626
Fax: 512-346-7953.
www.renaissancehotels.com
As well as a restaurant this hotel also has a pool, spa and workout facilities. Specialty shops and restaurants nearby. **$$$**
Radisson Hotel on Town Lake
111 E. Cesar Chavez, 78701
Tel: 512-478-9611, 800-333-3333
Fax: 512-473-8399
www.radisson.com/austintx
Fitness center and pool, 303 rooms and 99 suites. **$$$**
Woodburn House B&B
4401 Ave. D, 78751
Tel: 512-458-4335

PRICE CATEGORIES

Price categories are for a double room for one night in high season:
$ = up to $50
$$ = $50–125
$$$ = $125–200
$$$$ = more than $200

ABOVE: the Gaylord Texan Resort in Grapevine.

Fax: 512-458-4319
www.woodburnhouse.com
Charming Victorian house with wrap-around porches, gourmet breakfasts; fax/computer available. **$$**

Bandera

Bandera Lodge
1900 Highway 16 S., 78003
Tel: 830-796-3093
Fax: 830-796-3191.
This motel-lodge has 44 rooms and a picnic area on the Medina River. Restaurant, pool and nearby golf course. **$**

Blanco

Blanco County Inn
902 Main St, 78606
Tel: 830-833-4502
www.blancocountyinn.com
Located in beautiful Texas Hill country, live music on the deck Saturday nights. **$$**
Swiss Lodge
1206 N. Main St
Blanco, 78606
Tel: 830-833-5528, 866-797-5634
Apartments have full kitchens. **$$**

Clifton

Cliffview Resort
180 County Rd 1802, 76634
Tel: 254-622-8897
Fax: 254-622-2339
www.cliffviewatlakewhitney.com
Individual cabins with kitchens. Pets allowed, boat rentals available. **$$–$$$**
Lakehaven B&B
321 County Rd 1630, 76634
Tel: 254-622-3449
www.lakehaven.biz
Beautiful lake views, gourmet breakfast served any time. **$$$**
Little Rocky Lodge
106 County Rd 1807, 76634
Tel: 254-622-3010
www.littlerockylodge.com
Waterfront accommodations, on-site restaurant. **$$–$$$**

Corsicana

Best Western Executive Inn
2100 E. Highway 31, 75109
Tel: 903-872-0020
Fax: 903-872-0024
www.bestwestern.com
New, nicely appointed hotel with swimming pool, fitness center, free cable with HBO, and guest laundry. Free "deluxe" continental breakfast serves warm items as well as cold, including a make-your-own-waffle station. Not too far from Navarro Pecan Co. and Russell Stover chocolate factory. Rooms available for disabled. **$$**
Holiday Inn Express Hotel & Suites
620 Bryans Way, 75110
Tel: 903-874-7440
Fax: 903-874-7473
Brand new hotel adjacent to the new Corsicana Crossing district, rife with shops and restaurants, and less than 2 miles from Collin Street Bakery, home of the world-famous Corsicana Fruitcake. **$$–$$$**
The Wicklow Inn
220 N. 14th St, 75110
Tel: 903-872-7311
B&B with the warm hospitality of a Celtic inn. It's an 1890s mansion that offers five elegant bedrooms in the main house and one in the carriage house. **$$–$$$**

Fredericksburg

Dietzel Motel
909 W. Main (Jct 290W & 87N), 78624
Tel: 830-997-3330.
www.dietzelmotel.com
20 simple but well-maintained rooms 1 mile (1.6 km) west of the town center. **$**
Fredericksburg Bed & Brew
245 E. Main St, 78624
Tel: 830-997-1646
Fax: 830-997-8026
www.yourbrewery.com
B&B with brewpub, *biergarten* and restaurant. 12 rooms with private bath. **$$**
Sunday House Inn
501 E. Main, 78624
Tel: 830-997-4484
Fax: 830-997-5607
www.sundayhouseinnandsuites.com
German-American hotel with a pool and ethnic restaurant. **$$**

Georgetown

Comfort Suites
11 Waters Edge Circle, 78626
Tel: 512-863-7544
Fax: 512-863-7545
Nicely appointed hotel has large rooms and is located 2 miles from Inner Space Caverns, 3 miles from the Candle Factory, and 10 miles from Lake Georgetown. **$$$**
Days Inn
209 I-35, 78628
Tel: 512-863-5572
Fax: 512-869-5301
www.texasdaysinn.com
Affordable yet nice, hotel is right off I-35.**$$**
Holiday Inn Express Hotel & Suites
600 San Gabriel Village Blvd, 78626
Tel: 512-868-8555
Fax: 512-868-1874
Plenty of space here, with ample suites that have both a king bed and a pull-out sofa sleeper. Rooms come equipped with microwaves and refrigerators. Two conference rooms. **$$**
Quality Inn
1005 Leander Rd, 78628
Tel: 512-863-7504
Fax: 512-819-9016
Rooms are big at this hotel that's walking distance to Innerspace Caverns and not far from historic downtown Georgetown, Lake Georgetown, and two golf courses nearby. **$$**

Glen Rose

Best Western Dinosaur Valley Inn & Suites
1311 N.E. Big Bend Trail, 76043
Tel: 800-280-2055/254-897-4818;
Fax: 254-897-4828
Rustic inn with huge free breakfast, cozy lobby fireplace, wrap-around porch with waterfall and fishpond. **$$–$$$**

Hillsboro

Comfort Inn
1515 Old Brandon Rd, 76645
Tel/fax: 254-582-3333
Free continental breakfast at this modest but reliable stay-over. Location is close to Hillsboro's downtown historic district, housing over 200 antique dealers. **$$**
Holiday Inn Express
1505 Hillview Dr., 76645
Tel: 254-582-0220
Fax: 254-582-1003
Great spot for those visiting the Prime Outlets of Hillsboro, with nearly 100 brand-name stores. Hotel has 53 guest rooms including two jacuzzi suites. Lake Whitney is 10 miles from Hillsboro. **$$**
Windmill B&B
441 Hill County Rd 2421E, 76645
Tel: 254-582-7373/800-951-0033
www.windmillbb.com
This 1910 Victorian-styled home is situated on a 21-acre (8.5-hectare) spread with pecan and oak trees, hammock in the backyard, walking trail, and rose garden with windmill. Full

breakfast served in large dining room; afternoon tea has desserts and fruit. **$$**

Kerrville

Days Inn
2000 Sidney Baker St, 78028
Tel: 830-896-1000
Fax: 830-896-3786
www.daysinn.com
Serviceable spot with pool, jacuzzi, complimentary continental breakfast. **$$**

Holiday Inn Express
2114 Sidney Baker St, 78028
Tel: 830-895-9500/888-400-9714
Fax: 830-895-9501
www.hiexpress.com
Good-size rooms, clean and comfortable, with separate seating areas, TVs, sleeper sofas, and wet bars. **$$**

Inn of the Hills Resort
1001 Junction Highway, 78028
Tel: 830-895-5000, 800-292-5690
www.innofthehills.com
Delectable buffets, Olympic-size swimming pool and ranch-style bar. Sunday brunch. **$$**

Y.O. Ranch Resort
2033 Sidney Baker St, 78028
Tel: 830-257-4440, 877-967-3767
Fax: 830-896-8189
www.yoresort.com
This older hotel is rich in character and filled with antiques, artifacts and remembrances of an era of cowboys and the old West. Rooms are faded and bathrooms are small, but the public spaces are impressive, including a good restaurant, grand lobby, and relaxing bar. **$$**

Luckenbach

The Full Moon Inn
3234 Luckenbach Rd, 78624
Tel: 800-997-1124, 830-997-2205
Fax: 830-997-1115
www.fullmooninn.com/
Historic property on 12 manicured acres (12 hectares) with only six rooms, all enchanting. Fresh flowers and full breakfast in the dining room. Children and pets are welcome. **$$$**

Salado

Holiday Inn Express
1991 N. Stagecoach Rd, 76571
Tel: 254-947-4004
Fax: 254-947-8831
www.hiexpress.com
Most modern hotel in quaint Salado, with relaxing pool and morning cinnamon rolls **$$$**

Stagecoach Inn
1 Main St, 76571
Tel: 254-947-5111
www.staystagecoach.com
Older luxury motel with 82 rooms, some with extra vanities and sinks; patios and balconies overlook a pool and jacuzzi. It's walking distance from the creek. Packages include a "Stay and Play" with golf at the Mill Creek Inn and Golf Club, designed by Robert Trent Jones, Jr. **$$**

Waco

America's Best Value Inn & Suites
115 Jack Kultgen, 76706
Tel: 254-754-1266
Fax: 254-755-8612
www.bestvalueinn.com
Work-out facilities, Continental breakfast. **$$**

Hilton Hotel
113 S. University Parks Dr., 76701
Tel: 254-754-8484
Fax: 254-752-2214
www.waco.hilton.com
On the Brazos River Walk. Tennis, whirlpool. **$$**

La Quinta Inn
1110 S. 9th St, 76706
Tel: 254-752-9741
Fax: 254-757-1600
www.lq.com
Close to the university. **$$**

Waxahachie

Chaska House B&B
716 W. Main St, 75165
Tel: 800-931-3390, 972-937-3390
www.chaskabb.com
Large, beautifully appointed rooms. Whirlpools-for-two in romantic setting. Phone, fax, wi-fi access, cable TV and DVD. **$$$–$$$$**

Days Inn
803 S. I-35E, 75165
Tel: 972-937-8223
www.daysinn.com
Free high-speed Internet. Pets allowed. Pool. **$$**

Holiday Inn Express
984 W. US-287 Bypass, 75165
Tel: 972-938-3304, 888-400-9714
Fax: 972-938-3300
www.hiexpress.com
Pool, fitness facilities, complimentary breakfast.

SAN ANTONIO AND ENVIRONS

San Antonio

Beckmann Inn & Carriage House
222 E. Guenther St, 78204
Tel: 210-229-1449
Fax: 210-229-1061
www.beckmanninn.com
Wrap-aaround porch Victorian home in King William Historic District. River Walk and Alamo both within walking distance. Full breakfast. **$$–$$$**

Bullis House Inn
621 Pierce St, 78208
Tel: 210-233-9426
Fax: 210-299-1479
www.bullishouseinn.com
Seven units. Spacious, fireplaces, chandeliers, gardens, full kitchen adjacent, near downtown, good value. **$$**

Crockett Hotel
320 Bonham, 78205
Tel: 210-225-6500/800-292-1050
Fax: 210-225-6251
www.crocketthotel.com
Historic central hotel with 204 rooms decorated in "Southwestern" style. **$$**

Days Inn Alamo-Riverwalk
902 E. Houston St, 78205
Tel: 210-227-6233
Fax: 210-228-0901
www.daysinn.com
50 units. One block from Riverwalk and Alamo. **$$**

Fairmount Hotel
401 S. Alamo, 78205
Tel: 210-224-8800, 877-365-0500
Fax: 210-475-0082
www.thefairmounthotel-sanantonio.com
Renovated Victorian building with wrought-iron verandas. Restaurant. **$$$**

The Historic Menger Hotel
204 Alamo Plaza, 78205
Tel: 210-223-4361, 800-345-9285
Fax: 210-228-0022
www.mengerhotel.com
Revered 1859 structure next to the Alamo, 350 rooms and spa/fitness centre. **$$$**

Marriott Riverwalk
889 E. Market St, 78205
Tel: 210-224-4555
Fax: 210-224-2754
www.marriott.com
Heated pool, saunas, 500 rooms on 30 floors. **$$$$**

Hilton Palacio del Rio
200 S. Alamo, 78205
Tel: 210-222-1400
Fax: 210-270-0761
www.palaciodelrio.hilton.com
A fully equipped modern hotel with Spanish touches, 481 units, on the River Walk. **$$$**

Ogé Inn Riverwalk
209 Washington St, 78204
Tel: 210-223-2353
Fax: 210-226-5812
www.ogeinn.com
An 1857 antebellum mansion with exquisite antiques. **$$$–$$$$**

Omni La Mansión del Rio
112 College St, 78205
Tel: 210-518-1000/800-292-7300
Fax: 210-226-0389
www.omnihotels.com
Spanish mission architecture; 337 units, on quiet portion of Paseo del Rio. Interpreters available. **$$$**

Sheraton Gunter Hotel
205 E. Houston St, 78205
Tel: 210-227-3241
Fax: 210-227-3299
www.gunterhotel.com
Historic hotel built in 1909; 322 units. **$$–$$$**

A Yellow Rose B&B
229 Madison St, 78204
Tel: 210-229-9903
Fax: 210-229-1691
www.ayellowrose.com
Six spacious guest rooms in a pretty Victorian house. Located in a peaceful King William Historic District neighborhood but within walking distance to downtown and the River Walk. **$$$**

PRICE CATEGORIES

Price categories are for a double room for one night in high season:
$ = up to $50
$$ = $50–125
$$$ = $125–200
$$$$ = more than $200

Comfort

Comfort Common
717 High St, 78013
Tel: 830-995-3030
Fax: 830-995-3455
www.comfortcommon.com
Exquisite architecturally renowned B&B. **$$**

New Braunfels

Gruene Mansion Inn
1275 Gruene Rd, 78130
Tel: 830-629-2641
Fax: 830-629-7375
www.gruenemansioninn.com
Overlooking Guadalupe River, with 25 antique-furnished rooms in restored barns. **$$$**

Historic Kuebler-Waldrip Haus & Danville Schoolhouse B&B
1620 Hueco Springs Loop, 78132
Tel: 830-625-8300, 800-299-8372
www.kueblerwaldrip.com
Consists of an 1847 wine merchant's house and a relocated old school. Full country breakfast and nearby water recreation facilities. **$$–$$$**

Hotel Faust
240 S. Seguin, 78130
Tel: 830-625-7791
Fax: 830-620-1530
www.fausthotel.com
Historic landmark hotel with its own brew pub **$$**

Prince Solms Inn
295 East San Antonio St, 78130
Tel: 830-625-9169
www.princesolmsinn.com
1898 hotel with 12 rooms furnished with antiques. Fine restaurant and garden. **$$**

Schlitterbahn Waterpark Resort
305 W. Austin St, 78130
Tel: 830-625-2351
Fax: 830-620-4873.
www.schlitterbahn.com
In the grounds of a 65-acre (26-hectare) waterpark. **$$**

HOUSTON AND EAST TEXAS

Houston

Comfort Inn Brookhollow
4760 Sherwood Lane, 77092
Tel: 713-686-5525
Fax: 713-686-5365
www.comfortinn.com
46 units, with outdoor pool and free breakfast. **$$**

Doubletree Hotel
at Allen Center, 400 Dallas St, 77002
Tel: 713-759-0202
Fax: 713-759-1166
www.doubletree.com
Located in the business district; 350 rooms with floor-to-ceiling windows. **$$$**

Fairfield Inn Marriott
Near the Galleria, 3131 W. Loop South, 77027
Tel: 713-961-1690
Fax: 713-627-8434
www.marriott.com
107 units and a whirlpool/spa. **$$**

Grant's Palm Court
8200 S. Main St, 77025
Tel: 713-668-8000
Fax: 713-668-7777
Elvis Presley was once a guest at this 1950s inn. Pool, spa, and restaurant nearby. **$**

Hilton Hobby Airport
8181 Airport Blvd, 77061
Tel: 713-645-3000
Fax: 713-645-2251
www.houstonhobbyairport.hilton.com
The Hobby has 305 units, some with jacuzzis. Health club, café and restaurant. **$$**

Holiday Inn NASA
1300 NASA Rd 1, 77058
Tel: 281-333-2500
Fax: 281-335-1578
www.houston-nasa.holiday-inn.com
Across the street from NASA. Pool, kids' playground, 224 rooms. Complimentary underground tram service to George Bush International Airport. **$$**

Hyatt Regency
1200 Louisiana St, 77002
Tel: 713-654-1234
Fax: 713-951-0934
www.hyatt.com
Downtown hotel with 977 units. Recent $15 million facelift. **$$$$**

Lancaster Hotel
701 Texas Ave., 77002
Tel: 713-228-9500
Fax: 713-223-4528
www.thelancaster.com
Luxurious hotel built in 1926, located in the downtown theater district; 84 rooms, each with CD player and complimentary wireless Internet access. **$$$$**

McLachlan Farm B&B
24907 Hardy Rd, Spring, 77383
Tel: 281-350-2400
Fax: 281-350-1011
www.macfarm.com
1911 farmhouse with six rooms in quiet country setting. **$$**

Marriott West Loop
by the Galleria, 1750 W. Loop South, 77027
Tel: 713-960-0111
Fax: 713-624-1560
www.marriott.com
With 300 rooms on 13 floors. Indoor pool, sauna, spa, restaurant. **$$$**

St Regis
1919 Briar Oaks Lane, 77027
Tel: 713-840-7600
Fax: 713-840-8036
www.starwood.com/stregis
Has 232 upscale units in River Oaks residential area. **$$$**

Sara's Bed & Breakfast Inn
941 Heights Blvd, 77008
Tel: 713-868-1130
Fax: 713-868-3284
www.saras.com
Victorian mansion with 12 rooms; no children under eight. **$$**

Springhill Estates by Marriott
Astrodome, 1400 Old Spanish Trail
Tel: 713-796-1000
Fax: 713-796-8055
www.marriott.com
Pool, sauna, exercise room, restaurant, and 191 rooms. **$$**

Sheraton Suites
Galleria, 2400 W. Loop South, 77027
Tel: 713-586-2444
Fax: 713-586-2445
www.sheratonsuiteshouston.com
There are 281 units, a pool, spa, exercise room and restaurant. **$$**

The Warwick
5701 S. Main St, 77005

BELOW: Sara's Bed & Breakfast Inn, Houston.

Tel: 713-526-1991
Fax: 713-526-0359
www.warwickhotelhouston.com
Pool, sauna, exercise room and restaurant. European-style decor. **$$$**

The Westin Oaks
5011 Westheimer, 77056
Tel: 713-960-8100
Fax: 713-960-6554
www.starwood.com/westin
Recently renovated; with 406 rooms on 21 floors in the Galleria. **$$$**

Beaumont

America's Best Value Inn-Hotel
2525 N. 11th St
Beaumont, 77703
Tel: 409-924-7300
Fax : 409-924-7373
www.bestvalueinn.com
Full service inn has 130 rooms and suites, outdoor pool, free Internet, business center, and fitness center. Close to gambling casinos in nearby Louisiana. Pet friendly. $ **$$–$$$**

Fairfield Inn Beaumont
2265 S. I-10, 77705
Tel: 409-840-5751
Fax: 409-840-5751
www.marriott.com
Complimentary hot breakfast, free local calls and a convenient fax service, indoor pool, and exercise room. **$$**

MCM Elegante Hotel
2355 S. I-10, 77705
Tel: 409-842-3600, 877-842-3606
www.mcmelegante.com
Find indulgence with mahogany poster beds and high thread-count linens. But it's business-friendly, too, with oversized work desks, ergonomic chairs, and high-speed wireless Internet access. There's free HBO, in-room movies, and Nintendo Game Cube. **$$$**

Jasper

Ramada Inn
239 E. Gibson St, 75951
Tel: 409-384-9021
Fax: 409-489-1181
In-room coffee maker and hairdryer. Rooms and facilities suitable for the disabled. Restaurant on site. **$$**

Super 8 Motel
2100 N. Wheeler St, 75951
Tel: 409-384-8600
Fax: 409-384-8608
Complimentary breakfast. In-room microwave oven, small refrigerator and wi-fi access. Outdoor pool. Rooms and facilities suitable for the disabled. **$$**

Jefferson

Hotel Jefferson
124 W. Austin St, 75657
Tel: 903-665-2631
Fax: 903-665-6222
www.historicjeffersonhotel.com
Converted from an 1850s cotton warehouse in the historic downtown district; 23 romantic rooms. Award-winning Italian restaurant. **$$**

Old Mulberry Inn B&B
209 Jefferson St, 75657
Tel: 903-665-1945, 800-263-5319
www.oldmulberryinn.com
Romantic Louisiana-style house located in the historic district. Five distinctively decorated rooms. **$$**

Pride House
409 E. Broadway, 75657
Tel: 903-665-2929
Fax: 903-665-3901
www.jeffersontexas.com
Stately Victorian mansion with high ceilings and 30 original stained-glass windows. Ten rooms, six in the original servant's quarters. **$$**

Liberty

Luxury Inn & Suites
3564 E. Highway 90, 77575
Tel: 936-336-8300
Outdoor pool, hot tub, children's pool, spa, barbecue and picnic area. Continental breakfast. Cribs available. 24-hour front desk, fax facilities. **$$**

Nacogdoches

Econo Lodge
2020 N.W. Loop 224,
Stallings, 75964
Tel: 936-569-0880
Fax: 936-569-0303
www.econolodge.com
68 rooms. Free breakfast. There are two golf courses, biking and hiking trails nearby. Boating and fishing are available at Lake Nacogdoches. **$**

Pine Creek Lodge
341 Pine Creek Rd, 75964
Tel: 936-560-6282
Fax: 936-560-1675
www.pinecreeklodge.com
17 rooms on a farm 10 miles (16 km) west of town. **$$$**

Paris

Holiday Inn
3560 N.E. Loop 286, 75460
Tel: 903-785-5545
Fax: 903-785-9510
www.holidayinn.com
114 rooms including 10 two-room suites with fully equipped kitchens. Data ports, high-speed wi-fi access. Business center, fitness center, nearby shopping. **$$**

Kings Inn Motel
1907 Lamar Ave., 75460
Tel: 903-739-8499
TV in room, smoke-free rooms available, air conditioning, irons, kitchens, high-speed Internet access, rollaway beds. **$**

Port Arthur

Holiday Inn
2929 Jimmy Johnson Blvd, 77642
Tel: 409-724-5000
Fax: 409-724-7644
www.holidayinn.com
Neat atmosphere thanks to the courtyard/tower decor, with 164 rooms, tropical outdoor swimming pool, large sundeck, gazebo and patio dining. Adjacent to Babe Zaharias golf course. **$$$**

Ramada Inn
3801 Highway 73, 77642
Tel: 409-962-9858
Fax: 409-962-9453
Lounge, complimentary breakfast, restaurant, garden, swimming pool, business services. **$$**

Studio 6 Port Arthur
3000 Jimmy Johnson Blvd, 77642
Tel: 409-729-6611
Fax: 409-729-8439
www.staystudio6.com
Data port, facilities for the disabled, elevator, kids stay free. Small pets allowed. Free local phone calls. **$$**

Rusk

Weston Inn and Suites
1600 N. Dickinson Dr., 75785
Tel: 903-683-8383
Fax: 903-683-8263
www.westoninnrusk.com
Smoking, non-smoking and disabled-friendly rooms available. Microwave and refrigerator, laundry facilities, outdoor pool, high-speed Internet connection. **$$**

San Augustine

Captain Downs House B&B
301 E. Main St, 75972
Tel: 936-275-2289
Mom & pop bed and breakfast in a historic building. **$$$**

Sour Lake

Economy Inn
1070 E. Highway 105, 77659
Tel: 409-287-3444
Serviceable no-frills pit-stop for Sour Lake, a former oil boomtown and the birthplace of Texaco. The town currently boasts a small dessert wine-maker, Bruno & George Winery. **$$$$**

Texarkana

Budget Host Northgate Inn
400 W. 53rd St, 75503
Tel: 903-793-6565
Free high-speed Internet, plus non-smoking meeting room. Swimming pool; pets allowed. Car rental desk. **$$**

Courtyard By Marriott
5001 N. Cowhorn Creek Loop, 75503
Tel: 903-334-7400
Fax: 903-334-7402
www.marriott.com
90 spaciousrooms in this non-smoking hotel, high-speed Internet access, workstation,microwave and mini refrigerator. **$$$**

PRICE CATEGORIES

Price categories are for a double room for one night in high season:
$ = up to $50
$$ = $50–125
$$$ = $125–200
$$$$ = more than $200

THE GULF COAST

Corpus Christi

Best Western Marina Grand Hotel
300 N. Shoreline Blvd, 78401
Tel: 361-883-5111
Fax: 361-883-3686
www.bestwesterntexas.com
Fully equipped, 11-story hotel across from the seawall, with bay and marina views. **$$–$$$**

Fairfield Inn by Marriott
5217 Blanche Moore Dr., 78411
Tel: 361-985-8393
Fax: 361-985-8393
www.fairfieldinn.com
Pool. Breakfast included. **$$**

Holiday Inn Emerald Beach
1102 S. Shoreline Blvd, 78401
Tel: 361-883-5731, 800-465-4329
Fax: 361-883-9079
www.holidayinncorpus.com
This large (368-room) hotel has a private beach area, health club, two restaurants, indoor/outdoor pool, free airport shuttle, free parking, a spa and golf course nearby. **$$$**

Villa del Sol
3938 Surfside Blvd, 78402
Tel: 361-883-9748, 800-242-3291
Fax: 361-883-7537
www.villa-delsol.com
Situated on the beach. Whirlpool/spa, kitchenettes, two pools and volleyball court. **$$**

Galveston

Flagship Hotel
2501 Seawall Blvd, 77550
Tel: 409-762-9000
Fax: 409-762-1619
www.flagshiphotel.com
Nautically themed hotel on a pier stretching 1,000 ft (300 meters) out to sea. **$$$**

Gaido's Seaside Inn
3802 Seawall Blvd, 77550
Tel: 409-762-9625
Fax: 409-765-9285
www.gaidosoffalveston.com
With 104 motel-style units, many of which have a sea view. Also a tiered flower garden. **$$**

Harbor View Inn
928 Ferry Rd, 77550
Tel: 409-762-3311
Fax: 409-762-6264
www.galveston.com/harborviewinn
With 49 rooms. Close to ferry. Kitchenettes available. **$**

Hotel Galvez
2024 Seawall Blvd, 77550
Tel: 409-765-7721
Fax: 409-765-5780
www.galveston.com/galvez
Historic seafront hotel run by the Wyndham chain. Features a sauna and whirlpool and 231 units. **$$$**

The Inn at 1816 Postoffice
1816 Postoffice St, 77550
Tel: 409-765-9444, 888-558-9444
www.inn1816postoffice.com
Restored Victorian residence in heart of historic East End district. **$$–$$$**

The Tremont House
2300 Ship's Mechanic Row, 77550
Tel: 409-763-0300
Fax: 409-763-1539
www.wyndham.com
Historic, European-style hotel, near the Strand. Part of the Wyndham chain. 119 Victorian-style rooms. **$$**

Moody Gardens Hotel
7 Hope Blvd, 77554
Tel: 409-741-8484
Fax: 409-683-4936
www.moodygardens.com
Impressive hotel in the Moody Gardens entertainment park. Surrounded by 242 acres (98 hectares) of gardens and pyramids. **$$$**

Kingsville

Best Western Kingsville Inn
2402 E. King Ave., 78363
Tel: 361-595-5656
Fax: 361-595-5000
High-speed Internet access, free local calls, complimentary newspaper and a complimentary full or continental breakfast. **$$$**

Econo Lodge
2203 E. King Ave., 78363
Tel: 361-595-7700
Fax: 361-516-0269
Wi-fi high-speed Internet, continental breakfast. Free local calls. Pet-friendly. **$$**

Rodeway Inn
3430 S. US-77 Bypass, 78363
Tel: 800-246-8357
76 rooms, swimming pool, free breakfast. Fitness facility, wheelchair access. Car rental desk, family rooms. Pets allowed. **$$**

Palacios

The Luther Hotel
409 S. Bay Blvd, 77465
Tel: 361-972-2312.
Historic 1903 hotel with 41 rooms and great views of the bay. **$$**

Moonlight Bay B&B
506 S. Bay Blvd, 77465
Tel: 361-972-2232/877-461-7070
Fax: 361-972-0463
www.moonlightbaybb.com
Eight rooms with indoor/outdoor verandas, bay views, casual elegance, gourmet breakfast. **$$**

Port Isabel

Queen Isabel Inn
300 S. Garcia St, 78578
Tel: 956-943-1468
Fax: 956-943-3574
www.queenisabelinn.com
National landmark property with seven rooms; private and quiet. Fully furnished kitchens. Beach gear provided, fishing pier. **$$–$$$**

Rockport

Hoopes' House
417 N. Broadway, 78382
Tel: 361-729-8424.
www.hoopeshouse.com
Restored Victorian house with eight rooms, swimming pool and hot tub.

Hunt's Court Motel
725 S. Water St, 78382
Tel: 361-729-2273.
www.tx-motels-review.com
25 units; waterfront with fishing pier. **$**

South Padre Island

Moonraker B&B
107 E. Marisol 78597
Tel: 956-761-2206
www.moonrakerbb.com
Three units on the beach; fishing, close to restaurants. **$$**

Motel 6
4013 Padre Blvd, 78597
Tel: 956-761-7911
Fax: 956-761-6339
www.motel6.com
52 units. A mile (1.5 km) north of downtown. **$**

Radisson Resort South Padre Island
500 Padre Blvd, 78597
Tel: 956-761-6511
Fax: 956-761-1602
www.radissonspi.com
With 190 beachfront units and lots of amenities. **$$**

BELOW: the palms and pyramids of Moody Gardens Hotel, Galveston.

RIO GRANDE VALLEY

Brownsville

Rancho Viejo Resort and Country Club
US-83 and Rancho Viejo Dr., 78575
Tel: 956-350-4000, 800-531-7400
Fax: 956-350-9681
www.playrancho.com
Complete resort made up of 22 villas set on a golf course. **$$**

Harlingen

Sun Valley Motor Hotel
1900 S. 77 Sunshine Strip, 78550
Tel: 956-423-7222
Fax: 956-428-6394
Budget hotel with 83 cottage-style units, most of them with carports. Large pool. **$**

McAllen

Microtel Inn
801 E. Expressway 83, 78501
Tel: 956-630-2727
Fax: 956-630-0666.
www.microtelinn.com
Free continental breakfast, and high-speed wi-fi Internet access in each room, outdoor pool. **$**
Renaissance Casa de Palmas Hotel
101 N. Main St, 78501
Tel: 956-631-1101
Fax: 956-631-7934
www.renaissancemcallen.com
Spanish colonial-style hotel with 165 units. So named because of the 92 palm trees in its grounds. A national landmark preserved structure. **$$**

Rio Grande City

Best Western Garden Inn and Suites
4758 Highway 83, 78582
Tel: 956-488-0866
Fax: 956-716-1611
Swimming pool, fitness center, high-speed Internet access. Combining American and Mexican culture. **$$–$$$**
Holiday Inn Express Suites
5274 E. Highway 83 and Blanco Rd, 78582
Tel: 956-487-7772
Fax: 956-488-2320
www.holidayinn.com
Wheelchair access, business center, data port, meeting room, swimming pool, family rooms, fitness facility. **$$**

Roma

Roma Inn
1776 E. Grant St, 78584
Tel: 956-849-3755
Two-story hotel built in the 1990s with 40 rooms, some suites with mini-refrigerator. A Mexican restaurant is conveniently located next door. **$$**

San Juan

Days Inn San Juan
112 W. Expressway 83, 78589
Tel: 956-782-1510
Fax: 956-782-1885
www.daysinn.com
Meeting space, pool, breakfast, Shuttle service available to McAllen

DEL RIO TO LAREDO

Eagle Pass

Hampton Inn
3301 E. Main St, 78852
Tel: 830-757-5565
Fax: 830-757-5512
www.hamptoninn.com
Cribs available, refrigerator, cable TV. Comfortable rooms. Business center. express check out, golf, laundry/valet services, gym, in-room movies. **$$**
La Quinta Inn
2525 Main St, 78852
Tel: 830-773-7000
Fax: 830-773-8852
www.lq.com
Rooms and facilities for the disabled, continental breakfast, boating, scuba diving, fishing, golf, outdoor pool, playground, sauna, tennis, modem, rollaway beds. Pets allowed. **$$$–$$$$**
Super 8 Motel
2150 Del Rio Blvd, 78852
Tel: 830-773-9531
www.super8.com
Disabled-friendly rooms, tennis, pool, bar/lounge. Barber's and beauty shop, business center, casino, fitness center/spa. Pets allowed. **$$–$$$**

Laredo

Family Garden Inn
5830 San Bernardo Ave., 78041
Tel: 956-723-5300
Fax: 956-791-8842
190 rooms with cable TV, microwave oven, refrigerator, high-speed wired and wireless Internet access. Complimentary continental breakfasts. **$$**
La Hacienda Motor Hotel
4914 San Bernardo Ave., 78041
Tel: 956-722-2441
Fax: 956-725-4532
98 units, and live tejano music Tues–Sun nights. **$**
La Posada Hotel
1000 Zaragoza St, 78040
Tel: 956-722-1701
Fax: 956-722-4758
www.laposadahotel.com
Classic Mexican colonial-style hotel. **$$**
Loma Alta Motel
3915 San Bernardo Ave., 78041
Tel: 956-726-1628
Fax: 956-724-4339
Budget hotel with facilities for the disabled. Pool. **$**

EL PASO, THE TRANS-PECOS AND BIG BEND

El Paso

Best Western Airport Inn
7144 E. Gateway Blvd, 79915
Tel: 915-779-7700
Fax: 915-772-1920
www.bestwestern.com
165 clean rooms, heated pool and a rose-filled courtyard. Airport shuttle. **$**
Camino Real Paso del Norte
101 S. El Paso St, 79901
Tel: 915-534-3000
Fax: 915-534-3024
www.caminoreal.com/elpaso
Historic, highly rated accommodations with 360 units. Health club, and the classiest bar in the city. International cuisine in the Dome restaurant. **$$$**
Chase Suite Hotel by Woodfin
6791 Montana Ave., 79925
Tel: 915-772-8000
Fax: 915-772-7254
www.woodfinsuitehotels.com
Close to the airport (7 miles/11 km from downtown), with complimentary continental breakfast. **$$–$$$**

Alpine

Antelope Lodge
2310 W. US-90, 79830
Tel: 432-837-2451
Fax: 432-837-3881
www.antelopelodge.com
Rustic comfort in a valley setting; cottages with kitchenettes. **$**
Fiesta Country Inn
1200 E. US-90, 79830
Tel: 432-837-2503.
Opposite the university with a pool, 15 rooms – some with kitchenettes – golf and tennis facilities nearby. **$**
The Corner House
801 E. Avenue E, 79830
Tel: 432-837-7161.

PRICE CATEGORIES

Price categories are for a double room for one night in high season:
$ = up to $50
$$ = $50–125
$$$ = $125–200
$$$$ = more than $200

ABOVE: one of the rooms at the Gage Hotel, Marathon.

Garden with a fountain. Delicious home-baked breads. Five comfortable rooms. **$**

Big Bend N.P.

Chisos Mountains Lodge
Basin Rural Station, 79834
Tel: 432-477-2291
www.foreverlodging.com
The only lodging inside the park, located high in the Chisos Mountains near trail heads. Open all year, the 72 smoke-free rooms include 6 stone cottages with stone floors, ceiling fans and 3 double beds. Rooms are equipped with coffee pots, refrigerators and microwaves. There is a convenience store, a restaurant, and a gift shop. **$$**

Fort Davis

Hotel Limpia
On the town square, 100 Main St, 79734
Tel: 432-426-3237/800-662-5517
Fax 432-426-3983
www.hotellimpia.com
Historic restored hotel, built in 1912; period furnishings, pool. With 39 non-smoking rooms, restaurant and cocktail lounge. **$$**

Indian Lodge
P.O. Box 1707, 79734
Tel: 432-426-3254
www.tpwd.state.tx.us/park/indian
The only hotel/restaurant owned by the state of Texas. Reservations must be made far in advance. You could always try just for lunch. **$$**

Old Texas Inn
Main St, 79734
Tel: 432-426-3118
Fax: 432-426-2368
www.oldtexasinn.com
Cowboy-style hotel with old-fashioned drugstore and soda fountain and a gift shop. Friday and Saturday nights are Barbecue Night in the restaurant. **$$**

Prude Ranch
N. Highway 118, 79734
Tel: 432-426-3202
Fax: 432-426-4401
www.prude-ranch.com
This old cattle ranch 6 miles (10 km) west of town is now a dude ranch with open-range horseback riding and a mountain resort. Cabins and motel units. Facilities include tennis courts and hot tub. **$$**

Stone Village Motel
Main St, 79734
Tel: 432-426-3941
Fax: 432-426-2281
www.stone-village.com
Mountain retreat close to Fort Davis National Historic Site. **$$**

Veranda Country Inn B&B
210 Court Ave., 79734
Tel: 432-426-2233
Fax: 432-426-3839
www.theveranda.com
Historic, country adobe home. 14 rooms with antique furnishings. Full breakfast. **$$**

Juárez

Holiday Inn
Lincoln Av., Zona Pronaf, 32315
Tel: 011-52656-6131310
or 915-892-7790
www.holiday-inn.com
170 recently renovated units. Pool, fitness center, restaurant and cocktail lounge.

Marathon

The Gage Hotel
101 Highway 90 West, 79842
Tel: 432-386-4205
Fax: 432-386-4510
www.gagehotel.com
Split between a historic 1920s hotel, a courtyard-based annex and a restored 1900 house. Mexican and Southwestern cuisine. **$$–$$$$**

Marfa

Cibolo Creek Ranch
HCR 67 Box 44, 79843
Tel: 432-229-3737, 866-496-9460
Fax: 432-229-3653
www.cibolocreekranch.com
Extending over 30,000 acres (12,140 hectares) in the Big Bend region. Horse riding, health spa, exercise facility, sauna, ranch activities. Meals included in room rates due to remote location. **$$$$**

The Hotel Paisano
207 N. Highland Ave., 79843
Tel: 432-729-3669
www.hotelpaisano.com
The James Dean room, from the movie *Giant*, is one of the most popular. 100-seat banquet room, full-service bar, private meeting and conference area. Indoor swimming pool, shopping and a *Giant* memorabilia room with the movie playing continuously. **$$$**

Thunderbird Hotel
601 W. San Antonio St, 79843
Tel: 432-729-1984
Fax: 432-729-1989
www.thunderbirdmarfa.com
Pool, fine-art collection, televisions with DVD players, record players, vinyl, CD and DVD library, i-Pod home radios, high-speed and wi-fi Internet access. Cable television. vintage typewriter, Polaroid cameras to borrow. **$$$**

Presidio

Three Palms Inn
Old Highway 67 N., 79845
Tel: 432 229-3211
Two-story motel with basic services – clean rooms, swimming pool – ranks as best overnighter in this Mexican border town. Convenient Oasis restaurant next door. **$$**

Terlingua

La Posada Milagro
100 La Posada Lane
Terlingua Ghost Town, 79852
Tel: 432-371-3044
www.laposadamilagro.com
Called "The Miracle Inn," this breathtaking guesthouse is built from stone nearly 100 years old, dating to the old Pancho

Villa mining days. The inn is a remote, almost spiritual retreat, affording views of the Chisos Mountains, Big Bend National Park, and sunsets fading in the majestic Texas sky. **$$–$$$**

Van Horn

Best Western Inn
1705 W. Broadway, 79855
Tel: 432-283-2410
Fax: 432-283-2143
www.bestwestern.com
Large family rooms and pool. **$$**

Best Western American Inn
1309 W. Broadway Blvd, 79855
Tel: 432-283-2030
www.bestwestern.com
All of the 60 rooms are at ground level. Facility includes swimming pool, continental breakfast, coffee maker, dataport, high-speed Internet access, and in-room refrigerators. **$$**

Days Inn
600 E. Broadway Blvd, 79855
Tel: 432-283-1007
Fax: 432-283-1189
www.daysinn.com
Business center, free breakfast, free high-speed Internet access, pool. Pets allowed. **$$**

Ramada Limited
200 Golf Course Dr., 79855
Tel: 1-800-2Ramada
www.ramadavanhorn.com
24-hour front desk, Dairy Queen, free parking, golf, rooms and facilities for the disabled, laundry/valet service, modem lines in rooms, no-smoking rooms, outdoor pool. Pets allowed. **$$**

AMARILLO, LUBBOCK & ENVIRONS

Amarillo

Baymont Inn & Suites
3411 W. I-40, 79109
Tel: 806-356-6800
Fax: 806-356-0401
www.baymontinns.com
Heated pool, business center, conference facilities. Free local calls, modem lines, cable TV, wheelchair accessible; 97 rooms. **$$**

Travelodge West
2035 Paramount Dr., 79109
Tel: 806-353-3541, 800-578-7878
Fax: 806-353-0201
www.travelodgewest.com
100clean, comfortable rooms, pool and lots of restaurants nearby. **$**

The Big Texas Motel
7701 I-40, 79118
Tel: 800-657-7177
Fax: 806-353-0201
www.travelodgewest.com
Old West themed motel with free limo service from the airport. **$$**

Canyon

Best Western Palo Duro
2801 4th Ave., 79015
Tel: 806-655-1818
Fax: 806-655-0204
www.bestwestern.com
All rooms are suites. Lots of extras including swimming pool, car rental desk, family rooms, wheelchair access, dataport, free high-speed Internet, hot tub. Free breakfast. Fitness facility. Pets are welcome. **$$–$$$**

Buffalo Inn
300 23rd St, 79015
Tel: 806 655-2124, 800 526-9968
www.buffaloinncanyon.com
Cable TV, microwave and refrigerator. Summer continental breakfast. **$$**

Holiday Inn Express Hotel & Suites
2901 4th Ave., 79015
Tel: 806-655-4445, 888-400-9714
Swimming pool, wheelchair access, meeting room, non-smoking. Family rooms. Fitness facility. Pets allowed. **$$**

Lubbock

Days Inn – Texas Tech
2401 4th St, 79415
Tel: 806-747-7111
Fax: 806-747-9749
www.daysinn.com
90 units. At the university. **$**

Inn of the South Plains
310 Ave. Q, 79415
Tel: 806-763-2861
Fax: 806-747-1020.
58 units. **$**

Lubbock Inn
3901 19th St, 79410
Tel: 806-792-5181/ 800-545-8226
Fax: 806-792-1319
www.lubbockinn.com
Cocktail lounge, outdoor

THE WEST

Abilene

Antilley Inn
6550 US-83, 79602
Tel: 325-695-3330
Fax: 325-695-9872
www.antillyinn.com
52 units, with continental breakfast served. **$**

Bolin's Prairie House B&B
508 Mulberry St, 79601
Tel: 325-675-5855
Fax: 325-677-4694
www.abilenebedandbreakfast.com
Historic downtown home, with four rooms decorated with antiques. Good breakfast. **$**

Clarion Hotel
5403 S. 1st St, 79605
Tel: 325-695-2150
Fax: 325-698-6742.
Comprising 180 units; well-kept rooms at a good price, facilities for the disabled, heated indoor pool, whirlpool, saunas. **$$**

BELOW: the indoor pool at Marfa's Hotel Paisano.

Albany

Albany Motor Inn
424 E. US-180, 76430
Tel: 325-762-2451

PRICE CATEGORIES

Price categories are for a double room for one night in high season:
$ = up to $50
$$ = $50–125
$$$ = $125–200
$$$$ = more than $200

www.texbesthotels.com
13 RV hook-ups available. Telephone hook-up access, cable, and dog kennels available. **$$–$$$**

Hereford Motel
557 W. US-180, 76430
Tel: 325-762-2224
www.texbesthotels.com
Clean, comfortable rooms. Two suites have a kitchenette. Satellite TV computer accessible telephone.
$$

The Ole Nail House Inn
357 S. 3rd St, 76430
Tel: 325-762-2928
800-245-5163
www.tx-hotels-review.com
Three upstairs rooms with private baths, and one lovely private cottage with excellent location. B&B.
$$–$$$

Big Spring

Holiday Inn Express
1109 N. Aylesford St, 79720
Tel: 432-263-5400/888-400-9714
24-hour front desk, business center, connecting rooms, copy service. Cribs available. Gym, golf, fax, in-room modem lines. Outdoor pool, refrigerator, rollaway beds.
$$

Comfort Inn
2900 E. I-20, 79720
Tel: 432-267-4553
Fax: 432-267-4553
Business center/services, complimentary coffee in lobby, continental breakfast, data ports, fax, high-speed Internet. Microwave. No-smoking rooms available. Pool. ADA-approved rooms available,
$$–$$$

Midland

Clarion Hotel & Conference Center
4300 W. Wall St, 79703
Tel: 432-697-3181
Fax: 432-694-7754
Amenities include indoor heated pool, free deluxe continental breakfast buffet, free Internet access. Gaming areas complete with billiards and ping-pong tables. Miniature golf course and playground. Free airport transportation.
$$$–$$$$

Fairfield Inn by Marriott
2300 Faulkner Dr., 79705
Tel: 432-570-7155
Fax: 432-570-7155
www.marriott.com
Non smoking, free wireless high-speed Internet. Complimentary hot breakfast. Crisp linens, thick mattresses, and fluffy extra pillows.
$$–$$$

Ramada Limited
3100 W. Wall St, 79701
Tel: 432-699-4144
www.ramada.com
Pets allowed, car rental desk, swimming pool, free breakfast, wheelchair access, Non smoking. Hot tub. **$$**

Odessa

Best Western Garden Oasis
110 W. I-20, 79761
Tel: 432-337-3006
Fax: 432-332-1956
www.bestwestern.com
Two-room suites available, pool, in-room modem lines, room service, cable TV, courtesy car. Disabled-friendly rooms/facilities. Fitness center/spa. Pets allowed. **$$–$$$**

Fairfield Inn & Suites by Marriott Odessa
3933 John Ben Shepperd Parkway, 79762
Tel: 432-363-1900
Fax: 432-363-0094
www.marriott.com
Rooms for the disabled, no-smoking rooms, 24-hour front desk, safe deposit box. Courtesy car, coffee maker in room. Pool. Modem lines in room. **$$**

MCM Elegante Hotel
5200 E. University Blvd 79762
Tel: 432-368-5885
Fax: 432-362-8958
www.mcmelegante.com/odessa.htm
Lots of indulgences here, including pillow-top mattresses, Bath & Body Work amenities, and in-room coffee pots with Starbucks coffee. Good business features include high-speed Internet access, desk with ergonomic chair, 24-hour security, and express check-out. **$$$**

Odessa Days Inn
3075 E. Business Loop 20, 79761
Tel: 432-335-8000
Fax: 432-335-9562
www.daysinn.com
Free breakfast, free high-speed Internet access. Pool, fitness center/spa, golf nearby. Rooms for the disabled. **$$**

San Angelo

Best Western
3017 Loop 306, 76904
Tel: 325-223-1273
www.bestwestern.com
Cable TV, no smoking rooms, pool, in-room modem lines. Pets allowed.
$$

Hampton Inn
2959 Loop 306, 76902
Tel: 325-942-9622
Fax: 325-947-8123
www.hamptoninn.hilton.com
Complimentary breakfast bar, hairdryers, refrigerator, indoor pool and spa, 24-hour coffee and tea, elevator, fax services, and cable TV. **$$**

Hawthorn Inn and Suites
1355 Knickerbocker Rd, 76904
Tel: 325-653-1500
Fax: 325-653-1501
www.hawthorn.com
Complimentary hot breakfast buffet, Wednesday night social hour. Outdoor pool and spa, fitness center. Dataport and voice mail. Cable TV and movie rental. Full kitchen suites. Sofa sleepers in all suites.
$$–$$$

San Angelo Inn and Conference Center
441 Rio Concho Dr., 76903
Tel: 325-658-2828
Fax: 325-658-8741
www.hotelsanangelo.com
Comfortable rooms, horse stables and pleasant restaurant. Amenities include cable/satellite TV, in-room movies, free high-speed Internet. **$$**

Sweetwater

Sweetwater Ranch House Motel
301 S.W. Georgia Ave., 79556
Tel: 325-236-6341, 800-622-5361
Fax: 325-235-1536
www.sweetwaterranchhouse.com
Cool ranch decor, horse stables on-site. Free high-speed wireless Internet. Cable TV. Swimming pool. Free full

BELOW: sites are often spacious in Texas campgrounds.

EATING OUT

RECOMMENDED RESTAURANTS, CAFES & BARS

What to Eat

Don't plan on dieting while in Texas: Texans love their food, and a visit here wouldn't be complete without sampling a good portion of it. Tex-Mex food has become synonymous with the state, and it's not all fire-breathingly hot, so even the most wary should give it a try.

Another Texas staple is the barbecue – usually huge chunks of beef (but sometimes pork and sausage) that are cooked slowly for hours over special wood such as hickory or mesquite to add the distinctive flavor. One of the state's celebrated barbecue joints is The Salt Lick at Driftwood, tel: 512-858-4959, www.saltlickbbq.com, 13 miles (20 km) west of Austin in the Hill Country.

The state dish of Texas is chili con carne, and you'll find it in abundance throughout the state. On average, some 15 chili competitions are held each month.

The "runner-up" to the state dish must surely be chicken-fried steak, an inexpensive steak covered with batter and fried, usually served with gravy and found on most Texas menus. And you musn't forget to try pecan pie.

Drinking

For a state with such a robust reputation for hearty living, it may come as a surprise to learn that about one-fifth of the 254 counties choose to be "dry," banning all alcoholic beverages. This rarely presents a problem for would-be drinkers, who merely drive a mile or two to a neighboring county where anything goes.

Three brands of **beer** brewed in the state qualify as "famous" – Pearl, Lone Star and Shiner. Arguments often ensue among locals as to which is best.

Texas **wines** have also acquired an excellent reputation over the years, and many will be found on menus throughout the state.

Tequila may well be the most popular liquor consumed, due to the proximity of Mexico, where it is made in vast quantities. Tequila-based margaritas are probably drunk in Texas more than anywhere else in the US.

Recently, the **micro-brewery** concept has taken hold, with the Belgian-style Celis from Austin having established a statewide reputation. Many "brewpubs" have decent food. Drinking-based places to try include:

Bitter End Bistro and Brewpub, 311 Colorado Street, Austin, tel: 512-478-2337.

Flying Saucer Draught Emporium, 111 E. 4th Street, Fort Worth, tel: 817-336-7468. Massive range of draught beers.

Ginger Man, 5607 Morningside Drive, Houston, tel: 713-526-2770. First pub in a chain with venues also in Austin, Dallas and Fort Worth. Loads of beers.

RESTAURANT LISTINGS

DALLAS/FORT WORTH AND ENVIRONS

Dallas

Abacus
4511 McKinney Ave.
Tel: 214-559-3111
www.abacus-restaurant.com/
Chic Uptown spot from celebrated chef-owner Kent Rathbun, who gives New American an Asian spin. Must-get: the lobster shooters. Fine dining in a relaxed atmosphere. **$$$**

Adolphus Hotel French Room
1321 Commerce St
Tel: 214-742-8200
Arguably the best French cuisine in town. **$$$**

L'Ancestral
4514 Travis St
Tel: 214-528-1081
Beautifully decorated "French country inn"; classic French cuisine. **$$$**

Aurora
4216 Oak Lawn Ave.
Tel: 214-528-9400
www.auroradallas.com
Many say that Avner Samuel, who owns this high-end food temple dedicated to foie gras, truffles, and all things exotic, is Dallas' top chef. **$$$**

Avanti
1445 Ross Ave.
Tel: 214-965-0055
Mediterranean cuisine. Ideal for lunch, surrounded by fountains and a waterfall. **$$**

Blue Mesa Grill
5100 Belt Line Rd, suite 500
Tel: 972-934-0165
www.bluemesagrill.com
New-Mexican take on Mexican food relying on good, fresh ingredients, with nearly 100 boutique tequilas. **$$**

ABOVE: the French Room at the Adolphus Hotel, Dallas.

Bob's Steak and Chop House
4300 Lemmon Ave.
Tel: 214-528-9446
Upscale steakhouse; oversized portions. **$$$**

Café Capri
15107 Addison Rd at Beltline
Tel: 972-960-8686
Stylish atmosphere, with excellent seafood and a live harpist. **$$$**

Café Izmir
3711 Greenville Ave.
Tel: 214-826-7788
Plentiful Middle Eastern food. **$$**

Café Pacific
24 Highland Park Village
Tel: 214-526-1170
Great seafood. **$$$**

Casa Dominguez
2408 Cedar Springs at Fairmont
Tel: 214-871-9787
Serving good Tex-Mex food since 1963. **$$**

Coal Vines
2404 Cedar Springs Rd
Tel: 214-855-4999
www.coalvines.com
Trendy-casual hot spot is the go-to for New York-style thin crust pizza, baked in a blazing-hot coal oven. **$**

Cock and Bull Wine Bar & Restaurant
6330 Gaston Ave.
Tel: 214-841-9111
Bistro-type food, pâté, pastas and delicious fish. **$$**

Daddy Jack's Wood Grill
2723 Elm St, Deep Ellum
Tel: 214-653-3949
Lobster, shrimp, wood-grilled steaks, rack of lamb, chicken. **$$**

Dakotas
600 N. Akard St
Tel: 214-740-4001
Seafood, wild game and poultry in appealing surroundings. **$$$**

Daniele Osteria
3300 Oak Lawn Ave.
Tel: 214-443-9420
www.danieleosteria.com
Dallas' most authentic Italian, with a dashing chef-owner and house-made pasta cooked perfectly. **$$**

Del Frisco's Double Eagle Steakhouse
5251 Spring Valley Rd
Tel: 972-490-9000
Fine steaks. **$$$**

Fireside Pies
2820 N. Henderson Ave.
Tel: 214-370-3916
www.firesidepies.com/home.asp
Scrumptious artisan pizza with delectable toppings such as Italian sausage, fat meatballs, and caramelized onions. Major patio scene. **$**

Fogo de Chao
4300 Belt Line Rd, Addison
Tel: 972-503-7300
Meat-oriented Brazilian restaurant. **$$$**

India Palace
12817 Preston Rd
Tel: 972-392-0190
www.indiapalacedallas.com
Probably the best Indian restaurant in Dallas, with perfect tikka masala and great atmosphere. **$$**

Korea House Restaurant
2598 Royal Lane
Tel: 972-243-0434
Classy Korean cuisine. **$$$**

La Duni
4620 McKinney Ave.
Tel: 214-520-7300
www.laduni.com
Sophisticated mom-and-pop does Latin food and gorgeous desserts. Sandwiches are served on puffy popovers, and the *cuatros leches* cake is divine. **$**

Lola the Restaurant
2917 Fairmount St
Tel: 214-855-0700
www.lola4dinner.com
Hands-down favorite among Dallas foodies acts as a laboratory for bright young chefs. Amazingly savvy wine list, too. **$$$**

Mercury Grill
11909 Preston Rd
Tel: 972-960-7774
www.mcrowd.com/mercurygrill.shtm
Stylish bistro fuses comfort and innovation. Signature dish is the couscous carbonara. **$$$**

Mi Cocina
77 Highland Park Village
Tel: 214-521-6426
www.mcrowd.com
Beloved local chain gives Tex-Mex an upscale spin; be sure to try the brisket tacos, with a side of queso. **$**

Momo's Pasta
3312 Knox St
Tel: 214-521-3009
Good neighborhood Italian restaurant. **$$**

Nick and Sam's
3008 Maple Ave.
Tel: 214-871-7444
www.nick-sams.com
Classy, elegant steakhouse has fine wines and steaks; free samples from the caviar bar. **$$**

Nobu
Hotel Crescent Court
Tel: 214-252-7000
www.noburestaurants.com
This spin-off of New York original serves pristine sushi in a breathtaking setting; check out the wall of polished stones. **$$$**

Oceanaire Seafood Room
13340 Dallas Parkway
Tel: 972-759-2277
www.theoceanaire.com
This seafood emporium feels like a steakhouse but it has the best fish in land-locked Dallas; located at the three-story Galleria affords the opportunity for a post-dinner shopping stroll. **$$$**

Pappas Bros. Steakhouse
10477 Lombardy Lane
Tel: 214-366-2000
www.pappasbros.com
An elegant prime steakhouse with a big-city feel and its own dry-aging room, thick, glistening steaks and irresistible desserts. **$$$**

Poppy's Garden Café
107 S. Church St, Mc Kinney
Tel: 972-562-8386
www.poppys-gardencafe.com
New American with Asian twist served in a grand, rustic old house that perfectly embodies the town's vintage vibe. **$$$**

Martin's Wine Bistro
3020 Greenville Ave.
Tel: 214-826-0940
Romantic dining, French cuisine, fine wine selections. **$$$**

The Mansion on Turtle Creek
2821 Turtle Creek Blvd
Tel: 214-559-2100
Award-winning American nouvelle cuisine. **$$$**

Trail Dust Steak House
10841 Composite Dr.
Tel: 214-357-3862
Live country music every night of the week. Five venues in Dallas/Fort Worth area. **$$**

York Street
6047 Lewis St
Tel: 214-826-0968
www.yorkstreetdallas.com
The food at this pocket-sized, chic restaurant is

nothing less than flawless, with careful presentation of the finest ingredients. **$$$**

Fort Worth

Al's
1001 N.E. Green Oaks Blvd, Arlington
Tel: 817-275-8918
Local hamburger favorite for 30 years. **$**

Angelo's Barbecue
2533 White Settlement Rd
Tel: 817-332-0357
A Texas institution, founded in 1958; award-winning barbecue and coldest beer. **$**

Benito's Restaurant
1450 W. Magnolia Ave.
Tel: 817-332-8633
The Yucatan brought to just south of downtown. **$**

Billy Miner's Saloon
150 W. 3rd St
Tel: 817-877-3301
Big burgers in rustic setting entices all types downtown. **$**

Cattlemen's Steak House
2458 N. Main St, Stockyards
Tel: 817-624-3945
The cowboys' choice. **$$**

Flying Saucer Draught Emporium
111 E. 4th St, downtown
Tel: 817-336-7468
"Rib-sticking" German fare says one of the local weeklies. Vast selection of beers. **$$**

Hedary's Lebanese
6323 Camp Bowie Blvd
Tel: 817-731-6961
www.hedarys.com
Authentic and delicious Lebanese cuisine; shish kebabs, hummus, shawarma and more.Sunday buffet.**$$**

J&J Oyster Bar
612 N. University Drive
Tel: 817-335-2756
An old favorite. **$$**

Joe T Garcia's
2201 N. Commerce St.
Tel: 817-626-4356
www.joets.com
Informal Tex-Mex spot with family-style dinners and no menu. **$**

Kimbell Art Museum Buffet
3333 Camp Bowie Blvd
Tel: 817-332-8451
www.kimbellart.org
The salads and sandwiches are enticing; the setting delightful. **$**

Kincaid's Hamburgers
4901 Camp Bowie Blvd
Tel: 817-732-2881
1946 grocery and butcher's-turned-restaurant; voted best in US. **$**

La Madeleine
2101 N. Collins St, Arlington
Tel: 817-461-3534
www.lamadeleine.com
Great all-day breakfasts and bistro fare at this charming French bakery. **$**

Lanny's Alta Cocina Mexicana
3405 W. 7th St
Tel: 817-850-9996
www.lannyskitchen.com
High-end Mexican in lovely minimalist setting, with powerful flavor combinations. **$$$**

Lonesome Dove
2406 N. Main St
Tel: 817-740-8810
www.lonesomedovebistro.com
"Cowboy" cuisine – buffalo burgers, wild-boar ribs – from colorful chef Tim Love. **$$$**

Massey's
1805 8th Ave.
Tel: 817-921-5582
Sooner or later you'll have to try Texas' ubiquitous chicken fried steak, so why not here? **$**

Paris Coffee Shop
704 W. Magnolia Ave.
Tel: 817-335-2041
Old-time atmosphere. Great pies. **$**

Reata
310 Houston St
Tel: 817-336-1009
www.reata.net
High-class cowboy cooking. Big steaks, shrimp enchiladas, cheese grits, dessert tamales and more. Dine indoors or under the stars, on the rooftop. **$$$**

Saint-Emilion
3617 W. 7th St
Tel: 817-737-2781
Stunning French country food in a cozy atmosphere. **$$$**

Spiral Diner
1314 W. Magnolia Ave.
Tel: 817-332-8834
Inventive, substantial vegan fare in the heart of Cowtown. Cool, comfortable surroundings. Ask about the Blue Plate Special. **$**

The Tandoor
532 Fielder N. Plaza, Arlington
Tel: 817-261-6604
Good Indian spot for lunch as well as dinner where you should leave room for dessert. **$$**

Denton

Hannah's Off the Square
111 W. Mulberry St
Tel: 940-566-1110
www.hannahsoffthesquare.com
Fine dining at a likeable, small-town price. **$$**

Grapevine

Tolbert's
423 S. Main St
Tel: 817-421-4888
www.tolbertsrestaurant.com
Home of the famed "bowl of red" chili. Stunning Texana decor. **$**

Ponder

Ranchman's Cafe
110 W. Bailey
Tel: 940-479-2221
Ranchman's is famous for steaks that hang over the platter, homemade pies, and baked potatoes that must be ordered in advance. **$**

CENTRAL TEXAS

Austin

Güero's Taco Bar
1412 S. Congress Ave.
Tel: 512-442-7688
Friendly taqueria serving great Mexican snacks and Margaritas. The substantial main dishes are good, too, and the tortillas are freshly made on the premises.**$**

Chez Nous
510 Neches St
Tel: 512-473-2413
French. **$$**

Chuy's
1728 Barton Springs Rd
Tel: 512-474-4452
www.chuys.com
Light-hearted Tex-Mex: one of four Chuy's in town. **$**

The County Line
6500 West Bee Cave Rd
Tel: 512-327-1742
www.countyline.com
Classic, acclaimed Texas-pit barbecue. **$$**

Eastside Café
2113 Manor Rd
Tel: 512-476-5858
www.eastsidecafeaustin.com
Continental, vegetarian; patio. **$**

Fonda San Miguel
2330 W. North Loop Blvd
Tel: 512-459-4121
www.fondasanmiguel.com
Colonial, indoor patio. Gourmet Mexican influences. **$$**

Green Mesquite
1400 Barton Springs Rd
Tel: 512-479-0485
www.greenmesquite.net
Good food, live music. **$**

Hudson's on the Bend
3509 Highway 620
Tel: 512-266-1369
www.hudsonsonthebend.com
Classy, continental cuisine, especially the game. **$$$**

Jeffrey's Restaurant and Bar
1204 W. Lynn St
Tel: 512-477-5584
www.jeffreysofaustin.com
Award-winning restaurant with international cuisine. **$$$**

Manuel's
310 Congress Ave.
Tel: 512-472-7555
Bustling Mexican. **$**

Mother's Café
4215 Duval St
Tel: 512-451-3994
www.motherscafeaustin.com
Enclosed garden patio, vegetarian food a specialty, popular with locals. **$**

The Old Pecan Street Café
310 E. 6th St
Tel: 512-478-2491

PRICE CATEGORIES

Price categories based on the cost of a meal for one without drinks:
$ = under $15
$$ = $15–30
$$$ = over $30

Charming, historic café with full menu. **$**

Shanghai River
2700 W. Anderson Lane
Tel: 512-458-9598
Bountiful Chinese buffet. **$**

Shoreline Grill San Jacinto Center
98 San Jacinto Blvd
Tel: 512-477-3300
www.shorelinegrill.com
Top-rated steak/seafood restaurant at the Four Seasons Hotel. **$$**

Taj Palace
6700 Middle Fiskville Rd
Tel: 512-452-9959
Close to airport, Indian cuisine. Lunch buffet **$**; ethnic Indian. **$$**

Threadgill's
6416 Lamar Blvd
Tel: 512-451-5440
301 W. Riverside Dr.
Tel: 512-472-9304
www.threadgills.com
Texas roadhouse café in two locations. Southern cuisine, Cajun, vegetarian. **$**

Vespaio
1610 S. Congress Ave.
Tel: 512-441-6100
Hip, upscale Italian. One of the city's hottest restaurants. **$$$**

Z-Tejas
1110 W. 6th St
Tel: 512-478-5355
9400-A Arboretum Boulevard
Tel: 512-346-3506
www.ztejas.com
Creative spicy cuisine. **$$**

Bandera

OST Restaurant
305 Main St
Tel: 830-796-3836
www.texasbob.com/eats/tbe_ost.html
Home-made home cookin', real good. **$**

Blanco

Blanco Riverside Bar & Grill
18 Main St
Tel: 830-833-0208
Country cooking with a nice view of the Blanco River. **$**

Clifton

Bunkhouse Barbeque
1003 S. Ave. G, Highway 6
Tel: 866-466-5324
www.bunkhouseb-b-q.com
Texas barbecue with great pork ribs. **$**

Corsicana

Roy's Café
106 N. Beaton St
Tel: 903-874-6791
Home-cooking with small-town hospitality. **$**

Fredericksburg

Altdorf
301 W. Main St
Tel: 830-997-7865
German food in grand old home with outdoor *biergarten*. **$$**

Fredericksburg Brewing Co.
245 E. Main St
Tel: 830-997-1646
www.yourbrewery.com
Bakery-cum-brewery in historic building with an enclosed "biergarten". **$$**

Fredericksburg Herb Farm
405 Whitney St
Tel: 830-997-8615
www.fredericksburgherbfarm.com
Herbs play a key role in this upscale New American eatery. **$$$**

Hill Top Café
11 miles (18 km) N. US-87
Tel: 830-997-8922
www.hilltopcafe.com
Former gas-station site serving a unique combination of Cajun and Greek. **$$**

Georgetown

Monument Café
1953 S. Austin Ave.
Tel: 512-930-9586
www.themonumentcafe.com
1940s diner with fine home cooking, from breakfast with squeezed juices to house-baked pies. **$**

Wildfire Restaurant
812 S. Austin Ave.
Tel: 512-869-3473
www.wildfiretexas.com
High end yet homey New American with Texan and Mexican accents. **$$$**

Glen Rose

Rough Creek Lodge
County Rd 2013
Tel: 254-965-3700, 800-864-4705
www.roughcreek.com
Fine wine-and-dine destination at rustic lodge resort. **$$$**

Hillsboro

El Conquistador
1516 Old Brandon Rd
Tel: 254-582-9864
Reliable Tex-Mex at an easy price. **$**

Colorado Street Grille
115 N. Colorado St, Whitney.
Tel: 254-694-7455
Quiet spot in nearby Whitney has upscale, big-city menu. **$$$**

Kerrville

Anne Marie's River View Restaurant
1001 Junction Highway
Tel: 830-895-5000
Gourmet restaurant attached to a business retreat with panoramic view of the Guadalupe River. **$$**

Big Earl's Texas Style Bar B Que
401 Sidney Baker St
Tel: 830-896-5656
Barbecue joint noted for stand-out ribs and spicy sausage. **$**

Branding Iron
2033 Sidney Baker St
Tel: 830-257-4440/877-967-3767
Steakhouse at historic Y.O. Ranch resort. **$$$**

Salado

Ambrosia Tea Room
102 N. Main St
Tel: 254-947-3733
Gift-shop teahouse with soups, salads and sandwiches. **$**

The Range
101 Main St
Tel: 254-947-3828
www.therangerestaurant.com
Mediterranean cuisine in grandly renovated home. **$$$**

Stagecoach Inn
401 S. Stagecoach Rd
Tel: 254-947-5111/800-732-8994
www.staystagecoach.com
Substantial home-style mains such as prime rib and fried chicken served with hot, fresh hush puppies in a historic dining room. Fixed lunch and dinner menus available. **$$$**

Waco

Buzzard Billy's
208 S. University Parks Dr.
Tel: 254-753-2778
www.buzzardbillys.com
Blackened fish and other Cajun dishes. **$$**

Diamond Back's
217 Mary Ave.
Tel: 254-757-2871
Southwestern cuisine plus steak. **$$**

Elite Circle Grille
2132 S. Valley Mills Dr.
Tel: 254-754-4941
www.elitecirclegrille.com
Old-timer with trademark Dr Pepper barbecue baby back ribs. **$**

Waxahachie

1879 Chisholm Grill
111 South College Street
Tel: 972-937-7261
www.chisholmgrill.com
Home cooking: Black Angus steaks, crunchy onion rings. **$$**

BELOW: barbecue beef brisket and trimmings.

SAN ANTONIO AND ENVIRONS

San Antonio

Asia Kitchen
1739 S.W. Loop 410
Tel: 210-673-0662
Chinese restaurant with attached fish market. **$**

Biga on the Banks
203 S. Saint Mary's St
Tel: 210-225-0722
www.biga.com
Foodie fave blends Asian with New American. **$$$**

Bistro Vatel
218 E. Olmos Dr.
Tel: 210-828-3141
www.bistrovatel.com
Perfect French in funky, Euro-styled environment. **$$$**

Boudro's
421 E. Commerce St, on the River Walk
Tel: 210-224-8484
Ribs, seafood; don't miss the smoked shrimp enchiladas. Barge dinners possible. **$$**

Cactus Flower Café
711 E. Riverwalk
Tel: 210-224-4555
Part of the Marriott Hotel. Tortilla soup, prime rib, sandwiches. **$$**

County Line
111 W. Crockett St, on the River Walk
Tel: 210-229-1941
Barbecue. Party barges organized. **$$**

Crumpets Restaurant & Bakery
3920 Harry Wurzbach Rd
Tel: 210-821-5454
Long-established restaurant, popular Sunday brunch. **$$**

Eyes Over Texas
Tower of the Americas
222 Hemisphere Plaza
Tel: 210-223-3101
Spectacular views from the revolving tower and some classy food. **$$$**

Guenther House
205 E. Guenther St
Tel: 210-227-1061
Century-old store, restaurant and museum; roof garden. **$$**

Hung Fong
3624 Broadway St
Tel: 210-822-9211
Favorite Chinese location, in business for 60 years. **$$**

La Fogata
2427 Vance Jackson
Tel: 210-340-1337
Mexican; nationally recognized as among the best. **$$**

Le Reve
152 E. Pecan St
Tel: 210-212-2221
www.restaurantlereve.com
Top-rated downtown gem serves up nouveau French. **$$$**

Lodge Restaurant of Castle Hills
1746 Lockhill Selma Rd
Tel: 210-349-8466
www.thelodgerestaurant.com
Gussied-up Texas food in converted mansion. **$$$**

Los Patios
2015 N.E. Loop 410 at Starcrest Drive
Tel: 210-655-6171
Tex-Mex and Southwestern in twin garden restaurant by the river. **$$**

Magic Time Machine
902 N.E. Loop 410
Tel: 210-828-1470
Theme park restaurant aimed at children. **$$**

Mama's Café
2442 Nacogdoches
Tel: 210-826-8303
Home-style food, nice atmosphere. **$**

Mi Tierra Café & Bakery
218 Produce Row in Market Square
Tel: 210-225-1262
Colorful, festive, time-honored restaurant with a bakery. **$**

Republic of Texas
526 Riverwalk at Commerce Street Bridge
Tel: 210-226-6256
Enormous steaks, Mexican dishes, margaritas. **$$**

Texas Land & Cattle Steakhouse
60 N.E. Loop 410 at McCullough
Tel: 210-342-4477
Authentic ranch house, stone fireplaces, covered patio, mesquite grill. **$$**

Thai Orchid
9921 W. I-10
Tel: 210-691-8424
Typical Thai, vegetarian, seafood. **$**

Tokyo Steak House
9405 San Pedro
Tel: 210-341-4461
Sushi bar and steaks. **$$**

Comfort

814, A Texas Bistro
713 High St
Tel: 830-995-4990
Reasonably priced bistro with steaks and seafood. BYO. **$$**

Gruene

Gristmill
1287 Gruene Rd
Tel: 830-625-0684
www.gristmillrestaurant.com
Open-air dining with "Cowboy brunch". The Gristburger comes with spicy queso sauce. **$$**

New Braunfels

Gruene River Grill
1259 Gruene Rd
Tel: 830-624-2300
www.gruenerivergrill.com
Eclectic food with patio dining. **$$**

Adobe Verde
1724 Hunter Rd
Tel: 830-629-0777
www.adobeverde.com
Robust Mexican restaurant; excellent margaritas. Live music Thur–Sun. **$$**

Huisache Grill
303D W. San Antonio St
Tel: 830-620-9001
Grilled meats and plain-spoken food in a small, unpretentious setting. **$$**

New Braunfels Smokehouse
140 S. Highway 46
Tel: 830-625-2416
www.nbsmokehouse.com
Landmark German spot ships its hickory-smoked meats all around the world. **$$**

Oma's Haus
541 Highway 46
Tel: 830-625-3280
Lots of wursts at this authentic German restaurant. **$$**

HOUSTON AND EAST TEXAS

Houston

Barry's Pizza & Italian Diner
6003 Richmond Ave.
Tel: 713-266-8692.
Pasta, pizzas and good-value lunch specials served in a spacious faux log-cabin. **$$**

Benihana of Tokyo
9707 Westheimer Rd
Tel: 713-789-4962
Also at 1318 Louisiana St
Tel: 713-659-8231
Communal dining; sushi. **$$**

Billy Blues Bar & Grill
6025 Richmond Ave. near Fountainview
Tel: 713-266-9294
Five-story landmark, barbecue served up with live blues. **$$**

Café Annie
1728 Post Oak Blvd
Tel: 713-840-1111
www.cafe-annie.com
Highly rated Southwestern temple, conducted by chef Robert del Grande – a local treasure. **$$$**

Dave and Buster's
6010 Richmond Ave.
Tel: 713-952-2233
Pool hall and grub. **$**

Dessert Gallery
3200 Kirby Dr.
Tel: 713-522-9999
Sara Brook's sexy desserts plus furniture as art; open late on weekends; lunch specials. **$**

Dimassi's
5064 Richmond Ave.
Tel: 713-439-7481
Middle Eastern cuisine. **$**

Doneraki
2836 Fulton
Tel: 713-224-2509
Authentic Mexican food, live mariachis (Mexican

PRICE CATEGORIES

Price categories based on the cost of a meal for one without drinks:
$ = under $15
$$ = $15–30
$$$ = over $30

ABOVE: beat the Texas heat with an ice-cream break.

street musicians). **$**
Golden Room Restaurant
1209 Montrose Blvd
Tel: 713-524-9614
Tasty Thai food. **$**
Goode Company Bar-B-Q
5109 Kirby Dr.
Tel: 713-522-2530
Also at 8911 Katy Freeway
Said to be best barbecue place in the city. **$$**
Kim Son
2001 Jefferson St
Tel: 713-222-2461
Vietnamese. **$**
McGonigel's Mucky Duck
2425 Norfolk St
Tel: 713-528-5999
As Irish as its name. Pub grub. **$**
Marina Bar & Grill
3000 NASA Rd, in Nassau Bay Marina
Tel: 281-333-9300
Fresh seafood, grilled steaks; view over water. **$$**
Maxim's
3755 Richmond Ave. at Timmons
Tel: 713-877-8899
French cuisine, piano bar. **$$$**
Ouisie's Table
3939 San Felipe St
Tel: 713-528-2264
Cozy ranch house with own herb garden. American cuisine. **$$**
Pappadeaux Seafood Kitchen
6015 Westheimer Rd
Tel: 713-782-6310
One of eight favored local Cajun spots. **$$**
Rainbow Lodge
1 Birdsall St near Memorial Park
Tel: 713-861-8666
Upscale fishing lodge with classy decor, lovely gardens, seafood and wild game. **$$$**
Rotisserie for Beef & Bird
2200 Wilcrest Dr.
Tel: 713-977-9524
American colonial cuisine, wild game, good wine list. **$$$**
Sammy's Lebanese Restaurant
5825 Richmond Dr.
Tel: 713-780-0065
Delicious Lebanese dishes including taboule, hummus, kibbie, and excellent falafel. **$**
The Bombay Palace
4100 Westheimer Rd
Tel: 713-960-8472
One of the renowned worldwide chain. **$$**
The Brownstone
2736 Virginia St
Tel: 713-520-5666
Long-established favorite. Elegant surroundings, opulently decorated. Top-notch food on offer, too. **$$$**
The Great Caruso Dinner Theater
10001 Westheimer Rd
Tel: 713-780-4900
Steaks, pasta, vegetarian food. Plus Broadway shows. **$$$**
This Is It
207 Gray St
Tel: 713-659-1608
Funny name but tasty soulfood. **$**
Vincent's Rotisserie
2701 W. Dallas St
Tel: 713-528-4313
Spit-roasted chicken, various meats and seafood. **$$**

Beaumont

Bryan's 797
797 N. 5th St
Tel: 409-832-3900
This French-Asian is considered the best restaurant in Beaumont. **$$**
Willy Ray's Bar-B-Q
145 N. I-10
Tel: 409-832-7770
www.willyraysbbq.com
This Texas barbecue joint has been written up in many national magazines. **$**

Jefferson

Auntie Skinner's Riverboat Club
107 W. Austin St
Tel: 903-665-7121
Cajun food with New Orleans riverboat ambience. **$$$**
Lamache's Italian Restaurant
124 W. Austin St
Tel: 903-665-6177
http://historicjeffersonhotel.com
Popular Italian has noteworthy desserts including double chocolate cake. **$$**
Stillwater Inn
203 E. Broadway St
Tel: 903-665-8415
http://stillwaterinn.com
Chef-owned restaurant in an 1890s Victorian house. **$$$**

Nacogdoches

Auntie Pasta's
211 Old Tyler Rd
Tel: 936-569-2171
www.auntiepastas.com
Homey Italian American and one of Nacogdoches' dressiest spots. **$$**
Café Fredonia (in the Fredonia Hotel)
200 N. Fredonia St
Tel: 936-564-1234/800-594-5323
www.fredoniahotel.com
Every Friday night there's a generous seafood buffet. **$$**
Java Jacks Coffee House
1122 North St
Tel: 936-560-3975
www.javajacks.com
Independently owned coffee house that serves sandwiches, too. **$**
Shelley's Bakery Café
112 N. Church St
Tel: 936-564-4100
Baked goods and lunch, with soups and sandwiches. **$**

Sabine Pass

Olde Time Diner
5404 S. Gulfway Dr.
Tel: 409-971-2573
Great lunch specials, and cheap! **$**

Texarkana

Bryce's Cafeteria
2021 Mall Dr.
Tel: 903-792-1611
Simple cafeteria that is a long-time local staple. **$**

PRICE CATEGORIES

Price categories based on the cost of a meal for one without drinks:
$ = under $15
$$ = $15–30
$$$ = over $30

THE GULF COAST

Port Bolivar

Steve's Landing
1284 Bay Vue Dr.
Tel: 409-684-1440
Oysters on the pier. Fried shrimp, cajun potatoes and salads. **$$**

Corpus Christi

Snoopy's Seafood Restaurant and Pier
13313 S. Padre Island Dr.
Tel: 361-949-8815
Fish and chips, and boiled shrimp. Local catch of the day, open lunch and dinner. **$**

Texas Roadhouse
2029 S. Padre Island Dr.
Tel: 361-854-9505
www.texasroadhouse.com
Steaks and ribs and an ocean breeze. **$$**

Galveston

Clary's
8509 Teichman Rd, off I-45
Tel: 409-740-0771
www.galveston.com/clarysseafood
Longtime family-owned seafood haven. **$$$**

Gaido's
3802 Seawall Blvd
Tel: 409-762-9625
www.gaidosofgalveston.com
Seafood fresh from the gulf, since 1911. **$$**

Miller's Landing
Seawall & 19th St
Tel: 409-763-8777
www.galveston.com/millerslanding
Overlooks the Gulf; seafood, steaks. **$$**

Ocean Grill Restaurant
2227 Seawall Blvd
Tel: 409-762-7100
www.galveston.com/oceangrill
On the water, mesquite-grilled seafood. **$$**

Saltwater Grill
2017 Post Office St
Tel: 409-762-3474
www.galveston.com/saltwatergrill
Mobs line up for terrific seafood, cooked in vast kettles. In a class of its own. **$$$**

The Original Mexican Café
1401 Market St
Tel: 409-762-6001
www.galveston.com/theoriginal
Serving Mexican food for 80 years. **$**

Palacios

Outrigger Restaurant
515 Commerce St
Tel: 361-972-1479
www.outriggerrestaurant.com
Fresh local seafood such as shrimp, oyster and flounder, plus home-baked pies. **$$**

Port Isabel

Gabriella's Ristorante Italiano
1506 Highway 100
Tel: 956-943-2141
www.gabriellasrestaurant.com
Terrific pizza, and be sure to check out the faux boat exterior. **$$**

South Padre Island

Bubba's Bar-B-Que
1313 Padre Blvd
Tel: 956-772-8000
All your barbecue basics: brisket, ribs, sausage, chicken, turkey and good sides. **$**

Ted's Restaurant
5717 Padre Blvd
Tel: 956-761-5327
Noteworthy fajitas and fantastic breakfast. **$**

RIO GRANDE VALLEY

Brownsville

Palm Court
2200 Boca Chica Blvd
Tel: 956-542-3575
A few Mexican-influenced dishes, fresh seafood, salads, soups, sandwiches and delectable desserts such as the Manhattan cheesecake. **$$**

McAllen

Bistro M
2900 N. 10th St
Tel: 956-683-0027
www.bistrom.net
Palpable European atmosphere with classic dishes such as Dover sole, rack of lamb and pork tenderloin. Indulgent desserts. **$$$**

Sahadi's
709 N. 10th St
Tel: 956-682-3419
www.sahadi.com
Half café, half grocery, with lots of Mediterranean dishes such as stuffed grape leaves and sticky, sweet pastries. Lunch and dinner specials and live entertainment on the weekend. **$**

Rio Grande City

Caros
205 N. Garcia St
Tel: 956-487-2255
Caro's has been serving Mexican food in Rio Grande City since 1937. Their claim to fame is the puffy taco. Substantial Mexican breakfasts are seved from 11am until 2pm. **$$**

DEL RIO TO LAREDO

Eagle Pass

Guva's Steak & Grill
2150 Del Rio Blvd
Tel: 830-773-2100
Reliable Tex-Mex with tacos and the like, but steak, too. **$$**

Laredo

Cotulla Style Pit Bar-B-Q
4502 McPherson Rd
Tel: 956-724-5747
Mexican-plus-barbecue equals heaven, with puffy stuffed chilis and pit-smoked goat. **$**

Desayunos Mar-La
5904 McPherson Ave.
Tel: 956-729-9878
www.desayunosmarla.com
Breakfast and lunch only, with biscuits, pancakes, and eggs. **$**

El Palenque Bar and Grill
7220 Bob Bullock Loop
Tel: 956-728-1272
Rib-sticking Mexican spot has estimable meatball soup and chicken enchiladas. **$$**

El Rancho Su Majestad El Taco
9720 McPherson Rd
Tel: 956-725-2553
www.elranchosumajestad.com
Grilled meats, chicken enchiladas, and cheesecake for dessert to the tune of wandering mariachis. **$$**

ABOVE: a spicy stew.

EL PASO, THE TRANS-PECOS AND BIG BEND

El Paso

Back Burner Bistro
7130 N. Mesa St
Tel: 915-587-5797
Upscale dining, including vegan dishes and superb wine list. **$$**

Chico's Tacos
1235 McRae Blvd
Tel: 915-592-8484
Authentic Mexican fix that is especially hot after the bars close. **$**

Forti's Mexican Elder
321 Chelsea St
Tel: 915-772-0066
www.fortismexicanrestaurant.com
Steak, seafood and chicken

Leo's Mexican Food
5103 Montana Ave.
Tel: 915-566-4972
An old family favorite. The tri-color enchiladas are delicious. **$**

Mesa Street Grill
2525 N. Mesa St
Tel: 915-532-1881
www.themesastreetgrill.com
Elegant New American spot with Southwestern touches and a solid wine list. **$$**

Alpine

Bread and Breakfast Bakery and Café
113 W. Holland Ave.
Tel: 432-837-9424
Killer breakfasts and baked goods. **$**

Edelweiss Brewery and Restaurant
209 W. Holland Ave.
432-837-9454
www.edelweissbrewery.com
In historic Holland Hotel with four homebrews on tap: perfect with its signature buffalo burgers. The Bavarian style pork roast is slowly cooked in a beer marinade. **$$**

La Casita
1104 E. Ave. H
Tel: 432-837-2842
Locals call this the best Mexican in town; try the brisket enchiladas. **$**

Reata
203 N. 5th St
Tel: 432-837-9232
www.reata.net/with_flash.html
Steaks, game and bacon-wrapped shrimp. Featuring Mexican accents. **$$$**

Big Bend N.P.

Chisos Mountains Lodge Restaurant
Basin Rural Station
Tel: 432-477-2291
The only place to eat in the park, with generous breakfast buffet, Tex-Mex and thick burgers, served on "Texas toast" (thickly sliced white bread, toasted and buttered). **$**

Fort Davis

Hotel Limpia Dining Room
101 Main St
Tel: 432-426-3241/800-662-5517
www.hotellimpia.com
Homey food in quaint hotel setting with roast beef, and house-made pies; serves alcohol. **$$**

Pop's Grill
43424 Highway 17
Tel: 432-426-3195
www.popsgrill.com
The owners' ancestry can be seen in the family crest and the kilt and bagpipe displays. Burgers, salad, chicken and catfish; one of the few places where alcohol is served. **$**

Rodney's Phat Burger
1200 N. State St
Tel: 432-426-2900
Burgers and shakes in a retro 1950s atmosphere. Vegetarian burgers are on the menu too. **$**

Fort Stockton

Bienvenidos
405 W. Dickinson Blvd
Tel: 432-336-3615
Reliable Tex-Mex. **$**

K Bob's Steakhouse
2800 W. Dickinson Blvd
Tel: 432-336-6233
Burgers, sandwiches and steaks. **$$**

Sarah's Café
106 S. Nelson St
Tel: 432-336-7700
Standard Tex-Mex elevated by warm, hospitable service. **$**

Juárez

Kentucky Club
629 Avenida Juárez
1930s bar, inimitable margaritas. **$**

Marathon

Café Cenizo
Gage Hotel
101 W. US-90
Tel: 432-386-4205
Steaks and Southwestern specialties include pumpkin-stuffed acorn squash, using ingredients from their on-site garden. Western decor and a good wine list, too. **$$**

Marfa

Blue Javelina
1300 W. San Antonio St
Tel: 432-729-1919
www.bluejavelina.com
Former gas station, transformed with glass and corrugated steel into artsy place. Small menu with Spanish-Mediterranean influences. **$$**

Jett's Grill
Hotel Paisano
207 N. Highland Ave.
Tel: 432-729-3838
www.hotelpaisano.com
Continental with Southwestern accents; Dinner and Sunday brunch only. **$$**

Maiya's
103 N. Highland Ave.
Tel: 432-729-4410
www.maiyasrestaurant.com
Upscale northern Italian – great house-made pizza dough – in chic digs. **$$$**

Pizza Foundation
100 E. San Antonio St
Tel: 432-729-3377
www.pizzafoundation.com
Sibling of Maiya's does thin-crust pizza in a renovated gas station. **$**

Presidio

El Patio Restaurant
513 O'Reilly St
Tel: 432-229-4409
Mexican food, plus lunch buffet, plus frosty beer. **$**

Terlingua

La Kiva
Big Bend Travel Park
Highway 170 at Terlingua Creek
Tel: 432-371-2250
Meaty menu. Try the brisket, with a side of coleslaw. Funky restrooms. **$**

ABOVE: chuck-wagon breakfast in the Panhandle.

Long Draw Pizza
Highway 170, 6.6 miles (10.6 km) west of Highway 118
Tel: 432-371-2608
Hand-made pizza that's good not just for remote Terlingua, but good on its own merit, with fine chunks of chicken, prosciutto, and blue cheese. **$**

Ms Tracy's Café
Highway 170
Tel: Tel: 432-371-2888
British expat runs the show here; decor and quirky patrons are half the fun. **$**

Starlight Theatre
Highway 170, 5 miles west of Highway 118, Terlingua Ghost Town
Tel: 432-371-2326
Mexican and Mediterranean food served in adobe setting. Live entertainment. **$$**

Van Horn

Chuy's Restaurant
1200 W. Broadway St
Tel: 432-283-2066
Tex-Mex and burgers. **$**

Papa's Pantry
515 Van Horn Dr.
Tel: 432-283-2302
Where the locals go for lunch. **$**

Tortilleria Lizy's Restaurant
400 E. Broadway
Tel: 432-283-1521
Tortillas made by hand on-site, with menudo (tripe soup) on Sundays. **$**

AMARILLO, LUBBOCK & ENVIRONS

Amarillo

Big Texan
7701 E. I-40
Tel: 806-372-5000
www.bigtexan.com
Probably the most famous restaurant in Amarillo, home of the 72-ounce steak, wherein, if you can eat it all, you get it for free. Rife with shlocky Texas curios. Kitschy fun. **$$**

Calico County Restaurant
2410 Paramount Blvd
Tel: 806-358-7664
Home-cooking plus Mexican. **$**

Cattle Call
7701 W. I-40, Suite 398
Tel: 806-353-1227/800-658-6097
www.cattlecall.com
Famous for barbecue and chicken-fried steak. Children's menu. **$$**

Lubbock

50-Yard Line Steakhouse
2549 S. Loop 289
Tel: 806-745-3991
http://50-yardline.com
Sports-crazy steakhouse has toned down its football-themed decor to focus on steaks, which come with blueberry muffins, a curious but nice twist. **$$**

Chez Suzette
4423 50th St
Tel: 806-795-6796
Special occasion destination does French in a pleasing environment. Hearty entrées and classic desserts. **$$**

La Diosa Cellars
901 17th St
Tel: 806-744-3600
www.ladiosacellars.com
Winery-bistro-coffee-bar has lovely menu and wines by the glass. **$$**

Lujan's Mexican Food
7006 University Ave.
Tel: 806-795-1602
Hole-in-the-wall Tex-Mex goes beyond the usual with spinach and bacon enchiladas, grilled pork chops and the like. **$$**

Manna Bread and Wine
2610 Salem Ave.
Tel: 806-791-5600
www.mannabreadandwine.com
Tapas, wine flights, and unique items such as crab-avocado-mango nachos and tilapia topped with pineapple salsa. **$$**

Orlando's Classic Italian Restaurant
2402 Ave. Q
Tel: 806-747-5998
Lubbock landmark with solid Italian-American food and the occasional Southwestern touch. **$$**

Lisa West's Double Nickel Steakhouse
5405 Slide Rd
Tel: 806-792-0055
High-end steak at a high-end price. Some of the locals may balk at a $35 T-bone, but the food and service are a cut above. **$$$**

THE WEST

Abilene

Joe Allen's Bar-B-Que
301 S. 11th St
Tel: 325-672-6082
www.joeallens.com
Family-owned barbecue spot has mesquite-smoked meats cooked for 18 hours until tender. They bake their own bread. **$**

Lytle Land & Cattle
1150 E. S. 11th St
Tel: 325-677-1925
www.lytlelandandcattle.com
Hand-cut steaks grilled over mesquite in warm, homey surroundings. **$$**

Perini Ranch
3002 Highway 89, Buffalo Gap
Tel: 325-572-3339, 800-367-1721
www.periniranch.com
Nationally famous steakhouse and rightfully so, with showpiece hand-cut mesquite-grilled peppered tenderloin steaks and unique side dishes and desserts such as the jalapeño cheesecake. Decor is beautifully authentic; check out the tin ceiling, salvaged from a blacksmith's shop on the ranch. **$$$**

Spano's Italian Restaurant
4534 Buffalo Gap Rd
Tel: 325-698-3704
Popular Italian has quaint, romantic atmosphere despite location near a mall; you can bring your own alcohol. **$**

Albany

Fort Griffin General Merchandise Beehive Saloon
525 W. US-180
Tel: 325-762-3034
Folksy spot with chicken-fried steak. **$**

Icehouse Restaurant
200 S. 2nd St
Tel: 325-762-3287
Located in an old icehouse, the specialty is Mexican hamburgers: ground beef rolled into a big tortilla, then topped with chile and cheese. **$**

Presley's Grill
233 N. Main St
Tel: 325-762-3362
Home-style food – served in an old home, no less – and noted for breakfast. **$**

Prairie Star Deli and Grill
225 Hill St
Tel: 325-762-9095
Terrific deli. **$**

Midland

Cancún Grill
2404 N. Big Spring St
Tel: 432-618-0390
Authentic Mexican with light, fresh dishes and lots of seafood. **$**

Hot Pit Pub and Grub
7400 W. County Road 116
Tel: 432-561-9301
Killer barbecue, especially the ribs and chicken. Fine sides include potato salad and coleslaw with a little Tabasco kick. **$**

The Garlic Press
2200 W. Wadley Ave.
Tel: 432-570-4020
Upscale bistro has broad menu with steaks, duck, even halibut cheeks. Good wine list and desserts. **$$**

Odessa

La Bodega
1024 E. 7th St
Tel: 432-333-4469
This Tex-Mex institution does wonderful chile rellenos (stuffed with cheese and accented with chopped pecans and raisins). Start with the nachos, piled high with seasoned ground beef. **$**

Yana's 615
615 N. Sam Houston Ave.
Tel: 432-332-4305
Delicate lunches and lots of desserts in little cottage. **$**

Sweetwater

Allen's Family-Style Meals
1301 E. Broadway St
Tel: 325-235-2060
Excellent home-cooking served family-style, with shared sides such as macaroni and cheese. Community picnic tables mean you'll rub elbows with strangers, but that's part of its Sunday-dinner charm. **$**

Big Boys Barbecue
2117 Lamar St
Tel: 325-235-2700
Rated by *Texas Monthly* magazine as one of the top three barbecue places in the state. Get the ribs "their way" and don't miss the desserts. **$**

Bucks Steaks & Bar-B-Que
103 SW Georgia Ave.
Tel: 325-235-4049
A little pricey, and skip the barbecue, but the steak's not bad and the salad bar reigns supreme. **$$**

La Cocina
907 W. Alabama Ave.
Tel: 325-235-2927
Little old house staffed by little old Mexican ladies making real-deal Mexican food. **$**

PRICE CATEGORIES

Price categories based on the cost of a meal for one without drinks:
$ = under $15
$$ = $15–30
$$$ = over $30

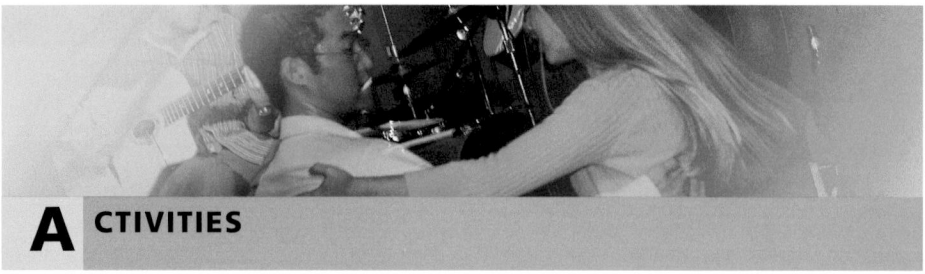

ACTIVITIES

FESTIVALS, THE ARTS, NIGHTLIFE, SHOPPING AND SPORTS

FESTIVALS

Dallas Arts District is the home of several free outdoor festivals held throughout the year. Visitors can enjoy the **Imagination Celebration** (a children's arts festival in April), the **Jazz Concert Series** in May, the Latin Jazz Festival in June and the Dallas **Dance Festival** in September.

Houston's ethnic celebrations include a Greek festival, a Chicano festival and an Asian-American festival, all held in October.

See Spectator Sports *(page 369)* for stock shows and rodeo listings.

January

Cotton Bowl Classic. Major college football game, nationally televised, Dallas. Tel: 214-634-7525.
Janis Joplin Birthday Bash, Port Arthur. Tel: 800-235-7822.
Texas Citrus Fiesta. Celebrates the ruby red grapefruit and other citrus fruits, Mission. Tel: 956-585-9724.

February

Charro Days with parades and a traditional Mexican rodeo, Brownsville. Tel: 956-542-4245.
Mardi Gras celebrations, Galveston. Tel: 888-425-4753. Also at Port Arthur, tel: 800-235-7822, Jefferson. Tel: 903-665-2672.
Washington's Birthday Celebration, Laredo. Tel: 956-722-0589.

March

Easter Fires Pageant. Celebrates the Easter bunny and religious traditions, Fredericksburg. Tel: 830-997-6523.
Oysterfest, Fulton. Tel: 361-729-5533.
Rattlesnake Roundup. Hunts, tours, demonstrations, Sweetwater. Tel: 325-235-5488.
South by Southwest. Texas-sized festival attracting hundreds of performers to Austin. Tel: 512-451-0754, www.sxsw.com

April

Arts and Jazz Festival, Denton. Tel: 940-565-0931, www.dentonjazzfest.com
Bluebonnet Trail Spring Celebration, Highland Lakes. Tel: 888-336-4748, www.visitennis.com
Buffalo Bayou Regatta. Texas' largest canoe race, Houston. Tel: 713-752-0314.
Fiesta San Antonio. Celebrated for more than a century. Tel: 210-227-5191, www.fiesta-sa.org
Germanfest. Polkas, strudel, sausage, etc., at Muenster. Tel: 940-759-2227.
Houston International Festival. Music, theater, food. Tel: 713-654-8808, www.ifest.org
Scarborough Faire. Jousting, juggling, living chess games and folkcraft, Waxahachie. Tel: 972-938-3247.
Worldfest. International film festival, Houston. Tel: 713-965-9955.

May

Cinco de Mayo celebrations at San Marcos, tel: 512-353-8482, and at Goliad, tel: 361-645-3563.
Cottonwood Arts Festival. Arts and crafts and musicians. Cottonwood Park, Richardson. Tel: 972-744-4580.
Mayfest. Family festival beside the Trinity River, Fort Worth. Tel: 817-332-1055.
Texas Live Oak Festival. Historic homes, arts and crafts, antiques, performances, Columbus. Tel: 979-732-6090.

June

Chisholm Trail Round Up and Pow Wow, Fort Worth. Tel: 817-625-7005.
Dog Days of Summer. Hundreds of dogs, parading, in costume, in contest, Denton. Tel: 888-381-1818.
Frontier Days & Rodeo Celebration, Van Horn. Tel: 432-283-2682.
Juneteenth. Marks the emancipation of Texas African-Americans on June 19 1865. Celebrations in various cities across the state, www.juneteenth.com
Texas. Musical pageant of Panhandle history, nightly Tuesday through Saturday from early June to mid-August, Palo Duro Canyon. Tel: 806-655-2181, www.texas-show.com.
Texas Folklife Festival. Food, music and many ethnic activities, San Antonio. Tel: 210-458-2224.
Viva El Paso! Outdoor musical drama Thursday to Saturday through Aug, El Paso. Tel: 915-565-6900.
Watermelon Thump. Arts and crafts, beer garden, melon judging and World Championship Seed Spitting Contest, Luling. Tel: 830-875-3214.

July

Great Texas Balloon Race. Competing hot-air champions, Longview. Tel: 903-237-4040, www.gtbr.net
Harambee African American Arts Festival. Arts and crafts, dancing, food, reggae, Houston. Tel: 713-524-1079.
Houston Shakespeare Festival. Free nightly in Hermann Park. Tel: 713-743-3003.

Texas International Fishing Tournament, South Padre Island. Tel: 956-943-8438.
West of the Pecos Rodeo, Pecos. Tel: 432-940-4777/800-588-BULL.

August

Gillespie County Fair, Fredericksburg. Tel: 830-997-2359, www.gillespiefair.com
Hotter 'n Hell Hundred Bike Ride. Thousands of peddlers, Wichita Falls. Tel: 940-322-3223, www.hh100.org
Houston International Jazz Festival. Outdoors. International groups. Tel: 713-839-7000.
Peach and Melon Festival, De Leon. Tel: 254-893-6600.

September

East Texas State Fair. Livestock, exhibits, arts and crafts, Tyler. Tel: 903-597-2501, www.statefairtyler.com
Fiesta Patrias. Hispanic celebration of Mexican independence, Houston. Tel: 713-926-2636.
Pioneer Days. Stockyards, Fort Worth. Tel: 817-626-7921.
Grapefest. Annual wine celebration in Grapevine, near Dallas. Tel: 817-410-3185.
National Championship Indian Pow Wow. Tribes from all over the US, Grand Prairie. Tel: 972-647-2331.
State Fair of Texas. through mid-October. Tel: 214-565-9931.
Texas Forest Festival. Arm wrestling, lumberjacks and a giant carnival, Lufkin Tel: 936-634-6305.
Washington County Fair, the state's oldest, Brenham. Tel: 888-273-6426, www.brenhamtexas.com.

October

Autumn Trails. Fall foliage celebration. Winnsboro. Tel: 903-342-1958.
CavOILcade. Parade, fishing tournament, pet show and more, Port Arthur. Tel: 498-983-1009.
East Texas Yamboree. Bike ride, yam-pie contest, fiddlers, antique car show, Gilmer. Tel: 903-843-2413, www.yamboree.com.
Asian American Festival, Houston. Tel: 713-861-8270.
Festival Chicano, Houston. Tel: 713-222-2783.
Halloween on Sixth St. Characters and costumes, Austin. Tel: 512-478-0098/800-926-2282.
International Chili Championship, Terlingua. Tel: 210-887-8827, www.chili.org/terlingua.html
Oktoberfest. German heritage festival, Fredericksburg. Tel: 830-997-4810.
Seafair. Gumbo cook-off, music, arts and crafts, boat race, crab contest, Rockport. Tel: 361-729-6445/800-242-0071. www.rockportseafair.com
Texas Renaissance Festival, Plantersville. Tel: 800-458-3435.

November

International Quilt Festival, Houston. Tel: 713-781-6864.
Regional Christmas Lighting, Hill Country. Tel: 830-997-6523.
Wonderland of Lights. Downtown is all illuminated, Marshall. Tel: 903-935-7868.

December

Campfire Christmas. At George Ranch Historical Park. Feasts and hayrides, Richmond. Tel: 281-342-0218.
Christmas Candelight Tour. A tour of charming homes, plus choral music, handbell ringers, brass bands, trolley rides, Jefferson. Tel: 903-665-7064, www.historicjefferson.com
Dickens on the Strand. Victorian-clad performers, choirs, handbell ringers, puppets, etc., Galveston. Tel: 409-765-7834.
Fiestas de las Luminarias. Riverside pageant, San Antonio. Tel: 210-227-4262.
Weihnachten. Christmas celebrations with a German spin, Fredericksburg. Tel: 830-997-6523.

THE ARTS

Art

The state's best art lies clustered in Houston and in Dallas/Fort Worth, though some of Texas' more famous museums lurk in unpredictable outposts such as the **Chinati Foundation**, a museum that put the remote small town of Marfa on the art world's map *(see page 278–9)* ; and the **Panhandle-Plains Historical Museum** in Canyon, home to displays on oil, the Old West, and Texan cultural heroes such as Buddy Holly.

Houston's **Menil Collection** is regarded as one of the best private collections in the world; meanwhile, the city's **Museum of Fine Arts** has recently expanded. Fort Worth's **Kimbell Art Museum** and **Modern Art Museum** are as noted for their stunning architecture as for their stellar collections. The **Nasher Sculpture Center** in downtown Dallas is a beautifully landscaped oasis, located a block away from the **Dallas Museum of Arts**.

What's on Listings

Entertainment listings are published in many of the daily city newspapers *(see page 373)*, and in alternative weeklies such as ***Dallas Observer***, ***Houston Press*** and ***Austin Chronicle***. Venues and events are also listed in ***Texas Monthly***. On-line newspaper ***Pegasus News*** (www.pegasusnews.com), covers the Dallas/Fort Worth area. A service called **Dallas Artsline**, tel: 214-522-2659, offers a complete listing of arts events, as do **local tourist offices** *(see page 375)*.

Music and Dance

The Dallas/Fort Worth cultural calendar is crowded with events. The **Morton H. Myerson Symphony Center** in the burgeoning arts district is the home of the **Dallas Symphony Orchestra**, tel: 214-692-0203, and the **Dallas Opera**, tel: 214-443-1000, which performs between November and February.

The **Performing Arts Center** at 5th and Walnut streets, tel: 972-205-2790, is the home of the **Garland Civic Theatre** and the **Garland Symphony**.

Further performing arts listings include:
The Texas Ballet Theater, tel: 817-763-0207/214-369-5200
Dallas' Black Dance Theatre, tel: 214-871-2390
The Fort Worth Symphony, tel: 817-665-6000
The Dallas Chamber Orchestra, tel: 214-321-1411
The Greater Dallas Youth Orchestra, tel: 214-528-7747

Lighter events are staged at the **Smirnoff Music Centre**, tel: 214-421-1111, in Dallas' Fair Park and the series of **Dallas Summer Musicals**, tel: 214-691-7200, also at Fair Park.

In Houston, the spectacular **Wortham Theater Center**, situated northeast of downtown, is home to the **Houston Ballet**, tel: 713-523-6300, www.houstonballet.org, and **Houston Grand Opera**, tel: 713-546-0246, as well as a variety of other activities. Nearby is **Jones Hall**, home to the **Houston Symphony**, tel: 713-224-7575, www.houstonsymphony.org and the **Society for the Performing Arts**, tel: 713-227-5134, which presents world-class orchestras, dance companies and solo artists, www.spahouston.org.

Houston's **Rice University** has its share of cultural activities with music and drama performances at the

Hermann Park amphitheater in summer, tel: 713-520-3292, and other venues, including the university's **Hamman Hall**.

It's also well worth making the relatively short trip to Galveston for a performance at the glorious Grand 1894 Opera House, tel: 800-821-1894, www.thegrand.com.

As befits a college town, **Austin** is also rich in classical music events, with regular performances by the **Austin Symphony Orchestra**, tel: 512-476-6064, www.austinsymphony.org and the **Austin Chamber Music Center**, tel: 512-454-7562, www.austinchambermusic.org.

Theater

Notable theater events in **Dallas** include the **Shakespeare in the Park Festival**, tel: 800-433-5747, www.shakespearedallas.com, held in Fort Worth's Trinity Park in July and August. Also worth a visit is the **Dallas Children's Theater**, tel: 214-978-0110.

Houston's **Wortham Theater Center** is the centerpiece of the city's compact Theater District, which also includes the 50-year-old award-winning **Alley Theatre**, tel: 713-228-8421, www.alleytheatre.org, which has earned a national reputation for original drama. Broadway shows are regularly presented at the downtown **Music Hall** on Bagby St in Houston by **Theatre Under the Stars**, tel: 713-558-2600.

NIGHTLIFE

Dallas/Fort Worth

Much of Dallas' liveliest nightlife, including clubs, bars, theaters and restaurants, is centered around Greenville Avenue, from the LBJ Freeway down to Ross Avenue, and Deep Ellum, the former industrial neighborhood in the 3500 block of Elm just east of the central Expressway. In Fort Worth, head for the stockyards area, where the **White Elephant Saloon** and **Booger Red's Saloon** along E. Exchange Avenue are among the spots offering live entertainment. Other nightspots in Dallas/Fort Worth include:

Billy Bob's Texas, Fort Worth Stockyards, tel: 817-624-7117, www.billybobstexas.com. The world's biggest honky tonk. Country stars, 40 bars, slot machines, barbecue, dance lessons and (real) bulls to ride Fri–Sat.

The Aardvark, 2905 W. Berry St, Fort Worth, tel: 817-926-1512.

Club Dada, 2720 Elm St, Dallas, tel: 214-744-3232. Rock and pop.

Dallas Alley, West End Marketplace, tel: 214-720-0170. Outdoor courtyard sometimes hosts free concerts.

Deep Ellum, Elm St, Dallas, tel: 214-748-4332. Has clubs, restaurants and underground music.

Gilley's, 1135 S. Lamar St, tel: 214-445-5397. Country venue immortalized in *Urban Cowboy*; home to a mechanical bull.

House of Blues, 2200 N. Lamar St, www.hob.com. Top-of-the-line rock venue with restaurant on site.

Palladium Ballroom, 1135 S. Lamar St. Top-quality live music venue located inside Gilley's *(see above)*.

Poor David's Pub, 1313 S. Lamar St, tel: 214-565-1295. Folk and country.

Sambuca Jazz Café, 2120 McKinney Avenue, tel: 214-744-0820. Top-notch food.

Sundance Square, tel: 817-255-5700, www.sundancesquare.com. Downtown Fort Worth has numerous restaurants, some outdoors with music.

White Elephant Saloon, 106 E. Exchange Ave, Fort Worth Stockyards, tel: 817-624-1887, www.whiteelephantsaloon.com. Old West saloon with nightly entertainment.

The Pour House Sports Grill, 209 W. 5th St, Fort Worth, tel: 817-335-2575.

Houston

Houston's nightlife is centered upon **Richmond Avenue**, north of the Southwest Freeway and west of US-610, a short walk from the Galleria. Among the dozens of clubs featuring rock 'n' roll, blues or Country and Western music, the best-known are **Billy Blue's Bar & Grill** and **Trail Dust Steak House**, both on the Richmond Avenue itself. There are dancehalls in the gay district of Montrose, with such lively clubs as **Pacific St**, tel: 713-523-0213, and **South Beach**, tel: 713-529-7623.

San Antonio

Most of the city's best nightlife can be found near the river, with dancing nightly at the **Republic of Texas Nightclub**, 526 Riverwalk, tel: 210-226-6256, and rowdy sing-alongs taking place at **Durty Nelly's Irish Pub**

Ticket Agents

Tickets for a wide variety of theater, dance and other performances are available through **Ticketmaster** (tel: 866-448-7849). Half-price tickets to some events on the day of the performance may be available. Call tel: 214-696-HALF OR 972-263-1061 for further information. **Front Gate** (tel: 888-347-8497) is an Austin-based ticket company that sells tickets to events in Texas and some parts of the South and Midwest. For schedules consult local paper listings.

Activities for Children

Houston's Space Center, 1601 NASA Parkway, tel: 281-244-2100, is one of the biggest family attractions with its interactive exhibits, IMAX films about being an astronaut (shown on a screen five stories high), a moon rock display and behind-the-scenes tour by tram. Another giant screen can be found in the **Wortham IMAX Theatre** at the **Museum of Natural Science**, which also includes a planetarium and a butterfly garden. Houston has a **Children's Museum** (1500 Binz St) with hands-on exhibits and mock-ups of ethnic villages.

The Dallas/Fort Worth area has a variety of amusement parks and attractions including the major **Six Flags Over Texas** and **Hurricane Harbor**, a family park featuring a plunging raft ride, whirlpools, wave pools, rain tunnels, and a sandy beach. Both of these are in Arlington. **The Sandy Lake Amusement Park** in Carrollton features paddle boats, miniature golf and a giant swimming pool. The five-mile journey on Fort Worth's **Forest Park MInI Train** is a pleasant way to slow the pace.

San Antonio has two theme parks: **Sea World of Texas**, 10500 Sea World Dr. off Loop 1604, tel: 800-700-7786, a 250-acre (100-hectare) park with killer whales, a shark-infested coral reef and a park with waterslides and exotic birds; and **Six Flags Fiesta Texas**, W. I-10 & Loop 1604, tel: 800-473-4378, with all the familiar attractions.

The **Austin Visitors & Convention Bureau**, tel: 800-926-2282, will send you a free brochure, *101 Things for Kids*, with information about activities such as watching the peacocks in **Mayfield Park**, shopping in a tiny grocery store in the **Children's Museum**, taking a miniature train ride in **Zilker Park,** or trying computer animation at the **Dougherty Arts Center**.

in the Hilton Palacio, which claims to hand out one ton of peanuts each week. The **Rivercenter Comedy Club**, tel: 210-229-1420 is a showcase for old and new performers.

Half-an-hour's drive away at New Braunfels is century-old **Gruene Hall**, tel: 830-629-5077, www.gruenehall.com, the oldest dancehall in Texas.

Austin

In this city of a mere 657,000 inhabitants, there are more than 100 live music venues, justifying Austin's boast of being "the live music capital of America." E. 6th St downtown is the main area.

For blues, try:
Antone's, tel: 512-320-8424.
Joe's Generic Bar, tel: 512-480-0171.
Ego's, tel: 512-474-7091, on nearby Congress Avenue.

Rock and pop fill the air at:
Fat Tuesday, tel: 512-492-9545.
Country and Western can be found at:
Broken Spoke, 512-442-6189.
Variety at:
The 311 Club, tel: 512-477-1630.
Maggie Mae's, tel: 512-478-8541.

And jazz at:
Jazz on 6th St, tel: 512-479-0474.
Pete's Peanut Bar & Piano Emporium, tel: 512-472-7383, where customers sing along.

These listings, of course, merely scratch the surface of what's available, because music venues are spread all over town.

Highly recommended is the veteran **Threadgill's**, tel: 512-451-5440, where diners share long tables and stomp their feet to a never-ending stream of live Country and Western groups.
The Austin Convention & Visitors Bureau distributes a free folder (also on-line at www.austin360.com), *101 Musical Things To Do*, which includes telephone numbers and listings for such seasonal events as Jerry Jeff Walker's Annual Birthday Party, (March), tel: 512-477-0036, and the summer outdoor concert series in Zilker Park, tel: 512-499-6700.

SHOPPING

Where to Shop

Dallas

Dallas boasts that it has more shopping centers per capita than any other US city.

Not only is it home to the internationally recognized specialty store **Neiman Marcus** and the retail giant **J.C. Penney**, but it is also the site of America's oldest shopping center, **Highland Park Village** (Preston Rd at Mockingbird Lane) where Victor Costa, internationally known for copying the designs of Paris couturiers, has a boutique. Avant-garde designer Todd Oldham is a Dallas native.

Most of the major names in retailing are represented in Dallas, many in the four-level **Galleria** (LBJ Freeway & Dallas Parkway), with 200 stores in a dramatic glass atrium supplemented by an ice rink and a Westin hotel. Other huge malls include **NorthPark Center** (Northwest Hwy at N. Central Expressway).

Love Field Antique Mall, tel: 214-357-6500, behind the Mobil station at the entrance to Dallas' Love Field airport, has 350 shops in addition to a collection of classic cars. As with everything else, there are many different specialties: The **Englishman's Interiors**, 14655 Midway Rd, Dallas, tel: 972-386-5996, www.englishmans.com has a vast array of Staffordshire pottery, Welsh dressers and other European furniture.

Fort Worth

Sundance Square, Main and Houston streets in downtown Fort Worth, is fun to visit with its collection of shops, restaurants, and museums set among red-brick sidewalks and charming courtyards.The **Stockyards Antique Mall**, 1332 Main St, Fort Worth, invites you to tour scores of shops in an 1890s hotel.

Austin

Austin's biggest mall, Highland Mall, is at 6001 Airport Blvd, tel: 512-451-2920, www.highlandmall.com, but there are also numerous little specialty stores, such as the **Turquoise Trading Post**, Burnet Rd at Koenig, which displays a large selection of Native American jewelry, including Zuni fetishes, Navaho Kachina dolls, medicine wheels and dreamcatchers. The more macabre-minded will enjoy the selection of skulls, hides and trophy mounts available at the Corner Shoppe, 5900 Lamar St.

As befits a college town – and state capital – Austin is proud of its literary leanings, pointing out that not only does it house branches of the big bookstore chains, such as **Borders** and **Barnes & Noble**, but also many independents, among them Congress Avenue Booksellers, Half Price Books – which deals in used books and music – and stores specializing in African-American literature: Folktales and Mitchie's Fine Black Art Gallery & Bookstore.

Clothing Chart

This table compares American, Continental and British clothing sizes. It's always advisable to try clothes on before buying as sizes can vary.

Women's Dresses/Suits

American	Continental	British
6	38/34N	8/30
8	40/36N	10/32
10	42/38N	12/34
12	44/40N	14/36
14	46/42N	16/38
16	48/44N	18/40

Women's Shoes

American	Continental	British
4.5	36	3
5.5	37	4
6.5	38	5
7.5	40	6
8.5	41	7
9.5	42	8
10.5	43	9

Men's Suits

American	Continental	British
34	44	34
–	46	36
38	48	38
–	50	40
42	52	42
–	54	44
46	56	46

Men's Shirts

American	Continental	British
14.0	36	14.0
14.5	37	14.5
15.0	38	15.5
15.5	39	15.5
16.0	40	16.0
16.5	41	16.5
17.0	42	17.0

Men's Shoes

American	Continental	British
6.5	–	6
7.5	40	7
8.5	41	8
9.5	42	9
10.5	43	10
11.5	44	11

Less than 30 minutes from Austin and an hour from San Antonio is **Prime Outlets San Marcos** (3939 S. I-35 900, San Marcos, tel: 512-396-2200/800-628-9465, www.primeoutlets.com), the largest factory outlet center in Texas, and one of the state's most popular travel destinations, with more than 130 stores offering big discounts on brand names such as Coach, Hugo Boss, Kate Spade and more.

San Antonio

Visitors to San Antonio's **North Star Mall** (Loop 410 between San Pedro and MacCullough) are invited to begin their browsing with a visit to the information booth to pick up a free shopping bag and a coupon booklet offering discounts at many of the 200 stores. These include such big names as Saks Fifth Avenue, Marshall Field's, Guess, Williams-Sonoma and Gap.

There are other malls, of which the most attractive architecturally is **Rivercenter**, 849 E. Commerce, adjoining the restaurants and IMAX theater in the heart of downtown. **La Villita**, the recreated Mexican village on the site of the original town, and **El Mercado** (514 W. Commerce) both offer specialty shops with Mexican arts and crafts.

Houston

There are more than 30 malls in the Houston area. In the city's southwest section, **Rice Village** draws the crowds with more than 300 stores ranging from familiar names to fashionable designer boutiques and funky mom-and-pop shops. There are also art and craft galleries and spas. Even bigger is the **Post Oak-Galleria** area uptown, which sports most of the big-name stores – including Neiman Marcus, Tiffany, Hermes, Marshall Fields, Saks Fifth Avenue – and claims to draw 10,000 visitors per day.

Three blocks east, the **Highland Village Shopping Center** also features upscale stores. For hard-to-find antiques and arty treasures, check out **The Heights**, whose streets (between 11th and 19th) are lined with Victorian structures and Craftsmen-style bungalows. Western wear is purveyed by **Rick's Ranchwear** (5085 Westheimer) and **Cavender's Boot City**, which has 11 separate locations in Houston alone. Call 800-256-9190 for nearest store.

El Paso

Shopping in El Paso is diverse given its proximity to both Juárez and New Mexico: gift shops and boutiques stand shoulder to shoulder with major department store chains. **Butterfield Trading Post**, tel: 915-771-7723, is an open-air market with Mexican and Southwestern handmade crafts. **Galeria San Ysidro**, tel: 915-544-4444, is a three-story market specializing in Mexican primitive art, plus objects from Morocco and Africa.

Shop Listings

Dallas

Highland Park Village, at Preston and Mockingbird, tel: 214-559-2740. The oldest of Dallas' many shopping centers and malls. With boutiques like Hermes, Tory Burch and Jimmy Choo, Highland Park claims to be Dallas' answer to Los Angeles' Rodeo Drive.

Neiman Marcus, 1618 Main, tel: 214-741-6911. There are several Neiman Marcus stores around town at various shopping malls, but this is the legendary original.

Hat Brands, 601 Marion Dr. in Garland, tel: 972-494-0511. Here you can get a good western hat for a very reasonable price.

Western paraphernalia is available in the shops at **Southfork Ranch** (3700 Hogge Rd, Parker, tel: 972-442-7800), location of the TV-famous Ewing Ranch.

BELOW: window-shop along the covered sidewalks of the Fort Worth Stockyards.

Fort Worth

Western wear is, of course, a big seller in these parts. Head for the Stockyards National Historic District where you will find several long-established Cowtown outfitters such as **M.L. Leddy's** (2455 N. Main St, tel: 888-565-2668) makers of fine boots and saddles; **Fincher's White Front,** (115 E. Exchange Ave., tel: 817-624-7302), and **Luskey/Ryon's Western Wear** (2601 N. Main St, tel: 817-625-2391). With 23 shops and restaurants located in renovated hog and sheep pens, **Stockyards Station** (140 E Exchange Ave.tel: 817-625-9715) delivers plenty of Cowtown atmosphere along with the western wear and souvenirs.

Boot fanciers often go directly to the **Justin Boot Company Factory Outlet Store** at 717 W. Vickery Blvd, tel: 817-654-3103. Founded in Fort Worth and headquartered in the town of Justin, the company also has branches in Dallas and Denton. A rival, **Cavender's**, 5600 S.W. Loop 820, tel: 817-294-4400, has stores all over the state.

Austin

Capitol Saddlery, 1614 Lavaca St, tel: 512-478-9309. Leather goods.

Tesoro's Trading Company, 209 Congress Avenue, tel: 512-479-8377.

Texas Custom Boots, 2525 S. Lamar Blvd, tel: 512-442-0926.

Texas Hatters, 5003 Overpass Rd, Buda, tel: 512-441-4287. Celebrity clients include Bob Dylan and Willie Nelson

San Antonio

Dillard's, at Alamo Plaza and Commerce, tel: 210-227-4343. One of San Antonio's most popular department stores. Also located at various shopping malls.

Kallison's Western Wear, 123 S. Flores, tel: 210-222-1364. Cowboy gear for all the family.

La Tienda, 123 Alamo Plaza, tel: 210-222-1588. Mexican imports.

Lucchese Boot Co., 255 E. Basse Rd, tel: 210-828-9419. Founded in 1883 by Italian immigrant Sam Lucchese.

Houston

Eagle Dancer "The American Indian Store", 159 S. Gulf Freeway at FM 518, League City 77573, tel: 281-332-6028.

The Galleria, 5075 Westheimer, tel: 713-621-1907. A three-story shopping mall with two hotels, a skating rink, 19 restaurants, four movie theaters, and high-end stores

Who Plays Where

Dallas Cowboys play football in Texas Stadium, Irving, tel: 972-554-6368.
Dallas Stars play hockey, Sept–April, at the American Airlines Center, tel: 214-273-5200, www.americanairlinescenter.com
Texas Rangers play baseball April–October in The Ballpark at Arlington, tel: 817-273-5100.
FC Dallas play soccer at Pizza Hut Park in Frisco, tel: 214-705-6700.
Dallas Mavericks play basketball at the American Airlines Center *(see above)*.
Houston Astros play baseball at Minute Maid Park, tel: 713-259-8000.
San Antonio Missions play baseball at Nelson Wolff Stadium, tel: 210-625-7275.
San Antonio Spurs play basketball at the Alamodome, tel: 210-207-3663.

such as Neiman Marcus, Chanel, Gucci, Gumps of San Francisco, Mark Cross, Tiffany & Co., Alfred Dunhill, Cartier and Fred Joaillier of Paris.
Stelzig's of Texas Western Store, 3123 Post Oak Blvd, tel: 713-629-7779. Another good western store; it even sells saddle blankets.
Paul Wheeler Boot Company, 4115 Willowbend Blvd, tel: 713-665-0224. Custom-made boots that are popular with the Houston oil-rich.

El Paso

Cowtown Boot Company, 11401 Gateway Blvd W., tel: 915-593-2929. Boots of all kinds.
Rocketbuster Boots, 115 S. Anthony St, tel: 915-541-1300. Beautifully hand-crafted boots.
Tony Lama Factory Store, 7156 Gateway Blvd E., tel: 915-772-4327. An outlet for these famous boots.

Juárez (Mexico, border)

Centro Commercial ProNaF, off 16 de Septiembre, east of downtown. A government-run center featuring Centro Artesanal, which offers items like Oaxacan pottery.
El Mercado Juárez, near downtown at 16 de Septiembre No. 103. This is the main city market.
Mercado Cuauhtenoc, one block off 16 de Septiembre between La Presidencia (City Hall) and Our Lady of Guadalupe Cathedral. A smaller version of El Mercado Juárez.

SPORTS

Participant Sports

Water Sports

There is canoeing, tubing and rafting on the Guadalupe River in Gruene. Contact the **Gruene River Company**, tel: 830-625-2800 or **Rockin R River Rides** in New Braunfels, tel: 830-629-9999. These activities are also available on the Rio Grande. Contact **Texas River Expeditions**, tel: 800-839-7238, www.texasriver.com or **Far Flung Adventures**, tel: 800-359-2627, www.farflung.com. Be sure to ask about the three-day gourmet raft trips with chef Francois Maeder (tel: 210-821-5600) in San Antonio – an excellent adventure.

Cycling

Planet Earth Adventures, tel: 800-923-4453, www.planetearthadventures.com has a reputation for well-organized multi-day cycle tours of the Davis Mountains, Hill Country and Bandera.

Golf

There are many golf courses in Dallas/Fort Worth area, including:
Bridlewood Golf Club, 4000 W. Windsor Rd, tel: 972-355-4800. A 7,000-yard (6,400-meter) course with lakes and a meandering creek.
Hyatt Bear Creek Golf and Racquet Club, Dallas/Fort Worth airport, tel: 972-615-6800. Trees line the fairways of two 18-hole courses.
Hank Haney Golf, 8787 Park Lane at Abrams, tel: 214-341-9600. Illuminated four-hole course, mini courses and driving range.
Gulch at Granbury, 25 miles (40 km) southwest of Fort Worth, Hwy 377, tel: 817-579-1515. Family park with mini-golf course, batting cages, practice range, picnic area.
L.B. Houston Municipal Golf Course, 11223 Luna Rd, Irving, tel: 214-670-6322.

And, in San Antonio:
Hyatt Regency Hill Country Golf Club, 9800 Hyatt Resort Dr, tel: 210-520-4040.
Westin La Cantera Golf Club, 16641 La Cantera Parkway. Home of the Westin Texas Open each September, tel: 210-558-4653.

Horseback Riding

Horseback riding can be found near downtown San Antonio in **Brackenridge Park** at 840 E. Mulberry. Also try **Fredricksburg Western Adventures** 830-644-2770, which offers guided and unguided trail rides, camera tours and ranch experiences of real cowboy life. Other centers include:
Skyline Ranch, 1801 E. Wheatland Rd, Dallas, tel: 972-224-8055
Texas Lil's Dude Ranch, 1125 S. Mulkey Lane, Justin, tel: 817-430-0192
Wagon Wheel Ranch, 816 Ruth Wall Rd, Grapevine, tel: 817-481-8284.

Spectator Sports

Horse Racing

Retama Park, N. 1-35 Selma, Texas (just north of San Antonio), tel: 210-651-7000.
Lone Star Park at Grand Prairie, 1000 Lone Star Parkway, Grand Prairie, tel: 800-795-7223.

Golf

The **Byron Nelson Championship** golf tournament brings world-class golfers to the Four Seasons Resort in Irving every April, tel: 972-717-0700.
The SBC Championship, a PGA tour event, is held every October at the Oak Hills Country Club, 5403 Fredericksburg Rd, tel: 210-698-3582.
The **Valero Texas Open**, one of the oldest pro events, comes to La Cantera Golf Club every September, tel: 201-345-3818.

Motor Racing

NASCAR racing goes on at San **Antonio Speedway**, 14901 S. Highway 16, tel: 210-628-1499; and at **Texas Motor Speedway**, 3545 Lone Star Circle, Fort Worth, tel: 817-215-8510.

Stock Shows and Rodeos

January: **Fort Worth Stock Show & Rodeo**. Takes over Cowtown for most of the month. Tel: 817-877-2400.
February: **San Antonio Stock Show and Rodeo**. Two weeks of events in early February. Tel: 210-225-5851.
March: The Houston **Stock Show and Rodeo** show is big in every sense. Tel: 832-667-1000; also in Mercedes in the Rio Grande Valley, (tel: 956-565-2456) and in San Angelo (tel: 325-653-7785).
Southwestern International PRCA Rodeo, El Paso. Tel: 915-532-1401.
Star of Texas Fair and Rodeo, Austin. Tel: 512-919-3000.
April–September: **Mesquite Championship Rodeo** Racing, roping, petting zoo and barbecues. every weekend. Tel: 800-833-9339.
June: **Texas High School Rodeo Finals**, June, in Abilene. Tel: 325-603-8086.

A – Z

A HANDY SUMMARY OF PRACTICAL INFORMATION, ARRANGED ALPHABETICALLY

A Admission Charges 370
B Budgeting for your Trip 370
Business Hours 370
C Climate 370
Crime and Security 371
Customs Regulations 371
D Disabled Travelers 371
E Embassies/Consulates 371
Emergency Numbers 371
Entry Requirements 371
Etiquette 371
G Gay and Lesbian Travelers 372
H Health and Medical Care 372
I Internet 373
L Lost Property 373
M Maps 373
Media 373
Money Matters 373
P Postal System 373
Public Holidays 374
Public Restrooms 374
R Religious Services 374
T Taxes 374
Telecommunications 374
Tipping 374
Tourist Information 374
W Websites 375

Admission Charges

Some of Texas' most famous sights – the **Grassy Knoll** in Dallas, the **Alamo** in San Antonio – are free. Otherwise, most museums charge $5 to $10 per adult, although many have free entry days during the week. **Houston Museum of Fine Arts** is free on Thursdays; **Dallas Museum of Art** is free on Tuesday nights and on the first Tuesday of every month. The **Lyndon B. Johnson Library and Museum** in Austin is free all the time. At the other extreme, the **Space Center** in Houston charges $18.95.

Budgeting for your Trip

Texas has options both cost-conscious and luxurious in accommodations, food, and transportation. At one end lie the low-priced motels and national restaurant chains where dinner is less than $10. Conversely, the major cities all have swanky restaurants and luxury hotels with penthouse suites whose daily rate runs up to $2,500. The average lies somewhere between. Travelers can expect to spend $100 to $125 per night for a room in a decent hotel; prices and selection drop in less urban areas. Allow $20–$25 per meal, although Texas' excellent "home-cooking" restaurants are cheaper. Dinner at a big-city restaurant with serious food starts at $50 per person.

Rental cars cost approximately $300 per week, including Texas tax and license, and a vague surcharge called a "facility fee." In addition, Texas applies higher add-on fees for cars rented from the airport than any other state, with mark-ups averaging more than 50 percent.

Greyhound is the major bus line, with routes to and from all of Texas' largest cities. Tickets range from $17.50 (Austin–San Antonio) to $37.50 (Dallas–San Antonio); to ride from Dallas to Houston is $35.

Business Hours

Offices: Mon–Fri 8am–5pm.
Banks: Mon–Fri 9/10am–3/4pm (although most have drive-through facilities that stay open longer). Some banks are open on Saturday morning.
Retail shops: Mon–Fri 10/11am–5/6pm, except in large shopping malls, when hours are extended to 8, 9 or 10pm and weekends. A few retail stores are always open.
Museums: many are closed on Mondays.

Climate

A uniform description of either winter or summer weather in Texas is impossible: while it's snowing in the Panhandle, people wintering on the Gulf Coast may be getting a tan at the beach; Central Texas may be baking in the late-summer heat while the Guadalupe Mountains feel the early-fall chill.

Average temperatures of 30–50°F (around 0–10°C) in winter and 70–90°F (20–30°C) in summer do not vary greatly around the state, but the humidity factor and elevation affect the comfort level considerably. Central Texas, East Texas, the Coastal Prairie and Rio Grande Valley are humid and close to sea level, so it is usually very hot and sticky in the summer, often climbing into the hundreds (100°F = 38°C) between May and October.

Although it doesn't usually snow or freeze in these areas, occasionally it does so in a big way. It is not unknown for cities as far south as Austin and San Antonio to be blanketed with snow, shutting down

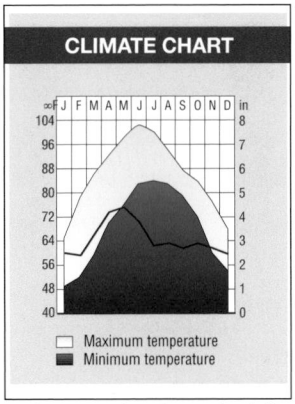

businesses and roads completely for the duration. In the Panhandle and the higher elevations of the Davis Mountains, the Guadalupe Mountains and the Big Bend area, where fall comes earlier than in the southern part of the state, there is little humidity except snow, which is common in the winters, sometimes causing roads and mountain areas to be closed to the public.

"Tornado Alley" runs through the state and peak twister season lasts from late spring to early summer.

Annual rainfall ranges from 8–16 inches (20–40 cm) in the dry Trans-Pecos region, to over 48 inches (122 cm) in the wettest parts of the state such as Houston and far East Texas. The best time for statewide travel is late Oct/Nov, March and April, and late May/early June. This will avoid, for the most part, Texas' hottest and coldest temperatures and the heaviest rainfall.

Crime and Security

While most people go about their business safely, the fact remains that Texas' largest cities – Houston, Dallas and San Antonio – rank highly on the top-10 list of cities with most crime in the United States. Houston and Dallas are currently among the top five cities for murder, rape and robbery. Do not walk a long way after dark in strange or deserted parts of town. Keep a watchful eye on your belongings. Do not leave your car unlocked in parking lots, and never leave your children alone. Smaller towns in Texas have much lower crime rates, but use the same precautions everywhere as you would in a big city.

Hotels usually warn you that they will not guarantee the safety of belongings left in your hotel room. If you have any valuables, you may want to lock them in the hotel safe.

To reach the police in an emergency dial **911**. For police non-emergencies dial **311**.

Customs Regulations

Meat or meat products, illegal drugs, firearms, seeds, plants and fruits are among the prohibited goods. Also do not bring in any duty-free goods which are worth more than $400 (returning US citizens) or over $100 (foreign travelers). Visitors over 21 may bring in 200 cigarettes, 3 lbs (1.3 kg) of tobacco or 50 cigars and 34 fl. oz (1 liter) of alcohol.

For a breakdown of up-to-date US Customs and Border Protection regulations, visit www.cbp.gov or telephone 202-354-1000.

Disabled Travelers

All public transportation, restaurants and public buildings provide wheelchair access and dedicated facilities for the disabled.

Embassies and Consulates

- **Australia** 5757 Woodway Dr., Houston, TX 77057, tel: 713-782-6009
- **Canada** 750 N. St Paul St, Suite 1700, Dallas, TX 75201, tel: 214-922-9806
- **United Kingdom** 2911 Turtle Creek Blvd, Dallas, TX 75219, tel: 214-521-4090. Wells Fargo Plaza, (19th Floor), 1000 Louisiana St, Suite 1900, Houston, TX 77002, tel: 713-659-6270

Emergency Numbers

For all emergencies requiring police, fire or ambulance dial **911**.

Road conditions on state highways, tel: 1-800-452-9292

Information on **evacuation routes**, **shelters** and **special-needs transportation**, tel: 211

Poison, tel: 1-800-764-7661 (Texas); 1-800-222-1212 (national)

American Red Cross, tel: 1-888-568-3318

Roadside assistance, tel: 800-525-5555

Texas crime stoppers, tel: 800-252-8477

To report a **missing person**, tel: 800-346-3243

Entry Requirements

Passports and Visas

A machine-readable passport, a passport-sized photograph, a visitor's visa, proof of intent to leave the US after your visit and (depending upon your country of origin) an international vaccination certificate, are required of most foreign nationals for entry into the US. Visitors from the UK staying less than 90 days no longer need a visa. Vaccination certificate requirements vary, but proof of immunization against smallpox or cholera may be necessary.

US citizens traveling by air between the US, Canada, Mexico, the Caribbean and Bermuda must present a current passport; a birth certificate and photo ID are no longer valid proof.

Due to increased security, the precise regulations for entry to the US change often, and vary for citizens of different countries. It's a good idea to check on the current situation before you travel, on the State Department website www.travel.state.gov or via a US Embassy or Consulate in your home country.

Etiquette

The key word here is "relaxed." Openness and natural friendliness rule. Don't be surprised when strangers smile broadly at you and ask how you are doing as you pass them in the street. You can expect almost everyone with whom you come into contact to ask how you are feeling, where you come from, where you are going and, if you prove to be a foreigner, whether you are married, how many children you have, what your job is and why you are here. Or they may just ask how you're "doin'."

This is not inappropriate behavior, personally invasive or presumptuous,

BELOW: sizzling Texas summer.

not even an attempt to begin a long, intimate conversation. It is natural friendliness and goodwill that prompts these genial greetings and enquiries from passers-by, waiters and sales people who suddenly become new Texas friends. Don't even be surprised at a congenial slap on the back to emphasize a point, or – particularly in South Texas – a friendly embrace in greeting.

One of the best things about Texas is the relaxed dress codes whether on city streets, at the shopping centre, at the symphony or theater, or in restaurants. Although some of the more expensive establishments in larger cities like Dallas and Houston require men to wear jackets and ties and women to have on dresses or dress pants, in most restaurants almost any attire is tolerated.

In most places where parties wearing jeans and T-shirts happen to be seated next to couples in evening dresses and tuxedos, both groups feel perfectly comfortable. If there is a rule for dress, it may be to wear whatever feels good.

Health regulations prohibit all animals, except guide dogs, in public eating places in Texas.

Gay and Lesbian Travelers

Texas' urban centers, especially Dallas, Houston and Austin, have large gay and lesbian populations, with corresponding businesses and services. Dallas' gay population is estimated at more than 120,000, while Houston's is estimated to be nearly 150,000. Both cities have gay neighborhoods around which the community is centered: Oak Lawn in Dallas, and the Montrose district in Houston.

Dallas has a weekly publication which comes out every Friday called *The Voice* (www.dallasvoice.com). Houston has a magazine called *OutSmart* (www.outsmartmagazine. com); Austin has two magazines: *Q Monthly* (www.qmonthlyaustin.com) and *SHOUT* (www.shouttexas.com). In addition, Houston has a comprehensive online guide at www.houstongayguide.com.

In September, Dallas hosts the annual **Alan Ross Texas Freedom Parade** (www.dallastaverrnguild.org/parade_info.asp), while Houston and Austin both have parades in June, called **Houston Pride** (www.pridehouston.org) and **Austin Pride** (www.austinprideparade.org). Austin is home to the annual **Gay & Lesbian International Film Festival** every fall (usually in late September; www.agliff.org), while Dallas has **Out Takes**, an annual lesbian and gay film festival in November (www.outtakesdallas.org/index.asp).

Dallas' **Cathedral of Hope** (www.cathedralofhope.com) is said to be the largest gay and lesbian church in the world.

Health and Medical Care

Depending upon the country from which you are traveling or through which you have just come, you may need an international vaccination certificate. Many types of over-the-counter medications are readily available, but if you're using prescription medication, it's best to bring extra, along with a spare pair of prescription glasses if you use them. Tap water is fine to drink, but if you're out camping in the more remote parts of some of the state's national parks or national forests, it is best to bring your own or use purifiers.

BELOW: seeing what's on.

Emergency Medical Services

Most cities have 24-hour pharmacies (often called drugstores) and minor emergency clinics, major emergency rooms at hospitals, and poison control centres. Look in the *Yellow Pages* or the inside cover of the telephone book, or **dial 411** for telephone operator assistance.

If you need to call an ambulance, many areas of Texas can gain access to the **emergency number 911** used in most parts of the country. A dispatcher will provide immediate first-aid information if needed, and send help. **If in a non-911 area, dial 0** for the telephone operator.

Pests

Because much of Texas is in the open (that is, all its small and sprawling cities together occupy only a tiny portion of the state), anyone who spends much time exploring it has a good chance of coming into contact with a poisonous animal. Avoidance is always the best strategy against threatening pests. If you are walking in a field, for example, loose clothing discourages ticks and chiggers from finding a spot in which to embed themselves. Tall, thick boots usually protect against stinging ground insects and reptiles. Once bitten or stung, however, there are a few procedures that will ease your suffering. The most important thing is to find what got you and, if possible, get it: taking the pesky pest with you to a doctor will help determine the correct remedy.

Watch out for loose mounds of dirt in grassy areas, which could house **fireants**. Once disturbed (test the area with a long stick), they will swarm at great speed and can be all over your legs in no time. Be careful with children as they may not think fast enough to brush off the ants once attacked.

The bite or sting of a **spider**, **ant** or **scorpion** is not usually fatal but it can cause a lot of pain and itching, and the area around it may swell. In most cases, discomfort gradually subsides. If extreme symptoms such as numbness, tingling, shooting pain, high temperature, low blood pressure, abdominal cramps, spasms, breathing difficulty, or problems focusing the eyes occur, see a physician at once. Remember that bringing the insect with you greatly aids the doctor.

Texans often call **chiggers** "red bugs." A salve from the drugstore may help relieve the itching, but you will just have to wait for it to go away. The same is true of the bite of the

mosquito, found by the million around water in low-lying areas.

Most **snakes** in Texas are not harmful to people and only strike in self-defense; entering a snake's territory and standing too close can agitate it enough to strike. Again, before fleeing in panic at least try to see what the snake looked like. A positive identification is extremely important for the physician making a treatment decision. Do not attempt any first-aid treatments such as freezing the limb, tourniquets or the outdated cut-and-suck method. Instead, go to the emergency center of the local hospital at once. **Coral snakes** are abundant in Texas and because of their beauty and relatively small size they are frequently picked up by children. Be sure to discourage children from picking up strange animals. **Rattlesnakes** and coral snakes have very different toxins, the toxin of the former attacking the nervous system and the latter primarily affecting the respiratory system. Treatment therefore consists of injecting very different antivenins, which makes identification extremely important. Snakes are not quite the omnipresent menace that strangers in Texas fear. They usually remain in fields or sand dunes and often hide under logs or in holes waiting to hunt at night or early in the morning.

Raccoons, **skunks**, **bats** and **squirrels** can all be found in Texas, but should not be touched; they are potential carriers of rabies, which is easily transmitted to people.

Portuguese man-of-war are found in their hundreds on Padre Island. Washed ashore, their blue balloon-like forms with long tentacles continue to pulsate for a while. If you are stung by their tentacles, either on shore, or in the water where they are harder to avoid, you may develop rashes and red welts. A few sensitive victims go into shock or endure fever, cramps and nausea. Some lifeguards treat these stings with meat tenderizer; others wash the area with sodium bicarbonate, boric acid, lemon juice or alcohol. If symptoms are severe, you should see a physician.

Insurance

You should never leave home without travel insurance to cover both yourself and your belongings. Your own insurance company or travel agent can advise you on policies, but shop around since rates vary. Make sure you are covered for accidental death, emergency medical care, trip cancelation and baggage or document loss.

Internet

Internet access is available at all FedEx Kinko's office-center locations. www.fedex.kinkos.com/locations/

Lost Property

Texas is too big and too hands-off organizationally to have a central repository for lost items. The best you'll find might be a form you can fill out such as the one offered by the Dallas Police Department (www.dallaspolice.net/content/11/66/uploads/lostpropformenglish.pdf).

For loss of credit cards, contact:
American Express: tel: 800-221-7282
MasterCard: tel: 800-307-7309
Visa: tel: 800-847-2911
Western Union: tel: 800-325-6000

Maps

Mapsco (www.mapsco.com) is the big map company of Texas. It publishes thick, complex binders of most major Texas cities. At approximately $40, they're not cheap; their level of detail would be useful primarily for those who will be driving around a city and need an explicit, page-by-page street guide.

The **Roads of Texas** is a more practical, one-volume set of detailed maps that covers Texas' entire road system (www.mapsco.com). The **Insight Fleximaps** to Dallas/Fort Worth, Houston and San Antonio are laminated and immensely durable.

Media

Print

Like many big American cities, Dallas and Houston have more than one daily newspaper, covering local, national and international news. There are also several weekly newspapers in most cities that cover local and, sometimes, state-wide news. Local newspapers include: *Dallas Morning News*, *El Paso Times*, *Fort Worth Star-Telegram*, *Galveston Daily News*, *Houston Chronicle*, *San Antonio Express-News* and *Waco Tribune-Herald*.

Current information on hotels, and all kinds of events and cultural activities, can be found in Texas periodicals. The Texas Department of Transportation, Box 149249, Austin, 78714, tel: 800-452-9292, publishes a monthly travel magazine, *Texas Highways*, at a moderate subscription fee. *Texas Monthly* is available at most newsstands.

There are also magazines dedicated to a particular city, such as *D Magazine* in Dallas. Bookstores display a wide array of books about Texas, from the *Texas Almanac* – covering every conceivable subject – to comprehensive bed-and-breakfast listings and cycling trip guides.

Broadcast Media

There are over 70 television stations and at least 550 AM and FM radio stations in Texas. Thanks to cable, satellite or pay television, programs from all over the world can be seen almost any hour of the day or night. The installation of cable in most hotels and motels and many homes means that how a particular station is found depends on where it appears on the cable to which they subscribe. Consult the newspaper for television listings. Radio listings are sometimes given in Sunday supplements of newspapers.

Money Matters

Foreign visitors are advised to take US dollar traveler's checks to Texas, since exchanging foreign currency – whether as cash or checks – can prove problematic. An increasing number of banks offer foreign exchange facilities, but this practice is not universal. Some department store chains offer foreign currency exchange.

Most shops, restaurants and other establishments accept traveler's checks in US dollars and will give change in cash. Alternatively, checks can be converted into cash at the bank.

Credit Cards are very much part of daily life in Texas. They can be used to pay for pretty much anything, and it is also common for car rental firms and hotels to take an imprint of your card as a deposit. Rental companies may oblige you to pay a large deposit in cash if you do not have a card.

You can also use your credit card to withdraw cash from ATMs (Automatic Teller Machines). Before you leave home, make sure you know your PIN and find out which ATM system will accept your card. The most widely accepted cards are Visa, American Express, MasterCard, Diners Club, Japanese Credit Bureau and Discovery.

Postal System

First-class postage is the same anywhere in Texas, or in the US, and bills arrive just as quickly in tiny Cut-and-Shoot as they do in big-city Dallas. Post offices open at 7, 8 or 9am and usually close at 5pm, Mon–Fri. Many of them are open for at least a couple of hours

on Saturday mornings, but they are all closed on Sunday.

There may also be coin-operated machines that dispense stamps whether the office is open or not. Rates are usually listed nearby. There are US Post Office Information numbers in the phone book, or call 411 and ask the operator.

Visitors can receive mail at post offices if it is addressed to them, care of "General Delivery", followed by the city name and (very important) the zip code. You must pick up this mail in person within a week or two of its arrival and will be asked to show some form of valid personal identification.

Public Restrooms

You will rarely find public restroom facilities. Restaurants and gas stations are the most obvious destinations, with McDonald's at the top of the list for cleanliness and ubiquity.

Religious Services

Texas' population is primarily Protestant in the north and east (with Baptists in the majority) and Catholic in the south and southwest. Other religions and ethical systems represented in the state include Buddhism, Hinduism, Islam, and Judaism. Consult the *Yellow Pages* or ask at the desk of your hotel for the nearest place of worship.

Taxes

Texas charges a **sales tax** of 6.25 percent on most purchases, from clothing to electronics to dining out. Individual cities then apply their own percentage, usually totaling approximately 2 percent. The only major nontaxable exception is food purchased from a grocery store.

Texas has higher add-on car rental fees than any other state. On average, airport travelers pay an average of 51.7 percent mark-up on a rate quoted by the rental car company.

Telecommunications

Telephones

To call from **city to city** in Texas, you must first find out the area code *(see box)*. The state's size requires that it be divided into different three-digit codes. The proliferation of fax machines and computers in recent years has resulted in more and more areas being re-assigned new area codes, often not long after they have been changed, so don't be surprised if an area code has changed from the one currently published.

To call from **one area to another**, dial 1 before the three-digit area code and the local seven-digit telephone number. If calling from a pay phone, you must first insert a coin to connect with the operator.

If you want to pay for the call with coins, a recorded voice will tell you how many to insert. Unless you have a credit card with the telephone company, your only other option is to call your party "collect" (reversing the charges).

Directory Assistance calls from pay telephones are free. However, to be connected to some of them you must first insert a coin, but as soon as you are connected with the operator it will be returned to you.

To get the information operator dial 411, but to get an **information operator** in another city, dial 1+area code of the city+555-1212.

For **local calls** from pay phones which accept coins, insert a coin and dial the seven-digit local telephone number. There is no time limit for local calls. Many businesses have toll-free (no charge) telephone numbers; these are always prefaced with 800 rather than an area code.

There are **Western Union cablegram offices** in most Texas cities. Look in the local telephone directory in the white pages (for major cities, there may be separate books for businesses and residences). Messages and money can be sent over the wires immediately. You must have identification, such as a driver's license, to receive money

Public Holidays

Banks, federal, state, county and city offices and private businesses often close during public holidays. Many stores remain open during weekends and holidays.

- **New Year's Day** 1 January
- **Martin Luther King Jr.'s Birthday** 15 January, although observed the third Monday in January
- **Presidents' Day** Third Monday in February
- **Easter Sunday** Late March/early April
- **Memorial Day** Last Monday in May
- **Independence Day** 4 July
- **Labor Day** First Monday in September
- **Columbus Day** Second Monday in October
- **Veteran's Day** 11 November
- **Thanksgiving Day** Fourth Thursday in November
- **Christmas Day** 25 December

Time Zones

Texas spans two time zones: Central Standard Time (Greenwich Mean Time minus six hours) and, in the extreme western corner of the state, Mountain Standard Time (Greenwich Mean Time minus seven hours). Daylight Saving Time is observed in almost every part of the state and begins at 2am on the first Sunday in April when clocks are advanced one hour, and ends at 2am on the last Sunday in October.

Tipping

Restaurant bills do not usually include a tip, unless you are in a group of five or more when a gratuity of 15 percent may be added to the total and unless the service is dreadful, you are obligated; otherwise tips of between 10 and 20 percent are expected.

Fifteen percent is a good rule of thumb when tipping for any service, including taxi rides and haircuts, although some Texans have not got used to tipping barbers. The owner of a hair salon is usually not tipped. Bellhops and parking attendants expect a dollar, shoeshiners more.

Tourist Information

Most cities in Texas have a Convention and Visitors' Bureau (CVB), which will provide you with brochures and maps, while elsewhere you must rely on the local chamber of commerce: these are oriented toward business people, but the staff are usually happy to help, particularly in tourist areas.

The ***Texas State Travel Guide***, published by the Department of Transportation, lists Texas cities with their attractions and is available free from P.O. Box 149249, Austin, TX 78714-9249, or by calling 800-452-9242. Information on road conditions and routes is also available from the same number. The "Media" section on page 373 gives details of Texas periodicals containing useful information for visitors to the state.

To request information on standard Texas travel, call or write the Tourism Division, Texas Department of Commerce, P.O. Box 12728, Austin, TX 78711, tel: 512-462-9191, or visit www.traveltex.com

Tourist Offices

Abilene, 1101 N. First St, TX 79601, tel: 325-676-2556; fax: 325-676-1630; www.abilene.com/visitors
Arlington, 1905 E. Randol Mill Road, tel: 817-265-7721; fax: 817-265-5640; www.arlington.org
Austin, 201 E. Second St, TX 78701, tel: 512-474-5171; fax: 512-583-7280; www.austintexas.org
Beaumont, 801 Main St, TX 77701, tel: 409-880-3749; fax: 409-880-3750; www.beaumontcvb.com
Corpus Christi, 1201 N. Shoreline Blvd, TX 78401, tel: 361-881-1888; fax: 361-887-9023; www.corpuschristicvb.org
Dallas, 1201 Elm St, TX 75270, tel: 214-571-1000; fax: 214-571-1008; www.dallascvb.com
Denton, 414 Parkway, TX 76201, tel: 888-381-1818; www.discoverdenton.com
El Paso, 1 Civic Center Plaza, TX 79901, tel: 915-534-0696; fax: 915-534-0686; www.elpasocvb.com
Ennis, 2 E. Ennis Ave, TX 75119, tel: 972-878-4748; fax: 972-875-1018; www.visitennis.org
Fort Worth, 415 Throckmorton St, TX 76102, tel: 817-336-8791; fax: 817-336-3282; www.fortworth.com
Galveston, 2428 Seawall Blvd, TX 77550, tel: 409-763-4311; fax: 409-770-0015; www.galvestoncvb.com
Granbury, 100 N. Crockett, TX 76048, tel: 800-950-2212; fax: 817-573-5789; www.granburytx.com
Grapevine, 1 Liberty Park Plaza, TX 76051, tel: 800-457-6338; fax: 817-410-3038; www.grapevinetexasusa.com
Houston, 901 Bagby, TX 77002, tel: 713-437-5200; fax: 713-227-6336; www.houston-guide.com
Laredo, 501 San Agustin, TX 78040, tel: 956-795-2200; fax: 956-795-2185; www.visitlaredo.com
Lubbock, 1301 Broadway, TX 79401, tel: 806-747-5232; fax: 806-747-1419; www.lubbocklegends.com
McKinney, 1650 W. Virginia, TX 75069, tel: 972-542-0163; fax: 888-649-8499; www.mckinneycvb.org
Midland, 109 N. Main, TX 79701, tel: 432-683-3381; fax: 432-682-9205; www.visitmidlandtx.com
Nacogdoches, 200 E. Main, TX 75961, tel: 936-564-7351; fax: 936-560-3920; www.visitnacogdoches.org
Odessa, 700 N. Grant St, TX 79761, tel: 432-333-7871; fax: 432-333-7858; www.odessacvb.com
Port Arthur, 3401 Cultural Center Dr., TX 77642, tel: 409-985-7822; fax: 409-985-5584; www.portarthurtexas.com
San Angelo, 500 Rio Concho Dr., TX 76903, tel: 325-655-4136; fax: 325-658-1110; www.sanangelotx.com
San Antonio, 203 S. St Mary's St, (2nd Floor), TX 78205, tel: 210-207-6700; fax: 210-207-6782; www.sanantoniocvb.com
San Marcos, 202 N. C.M. Allen Parkway, TX 78667, tel: 512-393-5900; fax: 512-393-5912; www.sanmarcostexas.com
South Padre Island, 600 Padre Boulevard, TX 78597, tel: 956-761-6433 or 800-so-padre; fax: 956-761-9462; www.sopadre.com
Waco, 100 Washington Ave, TX 76702, tel: 254-750-5810; fax: 254-750-5801; www.wacocvb.com

Local Dialing Codes

Abilene	325
Amarillo	806
Austin	512
Corpus Christi/ Padre Island	361
Dallas	214, 469, 972
Del Rio	830
El Paso	915
Fort Worth	682, 817
Galveston	409
Lake Jackson	979
Laredo/McAllen	956
Lufkin/Huntsville	936
Houston	281, 713, 832
San Antonio	210
Tyler	903
Waco	254

Tour Operators

Gray Line tours are available in many Texas towns and cities. For specific information call 800-472-9546, Other companies include:
Adventure Tours
Tel: 800-638-9040.
Central West of Texas, 3426 W. Gilbert Road, Grand Prairie 75050, Tel: 972-399-1059.
Discover Houston Tours
P.O. Box 230183, Houston 77223. Tel: 713-222-9255.

Websites

- **www.austintexas.org**
Austin Texas. Visitor information including Austin attractions, accommodations, vacation packages, activities, events, dining, music venues, and much more.
- **www.corpuschristi-tx-cvb.org**
Corpus Christi. Accommodations, attractions, activities, tour planning and travel information.
- **www.dallascvb.com/visitors**
Dallas Convention & Visitors Bureau. Information for business/leisure visitors in things to see and do, dining, shopping and events.
- **www.elpasocvb.com**
El Paso Convention and Visitors Bureau. Information on El Paso Convention Center, visitors information, travel and tourism, dining, attractions, excursions, hotels, day trips, and concert auditoriums, including a link in Spanish.
- **www.fortworth.com**
Fort Worth. For tourists and business travelers, information on where to stay, events, museums, downtown, the Stockyards, Texas Motor Speedway, and more.
- **www.galveston.com**
Galveston. Visitor information, where to stay, what to do, getting around.
- **www.visithoustontexas.com**
Visit Houston. Information from the greater Houston Convention and Visitors Bureau for visitors, meeting planners and travel agents.
- **www.lubbockcvb.com**
Lubbock. Lodgings, attractions, events, shopping, dining, transportation and sports.
- **www.sanantoniocvb.com**
San Antonio. Events, attractions, activities, parks, restaurants, tours, shopping, sports.
- **texana.texascooking. com/cal/db**
Texas festivals, cook-offs and rodeos
- **www.governor.state.tx.us/divisions/music/events/**
Texas music events.
- **www.texas-best.com/texasbest/annual**
Texas best annual events.
- **www.tpwd.state.tx.us/spdest/**
Texas state parks and destinations.

What to Bring

For clothing, fabrics such as cotton, linen and wool provide the best comfort in the Texas climate. Go particularly light in summer, but because of varying altitude and cool breezes, a sweater may be needed in the evening. The midwinters of Central and East Texas, the Coastal Prairie and the Rio Grande Valley usually require only a lightweight coat. In the mountains, High Plains and Panhandle, winters can be so severe that you need layers of warm clothes.

Texans are very casual dressers and away from the office blue jeans are the norm. They are worn almost anywhere, anytime of the day, dressed up or down by changing a shirt, sweater, jacket or accessories. People in Dallas and Houston dress formally for some evening events, but casual pants and dresses for women and shirt-sleeves or tieless shirts and jackets for men are acceptable almost anywhere you go.

FURTHER READING

General

1001 Texas Place Names by Fred Tarpley (University of Texas Press, 1988)
A Personal Country by A.C. Greene (Texas A & M Press, 1979)
Backroads of Texas by Ed Syers (Gulf Publishing, 1988)
The Best of the Old West by Ron Butler (Texas Monthly Press, 1983)
Bridges Over the Brazos by Jon McConal (TCU Press, 2005)
Cattle Kings of Texas by C.K. Douglas (Cecil Baugh, Dallas, 1939)
The Chisholm Trail by Wayne Gard (University of Oklahoma Press, 1954)
Cow People by J. Frank Dobie (Little, Brown & Co., 1964)

Feedback

We do our best to ensure the information in our books is as accurate and up-to-date as possible. The books are updated on a regular basis, using local contacts, who painstakingly add, amend and correct as required. However, some mistakes and omissions are inevitable and we are ultimately reliant on our readers to put us in the picture.

We would welcome your feedback on any details related to your experiences using the book "on the road". Maybe we recommended a hotel that you liked (or another that you didn't), as well as interesting new attractions, or facts and figures you have found out about the country itself. The more details you can give us (particularly with regard to addresses, e-mails and telephone numbers), the better. We will acknowledge all contributions, and we'll offer an Insight Guide to the best letters received.

Please write to us at:
Insight Guides
PO Box 7910
London SE1 1WE
United Kingdom
Or send e-mail to:
insight@apaguide.co.uk

The Cowboy Encyclopedia by Richard W. Slatta (ABC-CLIO, 1994)
Encyclopedia of the American West, eds. Charles Phillips and Alan Axelrod (Simon & Schuster, 1996)
A Guide to the Lone Star State, WPA guide; revised edition edited by Harry Hansen (Hastings House, 1970)
How Come It's Called That? by Virginia Madison & Hallie Stillwell (October House, 1958)
Journey Through Texas by Frederick Law Olmsted (1860: republished 1969 by Burt Franklin, NY)
Kinky Friedman's Guide to Texas Etiquette: Or How to Get to Heaven or Hell Without Going Through Dallas-Fort Worth by Kinky Friedman (Cliff Street Books, 2001)
Legends of the Dallas Cowboys Cody Monk (Sports Publishing, 2004)
Life on the King Ranch by Frank Goodwyn (Texas A & M University Press, 1993)
The Longhorns by J. Frank Dobie (Bramhall House, 1961)
A New Handbook of Texas (Texas State Historical Association, 1996)
Smithsonian Guide to Texas and the Arkansas River Valley by Alice Gordon (Stewart, Tabori & Chang, 1998)
The Texas Coast by Robert R. Rafferty (Texas Monthly Press, 1986)
Texas Rangers by Stephen Hardin, Richard Hook (Osprey, 2000)
The Tex-Mex Cookbook by Robb Walsh (Broadway Books, 2004)
They Called Them Greasers by Arnoldo De Leon (University of Texas Press, 1983)
Twelve Years in the Saddle with the Texas Rangers by W.J.L. Sullivan (University of Nebraska Press, 2001)
Where Texas meets the Sea by Brian Wooley (Pressworks, Dallas, 1985)
The Wine Roads of Texas by Wes Marshall, Robert Mondavi and Fess Parker (Maverick Publishing Co., 2007)

History & Current Affairs

Cowboy Culture: A Saga of Five Centuries by David Dary (Avon Press, 1982)
Early Times in Texas by J.C. Duval (Stock-Vaughn Co., 1892)
The Galveston That Was by Howard Barnstone (MacMillan, 1966)
The German Texans by Glen E. Lich (Institute of Texas Cultures, 1981)
The Great Galveston Disaster by Paul Lester (Pelican, 2000)
Gone to Texas: A History of the State by Randolph B. Campbell (Oxford University Press, 2003)
The Handbook of Waco and McLennan County, Texas, edited by Dayton Kelley (Texian Press, 1972)
Houston: A History by David G. McComb (Univ. of Texas Press, 1981)
The Illustrated History of America's Great Department Stores by Robert Hendrickson (Stein & Day, 1979)
Isaac's Storm: A Man, a Time, and the Deadliest Hurricane in History by Eric Larson (Crown, 1999)
Lone Star: A History of Texas and the Texans by T.R. Fehrenbach (Da Capo Press, 2000)
The Men Who Wear the Star: **The Story of the Texas Rangers** by C.M. Robinson (Modern Library, 2001)
North Toward Home by Willie Morris (Delta, 1976)
Oil in Texas: The Gusher Age 1845–1945 by Diana Davids Olien and Roger M. Oliens (University of Texas Press, 2002)
People & Places in the Texas Past by June Rayfield Welch (GLA Press, 1974)
Sam Houston's Texas pictures and text by Sue Flanagan (University of Texas Press, 1964)
San Antonio. A Historical and Pictorial Guide by Charles Ramsdall (University of Texas Press, 1976)
The Shipwrecked Men (Great Journeys), by Alvar Nunez Cabeza de Vaca (Penguin, 2007)
Storm Over Texas: The Annexation Controversy and the Road to Civil War, by Joel H. Silbey (Oxford University Press, 2006)
Texas: 1876, edited by Robert S. Gray. (Cordovan Press, 1974)
Texas: A Bicentennial History by Joe B. Frantz (W.W. Norton & Co., 1976)
Texas Women on the Cattle Trails ed. Sara R. Mass (Texas A&M University, 2006)
The Texas Almanac (Dallas Morning News)
The Years of Lyndon Johnson: The Path to Power by Robert A. Caro (Vintage, 1983)

Art & Architecture

Center: A Journal for Architecture in America (Center for the Study of American Architecture)
Harwell Hamilton Harris by Lisa Germany Austin (Center for American Architecture, 1985)
Talking with Texas Writers by Patrick Bennett (Texas A & M Press, 1980)
Texas Catalog: Historic American Buildings Survey by Paul Goeldner (Trinity University Press, 1974)
Texas Museums: A Guide-book by Ron and Paula Tyler (University of Texas Press, 1983
Texas Then & Now by Richard Reynolds (Westcliffe Publishers, 2005)
Texas Towns and The Art of Architecture by Richard Payne (Texas State Historical Association, 2006)

Natural History

The Explorer's Texas: The Lands and Waters by Del Weniger (Eakin 1984)
A Field Guide to the Birds of Texas by Roger Tory Peterson (Houghton Mifflin Company, 1963)
The Guadalupe Mountains of Texas by Alan Tennant (University of Texas Press, 1980)
Roadside Geology of Texas by Robert Sheldon (Mountain Press, 1979)
Texas Weather by George W. Bomar (University of Texas Press, 1983)
Touring Texas Gardens by Jessie Gunn Stephens (Republic of Texas Press, 2002)
Wildflowers of Texas: A Field Guide by Geyata Ajilvsgi (Shearer Publishing, 1984)

Other Insight Guides

Nearly 200 companion titles to this volume cover every continent. More than 30 of the titles are devoted to North America and include: ***Arizona and the Grand Canyon***, ***New Mexico***, ***Utah***, ***American Southwest***, ***US National Parks West***, ***USA on the Road***, ***USA: The New South*** and ***North American and Alaskan Cruises***.

There are also over 100 *Pocket Guides*, designed to assist the traveler with a limited amount of time to spend in a destination. The carefully planned one-day itineraries written by a local resident make a location easily accessible, and each book contains an easy-to-use full-size pull-out map.

In addition, more than 80 *Compact Guides* offer the traveler a highly portable encyclopedic travel guide packed with carefully cross-referenced text, photographs and maps.

Armchair Travel

Movies/Videos

Many of the state's major towns and cities have established their own Film Commissions, as the state has grown increasingly popular with moviemakers. Almost everybody has seen a movie with Texas as its main location. If not, here are a few to see:
The Alamo, 1960.
All the Pretty Horses, 2000.
The Best Little Whorehouse in Texas, 1982.
Big Country, 1982, starring Charlton Heston, Gregory Peck, Burl Ives and Jean Simmons.
Blood Simple, a 1984 Coen brothers film.
Bonnie & Clyde, 1967, starring Warren Beatty and Faye Dunaway.
Born on the Fourth of July, a 1989 Oliver Stone film starring Tom Cruise.
Dancer, Texas Pop. 81, 1998.
Giant (Elizabeth Taylor, Rock Hudson, James Dean), shot at Marfa in 1956.
Glory Road, 2006.
Happy, Texas, 1999.
Honeysuckle Rose, 1980, with Willie Nelson.
Idiocracy, 2006.
The Last Picture Show, a Peter Bogdanovich film written by Texan Larry McMurtry.
Letter from Waco, 1996, documentary.
The Newton Boys, 1998.
Paris, Texas, a 1984 Wim Wenders film.
The Positively True Adventure of the Allegedly Texas Cheerleading Mom, a Michael Ritchie film, 1993.
Texas Rangers, 2001.
Texasville, 1990, another Bogdanovich film.
The Three Burials of Melquiades Estrada, 2005.
The Trip to Bountiful, 1985.

Television

Notable television series that have presented a view (sometimes greatly exaggerated) of Texas life, past and present:
Austin City Limits, 1975–.
Austin Stories, 1997.
Dallas, 1978–91.
Houston Knights, 1987–8
King of the Hill,1997–.
Lonesome Dove, 1989 (plus sequels *Return To Lonesome Dove*, *Streets of Laredo* and *Lonesome Dove: The Series*.
Tales of the Texas Rangers, 1958–9.
The Texan, 1958–60.
Walker, Texas Ranger, 1993–2001.

Discography

The following are considered to be among the best of recorded Texas music available.
Buddy Holly, *Buddy Holly: From The Original Master Tapes* (MCA)
Lightning Hopkins, *Texas Blues* (Arhoolie)
Blind Lemon Jefferson, *King of the Country Blues* (Yazoo)
Willie Nelson, *Red-Headed Stranger* (Columbia)
Roy Orbison, *The Legends: Roy Orbison* (CBS Special Products)
Big Mama Thornton, *Hound Dog: The Peacock Records* (MCA)
Stevie Ray Vaughan & Double Trouble, *Couldn't Stand the Weather* (Epic)
T-Bone Walker, *The Complete Imperial Recordings* (EMI)
Various artists, *Tejano Roots/Raices Tejanas* (Arhoolie)
Various artists, *Texas Music Vols. 1, 2 & 3* (Rhino)

Art & Photo Credits

American Friends Service Committee 67
Andy Jackson/Alamy 157
AP/PA Photos front flap top, 51, 91, 245, 279, 371
The Art Archive/Bill Manns 70, 80
Austin American-Statesman/WpN 7TL & TR, 95
Brian Cahn/WpN 94
Bruce Bernstein, Courtesy of Princeton Library, NJ 24/25, 29, 30L&R, 38
Byrd Williams 20, 76/77, 112, 121 & T, 122, 124, 125L, 134, 135, 136, 368
Carolyn Brown/Image Bank 124T
Chris Shinn/Mira 66
Christopher B. Kuhn 329
Dallas CVB 356
Dave G Houser 4BL, 9CL, 21, 101, 108/109, 110/111, 174, 213, 255, 268
David Kennedy 8T
David Redfern/Redferns 175T
D.W Hamilton/Image Bank 40
Eleanor S Morris 137, 147, 153, 225T, 238T, 247
F. Poelking/Still Pictures 6B
Frank Whitney/Image Bank 303
Gaylord Texan 346
Getty Images 54, 92, 93L & R
Getty Images/Aurora Creative 309
Grant V Faint/Image Bank 14
Greg Smith/Corbis 62
Harald Sund/Image Bank 48, 286T
Houston CVB 205, 348
Hyatt 344
The Image Works/TopFoto 160L
Index Stock 208T, 258
iStockphoto.com 6CL, 163
Jack Hollingsworth 1, 2/3, 4BR, 10/11, 12/13, 19, 22, 33, 39, 43, 46/47, 71, 72, 74, 75, 79, 81, 82, 83, 84, 86, 88/89, 98, 116/117, 125R, 127 & T, 128 & T, 129, 130, 131, 133T, 138, 139, 140, 141T, 144, 154, 159, 167, 183, 184T, 186, 187, 189, 190R, 191, 192L, 193, 194, 200/201, 203, 205T, 207, 208, 209, 210, 216/217, 219, 221, 228T, 230/231, 235, 241, 242, 243, 244, 277, 280, 296, 297, 300, 302, 307, 308, 310T, 313, 314, 328, 329T, 330
Jan Butchofsky-Houser 5B, 187T, 301T
Jose Fuste Raga/Corbis 96/97
Joseph Savant/Image Bank 123
Joel Glenn/Image Bank 265
Kathy Adams Clark/KAC Productions 147T, 149T, 221T, 246T, 251T, 282, 291T, 333
Kenneth Breisch 148R, 149, 188L, 192, 233, 237, 253, 285, 322, 332
Laurence Parent 2B, 35, 68, 100R, 145, 156, 158, 161T, 223, 228, 248, 254, 272, 273, 288, 301, 304, 305, 316/317, 319, 325, 326, 332T, 334
Laurent Grandadam/Robert Harding 56/57
LOOK Die Bildagentur der Fotografen GmbH/Alamy 168/169
Mark Langford/Mira 191T
McAllen Monitor/WpN 251
Mike Blake/Reuters/Corbis 9TR
Nancy Boghossian Keeler 161
Neiman-Marcus 126
New York Times/Redux/eyevine spine, back cover left, 53, 284, 360, 361
Paul Vozdic/Rex Features 274T
Peter A. Calvin 65
P. Frischknecht/Still Pictures 291
Peter Gottschling/KAC 28, 34, 254T
Peter Newark's American Pictures 26, 41, 42, 44, 73L&R, 164, 260T, 260, 275T
Pictures Colour Library 212, 239
Randy Green 103, 142/143, 173
Rankin Harvey/Houserstock 55, 133, 150, 206, 312, 314T
Rex Features 52, 129T, 162, 222, 244T
Rex Features/Sipa Press 50L, 50R
Richard Carson/Reuters/Corbis 211
Richard Cummins/Corbis back flap bottom
Robert Fried 18, 99, 196
Robert & Linda Mitchell 16/17, 32, 105, 134T, 141, 155, 158T, 165, 170, 171, 172T, 175, 176, 180/181, 182, 185, 197, 227, 249, 263, 269, 270T, 293, 298T, 306, 311, 315
Rob Howard/Corbis 8B
The Ronald Grant Archive 279T
Ruben Guzman 58, 100L, 102, 226, 242, 246, 250L&R, 252
Russell Thompson/Archive Photos 166
Sean Sprague/Still Pictures 64, 266/267, 274, 275
Spectrum Colour Library 4/5
Steve Vidler/Jupiter Images 119
Stewart Cohen/WpN 118
Superstock 358
Texas Highway Department 31, 123, 148L, 151, 152, 218, 225, 259, 261, 318, 331
Texas Tourism 6T, 7B, 60, 85, 90, 278T, 281, 283, 310, 341, 350, 352, 353, 354, 362, 372
Texas Tourist Development Agency (Michael Murphy) front flap bottom, 36/37, 190L, 240, 256/257, 262, 276, 284T, 289, 323, 327, 335
(Richard Reynolds) spine, back cover center, back flap top, 59, 61, 106/107, 195, 229, 238, 271, 294/295, 324
(Henry Seawell) 160R
Tony Stone Worldwide 49, 78
Topham/ImageWorks 27, 292
Topham Picturepoint 306T, 325T
Travelsite/Global 283T
Viesti Associates 287
Wesley Bucxe/Rex 274T
William D Adams back cover right, 23, 45, 87, 104, 151T, 165T, 177, 202, 224, 232, 264, 299, 334T, 336
Wolfgang Kaehler/Corbis 188R

Picture Spreads

Pages 178–179
Top row, L–R: Dave G Houser, Rankin Harvey, Eleanor S Morris, Robert & Linda Mitchell.
Center row, L–R: Robert & Linda Mitchell, William D Adams.
Bottom row, L–R: Robert & Linda Mitchell, Jack Hollingsworth, Jack Hollingsworth.
Pages 198–199
Top row, L–R: Laurence Parent, Robert & Linda Mitchell, Jack Hollingsworth, Robert & Linda Mitchell.
Center row, L–R: Dave G Houser, Dave G Houser.
Bottom row, L–R: Robert & Linda Mitchell, Dave G Houser, Dave G Houser, Robert & Linda Mitchell.
Pages 214–215
Top row, L–R: NASA, Southern Photos, Topham Picturepoint, Robert & Linda Mitchell.
Bottom row, L–R: NASA, Fred Mawer, NASA, NASA, NASA.
Pages 294–295
Top row: All Robert & Linda Mitchell.
Center row: Spectrum Colour Library.
Bottom row, L–R: Kathy Adams Clark, Robert & Linda Mitchell, Robert & Linda Mitchell, Topham Picturepoint.

Map Production: Colourmap Scanning Ltd

© 2007 Apa Publications GmbH & Co. Verlag KG (Singapore branch)

INSIGHT GUIDE
TEXAS

Cartographic Editor **Zoë Goodwin**
Production **Linton Donaldson**
Design Consultants
Carlotta Junger, Graham Mitchener
Picture Research **Hilary Genin**

INDEX

Numbers in italics refer to photographs

A

Abilene 302–3
Buffalo Gap Historic Village 303
Historical Museum 302
Taylor County Exposition Center 302
Acadians 64
accommodations 343
Acuña, Manuel 259
Adair, John 311
Aeromotor Windmill 141
African-Americans 65–6
agriculture 22, 250
fruit growing 22, 173, 250
Ailey, Alvin 22
Alabama-Coushatta Indian Reservation 66, 229, 323
Alamo *see under* **San Antonio**
Alamo Village Movie Location *195*, 196
Albany 299–301
Alibates flint 331
Allen, Augustus and John 205
alligators *221*, 222, 294
Allred, James 74
Alpine 283
Amarillo 309
Amarillo Livestock Auction (tours/auction) 310
Big Texan Steak Ranch *308*, 309
Cadillac Ranch 310
Don Harrington Discovery Center 309
Old San Jacinto 309
Working Ranch Cowboys Association 309
American Institute of Architecture 240
amusement parks
Moody Gardens (Galveston) 241
Six Flags AstroWorld (Houston) 211
Six Flags Over Texas (Arlington) 138
Anglo immigrants 59, 64
Anglo-Americans 31, 100
Anglo-Southern (or Anglo-Celtic-Southern) culture 59, 60
aquariums
Dallas Aquarium 128
Dallas World Aquarium & Zoological Garden 123
Texas State Aquarium (Corpus Christi) 244
architects
Barnes, Edward Larrabee 123
Burgee, John 121, 135, 209
Cook, William David 124
Gordon, James Riley 100, *104*, 145
Johnson, Philip 103, 104, 121, 135, 136, 205, 208, 209, 243
Kahn, Louis 104, 135
Mies van der Rohe, Ludwig 207
Piano, Renzo 124
Pei, I.M. 103, 104, 120, 121, 124, 205
Pelli, Cesar 209
Schwarz, David 123, 134, 138
Wright, Frank Lloyd 125
architecture, contemporary 99–104
see also **freeway architecture**
Arlington 138–9
Air Combat School 138
Arlington Museum of Art 139
Johnson Plantation Cemetery 139
Legends of the Game Museum 138
Living Science Center 139
Louis Tussaud's Palace of Wax & Ripley's Believe It or Not! 138
Rangers Ballpark 138
Six Flags Hurricane Harbor (water park) 138
Six Flags Over Texas (amusement park) 138
theaters 139
Traders Village Flea Market 139
art galleries *see under* **museums, art galleries and halls of fame**
artists 54, 309–10
Asian immigrants 67
***Atalanta* railroad car** 228
Austin 32, 91, 162–6
6th Street block (Old Pecan Street) *162*, 166
Austin Children's Museum 165
Austin Museum of Art (Laguna Gloria) 165
Austin Visitor's Center 164
Barton Springs Pool 164–5
bat colony 164, *165*
Congress Avenue Bridge 164
Driskill Hotel 101, 166, *167*
French Legation Museum 166
Governor's Mansion *154*, 164
Hamilton Pool *157*
Lady Bird Johnson Wildflower Center 166
Lyndon B. Johnson Library and Museum 166
movie making 52
music 162
Neill-Cochran House 165
O. Henry Home 165
South By Southwest 162
State Capitol *163*, 164
swimming 165
tours (walking) 164
Town Lake 164
Austin City Limits 92, 162
Austin, Moses 31, 157
Austin, Stephen Fuller 31, 71, 165, 241
Autry, Gene 82

B

Balcones Fault Zone 161
Balli, Padre Nicolas 245
Bandera 171
barbecues 62, 66, 300
barbed wire 43–4, 82
Barnes, Will C. 44
Barrow, Clyde 74, 124, 133
Barton Warnock Environmental Educational Center 281
Basilica of Our Lady of San Juan (*Virgen de Los Lagos*) 253
Bass, Perry 133
Bass, Sam 161
bat colonies 164, 294
Bates, Ali 331
Battleship *Texas* 212
beaches *see* **Gulf Coast**
Bean, Judge Roy *260*, 261
Beaumont 219
Béjar (Bexar) 192
Belton 155
Ben Bolt 246
Best Little Whorehouse in Texas 166
Bettina 61
Big Bend National Park 289–92
accommodations 289
Castolon 292
Chisos Basin 289
Chisos Mountains Lodge 289
Fern Canyon 292
Johnson Ranch House 292
Mariscal Canyon 292
Mariscal Mine 292
Panther Junction 289
Rio Grande Village 289
River Road 292
Santa Elena Canyon 292
trails 290–2
visitors' center 289
water 290
Big Ranch Country 21
Big Spring 304–5
Big Tex *10–11*
Big Thicket 323
bird watching 172, 244, 254
birds 244, 245, *246*, *254*, 289, *327*
see also under individual parks 319–34
Black Chinese 67
blacks 66, 67
cowboys 84
music 93
Blanco 175
Boca Chica Beach 246, *254*
Bode, Elroy 273
Bohlin, Ed 133, 134
Bolivar 235
Bolivar Point Lighthouse 235
Bolivar, Simon 235
Bonham 229
Bonnie and Clyde 74, 124, 133
Bonnie and Clyde 52

Booth, John Wilkes 148, 171
Borglum, Gutzon 242
Bosque County 150
botanic gardens *see* **gardens and botanic gardens**
Boundary Act 32
Bowie, Colonel James 185
branding cattle *40*, 40–1, 42, 81
Brinkley, Dr John R. 260
Browning, Robert and Elizabeth Barrett 151
Brownsville
Brownsville Heritage Complex 254
Costumes of the Americas Museum 254
Gladys Porter Zoo 254
Historic Brownsville Museum 254
Brueske, Judith M. 287
Bruni, Antonio Mateo 263
Bryan, John Neely *21*, 119
Bryan/College Station 159
buckaroo 22
Bucksnort 158
buffalo 303
Buntline, Ned 79
Burnet 176
Burnett Bay 212
Bush, George 159
Bush, George W. 51
Butch Cassidy 131

C

Cabeza de Vaca, Alvar Núñez 29, 30, 65
Cactus Jack 196
Caddo confederations 29
Cadillac Ranch (10 Cadillacs) 310
Cajun immigrants 63–4
Cajun Triangle 219
Calvert 67, 158
Calvert, Robert 158
Camp Verde 173
Campeachy 236
camping *see under individual parks* 319–34
Candelaria 280
Canyon 309
canyons
Boquillas Canyon 292
Fern Canyon 292
Mariscal Canyon 292
McKelligan Canyon 273
McKittrick Canyon 329
Palo Duro Canyon 310
Santa Elena Canyon 292
Yellowhouse Canyon 314
Capote Falls 280
Castroville 188
cattle 34, 39–44, 131, 194
see also **branding, longhorn cattle**
breeds 44
shipping 43
unbranded 42
cattle drives *see* **trail drives**
Cattleman's Association 41
cattlemen *38*, 39
cave paintings *see* **pictographs**
caves and caverns *160*
Bracken Cave (bat colony) 164
Carlsbad Caverns 329
Cascade Caverns 176
Caverns of Sonora 176
Inner Space Cavern 160–1
Longhorn Cavern 176
Natural Bridge Caverns 176
Ney Cave 176
cemeteries
Acton Cemetery 319
Buffalo Gap Cemetery 303
D'Anis Cemetery (Castroville) *160*
Concordia Cemetery (El Paso) 272
First Street Cemetery (Waco) 152
Glenwood Cemetery (Houston) 211
Johnson Plantation Cemetery (Arlington) 138
Lubbock Cemetery 312
Old Round Rock Cemetery *161*
Central Texas 20, 22, 145, 155
see also **Hill Country**
Cherokees 32, 67, 225
Chihuahuan Desert 282, 306, 329
Chihuahuan Desert Research Institute 284
Chillada, Eduardo 124
Chinese immigrants 67
Chisholm, Jesse 194
Chisholm Trail 131 *140*, 194
Cisneros, Henry 195
Civil War 33, 34, 221, 225, 236, 254
Civilian Conservation Corps (CCC) 319
Clayton, Nicholas 100
Clifton 150
clothes, traditional 49
cowboy 80–1
Clyde, Vander 161
Coastal Plains 235
Coastal Prairie 235
colonists *see* **immigration**
Colt, Samuel 72, *73*
revolver 72
Comanche War Trail 279, 305
Comanches 34, 310
Comfort 62, *63*, 174, 196
Comstock 261
Confederacy 33, 34, 226
Confederate Gun Factory (Rusk) 225
Conger, Roger 150
cookoffs *see* **festivals**
Cooper Jr, Madison 152
Coronado, Francisco Vasquez de 39, 310
Corpus Christi 242–4
Art Museum of South Texas 243
Asian Cultures Museum 243
Bayfront Arts and Sciences Park 243
Corpus Christi Beach 243
Corpus Christi Museum of Science and History 243
Harbor Bridge 243
Magee Beach 244
North Beach 243
Seawall 242
Texas State Aquarium 244
USS *Lexington* 244
Corsicana 34, 147
Cos, General Martin Perfecto de 192
cotton 34, 145, 158
Cowboy Poetry Gathering 283
cowboys *14*, 22, 49, *78*, 79–86, 131
see also **rodeos, Old West and western shows**
black 84
boots 80, 141
capital of the world 171
costume 80–1
festivals 178
museums 86, 135, 208, 309
singing 79–80, 82
working *76–7*, 79, 86, 241, *313*
cowgirls
museum 137
Craig, George 221–2
Crockett, Davy *30*, 34, 185
wife's grave *319*
Cullen, Ezekiel W. 223
culture 36
customs *see* **festivals**
Czech immigrants 63, 147, 156
music 95

D

Dalhart 311
Dallas 51, *98*, 103, 119–29
see also **Irving**
African-American Museum 129
Age of Steam Railroad Museum 129
American Airlines Center 122
Artists Square 124
Bank of America Plaza 121
Belo Mansion 124
Cabin of John Neely Bryan *21*, 119
Cathedral Santuario de Nuestra Guadalupe 124
City Hall 103, 120
Convention Center 119
Cotton Bowl Stadium 128
C.R. Smith Museum (American Airlines) 127
craft shows 124
Crescent Court 125
Dallas Aquarium 128
Dallas Communications Complex 127
Dallas Museum of Art (DMA) 123
Dallas Museum of Natural History 128
Dallas Symphony Orchestra 124
Dallas World Aquarium & Zoological Garden 123
Dallas Zoo 129
Dallas/Fort Worth International Airport 127
Deep Ellum 127
Fair Park *127*, 128–9
Farmers' Market 129
Galleria 125
Greenville Avenue 127

Highland Park Village 124
Hyatt Regency Hotel 119
John F. Kennedy Memorial 121
J.P. Morgan Chase Tower 121
Kalita Humphreys Theater 125
light rail system (DART) 119
local economy/businesses 120, 121
Magnolia Hotel 121
McKinney Avenue 124
Mansion on Turtle Creek 125
Meadows Museum (at SMU) 125
Mesquite 129
Mockingbird Station 124
Morton H. Meyerson Symphony Center 124
music venues 127
Nasher Sculpture Center 124
Neiman Marcus department store 121
Old City Park 129
Pioneer Plaza 119
Reunion Arena 119
Reunion Tower 119
rodeos 129
sculptures 120, 124
shopping 124, 125
Sixth Floor Museum 121
Southern Methodist University (SMU) 125
Southfork Ranch *53*, 129
streetcars 124
Texas Discovery Gardens 128
Texas Hall of State 128
Texas School Book Depository 121
Thanksgiving Square 121, *125*
Thanksgiving Tower 121
The Conspiracy Museum 122
The Science Place 128
Trammell Crow Building 124
Wells Fargo Building 121
West End 121, *122*
Dallas *53*, 54, 129
Dart, Isom 84
Daughters of the Republic of Texas (DRT) 186
Davis, Jefferson 173
Deadwood Dick 84
Decatur *105*
Del Rio 259–61
denims (Levi-Strauss) 80
Denison 229
Denton 141
dinosaurs 149, 331
Dobie, J. Frank 82
Dr Pepper *150*, 151
tour of plant 151
Driscoll, Clara 186
Dublin 151
dude ranches 86, 171
Dunlap, S.M. 148

E

Eagle Pass 261, 262
Eakins, Thomas 136
East Texas 20, 21–2, 34, 59, *216–17*, 219–29
Eastland 299
economy, Texan 51, 53, 338
see also under individual towns
Eisenhower, General Dwight D. 212
Eisenhower Birthplace 229
El Camino Real (The King's Highway) 224, 225, 271
El Paso 269–75
Border Patrol Museum 274
Centennial Museum 273
Chamizal (park) 275
Chamizal Memorial 275
Concordia Cemetery 272
Fort Bliss Replica Museum 274
guidebook/tours 274
Magoffin Home State Historic Site 272
McKelligan Canyon 273
missions 198, 199
Museum of Art 274
San Jacinto Plaza 273
Texas-El Paso University 273
The Star on the Mountain 273
Transmountain Road 274
University of Texas at El Paso (UTEP) 272
Visitors' Bureau 274
Wilderness Park Museum 274
Wyler Aerial Tramway 274
El Paso-Juárez 271, 275
Ellison, Robert Reed 287
Ellwood, Isaac 221
empresario 31
Enchanted Rock Archives 173
Ennis 147
Enron 27, 203
Estebanico 65
Exotic Wildlife Association 172

F

Falcon Lake 264, 327
Fannin, Col. James 241
Far West Texas 278
Farmers' Alliance 157
Father of Texas 31, 157
Faver, Don Milton 289
Fehrenbach, T.R. 33, 44
Fence Cutting War 44
fencing 43–4, 82
festivals 63, 178–9
see also **rodeos, Old West and western shows**
Brazos River Festival (Waco) 152
Cajun Festival (Medina Lake) 173
Fandangle (Albany) 300
Fiesta (San Antonio) 185, 193
Forest Festival (Lufkin) 223
Grapefest (Grapevine) 140
Great Turkey Escape Festival (Johnson City) 175
International Chili Cookoff (Terlingua) 281
Kerrville Folk Festival 95, 171
Laredo 264
Mardi Gras (Galveston) 239
National Polka Festival (Ennis) 147
Shakespeare Festival (Odessa) 306
South by Southwest (SXSW) (Austin) 95, 162, 163
Texas International Apple Festival (Medina) 173
fiddle contests 91
fishing 160, 173, 235, 238, 242, 259
see also under individual parks 319–34
Five States of Texas 20
food 62, 63, 64
Deluxe fruit cake 147
fests 178
Tex-Mex 65, 265
Ford, O'Neil 102, 103
forests *see* **national forests**
Forreston 147
Fort Concho 305
Fort Davis 284
Fort Duncan 262
Fort Fisher 150
Fort Griffin 301
Fort Hood 155
Fort Leaton 279
Fort Phanton Hill 302
Fort Sam Houston 186
Fort Stockton 276
Fort Worth 82, 131–7
Amon Carter Museum 103, 136
Bass Performance Hall 134
Billy Bob's Texas 133
Botanic Garden 137
Casa Mañana 137
Cattle Raiser's Museum 135
Cowtown Coliseum 133, *137*
Cultural District 135–7
Fire Station No. 1 135
Fort Worth Museum of Science and History 137
Fort Worth/Tarrant County Convention Center 135
Fort Worth Zoo 137
Grapevine Vintage Railroad 133
Hell's Half Acre 131
Kimbell Art Museum *102*, 104, 135–6
Log Cabin Village 137
Modern Art Museum 136
Livestock Exchange *131*
murals *20*, 134
National Cowgirl Museum & Hall of Fame 137
Outlet Square 134
shopping 134
Sid Richardson Collection of Western Art 133
Stockyards (western festival) *8–9*, *36–7*, *130*
Stockyards Hotel 133
Stockyards National Historical District 131
Sundance Square 133, 134
Tarrant County Courthouse *135*
Thistle Hill 135
Vintage Flying Museum 137
Water Gardens 135
Western Triangle 133
White Elephant Saloon 131
Will Rogers Memorial Center 135
Fortune 500 companies 121

fossils 278, 289
see also **dinosaurs**
Fredericksburg *99*, 174
freeway architecture 205
French explorers/settlers 30, 64, 119
frontier 49
forts 301, 333–4
frontiersmen 79, 228

G

Galveston 235–41
1900 hurricane 233, 237
Ashton Villa 240
Bishop's Palace *101*, 240
Broadway 237
Elissa 238
fishing 238
Galveston County Beach Pocket Park 240
Galveston County Historical Museum 239
Galveston Island State Park 240, 328
Galveston Pier *238*
Grand 1894 Opera House 239
Lone Star Flight Museum 241
Mardi Gras 239
Mardi Gras Museum 239
Michael B. Menard Home 240
Moody Gardens (amusement park) 241
Moody Mansion 240
Ocean Star Offshore Drilling Rig and Museum 239
Railroad Museum 239
restaurants 238
Rosenberg Library 240
seawall 237, 238
shopping 238
Stewart Beach 237
Strand district *35*, *235*, 238, 239
Texas Seaport Museum 238
tourist office 238
trolley 238
West Beach 238
Galvez, Bernardo de 237
Garcia's Ranch 249
Gard, Wayne 43, 194
gardens and botanic gardens
Botanic Garden (Fort Worth) 137
Grapevine Heritage Garden 141
Lady Bird Johnson Wildflower Center (Austin) 166
Municipal Rose Garden (Tyler) 225
Texas Discovery Gardens (Dallas) 128
Water Gardens (Fort Worth) 135
Garner, John Nance (Cactus Jack) 196
gas *see* **oil and gas**
gem/mineral hunting 281
Gentling, Scott and Stuart 134
Georgetown 160
German immigrants/settlers 61–3, 100, 174, 188, 196
Giant 52, 279
Giddings, Mrs. W.T. 287
Gilchrist 235
Glen, Robert 127
Glen Rose 148
Glidden, Joseph F. 44
Gold Texas Conservation Passport 324
Goliad 241
Goodnight, Charles 39, *44*, 84, 277, 303, 311
Gould, Jay 228
Goyen, William 21
Gran Quivira 30
Grange organization 157
Grapevine 139–41
Grapevine Lake 141
Great East Texas Oil Field 225–6
Great Plains 313
Greene, Graham 188
Grey, Zane 277
Griffith, Thomas 151
Gruene 196
Gulf Coast 233–46
Gulf Coast Railroad 221

H

Haas, Richard 134
halls of fame *see* **museums, art galleries and halls of fame**
Hamer, Frank 74
Hardin, John Wesley *73*, 272
Harlingen 254
Hayes, Captain John Coffee "Jack" 72, 73
Headless Horseman 246
Heizer, Michael 208
Henderson 225
Hendrickson, Robert 126
Hidalgo 252
Higgins, Patillo 219
Highway 21 225
Highway 81 194
hiking
see also under individual parks
Big Bend National Park 290–2
Hill Country 171–7
state parks 325–6
Hillsboro 148
Hispanics 263, 271
immigrants 60, 64–5
historic houses 330
Beaumont 221
Chestnut Square (McKinney) 129
Galveston 240
Gingerbread Trail (Waxahachie) 145
Grapevine 139
Henderson 225
Highlands Mansion (Marlin) 158
Jefferson 227
Maxey House State Historical Park (Paris) 228
Port Arthur 221
Robertson Plantation House (Salado) 157
Sam Houston Park (Huntsville) 330
San Antonio 187
San Augustine 223
Waco 152
historic sites *see* **state historical parks and historic sites**
historical parks *see* **state historical parks and historic sites**
history 26–7, 29
Lone Star State 19–22
16th–19th century 29–34
20th century 49–54
Hogg, Ima 207
Hogg, James Stephen 208
Holly, Buddy (Charles Hardin Holley) 312
grave (Lubbock) 312
museum 314
Homer, Winslow 136
Hopkins, James 221–2
Horn, Tom 84
horse wranglers 39, 84
houses, traditional 100
Houston *12–13*, *104*, *200–1*, 203–12, 214–15
Allen's Landing Park 205
Alley Theater 205
American Cowboy Museum 208
Bayou Bend 207
Beer Can House 208
Blaffer Gallery 208
Broken Obelisk 206
Buffalo Bayou 205
Channel turning basin 212
Children's Museum 207
Cockrell Butterfly Center *206*, 207
Contemporary Arts Museum (CAM) 207
Cullen Sculpture Garden 207
Diho Supermarket 212
ethnic mix 203
Fiesta Market 210
freeway architecture 205
Galleria *202*, 209
Garden Center 207
gay community 206
Glenwood Cemetery 211
Hermann Park 207, *210*
Holocaust Museum 207
Houston Center for Photography 206
Houston Symphony 205
Houston Zoological Gardens 207
ice-skating 209
Johnson Space Center 212, 214, 215
Jones Hall 205
J.P. Morgan Chase Tower 104, 121, 205
Lillie and Roy Cullen Gallery of Earth Science 207
Livestock Show and Rodeo *62*, 211
Loop 205
Market Square 205
Menil Collection 206
Minute Maid Park 205
Montrose district 205
Museum District 206
Museum of Fine Arts (MFA) 207
Museum of Natural Science 207

National Museum of Funeral History 208
neon signs 210
New Chinatown (Bellaire Corridor, Diho Area) 212
Old Chinatown 211
One Shell Plaza 103
Orange Show 208
Pennzoil Place 103, 205
planetarium 207
Reliant Astrodome (Harris County Domed Stadium) *211*
Reliant Park 211
Reliant Stadium 211
Republic Bank 104
restaurants 209–10, 212
Rice University *101*, 208, *209*
Rice University Art Gallery 208
Rice Village 208
River Oaks 209
River Oaks Theatre 209
Rothko Chapel 206
sculpture *207*, 208
Ship Channel *34*, 212
shopping 209
Space Age Museum 207
sports 205, 207, 211
Tenneco skyscraper 103
Texas Medical Center 208
The Heights 210
Tien-Hou Taoist Temple 211
tours (harbor) 212
Tranquility Park 205
underground tunnels/ subterranean city 205
Visitor Information Center 205
Williams Tower 104, 209
Wortham IMAX Theater 207
Wortham Theater Center 205
Houston and Texas Central Railroad 119
Houston Creek 147
Houston, Sam *30*, 32, 33, 72, 221
grave (Huntsville) 222
Huddleston, Ned 84
Hughes, Howard (grave) 211
Hunt 171
Huntsville 222
hurricane of 1900, Galveston 233, 237. 239
Hutchison, Kate Bailey 51

I

Ikard, Bose 84
immigration 31, 33, 34, 59–67
festivals 178, 179
Indian Territory 194
Indianola 242
Indians 32, 72
see also **Native Americans** *and under individual tribes*
Industry 61
Ingram 172
Institute of Texan Cultures 86, 191
International Bridge 252, 254
Irish immigrants 60
Irving 127
Flower Clock 125
Heritage Park 127
Irving Arts Center 127
Las Colinas 125, 127
Main Street 127
Mandalay Canal 127
movie studio/tour 127
Mustang Sculpture Exhibit 127
Mustangs of Las Colinas *55*, *127*
sculpture garden 127
Texas Stadium 127
Italian immigrants 64, 158
Italy 147–8
Iwo Jima War Memorial (Harlingen) 254

J

Japanese settlers 67
Jarrell 160
Jasper 222
Jefferson 227–8
Annual Historical Pilgrimage 227
City Trolley tours 227
Excelsior House Hotel 227
historic homes 227
Jefferson Landing 228
river tour 228
The Freeman Plantation 227
trolley tours 227
Jefferson Landing 228
Jennings, Waylon 92, 174
Jewish immigrants 64
Johnson City 102, 175
Johnson, Lady Bird 166
Johnson, Lyndon Baines 50, 166
Boyhood Home 175
Johnson, Sam 186
Johnson Space Center 212, 214–5
Joplin, Janis 221, *222*
Jordan, Terry 66
Journey Through Texas 61
Juárez, Benito *275*
Judd, Don 279
Juneteenth (Emancipation Day) 236

K

Karankawas 29
Kemah-Seabrook area 240
Kennedy, John F. *50*, 121, 122
museum 121
Kerrville 171–2
Kickapoo Indians 67, 262
Kilgore 226
Rangerette Showcase 226
Killeen 155
Kimbell, Kay 136
King, Edward 59
King, Martin Luther (memorial) 206
King, Richard 83
Kingsville 245
Kuhnert, Wilhelm 137

L

***la frontera* (Texas/Mexico border)** 269
La Grange 166
La Reunion 119
La Salle, René Robert Cavelier, Sieur de 30, 64
Lafitte, Jean 63, 235, 236
museum 239
Lafitte, Pierre 236
Lajitas *106–7*, 280
Lake Amistad 259, 327
Lake Bardwell 147
Lake Sabine 221
Lake Texoma *228*, 229, 324
lakes 147, 166, 324, 325
see also under individual lake names
Lamar, Mirabeau 32, 72
Langtry, 261
Langtry, Lily *260*, 261
Laredo 263
Latin colonies 62
Leaton, Ben 279, 334
Liberty 222
Llano Estacado (Staked Plains) 313
Lomax, John A. 40, 79, 91
Lonesome Dove 52, 84, 196, 277
Longabaugh, Harry 131
longhorn cattle 39, *41*, 44, *45*, 194
official State of Texas herd 44, 149, 301
preservation of 171
Longview 226
Los Ebanos hand-drawn ferry *250*
Loving, Oliver 84, 277
Loving county 276
Lubbock 313–14
Buddy Holly 312, 314
Buddy Holly Center 314
Canyon Lakes Project 314
Historic Depot District 313
Lubbock Lake Landmark 314
Moody Planetarium 314
National Ranching Heritage Center 86, 313
OMNI Theater 314
Science Spectrum (museum) 314
Stubblefield, C.B. 314
Texas Tech Museum 313
Texas Tech University 86, *311*, 313
Lucas, Anthony F. 219
Lucas Gusher 219
Luckenbach 174–5
Lufkin 223
Lyndon B. Johnson Space Center 212, 214, 215

M

Mackenzie, General Ranald 310
Magic Valley 250
Mansfield Cut 245
Marathon *281*, 283
Marcus, Carrie 126
Marcus, Herbert 126
Marcus, Stanley 126
Marfa 278–9, *287*
Lights 287
Marlin 158
Marsh, Stanley 310
Marshall 226
Matagorda Bay 30
Maverick, Mary 193
Maverick, Samuel 41, 42

Mavericks (unbranded cattle) 41
Maximilian I 166
McAllen 251–2
McCamey 286
McCoy, Joseph G. 43
McDonald, Captain Bill 71
McDonald Observatory *276*, 284
  Star Parties 284
McKinney 129
McKissack, Jeff 208
McMurtry, Larry 52, 65, 79
Meadows, H. Algur 125
Medina 173
Menard, Michael B. 240
Menger, William 190
mesquite 300
Mexican border 252, 254, 269
  Border Patrol museum 274
  border regulars 269–70
  trade 264
Mexican Cultural Institute 192
Mexican undocumented immigrants 253, 269
Mexican War 254
Mexico
  Ciudad Acuña 259
  Ciudad Juárez 274–5
  Ciudad Miguel Alemán 249
  doctors/clinics 253
  historic rate of exchange 270
  Juárez *see* Ciudad Juárez
  Mier 249
  Nuevo Laredo 263, 264
  pedestrian/automobile crossing bridges 275
  Piedras Negras (Black Rocks) 262
  rebellion against 31, 32
  Reynosa 39, 52
  shopping *see under individual towns*
Michener, James 49
Midland 305–6
Milano 158
Milford 148
mission trails 198, 199
missions 30, *99*, 184, 196, 198–9, 271
  Guadalupe Mission 271
  Mission Concepción *198*
  Mission Espada 198
  Mission Espiritu Santo 39, 241
  Mission San Antonio de Valero (Alamo) 184, *185*, 198
  Mission San José (Queen of the Missions) 198
  Mission San Juan 198
  Mission Señora de los Ais (Dolores Mission) 223
  Oblate Mission 251
  San Augustín de la Isleta del Sur 271
  Socorro Mission *198*, 271
  Ysleta Mission 199
Mountain Home 171
mountains and mountain peaks
  Chinati Peak 279
  Chisos Mountains 281, *288*
  Davis Mountains 285
  El Capitan Peak 286, *329*
  formation of 285
  Franklin Mountains 285
  Guadalupe 286
  Guadalupe Peak 286, 329
  Mount Livermore 285
movie locations, movie studios and movie-making 52
  Alamo Village Movie Location *195*, 196
  Dallas Communications Complex 127
  Denton 141
  Pecos region 277
  Roma 249
  Waxahachie 145
***mulatto* population** 65
Munson, Thomas Volney 177
museums, art galleries and halls of fame
  1st Cavalry Museum (Fort Hood) 155
  2nd Armored Division Museum (Fort Hood) 155
  African-American Museum (Dallas) 129
  Age of Steam Railroad Museum (Dallas) 129
  American Airpower Heritage Museum of the Commemorative Air Force (Midland) 305
  American Cowboy Museum (Houston) 208
  American Quarter Horse Hall of Fame and Museum (Amarillo) 309
  Amon Carter Museum (Fort Worth) 103, 136
  Arlington Historical Society Museum 139
  Arlington Museum of Art 139
  Art Museum of South Texas (Corpus Christi) 243
  Ashton Villa (Galveston) 240
  Asian Cultures Museum (Corpus Christi) 243
  Austin Children's Museum 165
  Austin Museum of Art (Laguna Gloria) 165
  Bell County Museum (Temple) 156
  Blaffer Gallery (Houston) 208
  Border Patrol Museum (El Paso) 274
  Bosque Memorial Park (Clifton) 150
  Buddy Holly Center (Lubbock) 314
  Cattle Raiser's Museum (Fort Worth) 135
  Centennial Museum (El Paso) 273
  Chamizal Memorial (El Paso) 275
  Children's Museum (Houston) 207
  The Conspiracy Museum (Dallas) 122
  Contemporary Arts Museum (CAM) (Houston) 207
  Corpus Christi Museum of Science and History 243
  Courthouse-on-the-Square Museum (Denton) 141
  Cowboy Artists of America Museum (Kerrville) 102, 172
  C.R. Smith Museum (Dallas) (American Airlines) 127
  Czech Heritage Society Museum (Temple) 156
  Dallas Communications Complex 127
  Dallas Museum of Art (DMA) 123
  Dallas Museum of Natural History 128
  Daughters of the American Revolution Museum (Denton) 141
  Dr Pepper Museum (Waco) *150*, 151
  East Texas Oil Museum (Kilgore) 226
  Edison Plaza Museum (Beaumont) 221
  Ellis County Museum (Waxahachie) 145
  Falls County Historical Museum (Marlin) 158
  Fannin County Museum of History (Bonham) 229
  Fire Museum of Texas (Beaumont) 221
  Fort Bliss Replica Museum (El Paso) 274
  Fort Duncan Museum (Eagle Pass) 262
  Fort Inglish Park (Bonham) 229
  Fort Russell (Marfa) 279
  Fort Stockton Museum 286
  Fort Worth Museum of Science and History 137
  French Legation Museum (Austin) 166
  Frontier Times Museum (Bandera) 171
  Galveston County Historical Museum 239
  Garner Memorial Museum (Uvalde) 196
  George Bush Presidential Library and Museum (A&M University, Bryan/College Station) 159
  George Paul Museum (Del Rio) 259
  Gish's Old West Museum (Fredericksburg) 174
  Hangar 10 Airplane Museum (Denton) 141
  Harold B. Simpson History Complex (Hillsboro) 148
  Heard Natural Science Museum (McKinney) 129
  Helen Marie Taylor Museum of Waco History 152
  Hill Country Museum (Kerrville) 172
  Historic Brownsville Museum 254
  Historical Museum (Abilene) 303
  Holocaust Museum (Houston) 207
  Institute of Texan Cultures (San Antonio) 86
  John Jay French Historic House Museum (Beaumont) 221

John Wayne museum (Alamo Village Movie Location) 196
Johnson Space Center (Houston) 212, 214, 215
Kimbell Art Museum (Fort Worth) *102*, 135–6
Ledbetter Picket House Museum (Albany) 300
Legends of the Game Museum (Arlington) (baseball) 138
Lone Star Flight Museum (Galveston) 241
Longhorn Museum (Pleasanton) 86
Louis Tussaud's Palace of Wax & Ripley's Believe It or Not! (Arlington) 138
Lyndon B. Johnson Library and Museum (Austin) 166
Mardi Gras Museum (Galveston) 239
McNay Art Museum (San Antonio) 196
Meadows Museum (Dallas) 125
Menil Collection (Houston) 206
Modern Art Museum (Fort Worth) 136
Moody Mansion (Galveston) 240
Moody Planetarium (Lubbock) 314
Museo de Arte e Historia (Ciudad Juárez, Mexico) 275
Museum of Art (El Paso) 274
Museum of Fine Arts (MFA) (Houston) 207
Museum of Natural Science (Houston) 207
Museum of Regional History (Texarkana) 228
Museum of the Gulf Coast (Port Arthur) 222
Nasher Sculpture Center 124
National Cowgirl Museum & Hall of Fame (Fort Worth) *76–7*, 86, 137
National Museum of Funeral History (Houston) 208
National Museum of the Pacific War (Fredericksburg) 174
National Ranching Heritage Center (Lubbock) 86, 313
Ocean Star Offshore Drilling Rig and Museum (Galveston) 239
The Old Jail Art Center (Albany) 300
Old Stone Fort Museum (Nacogdoches) 224
Palm House Museum (Round Rock) 161
Panhandle-Plains Historical Museum (Canyon) 86, 309
Petroleum Museum (Midland) 305
Pioneer Museum Complex (Fredericksburg) 174
Presidential Museum (Odessa) 306
Railroad and Cultural Heritage Museum (Ennis) 147
Railroad and Pioneer Museum (Temple) 156
Railroad Museum (Galveston) 239
R.G. Le Tourneau Museum (Longview) 226
Rice University Art Gallery (Houston) 208
Sam Rayburn House Museum (Bonham) 229
San Antonio Museum of Art 196
San Jacinto Monument museum 212
Sanders-Metzger Gun Collection (A&M, Bryan/College Station) 159
The Science Place (Dallas) 128
Science Spectrum (Lubbock) 314
Sid Richardson Collection of Western Art (Fort Worth) 133
Sixth Floor Museum (Dallas) 121
Smitty's Joke Box Museum (Pharr) 252
Somervell County Museum (Glen Rose) 149
Space Age Museum (Houston) 207
Spindletop-Gladys City Boomtown Museum (Beaumont) 219
Star of the Republic Museum (Washington-on-the-Brazos) 159
Stark Museum of Art (Orange) 222
Strecker Museum (Waco) 151
Texas Energy Museum (Beaumont) 219
Texas Forestry Museum (Lufkin) 223
Texas Ranger Museum & Hall of Fame (Waco) *72, 75, 151*, 152
Texas Tech Museum (Lubbock) 313
The Trail Drivers Association (San Antonio) 86
Vintage Flying Museum (Fort Worth) 137
West of Pecos Museum (Pecos) 286
Whitehead Memorial Museum (Del Rio) 260
Wilderness Park Museum (El Paso) 274
Will Rogers Memorial Center (Fort Worth) 135
Witte Museum (San Antonio) 195
XIT Museum (Dalhart) 86
Ye Olde Clock Museum (Pharr) 252
music 91–5
blues 93, 127
blues-rock 94
Cajun 95, 221
conjunto 94, 95
country 91, 92
festivals 95, 171–2, 178
hip-hop 94
recordings 95
Tejano 95
Tex-Mex 94, 95
Western Swing 92
Mustang Island 244
Muybridge, Eadweard 136

N

Nacogdoches 223–4
La Calle del Norte 224
Millard's Crossing 224
Old Stone Fort Museum 224
Sterne-Hoya Home 224
Nameless 148
NASA 214–15
Nashville 157
national forests 229
Angelina National Forest 319
Big Thicket National Preserve 229
Davy Crockett National Forest 319
Sabine National Forest 322
Sam Houston National Forest 322
national parks *see* **state parks and national parks**
national recreation areas
Amistad National Recreation Area 259, 327
Lake Meredith National Recreation Area 217
National Register of Historical Places 140
National Society of Colonial Dames of America 165
Native Americans 29, 66–7, 195, 223, 282, 305
see also **cave paintings, pictographs** *and under individual tribe names*
and missions 199
museum 274
Pow-Wow 179
Reservation 323
natural areas and nature centers
see also **wildlife**
Armand Bayou Nature Center 212
Big Bend Ranch State Natural Area 280, 281
Enchanted Rock State Natural Area *173*, 173–4, 329
Hill Country State Natural Area 176
Lost Maples State Natural Area 176, 330
Riverside Nature Center 172
nature centers *see* **natural areas and nature centers**
Navarro, José Antonio 147, 187, 188
Neiman, Al 126
Neiman Marcus 54, 121, 126
Nelson, Willie 92
New Braunfels 63, 196
Norse 150
North Texas 20, 22
Norwegian settlers 150
museum 150

O

O'Conór, Hugo 60
O'Daniel, Governor W. Lee (Pappy) 193
Odessa 306
Odessa Meteor Crater 306
O. Henry 165

oil and gas 19, 34, 49–51
Abilene 302
Beaumont 219
Corsicana 147
East Texas 225, 226
Houston 203
Midland 305–6
Ranger 298
oil refineries
hard-hat tours (Port Arthur) 222
oilfields 49, 50
O'Keeffe, Georgia 309–10
Old West *see* **rodeos, Old West and western shows**
Olmsted, Frederick Law 61, 62, 71, 100, 183, 193
Oñate, Juan de 271
Orange 222
Oswald, Lee Harvey 121, 122
Outlaws 92

P

Padre Island *230–1, 245,* 328
Padre Island National Seashore 328, *330*
Palacios 242
Panhandle of Texas 21, 29, 309
Panna Maria 63, *192*
Paris 228–9
Parker, Bonnie 74, 124, 133
Parker, Chief Quanah 34, 310
Parker, George 131
Parker's Fort 333
Old Fort Parker Historic Preservation 333
parks
Davy Crockett Memorial Park 225
Galveston County Beach Pocket Park 240
Ramsey Nature Park 254
Pasadena-Baytown Industrial Corridor 212
patrón system 41
Patterson, Paul 277
Patton, George 280
Pecos 286
Pecos Bill 277
Pecos river 277
Penick, Stuart T. 289
Permian Basin Oil Field 305
Perot, Ross 124
Pershing, General Jack 280
Petrified City 149
Pharr 252
Pickett, Bill 84
pictographs 259, 271, 291, *318, 332*
Piney Woods 219, 225
Piper, Edward 39
pirates 236
Plains tribes 29
plantlife (desert) 282
Polish immigrants 60, 63
Port Aransas 244
Port Arthur 221–2
Museum of the Gulf Coast 222
Pompeiian Villa 221
Rainbow Bridge 222, *223*
Rose Hill Manor 222
White Haven 222
Port Isabel 246
Port Isabel Lighthouse 246
Port O'Connor 242
Porter, William Sydney (O. Henry) 165
Post *16–17,* 314
Post, Charles W. 314
prairie dogs 294, 314
prehistoric sites 331–2
see also **pictographs**
Presidio 280
Professional Rodeo Cowboys Association (PRCA) 85
Project X-Ray 176
Pryor brothers 43
pump jacks *16–17,* 21

R

raft trips 280
ranches
Dos Vaqueros (working cowboys) 242
dude 86, 171
Heep Ranch *156*
King Ranch (tours) *45,* 83, 246
Kokernot 06 85
LBJ Ranch (tours) 175
LH7 Ranch (tours) 171
Mission Espiritu Santo 39
Samuel Maverick's 42
Southfork Ranch (tours) 129
XIT Ranch 83, 311
YO Ranch 86, 171
ranching 21, 82
see also cattle
National Ranching Heritage Center (Lubbock) 313
sheep/goats 21, 44
Spanish influence/vocabulary 30, 80
Ranger 298–9
rattlesnake roundup 304
Rawhide 289
Rayburn, Sam 229
Refugio 241
religious broadcasting 260
Remington, Frederic 44, 133, 136
Republic of Texas 20, 32, 60, 72, 241
black bean incident 249
Galveston 236
Runaway Scrape 158
San Jacinto 185
Republic of the Rio Grande 263
museum 263
restaurants 355
Revere, Paul 190
revolver, Colt 72
Richards, Ann *50,* 51, 152
Richardson, Sid W. 44, 133
Rio Grande City 249–50, *252*
Rio Grande (Rio Bravo) river 253, 269
Rio Grande Valley 22, 249–54
economy 22, 250–1
Robertson, A.C. Eck 91
Robertson, E.S.C. 157
Robertson, Sterling Clack 157, 158
rock art *see* **pictographs**
rock hunters 281
Rockport-Fulton area 244
rodeo performers 84, *85,* 85–6
rodeos, Old West and western shows
Abilene 302
Bandera 171
Buffalo Gap Historic Village 303
Cowboy Morning 311
Cowtown Coliseum (Fort Worth) 133
Dalhart 311
Livestock Show and Rodeo (Houston) 211
Mesquite (Dallas) 129
Old West Show 311
Pecos 286
Texas Cowboy Reunion (Stamford) 301
World Championship Ranch Rodeo 309
Roebling, Thomas 151
Rogers, Roy 82, 134
Rollover Pass 235
Roma 249
Roosevelt, President T. 190, 193
Rose Capital of America 225
Rothko, Mark 206
Round Rock 161
Ruffini, Frederick E. 101
Ruiz, Francisco 195
rural communities 21
Rusk *224,* 225
Russell, Charles M. 44, 133, 136

S

Sabine–Neches Ship Channel 221
Sabine Pass 221
Salado 156
Saligny, Comte Alphonse Dubois de 166
Sam Rayburn Reservoir 319
San Angelo 305
San Antonio 62, 82, 183–96
Alamo *24–5,* 31, 99, 184–6, *185,* 198
Alamo Plaza 186
Arneson Theater 192
Aztec Theater 189
Blue Star Art Space 189
boat rides 184
Brackenridge Park 195
Buckhorn Saloon and Museum 191
Convention & Visitors' Bureau 193
Fiesta 186, 193
Hemisfair Park 191–2
Hilton Palacio del Rio 191
Historic Menger Hotel 190, *191*
José Antonio Navarro House 187
King William District 189
La Villita (Little Village) 192
Louis Tussaud's Plaza Wax Theater 191
Market Square 187, *186, 187*
McNay Art Museum 196

Menger Hotel 190
Milam Building 187
missions 198
music 193, 196
River Walk *180–1*, 183, 184, *189*
Rivercenter Mall 189
San Antonio Missions National Historical Park 196
San Antonio Museum of Art 196
San Antonio Zoo 195
San Fernando Cathedral 188, *196*, *197*
Science Treehouse 195
Spanish Governor's Palace 188
Steves Homestead *188*, 189
Sunset Station 192
The Texas Adventure 191
The Trail Drivers Association museum 86
tours 184, 187, 189
Tower Life building *182*
Tower of the Americas *192*
Trinity University 102
VIA streetcars 187
Visitor's Center 186, *193*
Witte Museum 195
San Antonio Conservation Society 189
San Antonio Current 193
San Antonio river 183, 184
San Augustine 223
San Diego 246
San Elizario 271
San Felipe Springs 259
San Jacinto 32, 185
Monument 212, *213*
museum 212
San Juan 253
San Ygnacio 249, *253*
sanctuary houses 269
Santa Anna, General 31, 32, 184, 186
Savings and Loan crisis 51
Scott, Winfield 135
Sea Turtle, Inc. 246
Serbin 63
settlers *see* **immigration**
Seven Cities of Cibola 30
Shafter 280
Shelby, General Joseph O. 262
Sheridan, General 277
Sherman 229
Shiner 166
Shrimp Capital of Texas 244
Sierra Blanca 278
Singer, John 245
sinkhole, East Texas 219
Siringo, Charlie 42
Sisterdale 62
Six Flags Over Texas 29
Republic of Texas 32
six-shooter 72
Slav immigrants 63
slavery 34, 66, 84, 236
snake sacking 162
snakes 295, 304
Socorro 271
Sonora 176
Sour Lake 219
South, Deep 59
South Padre Island *244*, *245*, 246
South Texas 20, 22
state parks 326–7
Spanish
architecture 99
colonization 30, 31
explorers 29, 30
influence 30
spas 158
Spindletop 34, 49, 219
Spoetzl Brewery 166
sports teams
Dallas Cowboys (football) 127
Dallas Mavericks (basketball) 119
Dallas Stars (hockey) 119
Houston Astros (baseball) 205
Houston Texans (football) 211
Texas Rangers (baseball) 138
Stamford 301
state capital *see* **Austin**
state flower *see* **Texas bluebonnet**
state historic parks and historic sites
Acton State Historic Site
Alibates National Monument 331
Battleship *Texas* State Historic Site 334
Caddoan Mounds State Historic Park 331
Fort Davis National Historic Site 284, 334
Fort Griffin State Park and Historic Site 301, 334
Fort Lancaster State Historic Site 334
Fort Leaton State Historic Site 280, 334
Fort McKavett State Historic Site 334
Fort Richardson State Historic Park and Site 334
Hueco Tanks State Historic Site 271, *318*, 332
Kreische Brewery State Historic Site 333
Lyndon B. Johnson National Historical Park 175
Magoffin Home State Historic Site 272
Monument Hill State Historic Site 333
San Antonio Missions National Historical Park 196, 333
San Jacinto Battleground State Historic Site 333, 334
Seminole Canyon State Historic Site *263*, 332
Washington-on-the-Brazos State Historic Park *333*
state parks and national parks 319–34
see also **parks**
Abilene State Park 328
Atlanta State Park 323
Bastrop State Park 330
Bentsen-Rio Grande Valley State Park 254, 327
Big Bend National Park 289–92
Big Spring State Park 305
Blanco State Park 326
Brazos Bend State Park 324
Caddo Lake State Park *227*, 323
Caprock Canyons State Park 329
Cleburne State Park 325
Daingerfield State Park 323
Davis Mountains State Park 285
Dinosaur Valley State Park 149, *331*
drinking water 290, 322
Eisenhower State Park 325
Fairfield Lake State Park 324
Falcon State Park 327
Fort Parker State Park 325
Galveston Island State Park 240, 328
Garner State Park 326
Gold Texas Conservation Passport 324
Goliad State Park 241, *332*, 333
Goose Island State Park 331
Guadalupe Mountains National Park *316–17*, 329
Guadalupe River State Park 326
Inks Lake State Park 326
Lake Arrowhead State Park 327
Lake Brownwood State Park 326
Lake Casa Blanca State Park 264
Lake Colorado City State Park 327
Lake Corpus Christi State Park 326
Lake Livingston State Park 323
Lake Meredith 327
Lake Mineral Wells State Park 324
Lake Somerville State Parks and Trailway 323
Lake Texana State Park 326
Lake Whitney State Park 324
Longhorn Cavern State Park 176
Mackenzie State Park 314
Martin Dies, Jr. State Park 322
Matagorda Island State Park and Wildlife Management Area 328
Meridian State Park 325
Mission Tejas State Park 332
Monahans Sandhills State Park 306
Mother Neff State Park 325
Mustang Island State Park 244, 328
Palmetto State Park 330
Palo Duro Canyon State Park 311, 329
Pedernales Falls State Park 326
Possum Kingdom State Park 324
Sea Rim State Park 328
Texas State Railroad State Park 225, 334
Tyler State Park 323
state recreation areas *see* **national and state recreation areas**
Staub, John F. 207
Stetson, John B. 81
Stilwell, Arthur 221
Summers, Robert 120
Sun Bowl (El Paso) 273
Sundance Kid 131

Surls, James 22
Sweetwater 304
Nolan County Coliseum 304

T

TAMIU Planetarium 264
Tavern Oak (Jasper) 222
taxes 32, 33
Taylor 162
Taylor, General Zachary 246
Tejanos 65
Tejas 30
Temple 155, 156
Terlingua *280*, 281
Texans 53, 59–67
Texarkana 228
Texas 178
Texas bluebonnet 166, 170
Texas Declaration of Independence 187, 195
Texas Motor Speedway (Denton) 141
Texas Oil Company (Texaco) 222
Texas & Pacific (T&P) Railroad 131, 297
Texas Parks and Wildlife Department 324
Texas Rangers 71–5, 150, 246
Hall of Fame *72*, *75*
Texas Revolution 31
Texas State Fair 6–7, 119, 128
Texas State Railroad *224*
Tex-Deutsch dialect 63
Texians 31
Thurber 297
Tigua (Tiwa) Indians 67, 271
Tillman's Lane 176
timber 219, 223
Tonkawa Indians 174
trail cattle 39
Trail Drivers Association 86
trail drives 39, 40, 43, 81, 82, 131, 171
Chisholm Trail 194
cook 40
trail boss 39, 40
trails *see under individual parks* *319–34*
Trans-Pecos 277–87
Travis, William Barret 185
tumbleweeds 306
turtles 246
Tyler 225

U

Union 32, 34
universities
Abilene Christian University 302
Baylor University (Waco) *144*, 151, 152
Hardin Simmons University (Abilene) 302
McMurry University (Abilene) 302
National Autonomous University of Mexico 183
Sam Houston State University 222
Southern Methodist University (SMU) (Dallas) 125
Sul Ross State University (Alpine) *277*, 283
Texas A&M University (Bryan/College Station) 159
Texas-El Paso University 272
Texas Tech University (Lubbock) 86, *311*, 313
Texas Women's University (TWU) (Denton) 141
Trinity University (San Antonio) 102
University of North Texas (Denton) 141
University of Texas (UT) (Austin) 158, 159, 166
University of Texas at El Paso (UTEP) 272
West Texas A&M University (Canyon) 309
urbanization 50, 54
U.S. camel corps 173
U.S. Immigration and Customs Enforcement Service (*la Migra*) 253
U.S. Navy 243

V

Valentine 281
Van Horn 278
Váró, Márton 134
Victoria 241
Vietnamese immigrants 67, 212
Villa, Pancho 272, 274
vineyards *see* **wines/wineries**
Viva Zapata 249

W

Waco 150–2
Armstrong Browning Library 151
Baylor University *144*, 151, 152
Dr Pepper Museum *150*, 151
First Street Cemetery 152
Helen Marie Taylor Museum of Waco History 152
Heritage Square 152
historic houses 152
Strecker Museum 151
suspension bridge 150–1
Texas Ranger Museum & Hall of Fame *72*, *75*, *151*, 152
Texas Sports Hall of Fame 152
The Governor Bill and Vara Daniel Historic Village 151
Tourist Information Center 152
Zoo 151
Waco tribe 150
Waggoner, W.T. 135
Walker, Captain Samuel 72
Walker, Jerry Jeff 175
Washington-on-the-Brazos 159
water sports and water parks
Corpus Christi 242
Lake Amistad 259
Lake Bardwell 147
Lake Georgetown 160
Grapevine Lake 141
Six Flags Hurricane Harbor (Arlington) 138
Waxahachie 145
Chautauqua Auditorium 145, *148*
Courthouse Square 145
Ellis County Courthouse 145, *147*, *148*
Ellis County Museum 145
Gingerbread Trail (historic houses) 145, *149*
Jenkins Home 145
movie-making 145
Nicholas P. Sims Library 145
Visitors' Bureau 145
Wayne, John 134
museum 196
Weldon, Dr Felix W. de 254
Wend immigrants 63
West 149
West Texas 20–1, 59, 297–306
wildlife 171, 172, 285, 294–5
wildlife parks and refuges
Aransas National Wildlife Refuge 245, *327*, 330
Black Gap Wildlife Management Area 283
Brazoria National Wildlife Refuge 241
Laguna Atascosa National Wildlife Refuge 254, 331
Matagorda Island State Park and Wildlife Management Area 328
Natural Bridge Wildlife Ranch 176
Ramsay Nature Park (Harlingen) 254
Sabal Palm Audubon Center and Wildlife Sanctuary 254
Santa Ana National Wildlife Refuge 254, 331
Sea Turtle, Inc. (South Padre Island) 246
Wills, Bob 93
wines/wineries 140, 177
Delaney Vineyards 140
Llano Estacado Winery (tours) 314
Val Verde Winery 259
Winter Texans *250*
Wister, Owen 79
women's rodeo 85
wool 44, 259
Wooley, Bryan 277
Working Ranch Cowboys Association 309
writers 22, 52, 79, 84

X–Z

XERF radio station 260
XIT Reunion 311
Ysleta 271
Zaharias, Babe Didrickson 221, 222
zoos
Cameron Park Zoo (Waco) 151
Dallas World Aquarium & Zoological Garden 123
Dallas Zoo 129
Fort Worth Zoo 137
Gladys Porter Zoo (Brownsville) 254
Houston Zoo 207
San Antonio Zoo 195
Texas Zoo (Victoria) 241